Quantitative Financial Risk Management

The Frank J. Fabozzi Series

Short Selling: Strategies, Risks, and Rewards edited by Frank J. Fabozzi

The Real Estate Investment Handbook by G. Timothy Haight and Daniel Singer

Market Neutral Strategies edited by Bruce I. Jacobs and Kenneth N. Levy

Securities Finance: Securities Lending and Repurchase Agreements edited by Frank J. Fabozzi and Steven V. Mann

Fat-Tailed and Skewed Asset Return Distributions by Svetlozar T. Rachev, Christian Menn, and Frank J. Fabozzi

Financial Modeling of the Equity Market: From CAPM to Cointegration by Frank J. Fabozzi, Sergio M. Focardi, and Petter N. Kolm

Advanced Bond Portfolio Management: Best Practices in Modeling and Strategies edited by Frank J. Fabozzi, Lionel Martellini, and Philippe Priaulet

Analysis of Financial Statements, Second Edition by Pamela P. Peterson and Frank J. Fabozzi

Collateralized Debt Obligations: Structures and Analysis, Second Edition by Douglas J. Lucas, Laurie S. Goodman, and Frank J. Fabozzi

Handbook of Alternative Assets, Second Edition by Mark J. P. Anson

Introduction to Structured Finance by Frank J. Fabozzi, Henry A. Davis, and Moorad Choudhry

Financial Econometrics by Svetlozar T. Rachev, Stefan Mittnik, Frank J. Fabozzi, Sergio M. Focardi, and Teo Jasic

Developments in Collateralized Debt Obligations: New Products and Insights by Douglas J. Lucas, Laurie S. Goodman, Frank J. Fabozzi, and Rebecca J. Manning

Robust Portfolio Optimization and Management by Frank J. Fabozzi, Peter N. Kolm, Dessislava A. Pachamanova, and Sergio M. Focardi

Advanced Stochastic Models, Risk Assessment, and Portfolio Optimizations by Svetlozar T. Rachev, Stogan V. Stoyanov, and Frank J. Fabozzi

How to Select Investment Managers and Evaluate Performance by G. Timothy Haight, Stephen O. Morrell, and Glenn E. Ross

Bayesian Methods in Finance by Svetlozar T. Rachev, John S. J. Hsu, Biliana S. Bagasheva, and Frank J. Fabozzi

The Handbook of Municipal Bonds edited by Sylvan G. Feldstein and Frank J. Fabozzi

Subprime Mortgage Credit Derivatives by Laurie S. Goodman, Shumin Li, Douglas J. Lucas, Thomas A Zimmerman, and Frank J. Fabozzi

Introduction to Securitization by Frank J. Fabozzi and Vinod Kothari

Structured Products and Related Credit Derivatives edited by Brian P. Lancaster, Glenn M. Schultz, and Frank J. Fabozzi

Handbook of Finance: Volume I: Financial Markets and Instruments edited by Frank J. Fabozzi

Handbook of Finance: Volume II: Financial Management and Asset Management edited by Frank J. Fabozzi

Handbook of Finance: Volume III: Valuation, Financial Modeling, and Quantitative Tools edited by Frank J. Fabozzi

Finance: Capital Markets, Financial Management, and Investment Management by Frank J. Fabozzi and Pamela Peterson-Drake

Active Private Equity Real Estate Strategy edited by David J. Lynn

Foundations and Applications of the Time Value of Money by Pamela Peterson-Drake and Frank J. Fabozzi

Leveraged Finance: Concepts, Methods, and Trading of High-Yield Bonds, Loans, and Derivatives by Stephen Antczak, Douglas Lucas, and Frank J. Fabozzi

Modern Financial Systems: Theory and Applications by Edwin Neave

Institutional Investment Management: Equity and Bond Portfolio Strategies and Applications by Frank J. Fabozzi

Quantitative Equity Investing: Techniques and Strategies by Frank J. Fabozzi

Probability and Statistics for Finance by Svetlozar T. Rachev, Markus Hoechstoetter, Frank J. Fabozzi, and Sergio M. Focardi

The Basics of Finance: An Introduction to Financial Markets, Business Finance, and Portfolio Management by Pamela Peterson Drake and Frank J. Fabozzi

Simulation and Optimization in Finance: Modeling with MATLAB, @Risk, or VBA by Dessislava Pachamanova and Frank J. Fabozzi

Emerging Market Real Estate Investment: Investing in China, India, and Brazil by David J. Lynn and Tim Wang

The Handbook of Traditional and Alternative Investment Vehicles: Investment Characteristics and Strategies by Mark J. P. Anson and Frank J. Fabozzi

Financial Models with Levy Processes and Volatility Clustering by Svetlozar T. Rachev, Young Shin Kim, Michele L. Bianchi, Frank J. Fabozzi

Complying with the Global Investment Performance Standards (GIPS) by Bruce J. Feibel and Karyn D. Vincent

Mortgage-Backed Securities: Products, Structuring, and Analytical Techniques, Second Edition by Frank J. Fabozzi and Anand K. Bhattacharya

Quantitative Credit Portfolio Management: Practical Innovations for Measuring and Controlling Liquidity, Spread, and Issuer Concentration Risk by Arik Ben Dor, Lev Dynkin, Jay Hyman, and Bruce D. Phelps

Analysis of Financial Statements, Third Edition by Pamela Peterson Drake and Frank J. Fabozzi

Quantitative Financial Risk Management

Theory and Practice

CONSTANTIN ZOPOUNIDIS
EMILIOS GALARIOTIS

WILEY

Library of Congress Cataloging-in-Publication Data

Zopounidis, Constantin.
    Quantitative financial risk management : theory and practice / Constantin Zopounidis, Emilios Galariotis.
      pages cm. – (The Frank J. Fabozzi series)
    Includes index.
    ISBN 978-1-118-73818-4 (hardback)
1. Financial risk management. I. Galariotis, Emilios. II. Title.
    HD61.Z67 2015
    332–dc23

Printed in the United States of America

10 9 8 7 6 5 4 3 2 1

This work is dedicated to our families for their support and encouragement, as well as for their understanding.

More specifically, Constantin Zopounidis wishes to dedicate this to his wife, Kalia, and children, Dimitrios and Helene.

Emilios Galariotis wishes to dedicate this to his wife, Litsa, his children, Irini and Vasileios, and his parents, Christos and Irini.

Contents

CHAPTER 9
Statistical Properties and Tests of Efficient Frontier Portfolios   242

C J Adcock

SECTION FOUR
Credit Risk Modelling

CHAPTER 10
Stress Testing for Portfolio Credit Risk: Supervisory Expectations and Practices   273

Michael Jacobs Jr.

CHAPTER 11
A Critique of Credit Risk Models with Evidence from Mid-Cap Firms   296

David E. Allen, Robert J. Powell and Abhay K. Singh

Preface

The book *Quantitative Financial Risk Management: Theory and Practice* provides an invaluable forum for creative and scholarly work on financial risk management, risk models, portfolio management, credit risk modeling, portfolio management, and financial markets throughout the world.

Quantitative financial risk management consists of economics, accounting, statistics, econometrics, mathematics, stochastic processes, and computer science and technology. The tools of financial management are more frequently being applied to manage, monitor, and measure risk, especially in the context of globalization, market volatility, and economic crisis.

The main objectives of this book are to advance knowledge related to risk management and portfolio optimization, as well as to generate theoretical knowledge with the aim of promoting research within various sectors wherein financial markets operate. Chapters will relate to one of these areas, will have a theoretical and/or empirical problem orientation, and will demonstrate innovation in theoretical and empirical analyses, methodologies, and applications.

We would like to thank the assistant editors Georgios Manthoulis and Stavroula Sarri for their invaluable help. We extend appreciation to the authors and referees of these chapters, and to the editors at John Wiley & Sons, Inc., for their assistance in producing this book.

The editors,
Constantin Zopounidis
Emilios Galariotis

About the Editors

Constantin Zopounidis is professor of Financial Engineering and Operations Research at Technical University of Crete in Greece, distinguished research professor at Audencia Nantes, School of Management (EQUIS, AMBA, AACSB) in France, senior academician of the Royal Academy of Doctors and the Royal Academy of Economics and Financial Sciences of Spain, and elected president of the Financial Engineering and Banking Society (FEBS).

His research interests include financial engineering, financial risk management, and multiple-criteria decision making. He has edited and authored more than 70 books in international publishers and more than 450 research papers in scientific journals, edited volumes, conference proceedings, and encyclopedias in the areas of finance, accounting, operations research, and management science. Prof. Zopounidis is editor-in-chief and member of the editorial board of several international journals. In recognition of his scientific work, he has received several awards from international research societies.

Emilios Galariotis is professor of Finance at Audencia Nantes School of Management (AMBA, EQUIS, AACSB) in France. He is the founder and director of the Centre for Financial and Risk Management (CFRM) and head of research in the area of Finance, Risk, and Accounting Performance at Audencia.

His academic career started at Durham University and head of research in the area of Finance, Risk, and Accounting Performance as well as co-chair of the department of Accounting and Finance at Audencia. UK. There, beyond his academic role. His academic career started at Durham University, UK (Top 100 in the world, 3rd oldest in England), he was also director of Specialized Finance Masters Programs. His research interests include behavioral finance and market efficiency, contrarian and momentum investment strategies, and liquidity.

His work has been published in quality refereed journals, such as (to mention only the most recent) the *European Journal of Operational Research, the Journal of Banking and Finance,* as well as the *Wiley Encyclopedia of Management.* Professor Galariotis is associate editor and member of the editorial board of several international journals, and member of the board of directors of the Financial Engineering and Banking Society and distinguished researcher at various research centers.

One

Supervisory Risk Management

CHAPTER 1

Measuring Systemic Risk: Structural Approaches

Raimund M. Kovacevic
ISOR, Department of Statistics and OR,
University of Vienna, Austria

Georg Ch. Pflug
ISOR and IIASA, Laxenburg

"Systemic risks are developments that threaten the stability of the financial system as a whole and consequently the broader economy, not just that of one or two institutions."
—Ben Bernanke, ex-chairman of the US Federal Reserve Bank.

The global financial crisis of 2007–2008, often considered as the worst financial crisis since the Great Depression of the 1930s, resulted in a change of paradigms in the financial and banking sector. These crisis years saw collapses of large financial institutions, bailouts of banks by governments, and declines of stock markets. Triggered by the U.S. housing bubble, which itself was caused by giving easy access to loans for subprime borrowers, financial distress spread over the banking sector and led to failure of key businesses and to the 2008–2012 global recession. Finally, this also contributed to the European sovereign-debt crisis, with lots of aftereffects in our present times.

Uncertainties about bank solvency, declines in credit availability, and reduced investor confidence had an impact on global stock markets. Governments responded with fiscal measures and institutional bailouts, which in the long term resulted in extreme public debts and necessary tax increases.

This negative experience demonstrates that the economy as a whole, but especially the financial sector is subject to risks, which are grounded in the interdependencies between the different economic actors and not in the performance of individual actors. This type of risk is generally called *systemic risk*. While aspects of systemic risk (e.g., bank run and contagion) were always an issue in discussions about the financial system, the recent crises have increased the interest in the topic, not only in academic circles, but also among regulators and central banks.

SYSTEMIC RISK: DEFINITIONS

If one aims at measuring—and in a further step managing and mitigating—systemic risk, it is important to start with a definition. However, despite the consent that systemic risk is an important topic, which is reflected by an increasing number of related papers and technical reports, there is still not a single generally accepted definition.

As a first step, one should distinguish between systemic and systematic risk. Systematic risks are aggregate (macroeconomic) risks that cannot be reduced by hedging and diversification. Systemic risk, on the other hand, is a different notion. It refers to the risk of breakdown or at least major dysfunction of financial markets. The Group of Ten (2001) gave the following, often cited definition:

> Systemic financial risk is the risk that an event will trigger a loss of economic value or confidence in, and attendant increases in uncertainly about, a substantial portion of the financial system that is serious enough to quite probably have significant adverse effects on the real economy. Systemic risk events can be sudden and unexpected, or the likelihood of their occurrence can build up through time in the absence of appropriate policy responses. The adverse real economic effects from systemic problems are generally seen as arising from disruptions to the payment system, to credit flows, and from the destruction of asset values.

This formulation describes many aspects related to systemic risk but can hardly be called a definition in the technical sense, as it is very broad and hard to quantify. In addition, it seems to confuse cause (confidence) and consequence (breakdown).

As an alternative, Kaufmann and Scott (2003) introduced the following definition:

> Systemic risk refers to the risk or probability of breakdowns in an entire system, as opposed to breakdowns in individual parts or components, and is evidenced by co-movements among most or all the parts.

In similar manner, but naming the cause and again considering larger consequences, the European Central Bank (2004) defines systemic risk as follows:

> The risk that the inability of one institution to meet its obligations when due will cause other institutions to be unable to meet their obligations when due. Such a failure may cause significant liquidity or credit problems and, as a result, could threaten the stability of or confidence in markets.

All discussed definitions focus on the banking or financial system as a whole, and relate systemic risk to the interconnectedness within the system. Often, they stress the risk of spillovers from the financial sector to the real economy and the associated related costs. This effect is emphasized even more after the financial crisis as described in the following definition of systemic risk from Adrian and Brunnermeier (2009):

> The risk that institutional distress spreads widely and distorts the supply of credit and capital to the real economy.

A similar definition can be found in Acharya et al. 2009.

Given the described diversity of definitions, which are similar but also different with respect to their focus, it is hard to develop universally accepted measures for systemic risk. Different definitions refer to different important nuances of systemic risk, which means that on the operational level a robust framework for monitoring and managing systemic risk should involve a variety of risk measures related to these different aspects. See Hansen (2012) for a deeper discussion of the basic difficulties in defining and identifying systemic risk.

We will focus on the first part of the definition by Kaufmann and Scott (2003), which summarizes the most important aspect of systematic risk in financial systems, without addressing more general economic aspects. Such an approach could be seen as "systemic risk in the narrow sense" and we state it (slightly modified) as follows:

Systemic risk is the risk of breakdowns in an entire system, as opposed to breakdowns in individual parts or components.

Three issues have to be substantiated, if one wants to apply such a definition in concrete situations: system, breakdowns, and risk.

System

In financial applications, the focus lies on parts of the financial system (like the banking system, insurance, hedge funds) or the financial system as a whole. Any analysis has to start with describing the agents (e.g., banks in the banking system) within the analyzed system. This involves their assets and liabilities and the main risk factors related to profit and loss.

For a systemic view, it is important that the agents are not isolated entities at all. Systematic risk can be modeled by joint risk factors, influencing all profit and losses. Systemic risk in financial systems usually comes by mutual debt between the entities and the related leverage.

Breakdowns

In single-period models, breakdown is related to bankruptcy in a technical sense—that is, that the asset value of an agent at the end of the period does not reach a certain level (e.g., is not sufficient to pay back the agents debt). A lower boundary than debt can be used to reflect the fact that confidence into a bank might fade away even before bankruptcy, which severely reduces confidence between banks. In a systemic view, it is not sufficient to look at breakdowns of individual agents: Relevant are events that lead to the breakdown of more than one agent.

Risk

Risk is the danger that unwanted events (here, breakdowns) may happen or that developments go in an unintended direction. Quantifiable risk is described by distributions arising from risk. For financial systems this may involve the probability of breakdowns or the distribution of payments necessary to bring back asset values to an acceptable level. Risk measures summarize favorable or unfavorable properties of such distributions.

It should be mentioned that such an approach assumes that a good distributional model for the relevant risk factors can be formulated and estimated. During this chapter, we will stick to exactly this assumption. However, it is clear that in practice it is often difficult to come up with good models, and data availability might be severely restricted. Additional risk (model risk) is related to the quality of the used models and estimations; see Hansen (2012) for a deeper discussion of this point.

FROM STRUCTURAL MODELS TO SYSTEMIC RISK

Structural models for default go back to Merton (2009) and build on the idea that default of a firm happens if the firm's assets are insufficient to cover contractual obligations (liabilities). Simple models such as Merton (2009) start by modeling a single firm in the framework of the Black–Scholes option pricing model, whereas more complex models extend the framework to multivariate formulations, usually based on correlations between the individual asset values. A famous example is Vasicek's asymptotic single factor model (see Vasicek 1987; 1991; and 2002), which is very stylized but leads to a closed-form solution.

In most structural default models, it is not possible to calculate the portfolio loss explicitly; hence, Monte Carlo simulation is an important tool for default calculations. Even then, the models usually make simplifying assumptions.

Consider a system consisting of k economic entities (e.g., banks), and let $A_1(t), A_2(t), \ldots, A_k(t)$ denote the asset processes—that is, the asset values at time t for the individual entities. Furthermore, for each entity i a limit D_i, the distress barrier, defines default in the following sense: default occurs if the asset value of entity i falls below the distress barrier:

$$A_i(t) < D_i. \tag{1.1}$$

The relation between asset value and distress barrier is usually closely related to leverage, the ratio between debt and equity.

Finally, let $X_1(t), X_2(t), \ldots, X_k(t)$ with

$$X_i(t) = A_i(t) - D_i \tag{1.2}$$

denote *the distance to default* of the individual entities. Note that alternatively the distance to default can also be defined in terms of $X_i(t)$ as a percentage of asset value, divided by the asset volatility (see e.g., Crosbie and Bohn 2003).

In a one period setup—as used throughout this chapter—one is interested at values $A_i(T), X_i(T)$ at time T, the end of the planning horizon. Analyzing systemic risk then means analyzing the joint distribution of the distances to default $X_i(t)$, in particular their negative parts $X_i(T)^- = \max\{-X_i(T), 0\}$, and the underlying random risk factors are described by the joint distribution of asset values $A_i(T)$.

Many approaches for modeling the asset values exist in literature. In a classical finance setup, one would use correlated geometric Brownian motions resulting in correlated log-normal distributions for the asset values at the end of the planning horizon. Segoviano Basurto proposes a Bayesian approach (Segoviano Basurto 2006); for applications, see also Jin and Nadal de Simone (2013). In this chapter, we will use copula-based models, as discussed later.

The second component of the approach, the distress barrier, is in the simplest case (Merton 2009), modeled just by the face value of overall debt for each entity. Other approaches distinguish between short-term and long-term debt (longer than the planning horizon). Usually, this is done by adding some reasonable fraction of long-term debt to the full amount of short term debt; see, for example, Servigny and Renault (2007).

Still, such classical credit default models (see, e.g., Guerra et al. 2013), although classified as systemic risk models, neglect an important aspect: Economic entities like banks are mutually indebted, and each amount of debt is shown as a liability for one entity but also as an asset for another entity. Default of one entity (a reduction in liabilities) may trigger subsequent defaults of other entities by reducing their asset values. We call such models systemic models in the strict sense.

Such approaches with mutual debt have been proposed, such as in Chan-Lau et al. (2009a; 2009b). Models neglecting this aspect are systemic models in a broad sense; in fact, they are restricted to the effects of systematic risk related to asset values.

The basic setup of systemic models in the strict sense can be described as follows: Let H^0_{ij} denote the amount of debt between entities i and j —that is, the amount of money borrowed by entity i from entity j. We also include debt to the nonbank sector, denoted by H_i for each entity i and credit C_i to the nonbanking sector, both repayable (including interest) at the end of the planning horizon, time T. Furthermore, $S_i(T)$ is the value at time T of other financial assets held by entity i. Then the asset value of entity i at the end of the planning horizon is given by

$$A^0_i(T) = S_i(T) + \sum_{j:j \neq i} H^0_{ji} + C_i, \qquad (1.3)$$

the distress barrier (in the simplest case) is

$$D^0_i = \sum_{j:j \neq i} H^0_{ij} + H_i, \qquad (1.4)$$

and the distance to default can be written as

$$X^0_i(T) = A_i(T) - D^0_i = S_i(T) + C_i + \sum_{j:j \neq i} H^0_{ji} - \sum_{j:j \neq i} H^0_{ij} - H_i. \qquad (1.5)$$

The random factors are the values $S_i(T)$ of financial assets, and (in an extended model) the credits C_i from outside the system, payable back at time.

Again, one could stop at this point and analyze the distances to default X^0_i, respectively the sum of all individual distances to default in the framework of classical default models. Systemic models in the strict sense, however, go farther.

Consider now all entities in distress (defaulted banks), that is, $I_D = \{i: X_i^0(T) < 0\}$. Each of these entities is closed down and the related debt has to be adjusted, because entity i cannot fully pay back its debts. In a simple setup, this can be done by reducing all debts to other entities as follows:

$$H_{ij}^1 = \left(1 - \frac{(X_i^0)^-}{D_i^0}\right) H_{ij}^0, \tag{1.6}$$

$$H_i^1 = \left(1 - \frac{(X_i^0)^-}{D_i^0}\right) H_i^0. \tag{1.7}$$

Here, the factor

$$LGD_i = (X_i^0)^-/D_i^0 \tag{1.8}$$

is an estimate for the loss given default of entity i.

It is now possible to calculate new asset values, new distress barriers, and new distances to default, after the default of all entities in I_D^0. For this purpose, we replace in (1.3) to (1.5) all occurrences of H_{ij}^0 by H_{ij}^1 and all occurrences of H_i^0 by H_i^1. This first default triggers further ones and starts a *loss cascade*: It may happen that after the first adjustment step new defaults can be observed, which results in a new set of bankrupt entities I_D^1 after the second round. In addition, bankruptcy of additional entities may reduce even further the insolvent assets of entities that already defaulted in the first round.

This process can be continued, leading to new values $X_i^k(T), H_{ij}^k, A_i^k(T)$, $D_i^k(T)$, and an augmented set I_D^k of defaulted entities after each iteration k. The loss cascade terminates, when no additional entity is sent to bankruptcy in step k, that is, $I_D^k = I_D^{k-1}$.

The sequences $[H_{ij}^k]$ and $[H_i^k]$ of debt are nonincreasing in k and, furthermore, are bounded from below by zero values for all components, which implies convergence of debt. At this point we have

$$S_i(T) + C_i + \sum_{j \neq i}\left(1 - \frac{X_j(T)^-}{\sum_{\substack{k \neq j}} H_{jk}^0 + H_j}\right) H_{ji}^0 - \sum_{j \neq i}\left(1 - \frac{X_i(T)^-}{\sum_{j \neq i} H_{ij}^0 + H_i}\right)(H_{ij}^0 + H_i)$$

$$= X_i(T)^+ - X_i(T)^- X_i(T)^+ \geq 0, X_i(T)^- \geq 0. \tag{1.9}$$

This system describes the relation between the positive and negative parts of the distances to default $X_i(T) = X_i(T)^+ - X_i(T)^-$ for all entities i. It holds with probability 1 for all entities. Note that previous literature, such as Chan-Lau et al. (2009a; 2009b), uses fixed numbers instead of the estimated loss given defaults in (1.9).

In fact, the system (1.9) is ambiguous, and we search for the smallest solution, the optimization problem

$$\min_{X(T)} \quad \mathbf{E}\left[\sum_i X_i(T)^-\right] \tag{1.10}$$

$$\text{subject to} \quad (1.9)$$

has to be solved in order to obtain the correct estimates for $X_i(T)^+$ and $X_i(T)^-$.

This basic setup can be easily extended to deal with different definitions of the distress barrier, involving early warning barriers, or accounting for different types of debt (e.g., short-term and long-term, as indicated earlier).

MEASURING SYSTEMIC RISK

The distances to default, derived from structural models, in particular from systemic models in the strict sense, can be used to measure systemic risk. In principle, the joint distribution of distances to default for all involved entities contains (together with the definition of distress barriers) all the relevant information. We assume that the joint distribution is continuous and let $p(x) = p(x_1, x_2, \ldots, x_k)$ denote the joint density of the distances to default $X_1(T), X_2(T), \ldots, X_k(T)$ for all entities.

Note that the risk measures discussed in the following are often defined in terms of asset value, which is fully appropriate for systemic models in the broader sense. In view of the previous discussion of systemic models in the strict sense, we instead prefer to use the distances to default or loss variables derived from the distance to default.

The first group of risk measures is based directly on unconditional and conditional default probabilities. See Guerra et al. (2013) for an overview of such measures. The simplest approach considers the *individual distress probabilities*

$$P_i^D = P(X_i(T) < 0)$$

$$= \int_{x_i < 0} \left[\int_{-\infty}^{+\infty} \cdots \int_{-\infty}^{+\infty} p\left(x_1, x_2, \ldots, x_k\right) dx_1 \cdots dx_{i-1} dx_{i+1} \cdots dx_k \, dx_i. \tag{1.11}\right.$$

The term in squared brackets is the marginal density of $X_i(T)$, which means that it is not necessary to estimate the joint density for this measure. In similar manner, one can consider joint distributions for any subset $I \subseteq \{1, \ldots, k\}$ of entities by using the related (joint) marginal density $p_I(x)$, which can be obtained by integrating the joint density $p(x)$ over all other entities, that is, $j \notin I$.

Joint probabilities of distress for a subset I can be achieved by

$$P_I^D = P(\forall i \in I : X_i(T) < 0) = \int\limits_{x_{i1} < 0} \cdots \int\limits_{x_{ik_I} < 0} p_I(x_{i_1}, \ldots, x_{ik_I}) dx_{i_1} \ldots dx_{ik_I},$$

(1.12)

where the set I contains the elements $i_1, i_2, \ldots, i_{k_I}$. Of special interest are the default probabilities of pairs of entities (see, e.g., Guerra, et al., 2013). Joint probabilities of distress describe tail risk within the chosen set I. If I represents the whole system (i.e., it contains all the entities), then the joint probability of distress can be considered as a tail risk measure for systemic risk (see, e.g., Segoviano & Goodhart, 2009).

Closely related are *conditional probabilities of distress*, that is, the probability that entity j is in distress, given that entity j is in distress, which can be written as

$$P_{j|i}^D = P(X_j(T) < 0 | X_i(T) < 0) = \frac{P_{\{i,j\}}^D}{P_i^D}.$$

(1.13)

These conditional probabilities can be presented by a matrix with $P_{j|i}^D$ as its *ij*th matrix element, the *distress dependency matrix*.

While conditional distress probabilities contain important information, it should be noted that they only reflect the two-dimensional marginal distributions. Conditional probabilities are often used for analyzing the interlinkage of the system and the likelihood of contagion. However, such arguments should not be carried to extremes. Finally, conditional probabilities do not contain any information about causality.

Another systemic measure related to probabilities is the probability of at least one distressed entity; see Segoviano and Goodhart (2009) for an application to a small system of four entities. It can be calculated as

$$P^1 = 1 - P(X_1 \geq 0, \ldots, X_k \geq 0)$$

(1.14)

Guerra et al. (2013) propose an asset-value-weighted average of individual probabilities of distress as an upper bound for the probability of at least one distressed entity. Probabilities of exactly one, two, or another number of distressed entities are hard to calculate for large systems because of the large number of combinatorial possibilities.

An important measure based on probabilities is the *banking stability index*, measuring the expected number of entities in distress, given that at least one entity is in distress. This measure can be written as

$$BSI = \frac{\sum_{i=1}^{k} P_i^D}{P^1}.$$ (1.15)

Other systemic risk measures based directly on the distribution of distances to default. Adrian and Brunnermeier (2009) propose a measure called *conditional value at risk*,[1] $CoVaR^=$. It is closely related to value at risk, which is the main risk measure for banks under the Basel accord.

$CoVaR^=$ is based on conditional versions of the quantile at level β for an entity j given that entity i reaches the α-quantile. In terms of distances to default, this reads

$$CoVaR_{\alpha,\beta}^=(j \mid i) = \inf \left\{ \gamma \in \mathbb{R} : P\left(X_j(T) \leq \gamma \mid X_i(T) = VaR_\alpha(X_i(T)) \right) \geq \beta \right\},$$ (1.16)

where

$$VaR_\alpha(i) = \inf \left\{ \gamma \in \mathbb{R} : P\left(X_i(T) \leq \gamma \right) \geq \alpha \right\}.$$ (1.17)

The contribution of entity i to the risk of entity j then is calculated as

$$\Delta CoVaR_\alpha^=(j \mid i) = CoVaR_{\alpha,\alpha}^=(j \mid i) - CoVaR_{0.5,0.5}^=(j \mid i).$$ (1.18)

That is, the conditional value at risk at level α is compared to the conditional value at risk at the median level. From all the $\Delta CoVaR_\alpha^=(j \mid i)$ values, it is possible to construct another kind of dependency matrix.

This idea can also be applied to the system as a whole: If $X_i(T)$ is replaced by $X(T) = \sum_{i=1}^{k} X_i(T)$, the distance to default of the whole system, (1.16) to (1.18), leads to a quantity $\Delta CoVaR_\alpha^=(j \mid i)$ that measures the impact of entity i on the system. In this way one is able to analyze notions like "too big to fail" or "too interconnected to fail."

In contrast to probability-based measures, $CoVaR$ emphasizes the role of potential monetary losses. This approach can be carried forward, leading to the idea that systemic risk should be related to the losses arising from

---

[1]Conditional value at risk should not be confused with general risk measure with the same name, which is also known as expected tail loss or average value at risk.

adverse events. Given a model for the distances to default $X_i(T)$, the overall loss of the system can be written as

$$L^{tot} = \sum_{i=1}^{k} X_i(T)^-. \tag{1.19}$$

L^{tot} covers all credit losses in the whole system, both from interbank credits and from credits to the public.

From the viewpoint of a state, this notion of total loss may be seen as too extensive. One may argue that only losses guaranteed by the state are really relevant. Definition (1.19) therefore depicts a situation in which a state guarantees all debt in the system, which can be considered as unrealistic. However, in most developed countries, the state guarantees saving deposits to a high extend, and anyhow society as a whole will have to bear the consequences of lost debt from outside the banking system. Therefore, a further notion of loss is given by

$$L^{sav} = \sum_{i=1}^{k} LGD_i \cdot H_i, \tag{1.20}$$

which describes the amount of lost nonbanking debt For the structural model, which has been described in the previous section, loss given default can be calculated using (1.8) and (1.9).

In general, the notion of loss depends on the exact viewpoint (loss to whom). We will therefore use the symbol L to represent any kind of loss variable in the following discussion of systemic risk measures.

An obvious measure is expected loss—that is, the (discounted) expectation of the risk variable L. For simple structural models like (1.2), this measure can be calculated from the marginal distribution of asset values, respectively, of distances to default. Modeling the joint distributions is not necessary. Note that this is different for the strict systemic model (1.9).

The expectation can be calculated with respect to an observed (estimated) model, or with respect to a risk-neutral (martingale) model. Using observed probabilities may account insufficiently for risk, which contradicts the aim of systemic risk measurement. Using risk-neutral valuation seems reasonable from a finance point of view and has been used, for example, in Gray and Jobst (2010) or Gray et al. (2010). However, it should be kept in mind that the usual assumptions underlying contingent claims analysis—in particular, that the acting investor is a price taker—are not valid if the investor has to hedge the whole financial system, which clearly would be the case when hedging the losses related to systemic risk.

Using expectation and the concept of loss cascades, Cont et al. (2010) define a *contagion index* as follows: They define first the total loss of a loss cascade triggered by a default of entity i and the contagion index of entity i as the expected total loss conditioned on all scenarios that trigger the default of entity i.

Clearly, the expectation does not fully account for risk. An obvious idea is to augment expectation by some risk measure ρ, which, with weight a, leads to

$$\pi_\rho(L) = E[L] + a\rho(L). \tag{1.21}$$

Typical choices of ρ are dispersion measures like the variance or the standard deviation. Such measures are examples of classical premium calculation principles in insurance. Further, more general premium calculation principles are for example, the distortion principle or the Esscher premium principle. For an overview on insurance pricing, see Furmann and Zitikis (2008). In the context of systemic risk, the idea to use insurance premiums was proposed in Huang et al. (2009). In this chapter, empirical methods were used for extracting an insurance premium from high-frequency credit default swap data. Even more generally, it should be noted that any monetary risk measure—in particular, coherent measures of risk—can be applied to the overall loss in a system. See Kovacevic and Pflug (2014) for an overview and references.

In this broad framework, an important class of risk measures is given by the *quantiles* of the loss variable L:

$$Q_\alpha(L) = \inf\{l : P\{L \le l\} \ge \alpha\}. \tag{1.22}$$

With probability α, the loss will not be higher than the related quantile.

Quantiles are closely related to the value at risk (VaR), which measures quantiles for the deviation of the loss from the expected loss. Note the slight difference between (1.22) and (1.17), because (1.17) is stated in terms of distance to default and (1.12) in terms of loss.

$Q_\alpha(L)$ can also be interpreted in an economic way, as follows. Assume that a fund is built up in order to cover systemic losses in the banking system. If we ask how large the fund should be, such that it is not exhausted, with probability α over the planning period, then the answer will be $Q_L(\alpha)$. This idea can also be reversed. Assume now that a fund of size q has been accumulated to deal with systemic losses. Then the *probability that the fund is not exhausted*,

$$F_L(q) = P(L \le q), \tag{1.23}$$

is a reasonable systemic risk measure. Clearly, $F_L(q)$ is the distribution function of the loss, and q is the quantile at level $F_L(q)$.

Unfortunately, quantiles do not contain any information about those $(1 - \alpha)100$ percent cases, in which the loss lies above the quantile. Two different distributions, which are equal in their negative tails, but very different in the positive tails, are treated equally.

The average value at risk (AVaR) avoids some drawbacks of quantiles. It is defined for a parameter α, which again is called level. The AVaR averages the bad scenario,

$$AVaR_\alpha(L) = E[L|L > Q_\alpha(L)]. \tag{1.24}$$

The latter formula justifies the alternative name conditional value at risk (CVaR), which is frequently used in finance. In insurance, the AVaR is known as conditional tail expectation or expected tail loss.

The effect of individual banks can be analyzed in obvious manner by defining conditional versions of the quantile or *AVaR* loss measures—that is, by conditioning the overall loss on the distance to default of an individual bank in the style of *CoVaR*; see (1.16).

SYSTEMIC RISK AND COPULA MODELS

The distinction between risk factors that are related to individual performances and risk factors that are a consequence of the interrelations of the economic agents has its parallel in a similar distinction for probability distributions or stochastic processes:

Suppose that $X_1(t), \ldots, X_k(t)$ describe the performance processes of k economic agents. The individual (marginal) processes are assumed to follow certain stochastic models as discrete Markov processes, diffusion models, or jump-diffusion models. The joint distribution, however, depends on the copula process, which links the marginal processes.

To simplify, suppose only a single-period model is considered and that the performance after one period is $X_1, \ldots, X_k$. If this vector has marginal cumulative distribution functions $F_1, \ldots, F_k$ (meaning that $P(X_i \leq u) = F_i(u)$), then the joint distribution of the whole vector can be represented by

$$P(X_1 \leq u_1, \ldots, X_k \leq u_k) = C(F_1(u_1), \ldots, F_k(u_k)), \tag{1.25}$$

where C is called the copula function. Typical families of copula functions are the normal copula, the Clayton copula, the Gumbel copula or—more generally—the group of Archimedean copulas.

While the marginal distributions describe the individual performances, the copula function models the interrelations between them and can thus be seen as representing the systemic component. In particular, the relation between underperformance of agent i and agent j can be described on the basis of the copula. To this end, we use the notion of conditional value at risk (CoVaR), as already described. Following Mainink and Schaaning (2014) we use the notations

$$CoVaR_{\alpha,\beta}^{=}(Y \mid X) = VaR_{\beta}(Y \mid X = VaR_{\alpha}(X))$$

for the notion of CoVAR introduced by Adrian and Brunnermeier (2009) and

$$CoVaR_{\alpha,\beta}(Y \mid X) = VaR_{\beta}(Y \mid X \leq VaR_{\alpha}(X))$$

for the variant introduced by Girardi and Ergün (2012). Keep in mind that we work here with profit and loss variables and not with pure loss variables. The latter variant can be expressed in terms of the conditional copula

$$C_{V \mid U \leq \alpha}(v) = \frac{P(V \leq u, U \leq \alpha)}{P(U \leq \alpha)} = \frac{C(\alpha, v)}{\alpha}.$$

Its inverse

$$C_{V \mid U \leq \alpha}^{-1}(\beta) = \inf \{v : C_{V \mid U \leq \alpha}(v) \geq \beta\}$$

and the marginal distribution of X can be used to write the $CoVaR$ in the following way:

$$CoVaR_{\alpha,\beta}(Y \mid X) = F_X^{-1}(C_{V \mid U \leq \alpha}^{-1}(\beta)).$$

For the $CoVaR_{\alpha,\beta}^{=}(Y \mid X)$, the conditional copula

$$C_{V \mid U = \alpha}(v) = \frac{\partial}{\partial v} C(\alpha, v)$$

is needed. With

$$C_{V \mid U = \alpha}^{-1}(\beta) = \inf \{v : C_{V \mid U = \alpha}(v) \geq \beta\}$$

one gets

$$CoVaR_{\alpha,\beta}^{=}(Y \mid X) = F_X^{-1}(C_{V \mid U = \alpha}^{-1}(\beta)).$$

Notice that both notions of $CoVaR$ depend only on the copula and the marginal distribution of X.

If underperformance of an agent means that its performance falls below an α-quantile, then $C_{V \mid U \leq \alpha}(\alpha) = \frac{C(\alpha,\alpha)}{\alpha}$ indicates the probability that the other agent also underperforms. $CoVaR_{\alpha,\alpha}(X_i \mid X_j)$ gives the necessary risk reserve for agent i to survive a possible default of agent j. For a system of k agents, the notion of $CoVaR_{\alpha,\beta}$ can be generalized in a straightforward manner to k components.

Example 1. Consider a financial institution A, which faces a gamma-distributed loss with mean 10 and variance 20. Then A's unconditional 99% VaR is 23.8.

If A's performance related to B's performance with a normal copula with correlation ρ, then A's conditional VaR (the CoVaR) increases with increasing ρ, see Table 1.1.

Example 2. Consider a system of seven banks, where the performances $X_i, i = 1, \ldots, 7$ are related by a normal copula stemming from a correlation matrix with all off-diagonal elements ρ (the diagonal elements are 1). Suppose that the first bank defaults if its performance drops below the 5 percent quantile. Given the copula, one may determine the number of other banks that also fall below the 5 percent quantile (i.e., default as a consequence of the first bank's default). Figures 1.1 and 1.2 show the distribution of these numbers for the choice of $\rho = 0, \rho = 0.2, \rho = 0.5$ and $\rho = 0.8$. One may observe that in the independent case ($\rho = 0$) the other banks are practically not affected by the default of one bank, while for higher correlated cases a contagion effect to other banks can be easily seen.

A very interdependent banking system carries a high systemic risk. It has therefore been proposed to limit the dependencies by creating quite independent subsystems. Example 3 gives evidence for this argument.

TABLE 1.1 Conditional VaR and correlation for example 1

ρ	0.0	0.2	0.5	0.8
$\text{CoVaR}_{0.99, 0.99}$	23.8	26.6	30.0	31.4

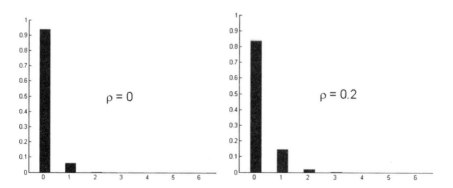

FIGURE 1.1 The distribution of the number of affected banks using the assumptions of Example 2. Left: the uncorrelated case ($\rho = 0$). Right: the weakly correlated case ($\rho = 0.2$).

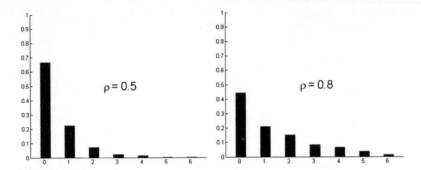

FIGURE 1.2 The distribution of the number of affected banks using the assumptions of Example 2. Left: the medium correlated case ($\rho = 5$). Right: the highly correlated case ($\rho = 0.8$).

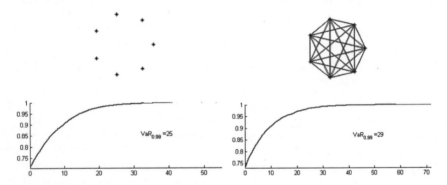

FIGURE 1.3 Left: All banks are independent, $\text{VaR}_{0.99} = 25$; Right: All correlations are $\rho = 0.2$, $\text{VaR}_{0.99} = 29$.

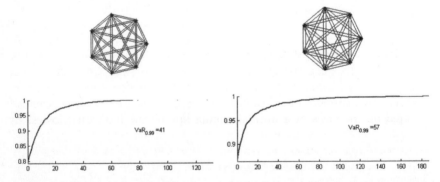

FIGURE 1.4 Left: All correlations are $\rho = 0.5$, $\text{VaR}_{0.99} = 41$; Right: All correlations are $\rho = 0.8$, $\text{VaR}_{0.99} = 57$.

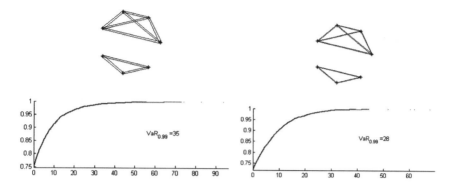

FIGURE 1.5 The system consists of two independent subsystems with internal correlations ρ. Left: $\rho = 0.2$, $\text{VaR}_{0.99} = 28$; Right: $\rho = 0.5$, $\text{VaR}_{0.99} = 35$.

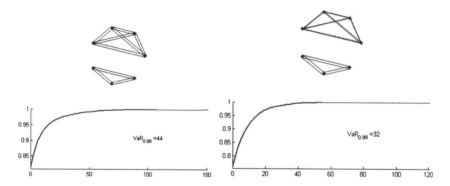

FIGURE 1.6 The system consists of two independent subsystems with internal correlations ρ. Left: $\rho = 0.8$, $\text{VaR}_{0.99} = 44$; Right: One subsystem has $\rho = 0.2$, the other $\rho = 0.8$, $\text{VaR}_{0.99} = 32$.

Example 3. Here, we consider seven banks, each of which has a performance given by a negative gamma distribution with mean 100 and variance 200, but shifted such that with probability 5 percent a negative performance happens, which means bankruptcy. The total losses of the system are calculated on the basis of a normal copula linking the individual losses. By assuming that the government (or the taxpayer) takes responsibility for covering total losses up to the 99 percent quantile, this quantile (the 99 percent VaR) can be seen as a quantization of the systemic risk.

In Figures 1.3 to 1.6, we show in the upper half a visualization of the correlations (which determine the normal copula) by the thickness of the arcs connecting the seven nodes representing the banks. The lower half shows the distribution of the total systemic losses, where also the 99 percent VaR is indicated. As one can see, the higher correlation increases the systemic risk. If the system is divided into independent subsystems, the systemic risk decreases.

CONCLUSIONS

Systemic financial risk is an important issue in view of the distress the banking systems all over the world have experienced in the recent years of crises. Even if breakdowns are prevented by the government, the related societal costs are extremely high.

We described the measurement of systemic risk, based on the structural approach originating from structural credit risk models. In particular, the cascading effects that are caused by mutual debt between the individual banks in the system were analyzed in detail. Furthermore, we related the notion of systemic risk to the copula structure, modeling dependency between the performances of the individual banks. The effects of different levels of dependency on the total systemic risk in terms of the value at risk of total losses were demonstrated by examples.

REFERENCES

Acharya, V., L. Pedersen, T. Phillipon, and M. Richardson. 2009. Regulating systemic risk. In *Restoring Financial Stability: How to Repair a Failed System*. Hoboken, NJ: John Wiley and Sons.

Adrian, T., and M. K. Brunnermeier. 2009. CoVar. In: Staff Report 348: Federal Reserve Bank of New York.

Chan-Lau, J., J. M. Espinosa-Vega, and J. Sole. 2009a. *On the use of network analysis to assess systemic financial linkages*. Washington, D.C.: International Monetary Fund, IMF.

Chan-Lau, J., M. A. Espinosa-Vega, K. Giesecke, and J. Sole. 2009b. A. Assessing the systemic implications of financial linkages. In: *Global Financial Stability Report*. Washington, D.C.: International Monetary Fund, IMF.

Cont, R., A. Moussa, and E.e.S. Bastos. 2010. Network structure and systemic risk in banking systems, s.l.: Preprint, electronic copy available at http://ssrn.com/abstract=1733528.

Crosbie, P. and J. Bohn. 2003. Modeling default risk: Moody's KMV.

European Central Bank. 2004. Annual Report, Frankfurt, available at http://www.ecb.europa.eu/pub/pdf/annrep/ar2004en.pdf.

Furmann, E., and R. Zitikis. 2008. Weighted premium calculation principles. *Insurance, Mathematics and Economics*, 459–465.

Girardi, G., and T. Ergün. 2012. Systemic risk measurement: Multivariate GARCH estimation of CoVaR. available at http://papers.ssrn.com/sol3/papers.cfm?abstract_id=1783958.

Gray, D. F., A. A. Jobst, and S. W. Malone. 2010. Quantifying systemic risk and reconceptualizing the role of finance for economic growth. *Journal of Investment Management* 8(2).

Gray, D., and A. A. Jobst. 2010. New directions in financial sector and sovereign risk management. *Journal of Investment Management* 8(1).

Group of Ten. 2001. The G10 Report on Consolidation in the Financial Sector, Chap. 3, http://www.imf.org/external/np/g10/2001/01/Eng/pdf/file3.pdf

Guerra, S. M., B. M. Tabak, R. A. Penaloza, and R. C. de Castro. 2013. Systemic Risk Measures. Working paper 321, Banco do Brasil, http://www.bcb.gov.br/pec/wps/ingl/wps321.pdf [Online].

Hansen, L. P. 2012. Challenges in identifying and measuring systemic risk, s.l.: National Bureau of Economic Research.

Huang, X., H. Zhou, and H. Zhu. 2009. A framework for assessing the systemic risk of major financial institutions. *Journal of Banking and Finance* 33: 2036–2049.

Jin, X., and F. Nadal de Simone. 2013. *Banking Systemic Vulnerabilities: A Tail-Risk Dynamic CIMDO Approach.* Banque centrale de Luxembourg.

Kaufmann, G. G., and K. E. Scott. 2003. What is systemic risk, and do bank regulators retard or contribute to it? *Independent Review* 7: 371–391.

Kovacevic, R., and G. Ch. Pflug. 2014. Measuring and Managing Risk. Chapter 2 In: *Investment Risk Management*, edited by K. Baker and G. Filbeck, Oxford University Press, Oxford, UK.

Mainink, G., and E. Schaaning. 2014. On dependence consistency of CoVaR and some other systemic risk measures. *Statistics and Risk Modeling.*

Merton, R. C. 2009. On the Pricing of Corporate Debt: The Risk Structure of Interest Rates. In: *Continuous Time Finance* (first published 1992). Wiley-Blackwell Publishing, New York, 388–412.

Segoviano Basurto, M. A. 2006. Consistent information multivariate density optimizing methodology, s.l.: London School of Economics, Discussion Paper 557.

Segoviano, M. A., and C. Goodhart. 2009. *Banking Stability Measures.* Washington, D.C.: International Monetary Fund.

Servigny, O. D., and O. Renault. 2007. *Measuring and Managing Credit Risk.* New York: McGraw-Hill.

Vasicek, O. 1987. Probability of loss on loan portfolios. K.M.V. Corporation 12(6).

_____. 1991. Limiting loan loss distribution. K.M.V. Corporation.

_____. 2002. Loan portfolio value. Risk, available at www.risk.net. December: 160–162.

CHAPTER 2

Supervisory Requirements and Expectations for Portfolio-Level Counterparty Credit Risk Measurement and Management

Michael Jacobs Jr., PhD, CFA[1]

Pricewaterhouse Cooper Advisory LLP

INTRODUCTION

A bank's *counterparty credit risk* (CCR) exposure quantifies how much money the counterparty might owe the bank in the event of default. The CCR quantity is broken down into *current exposure* (CE), which measures the exposure if the counterparty were to default today, and *potential exposure* (PE), which measures the potential increase in exposure that could occur between today and some time horizon in the future.

The time of default is typically modeled as a stochastic stopping time. As opposed to the known CE, the PE must be estimated, usually by simulation. First, the *expected positive exposure* (EPE) is computed by simulating a large number (on the order of 10^2 to 10^3) of different paths for the various underlying future prices in the possible market environments, using a so-called regularized variance-covariance matrix. Then the system prices each of the derivative transactions on each path for each sample date,[2] computes collateral call amounts based on relevant marked-to-market (MTM) calculations,

---

[1]The views expressed herein are those of the author and do not necessarily represent a position taken by Pricewaterhouse Cooper Advisory LLP.

[2]Typical sample dates are: daily for the first two weeks, once a week out to a quarter, once a month out to a year, once a quarter out to 10 years, and once a year up to 50 years.

applies the portfolio effects of netting and collateral, and aggregates exposure results to compute the average exposure along a term structure.

While an EPE may be a good indicator of the cost to replace a contract should the counterparty default, EPE is not helpful in the trade inception approval process because of its volatility and the need for a high confidence interval. Therefore, many banks will also report a very high percentile (e.g., 97.7th or 97.5th) of the exposure distribution over a large number of paths.

Note that these peaks in exposure profiles are not simply added over different products for a given counterparty, as these peaks may happen at different points in time. Rather, the time profiles of exposures are summed over products traded with a single counterparty, and the peak of that time profile is the summary PE measure. This methodology is conservative, as PEs are simply added over counterparties, while the bank may enter trades that mitigate each other in terms of PE with different counterparties.

We can readily see that CCR measurement necessarily combines the tools of standard market risk measurement with the tools of standard credit risk determination, a unique challenge to both. This frequently requires calculating *probability-of-default* (PD), *loss-given-default* (LGD), *exposure-at-default* (EAD), and a credit rating of the counterparty.[3]

The *credit valuation adjustment* (CVA) is defined as the product of the EPE times the LGD times the *cumulative mortality rate* (CMR), where the CMR is simply a multi-period PD rate. This is structurally equivalent to pricing EPE as the contingent leg of a *credit default swap* (CDS) by applying the counterparty spread to it. Such a spread is either a market quote if the name has a bespoke traded CDS, or a pseudo-CDS spread computed along a grid arrayed by region, industry, rating, and tenor. In the worst case, bond or loan spreads are used, giving rise to basis risk. It can be recognized that it is this part of the process that joins the market and the credit risk aspects of the algorithm. Practices for measuring market risk are used in mapping derivatives exposures to a set of market risk factors (e.g., spreads, volatilities, or correlations), simulating those factors out to a forward-looking time horizon, and determining the distribution of the level of exposures over various realizations of these risk factors in the simulation. Separately, standard credit risk processes provide assessments of the credit quality of the counterparty, such as PD and LGD estimation.

Direct or originating businesses (i.e., trading desks) are viewed as credit portfolios: As their positions get in the money, this gives rise to CCR, since

---

[3] See Araten and Jacobs 2001; Araten, Jacobs, and Varshney 2004; Araten, Jacobs, Varshney, and Pellegrino 2004; Carey and Gordy 2004; Carey and Hrycay 2001; Frye and Jacobs 2012; Jacobs 2010a, b; Jacobs and Kiefer 2010; and Jacobs, Karagozoglu, and Layish 2012.

the counterparty may default while owing money to the bank. The CVA represents a daily MTM transfer price of default risk charged to the originating business for insuring default risk, which is the price of a pseudo-CDS hedge with the EPE as underlying notional. The group (e.g., the market risk management department) that sells insurance to the business at inception of the trade will cover any loss due to counterparty default. As the exposure rises, due to either an increase in the position or a decrease in the credit quality of the counterparty, the CVA increases as it is marked to market. On the other hand, a profit is reported if the CVA decreases, due either to the bank's position becoming less in the money, an improvement in the counterparty's credit rating, or just the passage of time without any credit event. However, no further credit-related charges or costs are incurred by the business. In the limit, the CVA disappears as the maturity of the derivative contract is reached, and payment—if any is due—is made to the bank.

Products that are new or too complex to be properly simulated within the main CCR engine are dealt with "offline." This usually means assigning them "risk factors" or more generally "add-ons" that are conservative and do not allow for netting; for this reason, such offline trades may account for up to 50 percent of the total exposure, although only 5 to 10 percent of trades made. The problem is that *the counterparty credit exposure* (CCE) is not sensitive to actual risk any longer: The sum of these add-ons may lead to the same measure of CCE for a set of offsetting trades as it does for a set of trades that have no offsets. Hence, these add-ons are really suited only for CCE with counterparties having single trades. Moreover, the large exposures they generate are not taken seriously by management, and these products do not undergo the complementary/downstream risk management processes such as stress testing, which results in risk measures that do not provide a comprehensive view of the risks that banks face. Worse still, management may increase limits for these products, aware that their CCR is overstated, thus defeating the purpose of these add-ons.

A relatively new but expanding practice is to model *debt valuation adjustment* (DVA) in the CCR framework, reflecting an institution's own option to default. Counterparties implicitly charge for an option to default, as when an institution holding a derivative position that is out of the money is in effect borrowing from the counterparty and implicitly pays for its outstanding liability through its credit spread. One way for a bank to fund its CVA would be to generate income from the sale of credit default swaps on itself, which cannot be done, hence the remaining portion of credit risk as reflected by the CVA. However, note that such "gut " appeal DVA stems from the realization that if a bank enters a par swap agreement with a counterparty that has the same credit spread, then theoretically, credit risk considerations should not enter the pricing decision (i.e., the CVA and DVA should cancel for both parties in the transaction).

Analogous to the CVA, scenarios for underlying market factors are generated and averaged over the resultant negative portfolio marked-to-market values (liabilities), taking into account legal netting and collateral agreements. The resulting *expected negative exposure*, floored at zero if a bank gets in the money in any given scenario, is what risk managers expect to owe its counterparties on its derivative portfolio at the time of its default. It is priced as the contingent leg of a credit default swap using the bank's bank spreads, assuming that all deals are netted where possible, reflecting the fact that within the bank's jurisdiction it is likely that its counterparties would legally seek to net all positions upon its default.

For collateral considerations, often two types of default are considered. First, consider the case in which a bank defaults idiosyncratically, and a "springing" unilateral collateral agreement is assumed. This reflects the likely behavior of counterparties, who upon a worsening of a bank's credit worthiness will either demand to enter into unilateral collateral agreements where there are none or renegotiate existing collateral agreements to terms favorable to them. Second, there is the case of a systemic default, where a bank's default is part of a broad economic downturn. In this case it is much less clear that counterparties will be able to impose or change collateral agreements in their favor, and thus springing collateral is not considered. The final expected negative exposure value is a weighted average of the two cases, such that the relative weight is the relative likelihood of an idiosyncratic as opposed to a systematic default. These weights could be determined by the relative intensities of default implied by a bank's par spread curve and its risk premium spread curve backed using a *capital asset pricing model* methodology.

REVIEW OF THE LITERATURE

Supervisory rules and guidance on CCR can be found in the Basel Committee on Banking Supervision (BCBS) frameworks of Basel I (BCBS, 1988); Basel II (BCBS, 2006); Basel III (BCBS, 2011); and BCSB (2012). The U.S. Office of the Comptroller of the Currency (OCC) and the Board of Governors of the Federal Reserve System (BOG-FRS) issued supervisory guidelines (OCC & BOG-FRS 2011). Kang and Kim (2005) provide simple closed-form pricing models for floating-rate notes and vulnerable options under the CCR framework, deriving closed-form pricing models for them and illustrating the impact of the counterparty default intensity on the prices of floating-rate notes and vulnerable options.

Brigo and Chourdakis (2009) consider CCR for credit default swaps when default of the counterparty is correlated with default of the CDS reference credit. They incorporate credit spread volatility, adopt stochastic intensity models for the default events, and connect defaults through a copula function. The authors find that both default correlation and credit spread volatility have a relevant impact on the positive CCR valuation adjustment to be subtracted from the counterparty risk-free price. Jorion and Zhang (2009) observe that standard credit risk models cannot explain the observed clustering of default, sometimes described as "credit contagion," and provide the first empirical analysis of credit contagion via direct counterparty effects. They find that bankruptcy announcements cause negative abnormal equity returns and increases in CDS spreads for creditors, and that creditors with large exposures are more likely to suffer from financial distress later, suggesting that counterparty risk is a potential additional channel of credit contagion. Arora, Gandhi, and Longstaff (2012) use proprietary data from 14 CDS dealers and find that counterparty risk is priced in the CDS market and the magnitude of the effect is small. Brigo, Capponi, Pallavicini, and Papatheodorou (2013) value bilateral CCR through stochastic dynamical models when collateral is included with possible rehypothecation. The authors show for credit default swaps that a perfect collateralization cannot be achieved under default correlation.

Brigo, Buescu, and Morini (2012) compare two different bilateral counterparty valuation adjustment formulas (an approximation based on subtracting the two unilateral credit valuation adjustment formulas as seen from the two different parties in the transaction) and a fully specified bilateral risk formula where the first-to-default time is taken into account. Finally, Acharya and Bisin (2014) study financial markets where agents share risks but have incentives to default and their financial positions might not be transparent, that is, not mutually observable. The authors show that a lack of position transparency results in a counterparty risk externality, which manifests itself in the form of excess "leverage" in that parties take on short positions that lead to levels of default risk that are higher than Pareto-efficient ones.

SUPERVISORY REQUIREMENTS FOR CCR

CCR is defined as the risk that the counterparty to a transaction could default or deteriorate in creditworthiness before the final settlement of a transaction's cash flows. Unlike a loan, where only a bank faces the risk of loss, CCR creates a bilateral risk of loss because the market value of a transaction can be positive or negative to either counterparty. The future market value of the exposure and the counterparty's credit quality are uncertain and may vary over time as underlying market factors change. The regulatory focus is on institutions with large derivatives portfolios setting their risk management practices as well as on supervisors as they assess and examine CCR management.

CCR is multidimensional, affected by both the exposure to and credit quality of the counterparty, as well as their interactions, all of which are sensitive to market-induced changes. Constructing an effective CCR management framework requires a combination of risk management techniques from the credit, market, and operational risk disciplines. CCR management techniques have evolved rapidly and improved over the last decade even as derivative instruments under management have increased in complexity. While institutions substantially improved their risk management practices, in some cases implementation of sound practices has been uneven across business lines and counterparty types. The financial crisis of 2007–2009 revealed weaknesses in CCR management of timely and accurate exposure aggregation capabilities and inadequate measurement of correlation risks. The crisis also highlighted deficiencies in monitoring and managing counterparty limits and concentrations, ranging from poor selection of CCR metrics to inadequate infrastructure.

The Basel II "Revised Framework" (BCBS 2004) was intended to promote a more forward-looking approach to capital supervision that encourages banks to identify and manage the risks they face. Treatment of CCR arising from over-the-counter (OTC) derivatives and repos in either trading or banking books was first set forth in an amendment to the original 1988 Basel Accord (BCBS 1988) treatments for the CCR of repo-style transactions. The Basel II framework (BCBS 2004) represents joint work with the International Organization of Securities Commissions (IOSCO) on the treatment of CCR for over-the-counter derivatives, repo-style transactions, and securities financing.

The regulations specify three methods for calculating EAD for transactions involving CCR: the internal model method (IMM), a standardized method (SM), and the (at-the-time existing) current exposure method (CEM).

Commonalities across Approaches to CCR

Positions that give rise to CCR exposures share certain generic characteristics. First, the positions generate a credit exposure—the cost of replacing the transaction if the counterparty defaults, assuming there is no recovery of value. Second, exposures depend on one or more underlying market factors. Third, transactions involve an exchange of payments or financial instruments identified with an explicit counterparty having a unique PD.

CCR for a position at any point in time equals a maximum of zero or replacement cost (market value) for each counterparty over tenure. This may include the use of collateral to mitigate risk, legal netting or "rights of offset" contracts, and the use of re-margining agreements. The fact that similar risk characteristics, products, and related activities with CCR are managed by institutions using similar methods and processes imply they may merit similar capital requirements. However, there are differences in rule treatment between OTC exposures and *securities financing transactions* (SFTs). SFTs include securities lending and borrowing, securities margin lending, and repurchase and reverse repurchase agreements.

The Basel II revised framework (BCBS 2004) already provides three methods for SFTs: a simple approach, a comprehensive approach with both supervisory and nonsupervisory haircuts, and a value-at-risk (VaR) model.

An *internal model method* (IMM) to CCR is available for both SFTs and OTC derivatives, but the nonmodel methods available for the latter are not applicable to the former. Institutions use several measures to manage their exposure to CCR, including *potential future exposure* (PFE), *expected exposure* (EE), and *expected positive exposure* (EPE). Banks typically compute these using a common stochastic model as shown in Figure 2.1. PFE is the maximum exposure estimated to occur on a future date at a high level of statistical confidence, often used when measuring CCR exposure against credit limits. EE is the probability-weighted average exposure estimated to exist on a future date. EPE is the time-weighted average of individual expected exposures estimated for given forecasting horizons (e.g., one year). EPE is generally viewed as the appropriate EAD measure for CCR as such are treated similarly to loans, and EPE reduces incentives to arbitrage regulatory capital across product types; therefore, internal and standardized model methods employ this for EAD.

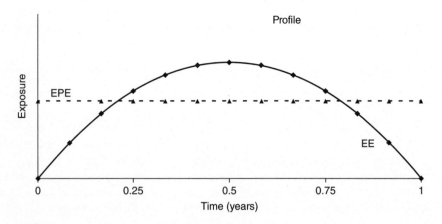

FIGURE 2.1   Expected positive exposure for CCR.

Consistent with the Basel I Revised Framework for credit risk, the EAD for instruments with CCR must be determined conservatively and conditionally on an economic downturn (i.e., a "bad state"; BCBS 1998). In order to accomplish such conditioning in a practical, pragmatic, and conservative manner, the internal and standardized model methods proposed scale EPE using "alpha" and "beta" multipliers. Alpha is set at 1.4 in both the internal model method and the standardized model method, but supervisors have the flexibility to raise alpha in appropriate situations. Banks may internally estimate alpha and adjust it both for correlations of exposures across counterparties and potential lack of granularity across a firm's counterparty exposures. The alpha multiplier is also viewed as a method to offset model error or estimation error. Industry and supervisors' simulations suggest alphas may range from approximately 1.1 for large global dealers to more than 2.5 for new users of derivatives with concentrated or no exposures. Supervisors proposed to require institutions to use a supervisory specified alpha of 1.4 with the ability to estimate a firm portfolio–specific alpha subject to supervisory approval and a floor of 1.2. To estimate alpha, a bank would compute the ratio of *economic capital* (EC) for counterparty credit risk (from a joint simulation of market and credit risk factors) to EC when counterparty exposures are a constant amount equal to EPE (see Figure 2.2). Under the internal model method, the resulting risk weight may be adjusted to reflect the transaction's maturity.

Banks may estimate EAD based on one or more bilateral "netting sets," a group of transactions with a single counterparty subject to a legally enforceable bilateral netting arrangement. Bilateral netting is recognized for purposes of calculating capital requirements within certain product

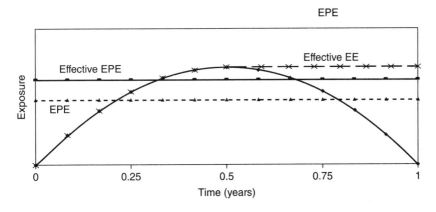

FIGURE 2.2 Effective EE and effective EPE for CCR.

categories: OTC derivatives, repo transactions, and on-balance-sheet loans/deposits. However, under the BCBS Amended Accord and Revised Framework, netting across product categories is not recognized for regulatory capital computation purposes. The intent is to allow supervisors discretion to permit banks to net margin loans secured by purchased securities and executed with a counterparty under a legally enforceable master agreement. This is not intended to permit banks to net across different types of SFTs or to net SFTs against OTC derivatives that might be included in a prime brokerage agreement. The Basel *cross-product netting rules* recognize such between OTC derivatives and SFTs subject to national supervisor determination that enumerated legal and operational criteria are widely met. A bank should have obtained a high degree of certainty on the legal enforceability of the arrangement under the laws of all relevant jurisdictions in the event of a counterparty's bankruptcy. It is also important that the bank demonstrate to the supervisory authority that it effectively integrates the risk-mitigating effects of cross-product netting into its risk management systems. Requirements are added to those that already exist for the recognition of any master agreements and any collateralized transactions included in a cross-product netting arrangement. Netting other than on a bilateral basis, such as netting across transactions entered by affiliates under a cross-affiliate master netting agreement, is not recognized for regulatory capital computation.

Summary of Regulatory Methods for CCR

The BCBS has articulated the principle that banks should be allowed to use the output of their "own estimates" developed through internal models in an advanced EAD. In order to achieve this, the regulators permit qualifying institutions to employ internal EPE estimates of defined netting sets of CCR exposures in computing the EAD for capital purposes. In general, internal models commonly used for CCR estimate a time profile of EE over each point in the future, which equals the average exposure over possible future values of relevant market risk factors (e.g., interest rates, FX rates). The motivation for this was the need for more consistent treatments and is particularly critical if banks may make use of their own estimates to calculate EAD through an internal model.

Relatively short-dated SFTs pose problems in measuring EPE because estimating a time profile of EE in an internal model only considers current transactions. For some SFT portfolios, the expected exposure might spike up rapidly in the first few days before dropping off sharply at maturity. However, a counterparty may enter new or roll over existing SFTs, generating new exposure not reflected in a current EE time profile. An additional problem arises when short-term are combined with long-term transactions, so that EE is U-shaped, which implies that if short-term transactions roll over, the decline in EE might understate the CCR amount. These issues can also apply to short-term OTC derivatives.

Effective expected positive exposure measurements always lie somewhere between EPE and peak EE. In the case of upward- versus downward-sloping EE profiles, effective EPE will equal EPE or peak EE, respectively. In general, the earlier that EE peaks, the closer effective EPE will be to peak EE; and the later that EE peaks, the closer effective EPE will be to peak EPE. Under the internal model method, a peak exposure measure is more conservative than effective EPE for any counterparty and can be used with prior supervisory approval. While banks generally do not use effective EPE for internal risk management purposes or in economic capital models, it can easily be derived from a counterparty's EE profile.

The consensus is that this is a pragmatic way of addressing rollover of short-dated transactions and differentiating counterparties with more volatile EE time profiles. EEs can be calculated based on risk-neutral or physical-risk factor distributions, the choice of which will affect the value of EE but not necessarily lead to a higher or lower EE. The distinction often made is that the risk-neutral distribution must be used for pricing trades, while the actual distribution must be used for risk measurement and economic capital.

The calculation of effective EPE has elements of both pricing (e.g., in the calculation of an effective maturity parameter) and simulation. Ideally, the calculation would use distribution appropriate to whether pricing or simulation is being done, but it is difficult to justify the added complexity of using two different distributions. Because industry practice does not indicate that one single approach has gained favor, supervisors are not requiring that any particular distribution be used.

Exposure on netting sets with maturity greater than one year is susceptible to changes in economic value from deterioration in the counterparty's creditworthiness short of default. Supervisors believe that an effective maturity parameter (M) can capture the effect of this on capital and the existing maturity adjustment in the revised framework is appropriate for CCR. However, the M formula for netting sets with maturity greater than one year must be different than that employed in the revised framework in order to reflect dynamics of counterparty credit exposures. The approach for CCR provides such a formula based on a weighted average of expected exposures over the life of the transactions relative to their one-year exposures. As in the revised framework, M is capped at five years, and where all transactions have an original maturity less than one year that meet certain requirements, there is CCR-specific treatment.

If the netting set is subject to a margin agreement and the internal model captures the effect of this in estimating EE, the model's EE measure may be used directly to calculate EAD as above. If the internal model does not fully capture the effects of margining, a method is proposed that will provide some benefit, in the form of a smaller EAD, for margined counterparties. Although this "shortcut" method will be permitted, supervisors would expect banks that make extensive use of margining to develop the modeling capacity to measure the impact on EE. To the extent that a bank recognizes collateral in EAD via current exposure, a bank would not be permitted to recognize the benefits in its estimates of LGD.

Supervisory Requirements and Approval for CCR

Qualifying institutions may use internal models to estimate the EAD of their CCR exposures subject to supervisory approval, which requires certain model validations and operational standards. This applies to banks that do not qualify to estimate the EPE associated with OTC derivatives but would like to adopt a more risk-sensitive method than the current exposure method (CEM). The standardized method (SM) is designed both to capture some certain key features of the internal model method for CCR and to provide a simple and workable supervisory algorithm with simplifying assumptions. Risk positions in the SM are derived with reference to short-term changes in valuation parameters (e.g., durations and deltas), and assumed open positions remain over the forecasting horizon. This implies that the risk-reducing effect of margining is not recognized, and there is no recognition of diversification effects.

In the SM, the exposure amount is defined as the product of two factors: (1) the larger of the net current market value or "supervisory EPE" times, and (2) a scaling factor termed *beta*. The first factor captures two key features of the internal model method (IMM) not mirrored in CEM with respect to netting sets that are deep in the money: The EPE is almost entirely determined by the current market value at the money (current market value is not relevant), and CCR is driven only by potential changes in values of transactions. By summing the current and add-on exposures, CEM assumes that the netting set is simultaneously at and deep in the money. The CEM derives replacement cost implicitly at transaction and not at portfolio level as the sum of the replacement cost of all transactions in the netting set with a positive value. The SM derives current market value for CCR as the larger of the sum of market values (positive or negative) of all transactions in the netting set or zero.

The second factor serves two purposes. First, as with the alpha in the IMM conditioning on a downturn, the beta addresses stochastic dependency of market values of exposures across counterparties as well as estimation and modeling errors. It also seeks to compensate for the fact that the first factor may at times be lower than the effective EPE under the IMM. This second concern is relevant for netting sets that are narrowly focused on certain risk areas (e.g., interest swaps that are mostly denominated in the same currency). Unless the netting set is very deep in the money, the effective EPE will exceed both the net current market value and the "supervisory EPE," as the latter is calibrated to transactions that are at the money. Supervisory EPE does not allow for basis risk, and price risk is reflected only by deltas, so beta is set considerably higher than alpha. However, some allowance is made for nonrecognition of diversification, which tends to make the first factor larger than effective EPE.

The recognition of hedging within netting sets is another key conceptual difference between the SM and IMM in comparison to the CEM. In CEM, the size of the netting effect depends not on hedging but on the portion of the transactions that is in the money: If none is out of the money, that implies no netting is recognized. For example, consider two at-the-market (ATM) and exactly identical but offsetting transactions with the same party subject to netting. Under the CEM there is positive exposure, whereas under either the SM or the IMM there is zero exposure. In general, the recognition of netting increases with the extent to which out-of-the-money transactions are present within a netting set.

Under the SM, supervisory EPE is determined by mapping to risk positions that represent certain key drivers of potential change in value, following a technique commonly employed in market risk modeling (e.g., delta/gamma hedging). Risk positions of the same category (e.g., the same currency) that arise from transactions within the same netting set, form a so-called hedging set within which hedging is fully recognized. Hedging sets are designed to capture general market risk. With respect to interest rate risk, there is no differentiation of the categories by the issuer of any underlying debt instrument. However, there is a differentiation with regard to the type of reference rate used—for example, sovereign versus corporate-issued instruments.

In the case of floating rate instruments, the sensitivity to interest rate changes with the remaining maturity is synonymous to the time to next adjustment. On the other hand, for equity price changes across issuers too different to permit netting at a national index level, netting is only permitted on an individual level. Nonlinear instruments require the capability of being represented in delta-equivalent form, which is compliant under the SM or the IMM. Unlike the CEM that considers only purchased options, in the SM sold options enter with negative signs and give rise to CCR. Modified duration/delta and an imperfect model of basis risk imply limited recognition of offsets by narrowed time bands of hedging sets.

Regulators expect that a bank's risk tolerance for CCR should be clearly articulated by its board through policies and a framework for establishing limits. Further, they expect that management should establish a comprehensive risk measurement and management framework consistent with this. At a minimum, supervisors require that policies should clearly address risk measurement, reporting, tools, processes, and legal and operational issues with respect to CCR. Furthermore, the view is that policies should be detailed and should contain an escalation process for the review and approval of policy exceptions. Banks are expected to report counterparty exposures at a frequency commensurate with the materiality and complexity of exposures. Reporting should include concentration analysis and CCR stress testing for an understanding of exposures and potential losses. Finally, reports should include an explanation of issues influencing accuracy and reliability of CCR measures.

Supervisory Guidance Regarding CCR

Given the complexity of CCR exposures, banks should employ a range of risk metrics for a comprehensive understanding of this risk. These metrics should be commensurate with the size, complexity, liquidity, and risk profile of the bank's CCR portfolio. Banks typically rely on certain primary metrics for monitoring, and secondary metrics for a more robust view, of CCR exposures. Banks should apply these metrics to single exposures, groups of exposures, and the entire CCR portfolio, and should be applying special assessing of their largest exposures.

CCR Supervisory Guidance: General Guidelines Sophisticated banks and large dealers should measure and assess the following:

- Current and potential exposure (both gross and net of collateral);
- Stressed exposure (broken out by market risk factors);
- Aggregate exposures and stressed exposure, as well as CVA, segmented by market factors;
- Additional relevant metrics, such as for credit derivatives, jump-to-default risk on the reference obligor, and economic capital usage;
- Correlation risks, such as wrong-way risk;
- Credit quality of collateral.

Banks' CCR systems should:

- Have sufficient capacity to aggregate at varying levels (industries, regions, products, business line, legal entity) or other groupings to identify concentrations;
- Be sufficiently flexible to allow for timely aggregation of all CCR exposures and other forms of credit risk;

- Calculate counterparty CE and PE on a daily basis on the previous day's position exchange of collateral;
- Include all trades at each level of aggregation.

Banks should consider the full range of credit risks in conjunction with CCR: on- and off-balance-sheet activities; contractual, noncontractual, contingent, and noncontingent risks; and underwriting and pipeline risks.

While a common metric across all risks is not required, banks should be able to view exposures to a given counterparty in one report. Such reports should exhibit consistency in exchange rate and account for legal enforceability of any netting agreements they may have to a counterparty. Management should have an understanding of the specific approaches used and the internal capital adequacy models should incorporate CCR.

CCR Supervisory Guidance: Concentrations Concentrations pose a significant concern as they can add to sudden increases in CCR with potentially large unexpected losses. Banks should have processes to identify, measure, monitor, and control concentrations at both a legal entity and firmwide basis. Concentration risk should be identified both quantitatively and qualitatively, as breaches of risk tolerance limits could result in material loss or damage to a bank's reputation. All credit exposures should be considered part of concentration management (e.g., loans, OTC derivatives, CDO tranches). Total credit exposures should include the size of settlement and clearing lines or other committed lines. CCR concentration management should identify, quantify, and monitor counterparty exposures with certain characteristics:

- Large exposures driven by a market factor, transaction type, or the same risk factors (*crowded trades*);
- Aggregations of risk exposures by industries/other obligor groupings, or geographic/country groupings sensitive similar macro shocks;
- Collateral concentrations, including a single counterparty or portfolios of counterparties;
- Noncash collateral for all product lines covered by agreements;
- *Special purpose entities* (SPEs), which represent payment capacity.

Banks with significant CCR should have a comprehensive, organizationally integrated stress-testing framework. This framework should inform day-to-day exposure/concentration management through identifying extreme conditions that could strain the bank's resources. No less than quarterly, management should evaluate test results for evidence of excessive risk and formulate the appropriate reduction strategy.

The severity of factor shocks should be consistent with the purpose of the stress testing. If the object is to test solvency, then banks should model historically extreme, but plausible, stressed market conditions and evaluate their impact on capital resources and earnings. On the other hand, if the purpose is day-to-day portfolio monitoring, hedging, and management of concentrations, then the scenarios should be of a lesser severity and of higher probability of occurrence. Furthermore, in stress tests, risk managers should challenge the strength of assumptions made about the legal enforceability of netting and the ability to collect and liquidate collateral.

Finally, a sound stress-testing framework should include the following elements:

- Measurement of largest counterparty impacts across portfolios and material concentrations within segments of a portfolio;
- Complete trade capture and exposure aggregation across all forms of trading at the counterparty level, including outside of the main credit system at frequencies consistent with that of tests;
- Stress of principal market risk factors individually for all material counterparties on a consolidated basis, and on at least a quarterly frequency;
- Tracking of concentrations in volatile currencies, particularly for repos and SFTs where liquidation large collateral may be difficult;
- Assessment of nondirectional risks from multifactor stress-testing scenarios, at a minimum addressing separate scenarios for severe economic or market events on the one hand, and a significant decrease in broad market liquidity on the other;
- Consideration of stressed joint exposures and counterparty creditworthiness at specific and group level in aggregate for the bank;
- If CVA methodology used, assurances that the stress test sufficiently captures additional losses from potential default, and basic stress testing of CVA to assess performance under adverse scenarios, incorporating any hedging mismatches;
- Concurrent stress testing of exposure and noncash collateral for assessing wrong-way risk;
- Identification and assessment of exposure levels for certain counterparties (e.g., sovereigns and municipalities), where the bank may be concerned about willingness to pay;
- Integration of CCR stress tests into firmwide stress tests.

CCR Supervisory Guidance: CVA   CVA can be defined as a fair value adjustment to transaction valuation reflecting a counterparty's credit quality. The market value of CCR and a market-based framework to understand and value CCR are embedded in all derivatives contracts when counterparties are subject to credit risk that includes default, downgrade, and credit spread risks. CVA may be unilateral, only reflecting the counterparty's credit quality, or bilateral, reflecting the bank's own credit quality as well.

Bilateral CVA is one-sided CVA plus a DVA. In the case of credit risk due to counterparties subject to default risk, one-sided CVA is typically used, but for pricing derivatives with a counterparty (or the market risk of derivatives transactions), a two-sided CVA should be used. CVA is not new but the importance has grown due to changes in accounting rules that require banks to recognize CVA in earnings. CVA has become a more critical component of modeling CCR to mitigate banks' exposure to the MTM impact of CCR.

CVA management should be consistent with sound practices for other material MTM risks and should include the following:

- Business units engaged in trades related to CVA management should have independent risk management functions.
- Systems for CVA risk metrics should be subject to the same controls as other MTM risks (e.g., independent validation and benchmarking through alternative modeling frameworks).
- CVA cost and risk should be allocated to the business unit of origination and be incorporated into the RAROC of a given business, respectively.
- CVA measurement and management frameworks should provide incentive for prudent risk-taking decisions and risk mitigation.
- CVA engines should measure sensitivities to changes in credit and market risk factors to determine material drivers of MTM changes (e.g., a regular test that CVA MTM sufficiently explained by these, including a backtesting of CVA VaR).

If a bank is hedging marked-to-market CVA, the framework or model should gauge the effectiveness of this activity through the measurement of basis risk and similar sensitivities, which is important to capture non-linearities (e.g., correlations between market and credit risk). Banking organizations with material CVA should measure the risk on an ongoing basis, including VaR models with CVA measurement capabilities. While currently in the early stages of development, such models may prove to be effective tools for risk management purposes. Key advantages of CVA VaR, as opposed to more traditional metrics, include the capture of CCR exposure variability, a counterparty's spread, and correlation. This is significantly more complicated than VaR for market risks as it should match the percentile and horizon and include all risks for the CVA change. All material counterparties covered by the credit valuation adjustment should be included in the VaR model. A CVA VaR calculation that keeps the exposure or counterparty PD static is not adequate, as this will omit dependence between the two variables and risk from the uncertainty of a fixed variable. The framework should assess the ability of the VaR measure to accurately capture the types of hedging used by the banking institutions.

Banking organizations with material CVA should measure the risk on an ongoing basis, including VaR models with CVA.

CCR Supervisory Guidance: Wrong-Way Risk *Wrong-way risk* (WWR) occurs when the exposure to a counterparty is positively correlated with the PD of the counterparty. *Specific* WWR arises from the nature of the transaction, while *general* WWR is attributed to counterparties' PD positively correlated to general factors.

WWR is an important aspect of CCR, since it has caused major bank losses and so should generally be avoided due to the increased risk. Banks need a process to systematically identify, quantify, and control both specific and general WWR across OTC derivative and SFT portfolios. Banks' senior management should maintain policies for both types of WWR with respect to tolerance limits, ongoing identification processes, escalation, and management of situations when there is a legal connection between the counterparty and underlying exposure. Banks should regularly perform WWR analysis for OTC derivatives at least at industry/regional levels and for SFTs on broad asset classes of securities.

CCR Supervisory Guidance: Limits Limits are an integral part of a CCR management framework and these limits should be formalized in CCR policies and procedures. For limits to be effective, a bank should incorporate them into an exposure-monitoring system independent of business lines. The system should perform ongoing monitoring of exposures and have risk controls that require action to mitigate exceptions. A review of exceptions should include escalation to a managerial level commensurate with the size or nature of mitigation.

Supervisors expect that a sound limit system should include several mandates:

- Regularly review limits by a designated committee and process to escalate approvals to higher levels depending on the size of counterparty exposures, credit quality, and tenor.
- Establish limits based on potential future exposure, other metrics, and market risk arising through CVA (which does not eliminate the need to limit CCR).
- Establish individual CCR limits based on peak exposures rather than expected exposures.
- Include peak exposures as appropriate for individual limit monitoring purposes, as they represent the risk tolerance for exposure to a single counterparty.

- Include expected exposure as an appropriate measure for aggregating exposures across counterparties in a portfolio credit model or for use within CVA.
- Take into consideration risk factors like counterparty credit quality, tenor of the transactions, and liquidity of the positions or hedges.
- Sufficiently automate monitoring processes to provide updated exposure measures at least daily.
- Monitor intraday trading activity for conformance with exposure limits and exception policies.
- Include monitoring of trade procedures and impact on limit utilization prior to execution, limit-warning triggers at specific utilization levels, and restrictions by credit risk management on allocation of limits.

CCR Supervisory Guidance: Collateral   Banks are expected to control the rehypothecation or other reinvestment of collateral received from counterparties, including the potential liquidity shortfalls resulting from the reuse of such collateral. In regard to the CCR associated with segregated margins, banks should perform a legal analysis concerning the risks of agreeing to allow cash to be commingled with a counterparty's own cash and rehypothecation. Policies and processes to monitor margin agreements with third-party custodians, as with bilateral counterparties, should identify the location of the account to which collateral is posted or from which it is received. Such policies should also obtain periodic account statements or other assurances that confirm the custodian is holding the collateral in conformance with the agreement. Furthermore, it is important that banks understand the characteristics of the account where the collateral is held (e.g., whether it is in a segregated account), as well as the legal rights of the counterparty or any third-party custodian regarding this collateral.

CCR Supervisory Guidance: Model Validation   A bank should validate its CCR models initially and on an ongoing basis, and this process should include the following standard elements (Jacobs 2010b):

- Evaluation of the conceptual soundness and developmental evidence;
- Ongoing monitoring including processes verification and benchmarking;
- An outcomes-analysis process that includes backtesting.

The validation process should identify key assumptions and potential limitations, assessing their possible impact on risk metrics across all components of the model subject to validation individually and in combination. The evaluation of conceptual soundness should assess quality of design and construction of CCR models/systems, including documentation and empirical evidence supporting the theory, data, and methods. Ongoing monitoring confirms that systems perform as intended and includes both process verification as well as the assessment of model data integrity and systems operation.

Benchmarking to intended outcomes assesses the quality of a given model. Benchmarking is a valuable diagnostic tool in identifying potential weaknesses with respect to a CCR model. This involves a comparison of the bank's CCR model output with that using alternative data, methods, or techniques. Benchmarking can also be applied to particular CCR model components, such as parameter estimation methods or pricing models. Management should investigate the source of any differences in output and determine whether gaps indicate model weakness.

Outcomes analysis compares model outputs to actual results during a sample period not used in model development. This is generally accomplished using backtesting and should be applied to components of models, risk measures, and projected exposure. While there are limitations to backtesting, especially for testing the longer time horizon predictions of a given CCR model, it is an essential component of model validation. Banks should have a process for the resolution of model deficiencies that are detected, including further investigation to determine the problem and an appropriate course of action. If the validation is not performed by staff that is independent from the developers, then independent review should be conducted by technically competent and independent personnel.

The scope of the independent review should include:

- Validation procedures for all components;
- The roles of relevant parties;
- Documentation of the model and validation processes.

This review should document its results, what action was taken to resolve findings, and its relative timeliness. Senior management should be notified of validation results and take appropriate/timely corrective actions. The board should be apprised of summary results, and internal audits should review and test models and systems validation and overall systems infrastructure as part of their regular audit cycle.

CCR Supervisory Guidance: Close-Out Banks should have the ability to effectively manage counterparties in distress, including execution of a close-out, with policies and procedures outlining sound practices (Jacobs, Karagozoglu, and Layish 2012). Requirements for hypothetical close-out simulations should be done at least once every two years for the bank's complex counterparties. Standards should be established for executing a close-out that addresses decision-making responsibilities, the sequence of critical tasks, and the speed and accuracy with which the bank can compile comprehensive counterparty exposure data and net cash outflows, including the capacity to aggregate exposures within a few hours.

The periodic review of documentation related to counterparty terminations and confirmations should require that the appropriate and current agreement defines the events of default, and that the termination methodology that will be used is in place, current, active, and enforceable. Management should document their decision to trade with counterparties that are either unwilling or unable to maintain appropriate and current documentation. Established close-out methodologies should be practical to implement, particularly with large and potentially illiquid portfolios. Dealers should consider using the "close-out amount" approach for early termination upon default in inter-dealer relationships.

There should be a requirement that the bank transmit immediate instructions to its appropriate transfer agent(s) to deactivate collateral transfers, contractual payments, or other automated transfers contained in "standard settlement instructions" in the event that counterparties or prime brokers default on the contract or declare bankruptcy.

CONCEPTUAL ISSUES IN CCR: RISK VERSUS UNCERTAINTY

In this section we will survey some of the thought regarding the concept of risk and consider how it applies to CCR. A classical dichotomy exists in the literature. The earliest exposition is credited to Knight (1921), who defines uncertainty as the state in which a probability distribution cannot be measured or is unknown. This is contrasted with the situation in which the probability distribution is known or knowable through repeated experimentation. Arguably, in economics and finance (and more broadly in the social or natural as opposed to the physical or mathematical sciences), uncertainty is the more realistic scenario that we are contending with (e.g., a fair vs. loaded die, or a die with an unknown number of sides). We are forced to rely on empirical data to estimate loss distributions, which is complicated by changing economic conditions that invalidate forecasts that our econometric models generate.

Popper (1945) postulated that situations of uncertainty are closely associated with, and inherent with respect to, changes in knowledge and behavior. This is also known as the rebuttal of the historicism concept, that our actions and their outcomes have a predetermined path. He emphasized

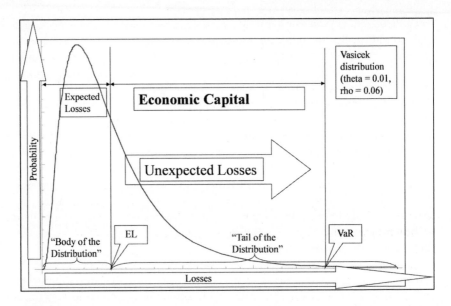

FIGURE 2.3 Stylized representation of economic capital.

that the growth of knowledge and freedom implies that we cannot perfectly predict the course of history. For example, a statement that the U.S. currency is inevitably going to depreciate if the United States does not control its debt, is not refutable and therefore not a valid scientific statement according to Popper (see Figure 2.3).

Shackle (1990) argued that predictions are reliable only for the immediate future. He contends that such predictions impact the decisions of economic agents, and this has an effect on the outcomes under question, changing the validity of the prediction (a feedback effect). This recognition of the role of human behavior in economic theory was a key impetus behind rational expectations and behavioral finance. While it is valuable to estimate loss distributions that help explicate sources of uncertainty, risk managers must be aware of the model limitation that a stress testing regime itself changes behavior (for example, banks "gaming" the regulators' CCAR process). The conclusion is that the inherent limitations of this practice is a key factor in supporting the use of stress testing in order to supplement other risk measures. Finally, Artzner et al. (1999) postulate some desirable features of a risk measure, collectively known as *coherence*. They argue that VaR measures often fail to satisfy such properties.

In light of these considerations, we may see a meta-problem that CCR exposure over long horizons (e.g., 10, 20, 30 years) may simply be inestimable. When trying to forecast prices one or more days ahead for trading

VaR purposes, or even one year ahead for other regulatory capital purposes (e.g., credit capital for banking book exposures), one is dealing with quantifiable risk. But when trying to forecast an exchange rate or a commodity price 30 years ahead, one is dealing with unquantifiable Knightian uncertainty. We take past history as a single homogeneous sample and believe that we have considerably increased our knowledge of the future from the observation of the sample of the past. For example, the study of the U.S. financial markets of the early twentieth century will certainly be of great help to an economic historian, but we should question any kind of inference that comes out of this analysis with respect to current applicability, as the structure of the institutions and the markets has changed to such a degree.

In order to illustrate this issue, consider the evolution of the rates markets in the United States. In the last 30 years, short-term interest rates in this jurisdiction went from nearly 20 percent at the peak of the 1980s bull market, to the very low single digits in the wake of the Fed's quantitative easing following the financial crisis. Therefore, we see how this non-stationarity can make past data quite irrelevant in such situations of dramatic regime change. However, this is not only a problem for long-dated FX or IR contracts, as trying to make multiyear commodity or equity forecasts can be seen as pointless endeavor. There exist no qualitative adjustments, such as the conservative factors applied by many large banks to exposures they can't really model within their main CCR engine, which can lend credence to this practice.

It has been said that what began with the best intentions from a collection of idealistic modeling enthusiasts has degenerated into pseudoscience at best and fraud at worst. In this view, the game is to disguise charlatanism under the veneer of mathematical sophistication, which leads to propositions that cannot be validated or refuted (as we are not dealing in controlled experimentation) and to the illusion that we understand markets. This self-attribution phenomenon usually gets worse with mathematical knowledge: The more complex the equations, the more we believe in our models. However, financial engineering still measures risks using models built on historical data as the core tool deployed to future events. We will just say at this point that the mere possibility of the distributions not being stationary makes the entire long-dated CCR estimation seem like a costly mind game. As we rely increasingly on models of increasing mathematical complexity, our confidence becomes greater that we have correctly modeled all price dynamics, and this may be a false sense of security. We see the phenomenon that new traders on the block dismiss past traders who blew up spectacularly as not sophisticated enough, and we are persuaded that their models are more refined and better able to forecast future market movements, until they blow up quite dramatically themselves.

CONCLUSIONS

In this paper, we have performed a survey of CCR, including the following elements. First, we have introduced various concepts in CCR measurement and management, including prevalent practices, definitions, and conceptual issues. Then, we have summarized various supervisory requirements and expectations with respect to CCR. This study has multiple areas of relevance and may be extended in various ways. Risk managers, traders, and regulators may find this to be a valuable reference. Directions for future research could include empirical analysis, development of a theoretical framework, and a comparative analysis of systems for analyzing and regulating CCR.

REFERENCES

Acharya V., and A. Bisin. 2014. Counterparty risk externality: Centralized versus over-the-counter markets. *Journal of Economic Theory* 149: 153–182.

Araten, M., and M. Jacobs Jr., 2001, May. Loan equivalents for defaulted revolving credits and advised lines. *The Journal of the Risk Management Association:* 34–39.

Araten, M., M. Jacobs, Jr., and P. Varshney. 2004, May. Measuring LGD on commercial loans: An 18-year internal study. *The Journal of the Risk Management Association:* 28–35.

Araten, M., M. Jacobs Jr., P. Varshney, and C. R. Pellegrino. 2004, April. An internal ratings migration study. *The Journal of the Risk Management Association:* 92–97.

Arora, N., P. Gandhi , and F. A. Longstaff, 2012. Counterparty credit risk and the credit default swap market. *Journal of Financial Economics* 103: 280–293.

Artzner, P., Delbaen, F., Eber, J.M., and D. Heath. 1997. Thinking coherently. *Risk* 10: 68–71.

Basel Committee on Banking Supervision (BCBS). 1988, June. International Convergence of Capital Measurement and Capital Standards: A Revised Framework. Bank for International Settlements, Basel, Switzerland.

_____. 2006, June. Basel II: International Convergence of Capital Measurement and Capital Standards: A Revised Framework: Comprehensive Version. Bank for International Settlements, Basel, Switzerland.

_____. 2011, June. Basel III: A global regulatory framework for more resilient banks and banking systems. Bank for International Settlements, Basel, Switzerland.

_____. 2012, December. Basel III counterparty credit risk and exposures to central—Frequently asked questions (update of FAQs published in November 2012. Bank for International Settlements, Basel, Switzerland.

Brigo D., C. Buescu, and M. Morini. 2012. Counterparty risk pricing: Impact of closeout and first-to-default times. *International Journal of Theoretical and Applied Finance* 15: 1250039.

Brigo D., A. Capponi, A. Pallavicini, and V. Papatheodorou. 2013. Pricing counterparty risk including collateralization, netting rules, rehypothecation and wrong-way risk. *International Journal of Theoretical and Applied Finance* 16: 1350007.

Brigo D., and K. Chourdakis. 2009. Counterparty risk for credit default swaps: Impact of spread volatility and default correlation. *International Journal of Theoretical and Applied Finance* 12: 1007–1026.

Carey, M., and M. Gordy. 2004. *Systematic Risk in Recoveries on Defaulted Debt: Firm-Level Ultimate LGDs.* Working paper, U.S. Federal Reserve Board.

Carey, M., and M. Hrycay. 2001. Parameterizing credit risk models with rating data. *Journal of Banking and Finance* 25: 197–270.

Frye, J., and M. Jacobs Jr., 2012. Credit loss and systematic LGD. *The Journal of Credit Risk*, 8 (1) (Spring): 109–140.

Jacobs, M. Jr., 2010a. An empirical study of exposure at default. *The Journal of Advanced Studies in Finance* 1(1).

_____. 2010b. Validation of economic capital models: State of the practice, supervisory expectations and results from a bank study. *Journal of Risk Management in Financial Institutions* 3 (4): 334–365.

Jacobs, M. Jr., and A. Karagozoglu. 2011. Modeling ultimate loss given default on corporate debt. *The Journal of Fixed Income* 21 (1): 6–20.

Jacobs, M. Jr., A. Karagozoglu, and D. Layish. 2012. Resolution of corporate financial distress: An empirical analysis of processes and outcomes. *The Journal of Portfolio Management*, Winter: 117–135.

Jacobs, M. Jr., M., and N. M. Kiefer. 2010. The Bayesian approach to default risk: A guide." In K. Boecker (ed.). *Rethinking Risk Measurement and Reporting.* London: Risk Books.

Jorion, P., and G. Zhang. 2009. Credit contagion from counterparty risk. *Journal of Finance*, 64: 2053–2087.

Kang, J., and H.-S. Kim. 2005. Pricing counterparty default risks: Applications to FRNs and vulnerable options. *International Review of Financial Analysis* 14: 376–392.

Knight, F. H. 1921. *Risk, Uncertainty and Profit.* Boston: Hart, Schaffner and Marx.

U.S. Office of the Comptroller of the Currency (OCC) and Board of Governors of the Federal Reserve System (BOG-FRS). 2011. Interagency Supervisory Guidance on Counterparty Credit Risk Management, June 29.

Popper, K. R. 1945. *The Open Society and Its Enemies.* New York: Routledge and Kegan.

Shackle, G. L. S. 1990. In J. L. Ford (ed.). *Time Expectations and Uncertainty in Economics: Selected Essays.* Northampton, MA: Edward Elgar Publishing.

CHAPTER 3

Nonperforming Loans in the Bank Production Technology

Hirofumi Fukuyama
Fukuoka University

William L. Weber
Southeast Missouri State University

INTRODUCTION

Nonperforming loans are an undesirable by-product of the loan production process for financial institutions. Although collateral requirements can substitute for a borrower's lower probability of repayment (Saunders and Cornett 2008), financial institutions must still incur a charge when borrower's default. However, any attempt to eliminate nonperforming loans to zero would likely require financial institutions to employ large amounts of inputs to monitor borrowers or would require financial institutions to forgo some profitable lending. Both of these alternatives are likely inefficient. Instead, since bank owners choose the level of risk they wish to undertake (Hughes, Lang, Mester, and Moon, 1996), financial institutions should be willing to accept nonperforming loans up to the point where the lost income (including principal) on the marginal nonperforming loan is just offset by the reduced monitoring costs or by the increased interest income on the loan portfolio. In fact, policies that promote bank competition by reducing entry restrictions have the effect of reducing loan losses as well as the operating costs of production (Jayaratne and Strahan, 1998). Such competition can also be an effective means of weeding out managers who are weak at originating and monitoring the loan portfolio (Berger and Mester, 1997).

Many researchers have incorporated nonperforming loans into the financial institution production technology in measuring managerial performance and the shadow price of nonperforming loans, and in this chapter we focus our attention on studies that have examined Japanese bank performance. In addition, we present a new model that is capable of estimating prices for desirable outputs such as loans and securities investments and the price or charge of undesirable outputs such as nonperforming loans. Our method is grounded in duality theory and employs the directional output distance function measured in cost space. We also simulate how managers can use the estimated directional output distance function to minimize nonperforming loans by optimally reallocating their budgets over time. Here, our idea is that bank managers might want to forgo expenditures on inputs in one period so that larger amounts of inputs can be purchased in a different period.

We apply our method to 101 Japanese city and regional banks that operated in fiscal years 2008 to 2012. The Japanese fiscal year starts on April 1 and ends on March 31 of the subsequent year. We choose the years 2008 to 2012, as those years comprise the most recent available five-year span of data. In the next section, we provide a review of research measuring Japanese bank performance that incorporates nonperforming loans in the production technology. The next section presents our method used to measure performance and recover the prices of the desirable outputs produced by financial institutions as well as the undesirable outputs consisting of nonperforming loans. We then present the data and estimates of regional bank performance and the prices of the various outputs. In addition, we show how bank managers can use the parameter estimates of the directional output distance function to optimally reallocate spending on inputs and the desirable outputs so as to minimize the sum of nonperforming loans over the five-year period.

SELECTIVE LITERATURE REVIEW

Distance Functions

The reciprocal of the Shephard (1970) output distance function gives the maximum proportional expansion in all outputs that can be feasibly produced given inputs. The output distance function can be estimated using data envelopment analysis (DEA)—a set of mathematical programming techniques developed by Charnes, Cooper, and Rhodes (1978) and Banker, Charnes, and Cooper (1984)—which have been used by numerous researchers to estimate bank efficiency. Berger and Humphrey (1997) and Fethi and Pasiouras (2013) provide extensive surveys of financial institution performance using DEA. Shephard distance functions can also be estimated parametrically using the deterministic linear programming method of Aigner and Chu (1968) or using stochastic frontier methods.

When nonperforming loans are accounted for in the bank production technology, the measurement of bank performance is complicated by the fact that bank managers typically want to simultaneously expand desirable outputs and contract undesirable outputs. Unfortunately, Shephard output distance functions expand both desirable and undesirable outputs. As an alternative to Shephard output distance function, the directional distance function can be used to measure performance. Chambers, Chung, and Färe (1996) extended Luenberger's (1992; 1995) benefit function used in consumer theory to derive the directional input distance function. Luenberger (1995) proposed a more general shortage function, which Chambers, Chung, and Färe (1998) adapted and termed the *directional technology distance function*. The last obvious extension is the directional output distance function, which gives the maximum expansion in desirable outputs and simultaneous contraction in undesirable outputs. Färe and Grosskopf (2000) provide further discussion of these directional distance functions.

Shadow Prices of Nonperforming Loans

To estimate the Shephard output distance function, the translog functional form has enjoyed widespread use in parametric estimation of efficiency (Färe, Grosskopf, Lovell, and Yaisawarng 1993; Coggins and Swinton 1996; Swinton 1998) and shadow prices of undesirable outputs. However, the output distance function expands both desirable outputs and undesirable outputs to the production possibility frontier, whereas most managers are concerned with expanding desirable outputs and contracting undesirable outputs. Although the directional output distance functions can satisfy these criteria, Chambers (1998) suggests a quadratic form as a second-order approximation to the true, but unknown function. The quadratic form can be parameterized to satisfy the translation property, whereas the translog form can only be parameterized to satisfy homogeneity.

Although DEA can be used to estimate the directional output distance function and recover the shadow price of nonperforming loans, the directional output distance function estimated via DEA is not twice differentiable (Färe, Grosskopf, and Weber, 2006), resulting in a situation where there may be a range of shadow price ratios that support an observed frontier combination of desirable and undesirable outputs. Instead, researchers have employed twice differentiable functional forms such as the quadratic to estimate the directional output distance function. Färe, Grosskopf, Noh, and Weber (2005) exploited the duality between the directional output distance function and the revenue function to recover the shadow prices of undesirable outputs. They illustrated their method with an application to the U.S. electric utility industry by treating sulfur dioxide emissions as an undesirable output. Similarly, Färe, Grosskopf, and Weber (2006) treated human risk–adjusted leaching and runoff of pesticides in the U.S. agricultural industry as two undesirable outputs and estimated their shadow prices. Fukuyama and Weber (2008a; 2008b) estimated the shadow price of nonperforming loans for Japanese banks using a directional output distance function with estimates from both DEA and a quadratic functional form. They found significant differences in the distributions of shadow prices estimated by DEA and by the quadratic form.

Japanese Bank Efficiency

Several studies have examined the efficiency of Japanese banks. Kasuya (1986) estimated a translog cost function for 13 Japanese city banks and 64 Japanese local banks during the period 1975–1985. Using bank revenues from loans and other activities as the two bank outputs, Kasuya found significant scope economies for city banks and some evidence of scope economies for local banks during the latter part of the period. In addition, Kasuya found scale economies for both city and local banks. Fukuyama (1993) decomposed overall technical efficiency into pure technical efficiency and scale efficiency for Japanese banks operating in 1992 and found that the gains to be realized from enhanced pure technical efficiency are more than the scale efficiency gains. Furthermore, Fukuyama found a positive relation between pure technical efficiency and bank assets. Fukuyama (1995) used DEA to estimate the Malmquist indexes of productivity change, efficiency change, and technological change for Japanese banks during 1989–1991, which corresponds to the years before and after the collapse of the Japanese real estate and stock market bubbles.

Miyakoshi and Tsukuda (2004) estimated a stochastic frontier model and found regional disparities in technical efficiency among regional banks similar to Fukuyama's (1993) finding on scale economies. Fukuyama and Weber (2005) estimated the potential gains in earnings and found that those earnings could be expanded by 16 to 25 percent from an optimal reallocation of physical inputs. Harimaya (2004) estimated technical efficiency and cost efficiency and found that cooperative Shinkin banks with a lower ratio of costs to deposits exhibit greater technical efficiency. Liu and Tone (2008) measured Japanese banking efficiency during 1997 to 2001 and found that banks appeared to be "learning by doing," as bank efficiency increased during the period.

Several researchers have taken into account risk factors such as nonperforming loans in their analyses of Japanese bank efficiency. Using Japanese bank data from 1992 to 1995, Altunbus et al. (2000) showed that bank scale economies are likely overstated if loan quality and bank risk-taking are not accounted for. Drake and Hall (2003) found substantial inefficiency and clear evidence of scale economies for small banks and diseconomies of scale for large city banks when nonperforming loans are ignored during 1992 to 1995. However, after controlling for nonperforming loans, the researchers found the extent of scale economies for small banks and scale diseconomies for large banks to be reduced. Hori (2004) controlled for nonperforming loans and used DEA to estimate cost efficiency for Japanese banks in 1994. He concluded that the average regional banks could have reduced operating costs by about 20 percent if they were able to minimize costs. In addition, he found the primary cause of cost inefficiency for regional banks to be pure technical inefficiency—the overuse of all inputs—rather than allocative inefficiency due to an inappropriate mix of inputs. Fukuyama and Weber (2008a, 2008b) estimated efficiency, technological change, and shadow prices for nonperforming loans for Japanese commercial banks and Shinkin banks during 2002 to 2004 and concluded that regional banks experienced faster technological progress than Shinkin banks. Fukuyama and Weber (2009) controlled for nonperforming loans and bank risk in their DEA model and found that the revenue-constrained Luenberger productivity indicator decreased during 2000 to 2001 and 2003 to 2006.

Drake, Hall, and Simper (2009) estimated a slacks-based efficiency measure and found evidence that significant differences in sample efficiency estimates, the dispersion of efficiency, temporal variations, and mean efficiency estimates across sectors depended on how researchers defined bank inputs and outputs. Perhaps one of the greatest specification issues concerns the treatment of deposits, which some researchers have specified as an output and other researchers have specified as an input. To address the specification of deposits issue, Fukuyama and Weber (2010) developed a network bank efficiency model, and Fukuyama and Weber (2013, 2014) extended it into a dynamic-network framework. The authors proposed a two-stage network technology where banks use labor, physical capital, and equity capital to produce deposits in a first stage of production, with those deposits then used as an input in the second stage of production to produce the final desirable outputs of loans and securities investments along with a jointly produced undesirable output in the form of nonperforming loans. The models take on a dynamic aspect in that the nonperforming loans generated in one period become an undesirable input that constrains what banks can produce in a subsequent period. These dynamic network models were applied to Japanese banks operating from 2006 to 2010. In conclusion, the implication of these studies is that incorporation of nonperforming loans in the efficiency analysis for Japanese banks is of great significance.

METHOD

Recent work by Färe, Grosskopf, Sheng, and Sickles (2012) and Cross, Färe, Grosskopf, and Weber (2013) exploited the duality between the directional input distance function and the cost function to recover the prices of non-market output characteristics. Their work is related to the hedonic pricing method of Rosen (1974), who showed in a theoretical model that the implicit prices of a bundle of product characteristics can be recovered such that the relative prices equal the consumer's marginal rate of substitution between the characteristics and the producer's marginal rate of transformation between the characteristics. We extend the work of Färe et al. (2012) and Cross et al. (2013) to recover output prices using a directional output distance function defined in cost space.

We model the production technology using the directional output distance function in cost space. Banks face a budget, c, that allows them to produce desirable outputs $y = (y_1, \ldots, y_M) \in R_+^M$ and jointly produced undesirable outputs $b = (b_1, \ldots, b_J) \in R_+^J$. The output correspondence (production possibility set) is given as

$$P(c) = \{(y, b) : c \text{ can produce } (y, b)\}. \tag{3.1}$$

The production possibility set $P(c)$ gives the various combinations of desirable and undesirable outputs that can be produced at a given budget or cost and has the following properties:

    i. $P(c) \subseteq P(c')$ for $c' \geq c$

    ii. If $(y, b) \in P(c)$ and $y' \leq y$, then $(y', b) \in P(c)$ (3.2)

    iii. If $(y, b) \in P(c)$ then for $0 \leq \theta \leq 1$, $(\theta y, \theta b) \in P(c)$.

Property (3.2)*i* means that the output correspondence does not shrink for producers that have a larger budget. Similarly, (3.2)*ii* corresponds to strong disposability of desirable outputs. Property (3.2)*iii* imposes weak disposability for the jointly produced desirable and undesirable outputs. That is, holding the budget constant, the opportunity cost of reducing the undesirable outputs is that less of the desirable outputs can be produced.

We use the directional output distance function to represent the production possibility set. This function scales outputs to the frontier of the production technology along the directional vector $g_y = (g_{y1}, \ldots, g_{yM})$ and $g_b = (g_{b1}, \ldots, g_{bJ})$. The directional output distance function is defined as

$$\vec{D}_o(c, y, b; g_y, g_b) = \max\{\beta : (y + \beta g_y, b + \beta g_b) \in P(c)\}. \tag{3.3}$$

The directional distance function finds the maximum additive expansion in outputs for the given directional vectors. We want to choose a directional vector that gives credit to producers that simultaneously expand desirable outputs and contract undesirable outputs. Therefore, we choose a non-negative directional vector for desirable outputs and a nonpositive directional vector for undesirable outputs: $g_y \geq 0$ and $g_b \leq 0$. Different directional vectors can be chosen, depending on the objectives of the manager or policy maker. A directional vector of $g_y = (y_1, y_2, \ldots, y_M)$ and $g_b = (-b_1, -b_2, \ldots, -b_J)$ would give the simultaneous maximum proportional expansion in desirable outputs and proportional contraction in undesirable outputs. A directional vector of $g_y = (1, 1, \ldots, 1)$ and $g_b = (-1, -1, \ldots, -1)$ would give the simultaneous maximum unit expansion in desirable outputs and unit contraction in undesirable outputs. If managers are interested in finding the maximum contraction in undesirable outputs holding desirable outputs constant, then $g_y = (0, 0, \ldots, 0)$ and $g_b < 0$ for undesirable outputs should be chosen. If managers are interested in finding the maximum expansion in desirable outputs holding undesirable outputs constant, then a choice of $g_b = (0, 0, \ldots, 0)$ and $g_y > 0$ would be appropriate.

When $\vec{D}_o(c, y, b; g_y, g_b) = 0$, the producer is on the frontier of $P(c)$; it cannot simultaneously expand desirable outputs and contract undesirable outputs given the budget with which to hire inputs. These producers are technically efficient for the given directional vectors, g_y and g_b. Inefficient producers have $\vec{D}_o(c, y, b; g_y, g_b) > 0$ with higher values indicating greater inefficiency.

The directional distance function inherits its properties from the production possibility set:

i. $(y, b) \in P(c)$ if and only if $\vec{D}_o(c, y, b; g_y, g_b) \geq 0$

ii. For $y' \leq y$ and $(y, b) \in P(c)$, then $\vec{D}_o(c, y', b; g_y, g_b) \geq \vec{D}_o(c, y, b; g_y, g_b)$,

iii. For $b' \geq b$ and $(y, b') \in P(c)$, then $\vec{D}_o(c, y, b'; g_y, g_b) \geq \vec{D}_o(c, y, b; g_y, g_b)$,

iv. For $c' \geq c$, then $\vec{D}_o(c', y, b; g_y, g_b) \geq \vec{D}_o(c, y, b; g_y, g_b)$

v. For $\alpha \in R_+$ and $(y, b) \in P(c)$, then $\vec{D}_o(c, y + \alpha g_y, b + \alpha g_b; g_y, g_b)$
$$= \vec{D}_o(c, y, b; g_y, g_b) - \alpha.$$

vi. $\vec{D}_o(c, y, b; g_y, g_b)$ is concave in (y, b).

$$(3.4)$$

These properties include feasibility $(3.4)i$, monotonicity conditions $(3.4)ii-iv$, the translation property $(3.4)v$, and concavity $(3.4)vi$.

We follow Färe and Primont (1995) and exploit the duality between the revenue function and the directional output distance function to obtain the prices that support the outputs on the production possibility frontier.

Let $p \in R_+^M$ represent the desirable output price vector and $q \in R_+^J$ represent the undesirable output price vector. The revenue function takes the form:

$$R(c, p, q) = \max_{y,b} \{py - qb : \ \ \vec{D}_o(c, y, b; g_y, g_b) \geq 0\}. \tag{3.5}$$

In (3.5), firms gain revenue of p for every unit of desirable output they produce but must also pay a charge of q for every unit of undesirable output they produce.

One way of recovering the shadow price of the undesirable output is by using the first-order conditions associated with the constrained maximization of 3.5. The first-order conditions imply that the ratio of prices equal the ratio of derivatives of the distance function with respect to the outputs:

$$\frac{q_j}{p_m} = -\frac{\partial \vec{D}_o(c, y, b; g_y, g_b)/\partial b_j}{\partial \vec{D}_o(c, y, b; g_y, g_b)/\partial y_m}. \tag{3.6}$$

Given knowledge of a single marketed output price, say p_m, the shadow price of the nonmarketed undesirable output, q_j, can be recovered using (3.6). However, this shadow pricing method requires the researcher to observe at least one marketed output price. In what follows below, we recover all prices without knowledge of a single market price.

Using the duality between the directional output distance function and the revenue function, we can write

$$c = py - qb = R(c, p, q) - \vec{D}_o(c, y, b; g_y, g_b)pg_y + \vec{D}_o(c, y, b; g_y, g_b)qg_b. \tag{3.7}$$

In words, (3.7) says that actual revenues ($py - qb$) are equal to maximum revenues $R(c, p, q)$ less a deduction for producing inefficient amounts of the desirable outputs in the amount of $\vec{D}_o(c, y, b; g_y, g_b)pg_y$ and a further deduction (since $g_b < 0$) for overproducing the undesirable outputs in the amount of $\vec{D}_o(c, y, b; g_y, g_b)qg_b$. Taking the gradient function of (3.7) with respect to desirable outputs and then again with respect to undesirable outputs yields

$$\begin{aligned} p &= -\nabla_y \vec{D}_o(c, y, b; g_y, g_b)pg_y + \nabla_y \vec{D}_o(c, y, b; g_y, g_b)qg_b \\ -q &= -\nabla_b \vec{D}_o(c, y, b; g_y, g_b)pg_y + \nabla_b \vec{D}_o(c, y, b; g_y, g_b)qg_b. \end{aligned} \tag{3.8}$$

Collecting terms in (3.8) yields

$$\begin{aligned} p &= -\nabla_y \vec{D}_o(c, y, b; g_y, g_b)(pg_y - qg_b) \\ q &= \nabla_b \vec{D}_o(c, y, b; g_y, g_b)(pg_y - qg_b). \end{aligned} \tag{3.9}$$

Multiplying the first equation in (3.9) by the desirable output vector y and the second equation in (3.9) by the undesirable output vector b yields

$$py = -\nabla_y \vec{D}_o(c, y, b; g_y, g_b)y(pg_y - qg_b)$$
$$qb = \nabla_b \vec{D}_o(c, y, b; g_y, g_b)b(pg_y - qg_b). \tag{3.10}$$

Subtracting the second equation in (3.10) from the first equation in (3.10) yields

$$c = py - qb = -[\nabla_y \vec{D}_o(c, y, b; g_y, g_b)y + \nabla_b \vec{D}_o(c, y, b; g_y, g_b)b](pg_y - qg_b). \tag{3.11}$$

Since $(pg_y - qg_b)$ is positive and since $c = py - qb$ is also positive, it must be the case that the term in brackets on the left-hand side of (3.11) is negative:

$$[\nabla_y \vec{D}_o(c, y, b; g_y, g_b)y + \nabla_b \vec{D}_o(c, y, b; g_y, g_b)b] < 0. \tag{3.12}$$

Solving (3.11) for $(pg_y - qg_b)$ yields

$$pg_y - qg_b = -\frac{py - qb}{\nabla_y \vec{D}_o(c, y, b; g_y, g_b)y + \nabla_b \vec{D}_o(c, y, b; g_y, g_b)b} \quad \text{or}$$
$$pg_y - qg_b = -\frac{c}{\nabla_y \vec{D}_o(c, y, b; g_y, g_b)y + \nabla_b \vec{D}_o(c, y, b; g_y, g_b)b}. \tag{3.13}$$

Finally, substituting (3.13) into (3.9) yields the pricing formulas for the desirable and undesirable outputs:

$$p = \frac{\nabla_y \vec{D}_o(c, y, b; g_y, g_b)c}{\nabla_y \vec{D}_o(c, y, b; g_y, g_b)y + \nabla_b \vec{D}_o(c, y, b; g_y, g_b)b} \quad \text{and}$$
$$q = \frac{-\nabla_b \vec{D}_o(c, y, b; g_y, g_b)c}{\nabla_y \vec{D}_o(c, y, b; g_y, g_b)y + \nabla_b \vec{D}_o(c, y, b; g_y, g_b)b}. \tag{3.14}$$

Since the denominator of (3.14) is negative via (3.12), and the monotonicity properties of the directional output distance function imply that $\nabla_y \vec{D}_o(c, y, b; g_y, g_b) \leq 0$ and $\nabla_b \vec{D}_o(c, y, b; g_y, g_b) \geq 0$, the pricing formulae (3.14) yield $p \geq 0$ and $q \geq 0$. The most significant result of (3.14) is that we do not need price information in contrast to the shadow pricing methods of Fukuyama and Weber (2008a; 2008b).

To implement the pricing formulae (3.14), we need to choose a functional form for the directional output distance function. Although DEA can be used to estimate dual shadow prices, DEA provides only a first-order approximation to the true but unknown production technology. In contrast, the translog functional form has been used as a second-order approximation to a true but unknown technology that can be estimated via Shephard output or input distance functions. However, the Shephard output distance function seeks the maximum expansion of both desirable and undesirable outputs. Since we want to give credit to banks that successfully expand desirable outputs and contract undesirable outputs, we choose a quadratic form for the directional output distance function. Although the translog form is suitable for modeling the homogeneity property of Shephard distance functions, the directional output distance function has the translation property that can be modeled using a quadratic form.

Given $k = 1, \ldots, K$ firms (banks) that produce in $t = 1, \ldots, T$ periods, the quadratic directional output distance function takes the form

$$
\vec{D}_o(c^t, y^t, b^t; g_y, g_b) = \alpha_o + \sum_{m=1}^{M} \alpha_m y_{km}^t + \frac{1}{2} \sum_{m=1}^{M} \sum_{m=1}^{M} \alpha_{mm'} y_{km}^t y_{km}^t
$$

$$
+ \sum_{j=1}^{J} \beta_j b_j^t + \frac{1}{2} \sum_{j=1}^{J} \sum_{j'=1}^{J} \beta_{jj'} b_{kj}^t b_{kj'}^t + \sum_{m=1}^{M} \sum_{j=1}^{J} \delta_{mj} y_{km}^t b_{kj}^t
$$

$$
+ \gamma_1 c_k^t + \frac{1}{2} \gamma_2 c_k^t c_k^t + \sum_{m=1}^{M} \theta_m y_{km}^t c_k^t + \sum_{j=1}^{J} \phi_j b_{kj}^t c_k^t + \sum_{t=2}^{T} \tau_t I_t. \tag{3.15}
$$

We allow for technological progress/regress by defining binary indicator variables, I_t, for each of the $t = 2, \ldots, T$ periods. For a given observation on budget, desirable outputs, and undesirable outputs (c, y, b), the sign of the coefficients τ_t tells us whether the distance of the observation to the period t frontier ($t \neq 1$) is further ($\tau_t > 0$) or closer ($\tau_t < 0$) than it is to the frontier in period $t = 1$. Positive values for τ_t indicate technological progress and negative values indicate technological regress. We impose symmetry on the cross-product effects, $\alpha_{mm'} = \alpha_{m'm}$ and $\beta_{jj'} = \beta_{j'j}$. The translation property is imposed by the following coefficient restrictions: $\sum_{m=1}^{M} \alpha_m g_{ym} + \sum_{j=1}^{J} \beta_j g_{bj} = -1$, $\sum_{m'=1}^{M} \alpha_{mm'} g_{ym'} + \sum_{j=1}^{J} \delta_{mj} g_{bj} = 0$, $m = 1, \ldots, M$, $\sum_{j'=1}^{J} \beta_{jj'} g_{bj'} + \sum_{j'=1}^{J} \delta_{mj} g_{ym} = 0$, $j = 1, \ldots, J$, and $\sum_{m=1}^{M} \theta_m g_{ym} + \sum_{j=1}^{J} \phi_j g_{yj} = 0$. Finally, the directional output distance function must be concave in outputs. Let the matrix $A = \begin{pmatrix} \alpha & \delta \\ \delta' & \beta \end{pmatrix}$ be the matrix of second-order and cross-product terms for the desirable and undesirable outputs, where $\alpha = \begin{pmatrix} a_{11} & \cdots & a_{1m} \\ \vdots & \ddots & \vdots \\ a_{m1} & \cdots & a_{mm} \end{pmatrix}$, $\beta = \begin{pmatrix} \beta_{11} & \cdots & \beta_{1J} \\ \vdots & \ddots & \vdots \\ \beta_{J1} & \cdots & \beta_{JJ} \end{pmatrix}$, and $\delta = \begin{pmatrix} \delta_{1j} & \cdots & \delta_{1J} \\ \vdots & \ddots & \vdots \\ \delta_{Mj} & \cdots & \delta_{MJ} \end{pmatrix}$.

For the directional output distance function to satisfy concavity, the matrix A must be negative semi-definite (Lau 1978, Morey 1986).

To estimate the directional distance function, we use the deterministic method of Aigner and Chu (1968). This method chooses coefficients so as to minimize the distance of each observation to the production possibility frontier:

$$\min \sum_{t=1}^{T} \sum_{k=1}^{K} \vec{D}_o(c_k^t, y_k^t, b_k^t; g_y, g_b) \text{ subject to}$$

i. $\alpha_{mm'} = \alpha_{m'm}, \quad m, m' = 1, \ldots, M, \quad \beta_{jj'} = \beta_{j'j}, \quad j, j' = 1, \ldots, J.$

ii. $\sum_{m=1}^{M} \alpha_m g_{ym} + \sum_{j=1}^{J} \beta_j g_{bj} = -1, \quad \sum_{m'=1}^{M} \alpha_{mm'} g_{ym'} + \sum_{j=1}^{J} \delta_{mj} g_{bj} = 0,$

$\quad m = 1, \ldots, M, \quad \sum_{j'=1}^{J} \beta_{jj'} g_{bj'} + \sum_{j'=1}^{J} \delta_{mj} g_{ym} = 0, \quad j = 1, \ldots, J,$

$\quad \sum_{m=1}^{M} \theta_m g_{ym} + \sum_{j=1}^{J} \phi_j g_{yj} = 0,$

iii. $\dfrac{\partial \vec{D}_o\left(c_k^t, y_k^t, b_k^t; g_y, g_b\right)}{\partial y_{km}^t} \leq 0, \quad m = 1, \ldots, M, \quad k = 1, \ldots, K,$

$\quad t = 1, \ldots, T,$

iv. $\dfrac{\partial \vec{D}_o(c_k^t, y_k^t, b_k^t; g_y, g_b)}{\partial b_{kj}^t} \geq 0, \quad j = 1, \ldots, J, \quad k = 1, \ldots, K, \quad t = 1, \ldots, T,$

v. $\dfrac{\partial \vec{D}_o(c_k^t, y_k^t, b_k^t; g_y, g_b)}{\partial c_k^t} \geq 0, \quad k = 1, \ldots, K, \quad t = 1, \ldots, T,$

vi. A is negative semi-definite,

vii. $\displaystyle\sum_{m=1}^{M} \dfrac{\partial \vec{D}_o(c_k^t, y_k^t, b_k^t; g_y, g_b)}{\partial y_{km}^t} \times y_{km}^t + \sum_{j=1}^{J} \dfrac{\partial \vec{D}_o(c_k^t, y_k^t, b_k^t; g_y, g_b)}{\partial b_{kj}^t} b_{kj}^t \leq 0,$

$\quad k = 1, \ldots, K, t = 1, \ldots, T,$

viii. $\vec{D}_o(c_k^t, y_k^t, b_k^t; g_y, g_b) \geq 0, \quad k = 1, \ldots, K, \quad t = 1, \ldots, T.$

$$(3.16)$$

In (3.4) we stated the properties of the directional output distance function and these properties are incorporated in (3.16). That each observation be feasible is given by the restriction (3.16)*viii*. The monotonicity conditions are incorporated in (3.16)*iii*, *iv*, and *v*. Restrictions corresponding to the translation property are given in (3.16)*ii*. The symmetry conditions for the quadratic form are given by (3.16)*i* and concavity is given by (3.16)*vi*. We impose concavity on the directional output distance function by decomposing the matrix A into its Cholesky factorization and imposing constraints on the Cholesky values of A.[1] The conditions in (3.16)*vii* ensure that the desirable and undesirable output prices are non-negative.

EMPIRICAL APPLICATION

Data Source and Data Description

Mergers, acquisitions, and regulatory closures have led to consolidation in the Japanese banking industry, and the trends among various bank types can be seen in Table 3.1. The data for Japanese banks were obtained via the Nikkei Financial Quest, which is an online data retrieval system that provides firm-level financial data. To estimate our model, we use pooled data on 101 banks during the five fiscal years of 2008 to 2012. The 101 banks include five city banks and 96 regional banks, which comprise first regional banks and second regional banks. In 2008 there were 64 first regional banks and 44 second regional banks. From 1971 to 2008, the number of second regional banks fell from 71 to 44 and by 2012 (the last year of our sample), the number of second regional banks had fallen to 41. Because of missing data, we deleted six regional banks from our sample: Tokyo Tomin Bank, Shinsei Bank, Kumamoto, Seven Bank, Tokushima Bank, Kagawa Bank, and Shinwa Bank. The bank names used in this study are provided in the Appendix 3.1.

Berger and Humphrey (1992) provide an overview of the various ways researchers have defined bank outputs and inputs. The asset approach of Sealey and Lindley (1977) includes bank assets such as loans and securities investments as the outputs of bank production, while the various deposit liabilities are inputs. In contrast to the asset approach, Barnett and

---

[1] The Cholesky decomposition is $A = TDT'$ where $T = \begin{pmatrix} 1 & 0 & \cdots & 0 \\ t_{21} & 1 & 0 \cdots & 0 \\ & & \ddots & \\ t_{m1} & t_{m2} \cdots & & 1 \end{pmatrix}$ and $D = \begin{pmatrix} d_{11} & 0 \cdots & 0 \\ \vdots & \ddots & 0 \\ 0 & \cdots & 0 & d_{mm} \end{pmatrix}$ is the matrix of Cholesky values. The necessary and sufficient condition for the matrix A to be negative semi-definite is all the Cholesky values are nonpositive (Morey 1986; Lau 1978).

TABLE 3.1 Trends in the Configuration of Japanese Banking Industry.

	1971	1980	1990	2000	2005	2008	2009	2010	2011	2012
City	14	13	12	9	6	6	6	6	6	6
Reg[1]	61	63	64	64	64	64	64	63	64	64
SecReg[2]	71	71	68	57	47	44	42	42	42	41
LTC	3	3	3	3	1	0	0	0	0	0
Trust[3]	7	7	16	31	21	20	19	18	18	16
Shinkin	483	461	451	372	292	279	272	271	271	270
Credit Co	524	476	408	281	172	162	159	158	158	157

Legend:
City: City banks (Toshi Ginko)
Reg: Regional banks
SecReg: Second regional banks (Dai-ni Chiho Ginko)
LTC: Long-term credit banks
Trust: Trust banks
Shinkin: Shinkin banks
Credit Co: Credit cooperative banks (Shinyo Kumiai)
Notes:
[1] The number of regional banks includes Sogo banks up until fiscal year 1980.
[2] Second regional banks are member banks of the Second Association of Regional Banks.
[3] Trust banks include foreign banks.
Source: Deposit Insurance Corporation of Japan (DICJ). Annual Report 2012/2013, p.184.
http://www.dic.go.jp/english/index.html

Hahm (1994) assume that banks produce the nation's money supply using a portfolio of loans and securities investment. The user cost approach of Hancock (1985) defines bank outputs as activities that add significantly to revenues and bank inputs as activities where there is an opportunity cost of production.

We follow the asset of approach of Sealey and Lindely (1977) in defining bank outputs. This approach has also been used by Fukuyama and Weber (2008a; 2008b; 2013; 2014) in studying Japanese bank efficiency. We assume that Japanese banks produce two desirable outputs and one undesirable jointly produced output by hiring inputs using their fixed budget (c). The budget (c = value of the inputs) equals total bank expenditures. In turn, total bank expenditures equal the sum of personnel expenditures, nonpersonnel expenditures, and interest expenditures. These expense categories are associated with the physical inputs of labor, physical capital, and raised funds.

Each of the outputs and the budget are in real terms, having been deflated by the Japanese GDP deflator. The desirable outputs are total loans (y_1) and securities investments (y_2). Financial Quest documents four categories of nonperforming loans: (1) risk management loans, which

TABLE 3.2 Descriptive Statistics for 101 Banks over 5 Years.

Variables	Mean	Std. Dev.	Min.	Max.
y_1 = total loans	4189690	10390770	160500	80928800
y_2 = securities investments	2374593	7805580	40200	71055100
b = nonperforming loans	110467	205376	10200	1777600
c = total expenditure	80241	214790	4310	2114750

[1]Total loans, securities investments, and total expenditure (personnel expenditure, nonpersonnel expenditure, and fundraising expenditure) are in millions of Japanese yen deflated by the Japanese GDP deflator (base year = 2005).

equal the sum of loans to bankrupt borrowers; (2) nonaccrual delinquent loans; (3) loans past due for three months or more; and (4) restructured loans. Risk management loans are items under banks accounts reported in the statement of risk-controlled loans. The sum of the four categories of nonperforming loans equals total nonperforming loans, which we take to be the jointly produced undesirable output (b_1).

Table 3.2 reports descriptive statistics for the pooled data. Total loans average 4.2 trillion yen and range from 0.16 trillion yen to 80.9 trillion yen. Securities investments average 2.4 trillion yen and range from 0.04 trillion yen to 71 trillion yen. Nonperforming loans average 0.11 trillion yen and range from 0.01 trillion yen to 0.21 trillion yen. As a percentage of total assets, nonperforming loans average 2.35 percent with a range from 0.5 percent to 5.2 percent. Nonperforming loans declined from 2.6 percent of total assets in 2008 to 2.2 percent of total assets in 2012. The average cost of production was 0.08 trillion yen, with the smallest regional bank incurring costs of only 0.004 trillion yen and the largest city bank incurring costs of 2.1 trillion yen.

Empirical Results

We estimate the quadratic directional output distance function for the directional scaling vectors, $g_y = (\bar{y}_1, \bar{y}_2) = (4.189690, \ 2.374593)$, and $g_b = \bar{b}_1 = 0.110467$, where $\bar{y}_1, \bar{y}_2, \bar{b}_1$ are the averages of total loans, securities investments, and NPLs reported in Table 3.2. While we provided the descriptive statistics of the financial variables in Table 3.2 in millions of yen, our estimation of the directional output distance function is carried out in trillions of yen. The estimated directional output distance function multiplied by the directional vector gives the simultaneous contraction in nonperforming loans, and expansion in total loans and securities investments. That is, the expansion in the desirable outputs will equal

$\vec{D}_o(c_k^t, y_k^t, b_k^t; g) \times g_y$ and the simultaneous contraction in the undesirable output will equal $\vec{D}_o(c_k^t, y_k^t, b_k^t; g) \times g_b$. Since the directional vector equals the averages of the desirable and undesirable outputs, the directional distance function is the amount that the outputs will change as a proportion of the mean.

Table 3.3 reports the parameter estimates for the quadratic directional output distance function. The sum of all 101 banks' inefficiencies over the five sample years equals 121.705.

One can easily check to see that the parameter estimates satisfy the translation property. For example, the first-order coefficients for the desirable and undesirable outputs multiplied by the directional vector must sum to negative one: $\alpha_1 g_{y1} + \alpha_2 g_{y2} + \beta_1 g_{b1} = -1$. Using the coefficients in Table 3.3 yields $-0.1742 \times 4.18969 - 0.0270 \times 2.374593 + 1.8638 \times (-0.110467) = -1$. Similarly, the translation restrictions for the second-order and cross-product terms can be shown to be satisfied.

TABLE 3.3 Estimates of $\vec{D}_o(c, y, b; g_y, g_b)^{1,2}$.

Parameter	Variable	Estimate
Objective	$\displaystyle\sum_{t=1}^{5}\sum_{k=1}^{101} \vec{D}_o(c_k^t, y_k^t, b_k^t; g)$	121.705
α_o	Constant	-0.0470
α_1	y_1	-0.1742
α_2	y_2	-0.0270
β_1	b_1	1.8638
α_{11}	$y_1 \times y_1$	-0.0005
$\alpha_{12} = \alpha_{21}$	$y_1 \times y_2$	0.0008
δ_{11}	$y_1 \times b_1$	-0.0003
α_{22}	$y_2 \times y_2$	-0.0014
δ_{21}	$y_2 \times b_1$	0.0005
β_{11}	$b_1 \times b_1$	-0.0002
γ_1	c	12.2277
γ_2	$c \times c$	-5.9945
θ_1	$y_1 \times c$	-0.0017
θ_2	$y_2 \times c$	0.0102
φ_1	$b_1 \times c$	0.1550
τ_2	T2	0.000
τ_3	T3	0.003
τ_4	T4	0.066
τ_5	T5	0.109

[1] The estimates are obtained based on data values in trillions of Japanese yen.
[2] The directional vectors are $g_y = (0.4189690, 0.2374593)$ and $g_b = 0.110467$.

To measure technological change we evaluate $\partial \vec{D}_O(\cdot)/\partial t \geq 0$. A positive value of this derivative means that holding the outputs and the budget constant, as time passes a bank, is further from the frontier, indicating technological progress. If the value is negative, then the bank exhibits technological regress. The estimated coefficients ($\tau_2 = 0.000$ (2009), $\tau_3 = 0.003$ (2010), $\tau_4 = 0.066$ (2011), $\tau_5 = 0.109$ (2012)) indicate that over time a given observation of outputs becomes further and further from the $P(c)$ frontier.

Table 3.4 presents the estimates of the directional output distance function, the number of frontier banks, and the prices for the two desirable outputs of loans and securities investments and the single undesirable output of nonperforming loans. Average inefficiency over the five-year period has a U-shape trending down from 0.33 in 2008 to 0.194 in 2010 and then rising slightly to 0.225 in 2012. For the five-year period, eight different banks[2] produce on the frontier with one bank on the frontier in 2008, 2009, and 2011, two banks on the frontier in 2010, and four banks on the frontier in 2012. Only one bank—Saitama Resona Bank—produced on the frontier in more than one year: 2011 and 2012.

The pooled price estimates for the desirable outputs average 3.7 percent for loans and 0.6 percent for securities investments. The price of loans reaches its maximum of 4.4 percent in 2010 and has a minimum of 2.9 percent in 2012. The price of securities investments ranges from 0.4 percent in 2012 to 0.7 percent in 2010. The charge on nonperforming loans averages 39.2 percent for the pooled sample and ranges from 47.3 percent in 2010 to 31.3 percent in 2012.

TABLE 3.4 Price Estimates and Inefficiency.

	2008	2009	2010	2011	2012	Pooled
$\hat{D}_o(c, y, b; g_y, g_b)$	0.330	0.232	0.194	0.226	0.225	0.241
# of frontier banks	1	1	2	1	4	9
$\hat{p}_1^*$	0.041	0.035	0.044	0.034	0.029	0.037
$\hat{p}_2^*$	0.006	0.005	0.007	0.005	0.004	0.006
$\hat{q}_1^*$	0.441	0.371	0.473	0.363	0.313	0.392

---

[2]The eight frontier banks are Saga Kyoei Bank in 2008, Toyama Bank in 2009, Howa Bank in 2010, Chiba Bank in 2010, Saitama Resona Bank in 2011 and 2012, Bank of Tokyo Mitsubishi-UFJ in 2012, Sumitomo Mitsui Bank in 2012, and Bank of Yokohama in 2012.

We further examine the estimates for a single bank, Tokyo Mitsubishi–UFJ Bank, which produced on the frontier in 2012. Tokyo Mitsubishi-UFJ bank is a large city bank that had costs of $c = 1.534$ trillion in 2012 and generated loans (y_1) equal to 80.9288 trillion yen, securities investments (y_2) equal to 70.3922 trillion yen, and nonperforming loans (b_1) equal to 1.7776 trillion yen. Its estimated prices in 2012 were $p_1 = 0.01996$, $p_2 = 0.0056$, and $q_1 = 0.26743$. Multiplying those prices by the respective outputs and summing yields revenues (and costs) of $p_1 y_1 + p_2 y_2 - q_1 b_1 = c = 0.01996 \times 80.9288 + 0.0056 \times 70.3922 - 0.26743 \times 1.7776 = 1.534$. Similar calculations hold for all other banks in all years.

Recent work by Färe, Grosskopf, Margaritis, and Weber (2012) investigated the issue of time substitution for producers. The goal of time substitution is to reallocate inputs or the budgets used to hire inputs across time so as to maximize production. The theoretical findings indicate that when there are increasing returns to scale, production should take place intensively in a single period and under conditions of decreasing returns to scale equal amounts of inputs should be employed in each period so as to maximize production. When technological progress occurs, firms should wait until later periods to use inputs, and when technological regress occurs, firms should use inputs earlier.

Here, we present a similar time substitution problem for Japanese banks. We use the parameter estimates of $\vec{D}_o(c_k^t, y_k^t, b_k^t; g)$ reported in Table 3.3 to simulate the effects of each bank optimally reallocating its budget c over time so as to minimize the sum of the undesirable output of nonperforming loans, while still producing a target level of the two desirable outputs. We choose the target for the desirable outputs to equal the actual output produced plus the estimated inefficiency in the output. That is, the target level of each output equals $y_{km,\text{Target}} = \sum_{t=1}^{5} (y_{km}^t + \beta_k^t g_{ym})$, $m = 1, 2$. We use nonlinear programming to solve the following problem for each of the 101 banks:

$$
\min_{b,y,c} \quad \sum_{t=1}^{T} b_k^t \text{ subject to}
$$

$$
\vec{D}_o(c_k^t, y_k^t, b_k^t; g) \geq 0, \quad t = 1, \ldots, T,
$$

$$
\sum_{t=1}^{T} y_{km}^t \geq y_{km,\text{Target}}, \quad m = 1, 2, \tag{3.17}
$$

$$
\sum_{t=1}^{T} c_k^t \leq c_{k,\text{Target}}
$$

where $c_{k,\text{Target}} = \sum_{t=1}^{5} c_k^t$ equals the sum of bank k's costs over the five-year period. In this problem the choice variables are the amount to spend in each period, c_k^t, and the amounts of the two desirable outputs, y_{km}^t, and jointly produced undesirable output of nonperforming loans, b_k^t, to produce each period. These variables are chosen so as to minimize the sum of nonperforming loans over the five-year period. The choices of c_k^t, b_k^t, and y_{km}^t, $m = 1, 2$ must also be feasible. That is, the choices must satisfy $\vec{D}_o(c_k^t, y_k^t, b_k^t; g) \geq 0$ in each year. We solve (3.17) for each of the 101 banks in our sample.

Table 3.5 presents the estimated optimal quantities for each period and Figures 3.1, 3.2, and 3.3 graph the optimal quantities of each output found as the solution to (3.17), the actual quantities, and the frontier quantities derived as $y + \hat{\beta} g_y$ and $b - \hat{\beta} g_b$, where $\hat{\beta}$ is the estimate of the directional output distance function from equation (3.16). Although the optimal quantities of the two desirable outputs summed over the five years equal the sum of the frontier quantities of the two desirable outputs and the sum of the optimal allocation of costs from (3.17) over the five years equals the sum of the actual costs over the five years, the optimal amount of nonperforming loans found as the objective function to (3.17) is less than the sum over the five years of the frontier amounts of nonperforming loans. The average amount of nonperforming loans is 0.11047 trillion yen. If banks were able to reduce inefficiency and produce on the frontier of the technology $P(c)$, they would have average nonperforming loans of 0.08369 trillion yen. If the average bank were then able to optimally reallocate its budget across the five years, the average amount of nonperforming loans would be 0.08080 trillion yen.

TABLE 3.5 Average Optimal Quantities Allowing Time Substitution (std. dev.) (trillions of yen).

	2008	2009	2010	2011	2012
Budget = $\bar{c}^t$	0.08061	0.07833	0.07877	0.08088	0.08262
	(0.2113)	(0.2068)	(0.2068)	(0.21719)	(0.2230)
Nonperforming loans = $\bar{b}^t$	0.09505	0.03112	0.04330	0.09526	0.13925
	(0.3830)	(0.0930)	(0.1247)	(0.5216)	(0.6251)
Loans = $\bar{y}_1^t$	5.17381	4.40290	4.56403	5.54095	6.31052
	(11.7869)	(9.2955)	(9.3587)	(13.7885)	(15.1249)
Securities investments = $\bar{y}_2^t$	2.94059	2.45514	2.55559	3.15367	3.62656
	(8.1413)	(6.9123)	(6.9351)	(9.4835)	(10.7685)

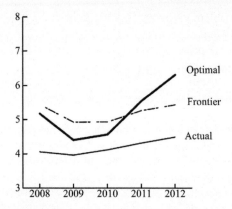

FIGURE 3.1 Actual, frontier, and optimal loans.

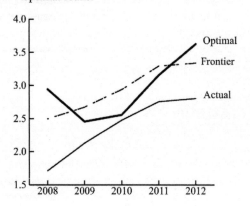

FIGURE 3.2 Actual, frontier, and optimal securities investments.

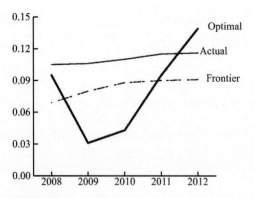

FIGURE 3.3 Actual, frontier, and optimal nonperforming loans.

The pricing problem given by (3.14) resulted in price estimates for the three outputs such that the value of the outputs equaled the cost of production. However, the price estimates typically varied for each bank in each year. Economic theory indicates that when relative prices vary across periods, firms can increase efficiency by reallocating production until the relative prices—the marginal rates of transformation—are equal in each period. The solution to (3.17) resulted in an allocation such that for each bank relative prices were equalized across the five periods. However, even after each individual bank reallocated across the five periods there was still some interbank variation in relative prices. Such a finding indicates that the banking system as a whole could further benefit by interbank reallocation of the budgets, with some banks expanding and some contracting until prices are equalized for all banks in all periods.

We also estimated (3.17) assuming that costs, nonperforming loans, and loans and securities investments should be discounted across time. We used a discount rate of 1 percent, which is the average yield on interest bearing liabilities among the banks in our sample. The results were largely the same as the undiscounted model, although a higher discount rates might cause larger differences.

SUMMARY AND CONCLUSION

Knowing the appropriate charge that must be borne for making a loan that becomes nonperforming provides important information to bank managers as they seek to determine the optimal bank portfolio. Although shadow pricing methods are well developed and can be used to recover charges for nonperforming loans, the method requires knowledge of one marketed output price and the marginal rate of transformation of outputs along a production frontier. In this paper, we presented a method that allows all prices to be recovered from a directional output distance function defined in cost space, which corresponds to the set of outputs that can be produced at a given cost. We estimated a quadratic directional output distance function using parametric methods and recovered prices for the desirable outputs of loans and securities investments and the charge on nonperforming loans for 101 Japanese banks during the period 2008 to 2012.

Our findings indicate that Japanese banks experienced technological progress during the period and that average bank inefficiency had a U-shaped trend, declining from 2008 to 2010, before rising slightly through 2012. We also found that the charge to be borne for nonperforming loans ranged averaged 0.39. We also used the estimates of the directional output distance function to simulate the effects of bank managers optimally reallocating their budgets across time. Actual nonperforming loans averaged 0.11047 trillion yen during the period. If bank managers were able to reduce inefficiency and produce on the production frontier nonperforming loans could be reduced to 0.083 trillion yen. Nonperforming loans could be reduced even further to 0.081 trillion yen if bank managers optimally allocated resources across time.

APPENDIX 3.1 BANK NAMES AND TYPE

AOZORA BANK	R	AWA BANK	R
SHINSEI BANK	R	HYAKUJUSHI BANK	R
MIZUHO BANK	C	IYO BANK	R
MIZUHO CORPORATE BANK	C	SHIKOKU BANK	R
BANK OF TOKYO-MITSUBISHI	C	BANK OF FUKUOKA	R
UFJ	C	CHIKUHO BANK	R
RESONA BANK	C	BANK OF SAGA	R
SUMITOMO MITSUI BANKING	R	EIGHTEENTH BANK	R
YACHIYO BANK	R	HIGO BANK	R
HOKKAIDO BANK	R	OITA BANK	R
AOMORI BANK	R	MIYAZAKI BANK	R
MICHINOKU BANK	R	KAGOSHIMA BANK	R
AKITA BANK	R	BANK OF THE RYUKYUS	R
HOKUTO BANK	R	BANK OF OKINAWA	R
SHONAI BANK	R	KIRAYAKA BANK	R
YAMAGATA BANK	R	KITA NIPPON BANK	R
BANK OF IWATE	R	SENDAI BANK	R
TOHOKU BANK	R	FUKUSHIMA BANK	R
77 BANK	R	DAITO BANK	R
TOHO BANK	R	TOWA BANK	R
GUNMA BANK	R	TOCHIGI BANK	R
JOYO BANK	R	KEIYO BANK	R
TSUKUBA BANK	R	HIGASHI NIPPON BANK	R
MUSASHINO BANK	R	KANAGAWA BANK	R
CHIBA BANK	R	TAIKO BANK	R
CHIBA KOGYO BANK	R	NAGANO BANK	R
BANK OF YOKOHAMA	R	FIRST BANK OF TOYAMA	R

DAISHI BANK	R	FUKUHO BANK	R
HOKUETSU BANK	R	SHIZUOKACHUO BANK	R
YAMANASHI CHUO BANK	R	AICHI BANK	R
HACHIJUNI BANK	R	BANK OF NAGOYA	R
HOKURIKU BANK	R	CHUKYO BANK	R
TOYAMA BANK	R	DAISAN BANK	R
HOKKOKU BANK	R	KANSAI URBAN BANKING	R
FUKUI BANK	R	TAISHO BANK	R
SHIZUOKA BANK	R	MINATO BANK	R
SURUGA BANK	R	SHIMANE BANK	R
SHIMIZU BANK	R	TOMATO BANK	R
OGAKI KYORITSU BANK	R	SAIKYO BANK	R
JUROKU BANK	R	EHIME BANK	R
MIE BANK	R	BANK OF KOCHI	R
HYAKUGO BANK	R	NISHI-NIPPON CITY BANK	R
SHIGA BANK	R	FUKUOKA CHUO BANK	R
BANK OF KYOTO	R	SAGA KYOEI BANK	R
SENSHU IKEDA BANK	R	HOWA BANK	R
NANTO BANK	R	MIYAZAKI TAIYO BANK	R
KIYO BANK	R	MINAMI-NIPPON BANK	R
TAJIMA BANK	R	OKINAWA KAIHO BANK	R
TOTTORI BANK	R	TOKYO STAR BANK	R
SAN-IN GODO BANK	R	SAITAMA RESONA BANK	R
CHUGOKU BANK	R		
HIROSHIMA BANK	R		

C=City, R=Regional

REFERENCES

Aigner, D. J., and S. F. Chu. 1968. On estimating the industry production function. *American Economic Review* 58: 826–839.

Altunbas, Y., M. Liu, P. Molyneux, and R. Seth. 2000. Efficiency and risk in Japanese banking. *Journal of Banking and Finance* 24: 1605–1638.

Banker, R. D., A. Charnes, and W. W. Cooper. 1984. Some models for estimating technical and scale inefficiencies in Data Envelopment Analysis. *Management Science,* 30: 1078–1092.

Barnett, W., and J-H. Hahm. 1994. Financial firm production of monetary services: A generalized symmetric Barnett variable profit function. *Journal of Business and Economic Statistics* 12 (1): 33–46.

Berger, A. N., and D. B. Humphrey. 1992. Measurement and efficiency issues in commercial banking. In *Output Measurement in the Service Industry,* edited by Z. Griliches, 245–300, Chicago: University of Chicago Press.

_____. 1997. Efficiency of financial institutions: international survey and directions for future research. *European Journal of Operational Research* 98: 175–212.

Berger, A. N., and L. J. Mester. 1997. Inside the black box: What explains differences in the efficiencies of financial institutions? *Journal of Banking and Finance* 21 (7): 895–947.

Chambers, R. G. 1998. Input and output indicators. In Färe, R., Grosskopf, S., Russell, R.R. (eds.), *Index Numbers: Essays in Honour of Sten Malmquist.* Dordrecht: Kluwer Academic.

Chambers, R. G., Y. Chung, and R. Färe. 1996. Benefit and distance functions. *Journal of Economic Theory* 70 (2): 407–419.

Chambers, R. G., Y. Chung, and R. Färe. 1998. Profit, directional distance functions and Nerlovian efficiency. *Journal of Optimization Theory and Applications* 95(2): 351–364.

Charnes, A., W. W. Cooper, and E., Rhodes. 1978. Measuring the efficiency of decision-making units. *European Journal of Operational Research* 2(6): 429–444.

Coggins, J. S., and J. R. Swinton. 1996. The price of pollution: a dual approach to valuing SO_2 allowances. *Journal of Environmental Economics and Management* 30: 58–72.

Cross, R., R. Färe, S. Grosskopf, and W. L. Weber. 2013. Valuing vineyards: A directional distance function approach. *Journal of Wine Economics* 8 (1): 69–82.

Drake, L., and M. J. B. Hall. 2003. Efficiency in Japanese banking: An empirical analysis. *Journal of Banking and Finance* 27: 891–917.

Drake, L., M. J. B. Hall and R. Simper. 2009. Bank modeling methodologies: A comparative non-parametric analysis of efficiency in the Japanese banking sector. *Journal of International Financial Markets, Institutions and Money* 19 (1): 1–15.

Färe, R., and S. Grosskopf. 2000. Theory and application of directional distance functions. *Journal of Productivity Analysis* 13 (2): 93–103.

Färe, R., S. Grosskopf, C. A. K. Lovell, and S. Yaisawarng. 1993. Derivation of shadow prices for undesirable outputs: a distance function approach. *The Review of Economics and Statistics,* 374–380.

Färe, R., S. Grosskopf, D. Margaritis, and W. L. Weber 2012. Technological change and timing reductions in greenhouse gas emissions. *Journal of Productivity Analysis* 37: 205–216.

Färe, R., S. Grosskopf, D. W. Noh, and W. L. Weber. 2005. Characteristics of a polluting technology: Theory and practice. *Journal of Econometrics* 126: 469–492.

Färe, R., S. Grosskopf, C. Sheng, and R. Sickles. 2012. Pricing characteristics: An application of Shephard's dual lemma, mimeo.

Färe, R., S., Grosskopf, and W. L. Weber. 2006. Shadow prices and pollution costs in U.S. agriculture. *Ecological Economics* 1 (1): 89–103.

Färe, R., and D. Primont. 1995. *Multi-Output Production and Duality: Theory and Applications.* Norwell, MA: Kluwer Academic.

Fethi, M. D., and F. Pasiouras. 2013. Assessing bank efficiency and performance with operational research and artificial intelligence techniques: A survey. *European Journal of Operational Research* 204 (2): 189–198.

Fukuyama, H. 1993. Technical and scale efficiency of Japanese commercial banks: A non-parametric approach. *Applied Economics* 25: 1101–1112.

_____. 1995. Measuring efficiency and productivity growth in Japanese banking: a nonparametric frontier approach. *Applied Financial Economics* 5: 95–107.

Fukuyama, H., and W. L. Weber. 2005. Modeling output gains and earnings' gains. *International Journal of Information Technology and Decision Making* 4 (3): 433–454.

_____. 2008a. Japanese banking inefficiency and shadow pricing. *Mathematical and Computer Modeling* 48 (11–12): 1854–1867.

_____. 2008b. Estimating inefficiency, technological change, and shadow prices of problem loans for Regional banks and Shinkin banks in Japan. *The Open Management Journal,* 1: 1–11.

_____. 2009. Estimating indirect allocative inefficiency and productivity change. *Journal of the Operational Research Society* 60: 1594–1608.

_____. 2010. "A slacks-based inefficiency measure for a two-stage system with bad outputs." *Omega: The International Journal of Management Science* 38: 398–409.

_____. 2013. A dynamic network DEA model with an application to Japanese cooperative Shinkin banks. In: Fotios Pasiouras (ed.) *Efficiency and Productivity Growth: Modeling in the Financial Services Industry.* London: John Wiley & Sons, Chapter 9, 193–213.

_____. 2014. Measuring Japanese bank performance: A dynamic network DEA approach. *Journal of Productivity Analysis.*

Hancock, D. 1985. The financial firm: Production with monetary and nonmonetary goods. *Journal of Political Economy* 93: 859–880.

Harimaya, K. 2004. Measuring the efficiency in Japanese credit cooperatives. *Review of Monetary and Financial Studies* 21: 92–111 (in Japanese).

Hori, K. 2004. An empirical investigation of cost efficiency in Japanese banking: A nonparametric approach. *Review of Monetary and Financial Studies* 21: 45–67.

Hughes, J. P., W. Lang, L. J. Mester, and C-G. Moon. 1996. Efficient banking under interstate branching. *Journal of Money, Credit, and Banking* 28 (4): 1045–1071.

Jayaratne, J. and P. E. Strahan. 1998. Entry restrictions, industry evolution, and dynamic efficiency: Evidence from commercial banking. *Journal of Law and Economics* 41 (1): 239–274.

Kasuya, M. 1986. Economies of scope: Theory and application to banking. *BOJ Monetary and Economic Studies* 4: 59–104.

Lau, L. J. 1978. Testing and imposing monotonicity, convexity and quasi-convexity constraints. In M. Fuss and D. McFadden, eds. *Production Economics: A Dual Approach to Theory and Applications* volume 1. Amsterdam: North Holland.

Liu, J., and K. Tone. 2008. A multistage method to measure efficiency and its application to Japanese banking industry." *Socio-Economic Planning Sciences* 42: 75–91.

Luenberger, D. G. 1992. Benefit functions and duality. *Journal of Mathematical Economics* 21: 461–481.

_____. 1995. *Microeconomic Theory*. Boston: McGraw-Hill.

Miyakoshi, T., and Y. Tsukuda. 2004. Regional disparities in Japanese banking performance. *Review of Urban and Regional Development Studies,* 16: 74–89.

Morey, E. R. 1986. An introduction to checking, testing, and imposing curvature properties: The true function and the estimated function. *Canadian Journal of Economics* 19 (2): 207–235.

Rosen, S. 1974. Hedonic prices and implicit markets: Product differentiation in pure competition. *Journal of Political Economy* 8(1): 34–55.

Saunders, A., and M. Cornett. 2008. *Financial Institutions Management: A Risk Management Approach.* 6th ed. New York: McGraw-Hill Irwin.

Shephard, R. W. 1970. *Theory of Cost and Production Functions.* Princeton: Princeton University Press.

Sealey, C., and J. T. Lindley. 1977. Inputs, outputs and a theory of production and cost at depository financial institutions, *Journal of Finance,* 33: 1251–1266.

Swinton, J. R. 1998. At what cost do we reduce pollution? Shadow prices of SO_2 emissions. *The Energy Journal* 19 (4): 63–83.

Risk Models and Measures

CHAPTER 4

A Practical Guide to Regime Switching in Financial Economics

Iain Clacher
Leeds University, UK

Mark Freeman
Loughborough University, UK

David Hillier
University of Strathclyde, UK

Malcolm Kemp
Nematrian Limited, UK

Qi Zhang
Leeds University, UK

A standard assumption in empirical finance is that logarithmic returns to a number of financial asset classes are independently and identically normally distributed (i.i.n.d.). This is convenient to work with analytically and underlies a number of the key theorems in asset pricing, including the Black–Scholes–Merton options pricing model. A further assumption is also commonly invoked that restricts the correlations between different financial assets to be constant over time. This, again, aids in determining closed-form solutions to optimal asset allocation problems.

Despite the mathematical appeal of this framework, it is well known that it does not accurately capture the real-world dynamics of asset returns. There are extensive literatures that document time-varying expected returns, time-varying volatility (heteroskedasticity), autocorrelation, fat-tailed distributions where outliers occur considerably more frequently than might be estimated under the assumption of normality (leptokurtosis), and time-variation in cross-sectional correlation when describing the actual price behavior of financial assets.

Markov regime switching models are one of a range of statistical techniques that capture these observed characteristics of asset returns in a manageable and easily interpretable way. In the next section we provide a brief overview of Markov regime switching models in an academic setting; we then go on to describe the basic mathematical properties of these models in the case when there is only a single asset as well as extending this to multiple assets before considering more complex calibrations. Finally, we look at the use of Markov models and the challenges that can occur in using these models in practice.

A BRIEF LOOK AT MARKOV REGIME SWITCHING IN ACADEMIC ECONOMICS AND FINANCE

This first section of this chapter is intended to provide a brief overview of the applicability of and contexts in which academic research in economics and finance has applied Markov regime switching models. Since Hamilton (1988) and Schwert (1989), the literature has grown exponentially with ever more sophisticated techniques being applied across a multitude of economic and financial settings. The following gives an indication of just how wide the range of settings in which regime switching has been effectively utilized in economic analysis: stock returns (e.g., Ang and Baekert, 2002a); exchange rate dynamics (e.g., Dahlquist and Gray, 2000); interest rates (e.g., Sims and Zha, 2006); option pricing (Boyle and Draviam, 2007); bond pricing (Elliot and Siu, 2009); and pension fund solvency (Abouraschi et al., 2014).

Interestingly, in his comprehensive review of the use of Markov regime switching in empirical finance, Guidolin (2012) finds that in choosing to employ a regime-switching framework for economic analysis, around 50 percent of papers use regime switching because of statistical considerations—that is, the use of a regime-switching framework is dictated by the data. The other 50 percent, however, pick a regime-switching framework on the basis of economic considerations (e.g., analyzing the business cycle). As Guidolin (2012) notes, these two differing approaches, therefore, lead to two very different types of paper. The first is a traditional horse race where regime-switching models are pitched against other types of modeling—for example, regime switching versus a linear benchmark model. The second are papers that are firmly rooted in economic theory.

Markov switching models are well suited to the analysis of economic and financial time series. Since Hamilton's (1989) paper analyzing the business cycle in the United States, the idea that such models can analyze different states, such as expansion and recession, around a long-run trend clearly corresponds to the actual experience of most economies. Crucially, regime-switching models, therefore, have an intuitive interpretation. Moreover, as Ang and Timmerman (2011) note, in the context of financial time series, identified regimes correspond to distinct states such as differing regulatory periods or changes to policy. Further, such models introduce the ability to capture extreme market movements, which is a common feature in financial time-series. Regime switch models are, therefore, suitable for analyzing a wide range of data in the presence of fat tails, skewness, and time-varying correlations.

Further, one of the standard assumptions of finance and asset pricing, as demonstrated by the Capital Asset Pricing Model, is that risk-return payoffs are positive and linear in a monotonic fashion. However, this once again does not correspond to real-life experience. Markets can remain flat for prolonged periods; markets can crash and remain low; or they can grow for sustained periods. Experience has shown repeatedly that the economy can be in a "good" state or a "bad" state (e.g., a boom or a bust). This links to the idea that the economy, or a market for that matter, can be in a period that has more certain, and by definition, more stable return growth, or it can be in a period of high uncertainty where returns are increasingly uncertain. Such differential risk-return trade-offs occur as a consequence of time-varying consumption growth (Whitelaw, 2000). From the point of view of investors, this introduces an additional risk that they may wish to manage when optimizing their portfolio, as the existence of "good" and "bad" regimes, which result in non-monotonic asset returns, increases uncertainty, even if portfolios are largely in the more stable "normal" regime (Ang and Timmerman, 2011).

As noted earlier there are a wide range of applications and settings in which regime switching can be utilized. We, therefore, focus, albeit briefly, on three key areas of academic interest within the regime-switching literature, namely, interest rates, exchange rates, and stock returns and asset allocation.

REGIME SWITCHING AND INTEREST RATE PROCESSES

We first focus on interest rate processes, as this is where the application of regime switching was first utilized by Hamilton (1988) in the analysis of the term structure of interest rates. A key finding of this research is that interest rate regimes are closely related to differing monetary policy regimes (Hamilton, 1988; Sola and Driffill, 1994; Bekaert et al., 2001; and Ang and Bekaert (2002b and 2002c). Such findings clearly show the applicability of regime-switching modeling to such a setting as one would fully expect interest rates to be linked to different monetary policy regimes. Moreover, prior research has shown that interest rate dynamics are related to inflation expectations (Evans and Wachtel, 1993); real interest rates (Garcia and Perron, 1996); and inflation risk premiums (Ang et al. 2008).

Within this area, the work of Ang et al. (2008) is of particular note. Prior research into interest rate regimes had only considered one factor, such as inflation expectations. As such, the analysis would examine states of high inflation, low inflation, deflation, and the probability of being in a given inflationary state. However, in their 2008 model, Ang et al. incorporate two inflationary regimes and two real rate determinants. Moreover, unlike prior research into the inflation risk premium—for example, Campbell and Viceira (2001) that considered a single regime with a constant inflation risk premium—Ang et al. (2008) incorporate a time-varying inflation risk premium into a four-state regime model. Their results show that, in general, real short-term interest rates for the United States are low (circa 1.3 *percent*) and inflation is high; however, neither interest rates nor inflation exhibit large amounts of volatility.

Consistent with the idea that regime-switching models capture shifts in policy, the results of Ang et al. (2008), found an increasing frequency of regimes with decreasing inflation in the United States. As they note, these regimes are characterized by a downward-sloping real yield curve and swift decreases in inflation, and are consistent with activist monetary policy, which increases real interest rates at the short end of the yield curve. Moreover, these results are in line with Clardia et al. (2000), Boivin (2006), and Cho and Moreno (2006), who demonstrated a structural break in U.S. monetary policy during in the post-Volker period.

REGIME SWITCHING AND EXCHANGE RATES

As with other financial time series, exchange rates follow long-run trends that have periods of very high short-term volatility (Ang and Timmermann, 2011). Consistent with prior literature in interest rate dynamics, such changes have been attributed to underlying government policy with regards to foreign exchange. For example, Froot and Obstfeld (1991) implement dynamic regime switching models for three scenarios where the government will restrict a currency float within a specific range; peg a currency at a specified future level; or unify a system of dual exchange rates. In considering these three policies, they show that regime-switching models are well specified for capturing such dynamics. Similarly, regime switching has been used by Dahlquist and Gray (2000) to examine the European Monetary

System (EMS), and they identified periods where currencies were weak and defended against speculation via interest rates, and periods where currencies were stronger and were characterized by a free-float.

The applicability of regime-switching models to exchange rates has been well documented. Many studies find that the U.S. dollar exhibits very stable long-run trends of appreciating for three to four years and then depreciating for a similar period (e.g., Engle and Hamilton, 1990; Bekaert and Hodrick, 1993). One of the interesting findings of the application of regime switching to exchange rates, and possible explanation for long-run trends, is the persistence of policy regimes. In foreign exchange, the duration of policy regimes can differ substantially. As Bollen et al. (2000) note, policy regimes in the United States, such as the Fed experiment, are long lived. However, in the case of the EMS, policy interventions in defending weak currencies are likely to spike due to the nature of the intervention by central banks to ward off speculative attacks. In this case, then, switches between regimes would be much more volatile, as it is not possible to predict when a speculative attack would occur.

As well as looking at the policy drivers of exchange rate regimes, other research has considered the linkage between changes in foreign exchange rates and stock returns (e.g., Jorion, 1990; Roll, 1992; Dumas and Solnik, 1992). The idea underpinning the link between currencies and stock returns is again intuitive. For international investors, their exposure is not only to the stock returns in foreign equity markets, but also to the domestic currency in which these returns are expressed. As a result, when significant market events occur, such as the onset of the global financial crisis in 2008, asset values tumble and foreign exchange volatility increases. Despite the clear logic of this setting, and the suitability of its characteristics for regime switching, the literature is inconclusive on this relationship. Jorion (1990) does not find any evidence of predictive power between changes in foreign exchange rates and stock return volatility. Conversely, Roll (1992) and Dumas and Solnik (1995) find strong evidence that foreign exchange volatility predicts stock returns. Recent work, applying more sophisticated modeling in a Markov framework, has found evidence that there is a dynamic linkage between exchange rates and stock returns in emerging markets (see, e.g., Chkili et al., 2011 and Chkili and Nguyen, 2014).

REGIME SWITCHING, STOCK RETURNS, AND ASSET ALLOCATION

Another major focus of regime switching models in academic finance is the predictability of stock returns. Early models, such as those of Hamilton and

Susmel (1994), build on the ARCH and GARCH models of Engle (1982) and Bollerslev (1986). The original models of Engle (1982) and Bollerslev (1986), failed to capture the sudden spikes that occur in equity returns. Hamilton (1994), therefore, allowed for the combination of the properties of ARCH models and regime switching, which better captured the severity of the spikes that occur in asset prices as shifts to different regimes occur. For example, utilizing a multivariate Gaussian regime switching model is well suited to modeling asset returns in extreme markets (Abouraschi, et al., 2014). As Ang and Bekaert (2002) show, these models capture the leptokurtosis present in asset returns, as well as the increased correlations that occur in bear markets.

Many early asset-pricing studies have found that asset returns are predictable and focused on a wide range of instruments, including default spreads, dividend yields, and term spreads (Ang and Timmerrmann, 2011). However, later studies have found that this predictability has declined through time (Welch and Goyal, 2008). In concluding, Welch and Goyal (2008) argue that almost none of the standard proxies that are used in asset pricing for predicting returns would have systematically allowed an investor to beat the market, and that the predictability observed in previous studies may never have been there. However, Henkel, et al. (2011) apply a regime-switching model to understand the changes in predictability that have been observed. Their results show that the greatest amount of predictability occurs in bear markets, which is consistent with the findings of Welch and Goyal (2008), who show that some of the past performance of models was due to the inclusion of severe downturns, such as the oil shock during the 1970s.

One further application that has been conducted in the literature is to examine regime switching for portfolios of stocks. Guidolin and Timmermann (2008) analyze individual portfolios in the presence of regime switches and the relation of these regimes across portfolios. The intuition, and the evidence presented, are compelling. As the authors note,

> A single-state model appears to be misspecified as means, correlations and volatilities of returns on these portfolios vary significantly across states. This finding is perhaps not so surprising given the very different episodes and market conditions—such as the Great Depression, World War II and the oil shocks of the 1970s—that occurred during the sample (1927–2005). It is difficult to imagine that the same single-state model is able to capture episodes of such (Guidolin and Timmermann, 2008, p. 18).

Their regime switching analysis shows that size and value premiums vary across regimes in similar directions. However, the gains to investors are regime dependent. For investors who start in a negative state, this adversely affects the hedging demands of investors, while starting in a positive state has a positive impact on hedging demands.

As the conclusion of Guidolin and Timmermann (2008) shows, there are clearly costs to investors from being "in the wrong place"—that is, in a portfolio that is not well suited to a particular regime. Ang and Bekaert (2002) examine portfolio choices for international investors, and analyze whether the benefits of international diversification are offset by the increased volatility and correlations that are observed in bear markets. Their results show international diversification to be beneficial even in bear market regimes, and that ignoring regime changes is costly.

Ang and Bekaert (2004) apply a regime switching approach to the International Capital Asset Pricing Model. In the analysis, they show that there are two distinct regimes: a volatile regime with low Sharpe ratios; and a low volatility regime with a high Sharpe ratio. From this result, if investors do not take account of regimes in their asset allocation, then they hold suboptimal portfolios on a mean-variance decision criterion. As a result, investors could improve their mean-variance position by selecting a better portfolio in the low volatility regime, while it would be better to hold a lower exposure to equity in the high volatility regime. While such a conclusion is intuitive, these regimes clearly exist, and so investors would be better off if they were aware of regime switches and undertook a more dynamic asset allocation.

Guidolin and Timmermann's (2008) analysis of international investments incorporated skewness and kurtosis into investor preferences. Their results demonstrate that the incorporation of regime switches into the asset allocation decision showed the presence of home bias in the asset allocation of a U.S. investor, which has been an anomaly in finance without any definitive explanation (e.g., Stulz, 1981; Black, 1990; Chaieb and Errunza, 2007). Moreover, once skewness and kurtosis were included into the model, the results for home bias strengthened considerably.

SINGLE-ASSET MARKOV MODELS

The standard Markovian assumption is that the world exists in a finite number of states, S. If $S = 2$, then, as will be discussed next, these can often be interpreted as bull and bear markets as understood by practitioners, but the framework can be extended to higher values of S. We denote the individual states by $i, j \in [1, S]$ and use the indicator variable $\delta_{jt} = 1$ to identify that the market is in state j at time t; the market must be in one and only one state at each given moment.

Within a Markov model, the probability that $\delta_{jt} = 1$ for any j depends only on the state that is prevailing at time $t - 1$. We state that $Prob(\delta_{jt} = 1 | \delta_{it-1} = 1) = \pi_{ij}$, which will be assumed to be constant. Markov models have no memory of previous states and no dependence of where the world has been before time $t - 1$. We let T, with elements π_{ij}, be the $S \times S$ transition probability matrix. Because we must end up in one, but only one state at time t, $\sum_{j=1}^{S} \pi_{ij} = 1$, each row of T must sum to one.[1]

Denote by Π the $1 \times S$-vector with elements Π_j that is the left eigenvector of T. This is the unique vector (the elements of which sum to unity) that remains unchanged by left-multiplication with T; $ST = S$. Each of the Π_js represents the proportion of time that the economy will spend in state j over an infinitely long time-horizon (for economically plausible Markov chains). Similarly, the expected length of time that we expect to spend in state j before switching out to any other state is given by $\sum_{t=1}^{\infty} t\pi_{jj}^{t-1}(1 - \pi_{jj}) = (1 - \pi_{jj})^{-1}$.

In this section, we assume that we are only considering the time-series properties of a single asset, whose returns are given by r_t. If $\delta_{jt} = 1$, then r_t is drawn from the fixed distribution $f_j(r)$, which can be any well-defined probability density function. In the simplest Markov models, which we consider here, it is assumed that these are i.i.n.d: $f_j(r) \sim N(\mu_j, \sigma_j)$, where both the mean and the variance of the normal distribution vary between states but remain constant for each individual regime. If the state of the world never changes ($\pi_{jj} = 1, \pi_{ij} = 0$ for $i \neq j$), then this framework becomes identical to the standard model. However, the potential for regime switching introduces a number of important features into the dynamics of modeled asset returns.

The conditional distribution of the return to the asset at time t contingent on being in state i at time $t - 1$ is defined by a mixture of S normal distributions with weights π_{ij}:

$$f(r_t|\delta_{it-1} = 1) = \sum_{j=1}^{S} \pi_{ij} f_j(r)$$

As a consequence, if we denote by $m_i^k = E[r_t^k|\delta_{it-1} = 1]$ the kth noncentral moment of the return at time t contingent on the state being i at time $t - 1$, then, by the law of iterated expectations:

$$m_i^k = \sum_{j=1}^{S} \pi_{ij} x_j^k \quad x_j^k = \begin{cases} \mu_j & k = 1 \\ \mu_j^2 + \sigma_j^2 & k = 2 \\ \mu_j^3 + 3\mu_j\sigma_j^2 & k = 3 \\ \mu_j^4 + 6\mu_j^2\sigma_j^2 + 3\sigma_j^4 & k = 4 \end{cases}$$

where x_j^k represents the kth noncentral moment of the normal distribution that describes the return in state j.

---

[1]Some sources define the transition probability matrix as the transpose of this definition, in which case the columns must sum to one.

Except in the situation where the probability of being in any given state next period is independent of the current state (when π_{ij} is independent of i for all j), it is clear that the mean, variance, and all higher moments of the distribution of returns next period depend on the current state. This allows for both time variation in the expected return and heteroskedasticity, which adds substantial empirical flexibility when compared against the standard model.

The unconditional noncentral moments of the distribution for returns one period ahead are given by $M^k = \sum_{i=1}^{S} \Pi_i m_i^k$, allowing for a closed-form solution for the unconditional mean (μ), standard deviation (σ), skewness (ς), and excess kurtosis (κ) of returns; $\mu = M^1, \sigma^2 = M^2 - \mu^2, \varsigma = (M^3 - 3\mu\sigma^2 - \mu^3)/\sigma^3$, and $\kappa = (M^4 - 4\varsigma\sigma^3\mu - 6\mu^2\sigma^2 - \mu^4)/\sigma^4 - 3$. In general this will lead to nonzero skewness and excess kurtosis for the unconditional distribution, again adding richness by potentially allowing for the fat-tailed nature of asset returns.[2] Markov models then become an alternate to extreme value theory as a way of capturing leptokurtosis.

We demonstrate the descriptive power of the Markov framework by considering nominal monthly logarithmic returns to the U.S. stock market index over the interval February 1871 to February 2014, which are presented in Figure 4.1.[3] The descriptive statistics for these data are mean = 0.72 *percent*, standard deviation = 4.07 *percent*, skewness = −0.39 and excess

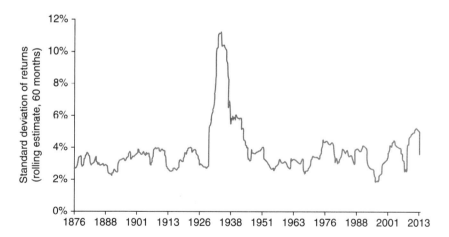

FIGURE 4.1 Standard Deviation of US Stock Returns 1871–2014.

---

[2] We can also calculate the value of these statistics for r_t conditional on $\delta_{it-1} = 1$ in an analogous way by replacing M^k with m_i^k in these expressions.

[3] Data are taken from Robert Shiller's website (http://www.econ.yale.edu/~shiller/data.htm).

kurtosis = 11.51. There are fat tails and clear evidence of time-varying volatility in the data as can be seen from Figure 4.1. Moreover, time-variation in expected returns for this market has been documented by Fama and French (2002), Lettau, Ludvigson, and Wachter (2008), and Freeman (2011), among others. The standard i.i.n.d. model clearly does not capture many of the characteristics of the observed data.[4]

To consider how Markov regime switching models might be used to capture more accurately the unconditional summary statistics of the underlying, we present estimates based on both two- and three-state versions of the framework. A review of the empirical techniques that can be used to estimate these models, and the steps and processes required, are clearly set out in Hamilton (1989), and this is the starting point for any reader who would want to utilize the techniques discussed. Econometric packages that will directly undertake the Markov estimation are available from http://bellone.ensae.net/download.html, the MSVARlib packages in Gauss by Benoit Bellone, on which the results that we report are based.

TWO-STATE ESTIMATION

When $S = 2$, the Markov estimates are $\mu_1 = -0.716\, percent$, $\sigma_1 = 8.018\, percent$, $\mu_2 = 1.111\, percent$, and $\sigma_2 = 2.906\, percent$. The transition probability matrix, T, has diagonal elements $\pi_{11} = 75.04\, percent$, $\pi_{22} = 97.44\, percent$. These six values are all that is required to determine a wide range of model-based summary statistics for asset returns. In Table 4.1, we report both the conditional and unconditional values of the mean, standard deviation, skewness, and excess kurtosis of the return to the market one period ahead and compare these to the equivalent descriptive statistics for the raw data.

From this it is clear that both time-varying expected returns and heteroskedasticity are introduced by allowing for asset returns to be described by a mixed normal distribution through a Markov regime switching process. The unconditional data also contain clear excess kurtosis. State 1 is a bear state with negative expected returns and high volatility, while State 2 has slightly above average returns and lower volatility. The proportion of time that the economy spends in State 1 (State 2) is $9.3\, percent$ ($90.7\, percent$), which is taken directly from S, the left eigenvector of T. The expected length of stay in each state on each visit is given by $(1 - \pi_{jj})^{-1}$, and this is equal to four months in State 1 and over three years in State 2.

---

[4]All of our statistics are monthly as we are using monthly data.

TABLE 4.1 Conditional and Unconditional Asset Returns Descriptive Statistics.

Descriptive Statistics	Conditional		Unconditional	Data
r_t	$\delta_{1t-1} = 1$	$\delta_{2t-1} = 1$		
Mean	−0.26%	1.06%	0.94%	0.72%
Standard Deviation	7.14%	3.16%	3.73%	4.07%
Skewness	−0.16	−0.25	−0.50	−0.39
Excess Kurtosis	0.63	2.62	4.47	11.51

At first sight, though, this calibration appears to be inconsistent with market equilibrium. If State 1 can be fully identified at the time it occurs, then all rational risk-averse investors would wish to immediately remove their money from the volatile stock market because of the negative expected returns in this state. This issue is at least in part overcome by the fact that the state variable δ_{jt} is not directly observable. Instead, the Markov estimation process produces values p_{jt}, which gives the probability that $\delta_{jt} = 1$. The expected return contingent on information available at time $t-1$ is given by $E_{t-1}[r_t] = \sum_{i=1}^{S} p_i m_i^1$, with similar expressions following for higher moments. For example, the Markov estimate for February 2014 is that $p_{1t} = 1.4$ *percent*, giving an expected return for March 2014 of 1.05 *percent*.

Figure 4.2 presents the average estimate of p_{1t} during the previous 60 months for the total horizon of the available data, 1876–2014.

As we might expect, p_{1t} takes its greatest values at times consistent with market participants' beliefs about the occurrence of bear markets: the 1930s, 1970s, and 2000s.[5] The appeal of Markov switching models becomes clear from this example. The basic framework is very similar to the standard model, with no requirement to move to more complex distributions than the normal. Markov models are therefore simple to explain intuitively to people familiar with the usual assumption of i.i.n.d. logarithmic asset returns. The considerably improved descriptive power comes purely from switching between states, and these have properties that are likely to be well recognized by those familiar with financial markets. The estimated timings of transition also correspond well with our historical understanding of the way in which the economy has moved between bull and bear markets. This combination of a simple extension from the standard model, intuitively appealing states, and

---

[5]It is worth noting that this is an ex-post statement and not an ex-ante statement, and so we do not know investor expectations beforehand.

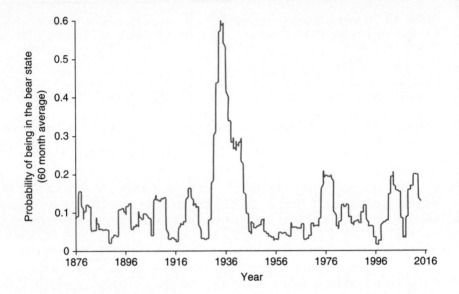

FIGURE 4.2   Probability of being in a Bear State (60 Month Average).

high descriptive accuracy lie behind the widespread use of Markov regime switching models in empirical finance.

THREE-STATE ESTIMATION

We can further enrich this model by incorporating a further state. Now the conditional and unconditional returns to the market next period are given by Table 4.2.

In principle, we can add more and more states to increase both the complexity of our underlying model and its ability to capture the unconditional moments of the underlying data. However, beyond a certain level, the benefits of parsimony begin to outweigh those of a richer regime setting. Standard model selection metrics, such as the Akaike Information Criterion (AIC), which are standard outputs from Markov estimation software, can be used to determine when there is overfitting from modeling too many states. For the two-, three-, and four-state models, the AIC are 2.754, 2.587, and 2.576, respectively. We should therefore, choose the lowest AIC, so the three-state calibration is preferred to the two-state calibration, and a four-state calibration is mildly preferred to the three-state calibration.

TABLE 4.2 Conditional and Unconditional Asset Returns Descriptive Statistics.

Descriptive Stats	Conditional			Unconditional	Data
r_t	$\delta_{1t-1} = 1$	$\delta_{2t-1} = 1$	$\delta_{3t-1} = 1$		
Mean	−1.53%	0.32%	2.17%	0.47%	0.72%
Standard Deviation	6.40%	2.76%	3.10%	3.92%	4.07%
Skewness	−0.21	−0.38	−1.09	−0.91	−0.39
Excess Kurtosis	0.20	2.78	5.12	3.59	11.51

MARKOV MODELS FOR MULTIPLE ASSETS

The extension of this framework to account for the joint time-series properties of multiple assets is straightforward. Denote individual assets by the subscripts a,b, let the expected return and standard deviation of returns to asset a at time t be given by μ_{at}, σ_{at} respectively, and let the correlation between the returns of asset a and b be given by ρ_{abt}. We further use Σ_t to denote the variance-covariance matrix at this time, with elements $\Sigma_{aat} = \sigma_{at}^2$ on the diagonal and $\Sigma_{abt} = \rho_{abt}\sigma_{at}\sigma_{bt}$ off the diagonal.

The usual Markov assumptions now hold, with $\mu_{at} = \mu_{aj}$ and $\Sigma_t = \Sigma_j$ for fixed values of μ_{aj}, Σ_j contingent on the state being j at time t; $\delta_{jt} = 1$. This setting not only captures time-varying expected returns and volatility, but also now potentially captures time-variation in cross-sectional correlations.

Take as an example the following three asset classes: 10-year UK Treasury bonds (gilts), an index of UK Treasury Inflation-Protected Securities (TIPS), and an index of world equity returns, all denominated in sterling, based on monthly returns for the interval December 1998 to December 2010. The descriptive statistics for these data are shown in Table 4.3.

Surprisingly, over this time period, there is no excess kurtosis in world equity returns as measured in sterling, although the TIPS returns distribution has a very fat tail. The correlation between equities and the other asset classes is also low, but there is some positive correlation between the two classes of fixed income securities.

If we set $S = 2$, then a Markov model captures this as follows, see Table 4.4.

State 1 is again a very clear bear state with extremely negative expected returns to world equities and with volatilities well above their unconditional values. A particularly notable feature is the high positive correlation in this

TABLE 4.3   Asset Returns Descriptive Statistics.

	World Equity	UK Gilts	UK TIPS
Mean Return	0.144%	0.474%	0.439%
Standard Deviation	4.747%	1.725%	0.803%
Skewness	−0.617	0.422	−0.323
Excess Kurtosis	−0.012	3.530	14.835
Correlation			
World Equity	1.000	−0.082	0.070
UK Gilts	−0.082	1.000	0.219
TIPS	0.070	0.219	1.000

TABLE 4.4   Asset Returns Descriptive Statistics (State 1).

	World Equity	UK Gilts	TIPS
Mean Return, μ_{a1}	−3.227%	1.867%	0.222%
Standard Deviation, σ_{a1}	7.738%	4.071%	2.609%
Correlation, ρ_{ab1}			
World Equity	1.000	0.669	0.487
UK Gilts	0.669	1.000	−0.020
TIPS	0.487	−0.020	1.000

TABLE 4.5   Asset Returns Descriptive Statistics (State 2).

	World Equity	UK Gilts	TIPS
Mean Return, μ_{a2}	0.365%	0.395%	0.454%
Standard Deviation, σ_{a2}	4.390%	1.421%	0.511%
Correlation, ρ_{ab2}			
World Equity	1.000	−0.270	−0.165
UK Gilts	−0.270	1.000	0.493
TIPS	−0.165	0.493	1.000

state between world equities and UK gilts—a characteristic that is completely obscured in the unconditional summary statistics.

State 2 is similar to state 2 in the single-asset example, as it corresponds to a mild bull market for world equities. Now the correlation between world equities and UK gilts is mildly negative. The transition probability matrix has diagonal elements $\pi_{11} = 86.82$ *percent*, $\pi_{22} = 99.28$ *percent*. This means that the economy spends approximately 5.2 *percent* of the time in state 1 and

94.8 *percent* in state 2 over the long run. The bull market state has an expected duration of almost 12 years, while for the bear market state, it is just over 7 months.[6]

This can again be further extended to multiple assets, N, and states, S, but the number of parameters that need estimation quickly gets large. There are $N(N + 1)/2$ values of Σ_i and N values of μ_a for each state, plus $S(S - 1)$ value for T, giving a total number of parameters of $S(N(N + 3)/2 + S - 1)$. So, with ten asset classes and four states, there are 272 parameters that require estimation. In nearly all potential applications this will be challenging to estimate robustly, and so, as the number of assets increases, the regime structure must become simpler to allow for effective estimation.

PRACTICAL APPLICATION OF REGIME SWITCHING MODELS FOR INVESTMENT PURPOSES

In these final sections, we explore the practical application of regime switching models for investment purposes—specifically, Markov switching models. A standard Markov switching model assumes two things:

1. The modeled world exists in only a finite number, S, of states each one of which is characterized by a suitable multivariate probability distribution (and if relevant other relationships) characterizing the (random) values that variables of interest may take within the model if the world is then in that state. Often, but not always, these distributions will be multivariate normal.
2. The probability of shifting from one state to another at the end of each time step is encapsulated in a $S \times S$ matrix, the transition matrix with elements π_{ij}. Typically, the π_{ij} are assumed to be time stationary unless there is strong evidence to the contrary.

INTUITIVE APPEAL OF SUCH MODELS

Markov switching models have several intuitive attractions for financial modeling purposes. These include:

1. They can be viewed as natural extensions of ones in which the modeled world is assumed to exist in just one state (the latter being a special case of a Markov switching model with $S = 1$ and $\pi_{11} = 1$).

---

[6]It is worth noting that the results for the one-state and two-state models are quite different, which highlights the need for a Markov model. If we thought they would be the same, or similar, then this would not be the appropriate econometric framework to undertake the analysis.

2. When $S > 1$ and even if each individual state in the Markov switching model is characterised merely by a multivariate normal distribution, unconditional outcomes typically exhibit heteroskedasticity, excess kurtosis, and other stylized features observed in real-life financial data.

3. Most other practical modeling approaches (perhaps all, if the Markovian approach is sufficiently general) can be approximated by Markov switching models, albeit potentially very complicated ones. For example:

   a. Suppose the world is not actually time varying. We can model this either as a single-state Markovian model with the distributional form applicable to that state being the one we want the world to exhibit or as a multistate Markovian model, each state of which involves, say, a multivariate normal distribution. This is because any multivariate distribution can be reproduced arbitrarily accurately (in a suitable sense) using merely a distributional mixture of suitably chosen multivariate normal distributions; see for example, Kemp (2011). If we adopt the latter approach then we can achieve the desired time stationarity by selecting the Markov transition matrix so that the probability of ending up in a given final state is the same whatever the initial state, by selecting π_{ij} so that for any given j it is the same for all i.

   b. Suppose the world is time varying but in a way that involves an infinite number of possible states. For example, it exhibits generalized autoregressive conditional heteroskedastic (GARCH) AR(1) behavior in which the volatility of some underlying process, σ, is allowed to take a continuum of values and is updated at time t by reference to its value at time $t - 1$ together with some random innovation occurring between $t - 1$ and t. We typically discretize time to approximate the reality of continuous time. We can likewise discretize σ, identifying different regimes for different discretized values that σ is now assumed to be capable of taking. In this instance we would probably also impose constraints on how the different states behave relative to each other, e.g., for a typical GARCH model we might constrain the states so that all features other than the underlying volatility are the same in each state. Of course, if we have $m > 1$ variables autoregressing at the same time, instead of discretising in one dimension we may need to discretise in m dimensions, vastly increasing the complexity of the model if it is specified in the form of a Markov switching model.

   c. Suppose the world is time varying but in a way that cannot be captured in a standard Markovian way via state transition probabilities between $t - 1$ and t that depend only on the state of the world at time $t - 1$. For example, transition probabilities might exhibit longer-term memories, might themselves be time varying, or might depend on the states of the world at times $t - 1, \ldots, t - n$. However, an nth order difference equation in a scalar $y_t = f(y_{t-1}, y_{t-2}, \ldots, y_{t-n})$ can be rewritten as a first order difference equation in the vector $\mathbf{v}_t = (y_t, y_{t-1}, \ldots, y_{t-n+1})^T$. We can likewise reexpress more complicated time dynamics by introducing additional "stacked" states characterized by which underlying states the world was in not just at time $t - 1$ but at one or more earlier times, again with the downside that this can exponentially increase the effective number of states included in the model.

IMPLEMENTATION CHALLENGES

Perhaps the most important practical challenges faced when implementing a Markov switching model for a real-life investor involve:

1. Selecting the "right" Markov switching model structure;
2. Calibrating the selected model type to suitable data;
3. Integrating the Markov switching model selected as per (1) and (2) with a sufficiently realistic model of the assets and liabilities of the investor in question; and
4. Drawing the right conclusions from the combined model in (3), if it is being used to make business or investment decisions, given the challenge of identifying robustly the state the world is currently in.

We discuss these challenges next, accepting that there is often overlap between them. As it is not unique to Markov switching models, we have assumed that the outputs of the Markov switching model align with the inputs needed by the investor's asset and liability model.

SELECTING THE "RIGHT" MODEL STRUCTURE

By this, we mean choosing the number of states we wish to consider, the overall structure of each state (e.g., the distributional family used to characterize the state, in contrast to the specific member of that family to be used in practice), the interrelationships (if any) between states that the model is constrained to exhibit, and so on.

The discussion in the section titled "Intuitive Appeal of Such Models" highlights that Markov switching models can approximate essentially any other type of econometric financial model. It also highlights that it is possible to get the same end answers using differently formulated Markov switching models. The flexibility inherent in Markov switching models almost inevitably means that the structure of any eventually selected model will be strongly influenced by the model creator's prior (i.e., expert) views on how the world "ought" to work.

There are, of course, statistical techniques that can to some extent guide such views. For example, we might adopt the principle of parsimony and penalize more complex models over less complex ones using tools such as the Akaike information criterion or the Bayes information criterion (see, e.g., Kemp (2011)). However, the range of possible Markov switching models is so large that, in practice, prior judgment will still play a strong part in framing such models. As always in investment, the key to a successful eventual outcome is a good understanding of the applicable market dynamics.

For the rest of this chapter, we will assume that the model creator has alighted on a sufficiently rich range of plausible model structures (probably based on prior heuristic analysis of applicable data and prior analysis of the economic rationales supporting the selected model structures) to stand a reasonable chance of selecting an appropriate model structure within the confines of his or her computing resources. We then highlight some of the issues that model creators should ideally bear in mind if they wish to select "intelligently" between these plausible model structures and to utilize them effectively for investment purposes. In this context, the range of plausible model structures to be selected from would typically include special cases not otherwise normally associated with Markov switching model approaches, such as a model that incorporates a single (perhaps non-Gaussian) state (which, as noted, is still technically a Markov switching model but with $S = 1$). This allows the model creator to validate whether it is worth including regime-switching features in the model in the first place, given the added complexities they introduce as also explored next. It should be noted that some of the issues discussed here are generic to model selection rather than being specific to Markov switching models.

CALIBRATING THE SELECTED MODEL TYPE TO SUITABLE DATA

Markov switching models face the same sorts of issues as other model types when it comes to calibrating model parameters, with the added complication that there are often greater numbers of parameters involved with a Markov switching model and/or more complicated constraints imposed on how these parameters can interact.

Perhaps the most fundamental challenge is to identify suitable data to use in the first place. Researchers often reach for past datasets because they are objective and relatively easily accessible. However, this assumes that the past will be a good guide to the future. For some purposes it may be better to calibrate to market-implied current estimates of distributional parameters or even to use forward looking data if applicable. Most forward-looking data (e.g., analysts' expected future returns or volatilities on different asset categories) involves expert judgment, introducing issues like those noted in the previous section. However, many of the potential applications of Markov switching models in a financial context are inherently forward-looking, especially if we are hoping to take financial decisions based on our model rather than merely attempting to understand what might have happened in the past. For such model uses, introducing some expert judgment is generally desirable, as long as the judgment really is "expert."

Even if we revert merely to using past data, we still need to ask ourselves whether the data we have available are representative of what might happen in the future. Even if it is, are some time periods within it more representative than others? For risk-management purposes, it is increasingly common to require that the dataset include a minimum proportion of "stressed" times. For example, if we would otherwise use a five-year dataset but conditions have been relatively benign over the whole of that period, then we might overwrite the earlier part of the dataset with data from further back in time deemed to relate to less benign conditions. Even for return-optimization purposes, there may be some parts of the data we think are more applicable now than other parts. Indeed, the inherent rationale for using regime-switching models is the recognition that different parts of the past have different characteristics, depending on the state the world was then in.

Assuming that such issues are adequately addressed, we then need to select parameters characterizing the model that best fit the (past) data. This would typically be done algorithmically (via suitable computer software), using some criterion of best fit, such as maximum likelihood. If the states are all multivariate normal, then one way of doing this is to use a Gaussian Mixture Model (GMM) approach as explained in, e.g., Press et al. (2007). The GMM approach identifies the set of S multivariate normal distributions that best represents the observed distribution of the data points from $t = 1$ to T. If there are m variables of interest in each state, then each of the T data points is an m dimensional random variable. Part of the output of the GMM algorithm is the probability $p_{t,k}$ that the observation at time t is from state k where $1 \leq j \leq S$. With enough observations and by comparing $p_{t-1,j}$ with $p_{t,j}$, we can derive a suitable transition matrix $\hat{\pi}_{ij}$ between the states that matches the observed likelihoods.

If at outset we haven't decided how many states to include in our model, then such a fitting might be repeated for several different values of S, potentially including penalties for reduced parsimony such as the information criteria referred to in the previous section. If constraints are applied to inter-relationships between individual states (e.g., we might require some means, volatilities, or correlations to be identical in two or more states), then the iteration steps within the basic GMM algorithm would need to be suitably refined and any information criterion scores adjusted accordingly.

Several open access or open source versions of the GMM algorithm are available to researchers who do not otherwise have access to this algorithm using commercial packages. These include the open access web-based MnGaussianMixtureModellingSA (http://www.nematrian.com/F.aspx?f= MnGaussianMixtureModellingSA) function in the Nematrian website's online function library (and corresponding spreadsheets). Although the GMM algorithm is normally associated with underlying Gaussian states, it can, in principle, be modified to target other distributional forms (by modifying the appropriate part of the algorithm that encapsulates the likelihood function for each individual state), but we are not aware at the time of writing of open access or open source variants that include such refinements.

Using computer software to carry out such calibrations hides complexities that ideally need to be borne in mind when applying such models in practice. These complexities include:

1. Underlying such algorithms are computerized searches for the maximum value of the function used in the best-fit criterion (e.g., here the likelihood function), and this function will almost always be multidimensional. Multidimensional maximization is generally an inherently hard computational problem, e.g., Press et al. (2007). In particular, if the function in question has more than one local peak, then practical maximization algorithms can converge to a spurious local maximum rather than to the desired global maximum. Typically such algorithms are seeded with initial parameter estimates selected by the user (or preselected by the software). One way of testing whether the algorithm appears to be converging to the desired global maximum is to run the algorithm multiple times starting with different initial parameter estimates and see whether the choice of seed affects algorithm output. Gaussian distributional forms tend to be better behaved (and simpler) than non-Gaussian alternatives in this respect, which tends to favor use of models that involve Gaussian underlying states even if economic theory might otherwise hint at more complicated model structures.

2. There is arguably an asymmetry in the way in which such an approach handles the state specification versus how it handles the transition matrix specification. Usually, we will have enough observations to be able to replicate exactly the observed transition probabilities $\hat{\pi}_{ij}$, so the maximum likelihood aspect of the problem formulation in practice primarily drives selection of the characterization of the individual states. However, this means that the calibrated model can end up flipping between states relatively quickly. This is implicit in a Markov switching approach in which the transition matrix depends only on the immediately

preceding state in which the world was in and also means that model results may be sensitive to choice of time step size. However it does not fully accord with an intuitive interpretation of what we mean by a "state." For example, when commentators talk about being in bear or bull markets, they usually have in mind a state of the world that is expected to persist for quite a few months even if they might be using monthly data to form their views.

3. There are inherent limitations on how accurately the fine structure of covariance matrices can be estimated from finite-sized time series (see, e.g., Kemp, 2011). These apply to Markov switching models as well as to simpler single-state multivariate normal models. Even when the time series are long enough, the fine structure may still in practice be largely indistinguishable from random behavior, making its selection again an exercise in expert judgment. This issue becomes more important when decision outputs from the model are materially affected by these limitations. Unfortunately, portfolio optimization, a common use for financial models, can fall into this category, particularly if the portfolio is being optimized after one or more important drivers of portfolio behavior (such as overall equity market exposure) has been hedged away; see Kemp (2011).

DRAWING THE RIGHT CONCLUSIONS FROM THE MODEL

The final challenge faced by modelers, or at least faced by those employing them, is interpreting the model output in an appropriate manner.

The extent of this challenge will depend heavily on exactly how the model might be used. For example, we might characterize model use for investment purposes under two broad types:

1. Reaching a specific investment decision at a particular point in time (e.g., selecting a specific asset allocation stance with the aim of maximizing reward versus risk).

2. Seeking generic understanding of likely future market behavior, such as potential range of outcomes for generic downside risk management purposes.

Perhaps the biggest challenge, if we wish to use a Markov switching model for decision-making purposes as in the first type just described, is to work out how best to identify the state of the world we are in at the point in time we are taking our decision. By design with a Markov switching model, different outcomes (over the short-term future) will have different likelihoods, depending on the current state of the world, so our ideal response at the current time should also vary, depending on which state we think we are currently in. If we can't actually tell which state we are in at any given point in time, then we might as well ditch using a Markov switching model and instead replace it with a single universal state endowed with the weighted average characteristics of the original differentiated states.

Of course, algorithms such as GMM do provide probabilities of being in a given state at any point in time, including the current time; see section titled "Calibrating the selected model type to suitable data." However, if we plan to use such output then we need to take seriously the second complication referred to in the section on Calibrating the Selected Model Type to Suitable Data. As we noted there, the GMM algorithm output typically results in average times within any given state that are modest multiples of the period length of the data being used to estimate the model. However, if the states are to have economic relevance, then we would not expect their average lifetimes to depend on the periodicity of the underlying data. Better, probably, is to use Markov switching models to identify individual states and then to seek out ways of associating different states with different exogenous variables.

For example, we might be able to characterize one of the states in our model as the "bear" state, and we might find that being in such a state has in the past typically been associated with pessimistic market newsfeeds (or high levels of implied volatility ...). We might then infer that if market news-feeds are currently pessimistic (or implied volatility is high ...), then we are currently likely to be in the bear state and react accordingly.

However, there are many possible exogenous variables we might consider in this context, and an ever-present risk of alighting on spurious correlations leading to incorrect decision making. As we have already highlighted, sophisticated modeling techniques such as Markov switching models are most useful when they are accompanied by a good understanding of market dynamics, including dynamics not directly captured by the model itself.

In contrast, the need to be able to identify what state of the world we are in at the current time is arguably not so important for more generic downside risk management purposes. For these sorts of purposes we might in any case start with a mindset that is skeptical of any ability to tell reliably which state we are in at the present time. To work out a value-at-risk (VaR) or other similar risk metric, we might then assume a suitably weighted probabilistic average of opening states or, if we wanted to be more prudent, whichever opening state gave the largest VaR for the relevant time horizon.

Finally, it should be noted that the inclusion of regime-switching elements into asset allocation models considerably complicates the mathematics of the underlying asset allocation problem, especially in relation to selection between risky asset classes. The problem becomes inherently time dependent and hence more sensitive to the utility of the investor in question (and how this might vary through time). This is because the risks and rewards of different strategies change through time and vary, depending on the then-state of the world. Issues such as transaction costs that may be glossed over with simpler time-independent models also take on added importance. This is because the optimal asset allocation can be expected to change through time as the state of the world changes.

REFERENCES

Abouraschi, N., I. Clacher, M. Freeman, D. Hillier, M. Kemp, and Q. Zhang. 2014. Pension plan solvency and extreme market movements: A regime switching approach. *European Journal of Finance*.

Ang A., and G. Bekaert. 2002. International asset allocation with regime shifts. *Review of Financial Studies* 15: 1137–1187.

_____. 2002. Regime switches in interest rates. *Journal of Business and Economic Statistics* 20: 163–182.

_____. 2002. Short rate nonlinearities and regime switches. *Journal of Economic Dynamics and Control* 26: 1243–1274.

_____. 2004. How do regimes affect asset allocation? *Financial Analysts Journal*, 60: 86–99.

Ang, A., and A. Timmermann. 2011. Regime changes and financial markets. *Netspar Discussion Paper Series*, #DP 06/2011–068.

Ang, A., G. Bekaert, and M. Wei. 2008. The term structure of real rates and expected inflation. *Journal of Finance* 63: 797–849.

Bekaert, G., and R. J. Hodrick. 1993. On biases in the measurement of foreign exchange risk premiums. *Journal of International Money and Finance* 12: 115–138.

Bekaert, G., R. J. Hodrick, and D. Marshall. 2001. Peso problem explanations for term structure anomalies. *Journal of Monetary Economics* 48: 241–270.

Black, F. 1990. Equilibrium exchange rate hedging. *Journal of Finance* 45: 899–908.

Boivin, J. 2006. Has U.S. monetary policy changed? Evidence from drifting coefficients and real-time data. *Journal of Money, Credit and Banking* 38: 1149–1174.

Bollen, N., S. F. Gray, and R. E. Whaley. 2000. Regime switching in foreign exchange rates: Evidence from currency option prices. *Journal of Econometrics* 94: 239–276.

Bollerslev, T. 1986. Generalized autoregressive conditional heteroskedasticity. *Journal of Econometrics* 31: 307–327.

Boyle, P. P., and T. Draviam. 2007. Pricing exotic options under regime switching. *Insurance Mathematics and Economics* 40: 267–282.

Campbell, J. Y., and L. M. Viceira. 2001. Who should buy long-term bonds? *American Economic Review* 91: 99–127.

Chaieb, I., and V. Errunza. 2007. International asset pricing under segmentation and PPP deviations. *Journal of Financial Economics* 86: 543–578.

Chkili, W., and D. K. Nguyen. 2014. Exchange rate movements and stock market returns in a regime-switching environment: Evidence for BRICS countries. *Research in International Business and Finance* 31: 46–56.

Chkili, W., C. Aloui, O. Masood, and J. Fry. 2011. Stock market volatility and exchange rates in emerging countries: A Markov-state switching approach. *Emerging Markets Review* 12: 272–292.

Cho, S., and A. Moreno. 2006. A small sample study of the new-Keynesian macro model. *Journal of Money, Credit and Banking* 38: 1461–1481.

Clarida, R., J. Cali, and M. Gertler. 2000. Monetary policy rules and macroeconomic stability: Evidence and some theory. *Quarterly Journal of Economics* 115: 147–180.

Dahlquist, M., and S. F. Gray. 2000. Regime-switching and interest rates in the European monetary system. *Journal of International Economics* 50: 399–419.

Ding, Z. 2012. An implementation of Markov regime switching models with time varying transition probabilities in matlab. Available at SSRN: http://ssrn.com /abstract=2083332

Dumas, B., and B. Solnik.1995. The world price of foreign exchange risk. *Journal of Finance* 50: 445–477.

Elliot, R. J., and H. Miao. 2009. VaR and expected shortfall: A non-normal regime-switching framework. *Quantitative Finance* 9: 747–755.

Elliot, R. J., and T. K. Siu. 2009. On Markov modulated exponential affine bond price formulae. *Applied Mathematical Finance* 16: 1–15.

Engle, R. F. 1982. Autoregressive conditional heteroscedasticity with estimates of the variance of United Kingdom inflation. *Econometrica* 50: 987–1008.

Engel, C., and J. Hamilton. 1990. Long swings in the dollar: Are they in the data and do markets know it? *American Economic Review* 80: 689–713.

Fama, E. F., and K. R. French. 2002. The equity premium. *Journal of Finance* 57: 637–659.

Freeman, M. C. 2011. The time varying equity premium and the S&P500 in the twentieth century. *Journal of Financial Research* 34: 179–215.

Froot, K. A., and M. Obstfeld. 1991. Exchange-rate dynamics under stochastic regime shifts. *Journal of International Economics* 31: 203–229.

Guidolin, M. 2012. Markov switching models in empirical finance. *Innocenzo Gasparini Institute for Economic Research, Bocconi University Working Paper Series* No. 415.

Guidolin, M., and A. Timmermann. 2008. Size and value anomalies under regime shifts. *Journal of Financial Econometrics* 6: 1–48.

Hamilton, J. D. 1988. Rational expectations econometric analysis of changes in regime: An investigation of the term structure of interest rates. *Journal of Economic Dynamics and Control* 12: 385–423.

_____. 1989. A new approach to the economic analysis of nonstationary time series and the business cycle. *Econometrica* 57: 357–384.

Hamilton, J. D., and R. Susmel. 1994. Autoregressive conditional heteroskedasticity and changes in regime. *Journal of Econometrics* 64: 307–333.

Heinen, C. L. A., and A. Valdesogo. 2009. Modeling international financial returns with a multivariate regime-switching copula. *Journal of Financial Econometrics* 7: 437–480.

Henkel, S. J., J. S. Martin, and F. Nardari. 2011. Time-varying short-horizon predictability. *Journal of Financial Economics* 99: 560–580.

Jorion, P. 1990. The exchange rate exposure of U.S. multinationals. *Journal of Business* 63: 331–345.

Kanas, A. Forthcoming. Default risk and equity prices in the U.S. banking sector: Regime switching effects of regulatory changes. *Journal of International Financial Markets, Institutions and Money*.

Kemp, M. H. D. 2011. *Extreme Events: Robust Portfolio Construction in the Presence of Fat Tails*. Hoboken, NJ: John Wiley and Sons.

Lettau, M., S. C. Ludvigson, and J. A. Wachter. 2008. The declining equity premium: What role does macroeconomic risk play? *Review of Financial Studies* 21: 1653–1687.

Roll, R. 1992. Industrial structure and the comparative behaviour on international stock market indices. *Journal of Finance* 47: 3–41.

Schwert, G. 1989. Why does stock market volatility change over time? *Journal of Finance* 44: 1115–1153.

Sims, C., and T. Zha. 2006. Were there regime switches in U.S. monetary policy? *American Economic Review* 96: 54–81.

Sola, M., and J. Driffill. 2002. Testing the term structure of interest rates using a stationary vector autoregression with regime switching. *Journal of Economic Dynamics and Control* 18: 601–628.

Stulz, R. (1981). On effects of barriers to international investment. *Journal of Finance* 36: 923–934.

Welch, I., and A. Goyal. 2008. A comprehensive look at the empirical performance of equity premium prediction. *Review of Financial Studies* 21: 1455–1508.

Whitelaw, R. 2000. Stock market risk and return: An equilibrium approach. *Review of Financial Studies* 13: 521–548.

CHAPTER 5

Output Analysis and Stress Testing for Risk Constrained Portfolios

Jitka Dupačová
Miloš Kopa
Department of Probability and Mathematical Statistics,
Faculty of Mathematics and Physics, Charles University,
Prague, Czech Republic

INTRODUCTION

The main feature of the investment and financial problems is the necessity to make *decisions under uncertainty* and *over more than one time period*. The uncertainties concern the future level of interest rates, yields of stock, exchange rates, prepayments, external cash flows, inflation, future demand, and liabilities, for example. There exist financial theories and various stochastic models describing or explaining these factors, and they represent an important part of procedures used to generate the input for decision models.

To build a decision model, one has to decide first about the purpose or goal; this includes identification of the uncertainties or risks one wants to hedge, of the hard and soft constraints, of the time horizon and its discretization, and so on. The next step is the formulation of the model and generation of the data input. An algorithmic solution concludes the first part of the procedure. The subsequent interpretation and evaluation of results may lead to model changes and, consequently, to a new solution, or it may require a what-if analysis to get information about robustness of the results.

In this paper, we shall focus on static, one-period models. Accordingly, let us consider a common portfolio optimization problem: There are I preselected investment possibilities that result from a preliminary security and portfolio analysis. The composition of portfolio is given by the vector of weights $x \in \mathbb{R}^I$ with components $x_i, i = 1, \ldots, I \sum_i x_i = 1$, and it should satisfy several constraints, e.g., $x_i \geq 0$ $\forall i$ (no short sales are allowed), or various bounds given by legal or institutional investment policy restrictions, bounds on the total number of assets in the portfolio, and so on. These constraints determine the set X of hard constraints, and they must be satisfied. The outcome of a decision $x \in X$ is uncertain. We suppose that it depends on a random factor, say $\omega \in \Omega$; the common assumption is that *the probability distribution P of ω is fully specified*. Given a realization of ω the outcome of the investment decision x is the return $h(x, \omega)$ or the loss $f(x, \omega)$ related with the decision x. However, the realization ω is hardly known at the moment of decision making, hence the goal function should reflect the random factor ω as a whole. The traditional approach is to use the expectations $E_P h(x, \omega)$ or $E_P f(x, \omega)$. The problem to solve would be then

$$\max_{x \in X} E_P h(x, \omega) \text{ or } \min_{x \in X} E_P f(x, \omega). \qquad (5.1)$$

Maximization of expected gains or minimization of expected losses means to get decisions that are optimal in average; possible risks are not reflected. Yet this need not be an acceptable goal. The present tendency is to spell out explicitly the concern for *hedging against risks* connected with the chosen (not necessarily optimal) decision $x \in X$. However, the concept of risk is hard to define. In practice, risk is frequently connected with the fact that the (random) outcome of a decision is not known precisely, that it may deviate from the expectation, and so on. Intuitively, the "outcome" may be the ex-post observed value of the random objective $h(\tilde{x}, \omega)$ or $f(\tilde{x}, \omega)$ for the chosen decision $\tilde{x}$; hence, a decision-dependent *one-dimensional* random variable. There are various types of risk, their definitions depend on the context, on decision maker's attitude, and they may possess many different attributes. Anyway, to reflect risk in portfolio optimization models, it is necessary to quantify it.

Risk and Deviation Functions

An explicit quantification of risk appears in finance since 1952 in the works of Markowitz (1952), Roy (1952), and others. Since the mid-nineties of the last century, various functions that describe risk, briefly *risk functions* or *deviation functions*, have been introduced and their properties studied—see, for example, Pflug and Römisch (2007), Rockafellar and Uryasev (2002), and Rockafellar, Uryasev, and Zabarankin (2006). Incorporating them into the portfolio optimization model makes the model more adequate but also much harder to solve. Moreover, inclusion of risk functions means to design suitable stress tests, to compare alternative choices of risk functions and of probability distributions by multimodeling, to develop stability and robustness analysis, and so on. Applicability of the existing output analysis techniques (e.g., Dupačová (1999, 2009), Dupačová, Hurt, and Štěpán (2002)), depends on the structure of the model, on the assumptions concerning the probability distribution, on the available data, and on hardware and software facilities.

Both in theoretical considerations and in applications, reasonable properties of risk functions are requested. Similarly, as the risk-neutral expected value criterion, risk functions R should not depend on realization of ω but they depend on decisions and on probability distribution P; the value of a risk function will be denoted $R(x, P)$. Coherence of R (monotonicity, translation invariance, positive homogeneity, and subadditivity (Artzner et al. 1999) is mostly expected. Risk functions value at risk (VaR), which is not coherent in general, and the coherent conditional value at risk (CVaR) are special cases of R. Monotonicity with respect to the pointwise partial ordering and subadditivity are evident requirements. Subadditivity, together with positive homogeneity, imply convexity of the risk function. Hence, duality theory can be used to prove that coherent risk functions R arise as the worst-case expectations for a family of probability measures G on Ω; for a finite set Ω the details can be found in Artzner et al. (1999), and the representation can be extended to a broader class of convex risk functions. In general, convexity of risk functions allows to keep a relatively friendly structure of the problem for computational and theoretical purposes, polyhedral property (CVaR introduced in Rockafellar and Uryasev, 2002), or polyhedral risk functions (Eichhorn and Römisch, 2005). It also allows to rely on linear programming techniques for risk-averse linear scenario-based problems.

In the classical mean-risk notion, a measure of risk expresses a deviation from the expected value. The original Markowitz mean-variance approach Markowitz (1952) was later enriched by alternative deviation functions such as semivariance, mean absolute deviation, or mean absolute semideviation. Recently, Rockafellar, Uryasev, and Zabarankin (2006) introduced general deviation functions $D(x, P)$ that preserve the main properties of standard deviation (nonnegativity, positive homogeneity, subadditivity, and insensitivity to a constant shift). Hence, contrary to the coherent risk functions, deviation functions are not affected by the expected value and can be interpreted as measures of variability. As shown in Rockafellar, Uryasev, and Zabarankin (2006), deviation functions are convex, and they correspond one-to-one with strictly expectation bounded risk functions (i.e., translation invariant, positively homogenous, subadditive risk functions satisfying $R(x, P) > -E_P f(x, \omega)$) under the relations:

$$R(x, P) = D(x, P) + E_P f(x, \omega) \text{ or } D(x, P) = R(x, P_c)$$

where P_c is the centered distribution derived from P. Using duality theory, one can express deviation functions in terms of risk envelopes. For a given x, each deviation function can be paired with the corresponding risk envelope $\mathcal{A}$. For a coherent deviation function the risk envelope $\mathcal{A}$ is nonempty, closed, and convex subset of $Q = \{A : A(\omega) \geq 0, EA = 1\}$. Hence, the risk envelope is a set of probability distributions and the dual representation of $D(x, P)$ is

$$D(x, P) = E_P f(x, \omega) - \inf_{A \in \mathcal{A}} E_{P'} f(x, \omega)$$

where $A(\omega) = \frac{dP'}{dP}(\omega) \; \forall \omega \in \Omega$. The dual expression assesses how much worse the expectation $E_P f(x, \omega)$ can be under considered alternative probability distributions P'. These alternative distributions depend on the probability distribution P unlike the risk envelope $\mathcal{A}$. More details can be found in Rockafellar, Uryasev, and Zabarankin (2006) or in a recent survey, Krokhmal, Uryasev, and Zabarankin (2011). Deviation functions, which can be evaluated using linear programming techniques (in scenario-based problems), mainly CVaR-type deviation functions, are very popular in empirical applications because of their tractability, even for a large number of scenarios.

Risk-Shaping with CVaR [Rockafellar and Uryasev (2002)] Let $f(x, \omega)$ denote a random loss defined on $X \times \Omega$, $\alpha \in (0, 1)$, the selected confidence level, and $F(x, P; v) := P\{\omega : f(x, \omega) \leq v\}$, the distribution function of the loss connected with a *fixed* decision $x \in X$. Value at risk (VaR) was introduced and recommended as a generally applicable risk function to quantify, monitor, and limit financial risks and to identify losses that occur with an acceptably small probability. Several slightly different formal definitions of VaR coincide for continuous probability distributions. We shall use the definition from Rockafellar and Uryasev (2002), which applies to general probability distributions: The *value at risk* at the confidence level α is defined by

$$\text{VaR}_\alpha(x, P) = \inf_v \{v \in \mathbb{R} : F(x, P; v) \geq \alpha\}. \tag{5.2}$$

Hence, a random loss greater than VaR_α occurs with probability equal (or less than) $1 - \alpha$. This interpretation is well understood in the financial practice.

However, VaR_α does not fully quantify the loss and does not in general satisfy the subadditivity property of coherent risk functions. To settle these problems, new risk functions have been introduced (see, e.g., Krokhmal, Palmquist, and Uryasev (2002)). We shall exploit results of Rockafellar and Uryasev (2002) to discuss one of them, the conditional value at risk.

Conditional value at risk at the confidence level α, CVaR_α, is defined as the mean of the α-tail distribution of $f(x, \omega)$:

$$F_\alpha(x, P; v) = 0 \text{ for } v < \mathrm{VaR}_\alpha(x, P)$$

$$F_\alpha(x, P; v) = \frac{F(x, P; v) - \alpha}{1 - \alpha} \text{ for } v \geq \mathrm{VaR}_\alpha(x, P). \tag{5.3}$$

According to Rockafellar and Uryasev (2002), $\mathrm{CVaR}_\alpha(x, P)$ can be evaluated by minimization of the auxiliary function

$$\Phi_\alpha(x, v, P) := v + \frac{1}{1 - \alpha} E_P(f(x, \omega) - v)^+$$

with respect to v. Function $\Phi_\alpha(x, v, P)$ is linear in P and convex in v. If $f(x, \omega)$ is convex function of x, $\Phi_\alpha(x, v, P)$ is convex *jointly* in (v, x). It means that $\mathrm{CVaR}_\alpha(x, P) = \min_v \Phi_\alpha(x, v, P)$ is *convex in x and concave in P*. In addition, $\mathrm{CVaR}_\alpha(x, P)$ is continuous with respect to α.

If P is a *discrete probability distribution* concentrated on $\omega^1, \ldots, \omega^S$, with probabilities $p_s > 0$, $s = 1, \ldots, S$, and x a *fixed* element of X, then the optimization problem $\mathrm{CVaR}_\alpha(x, P) = \min_v \Phi_\alpha(x, v, P)$ has the form

$$\mathrm{CVaR}_\alpha(x, P) = \min_v \left\{ v + \frac{1}{1 - \alpha} \sum_s p_s \left(f\left(x, \omega^s\right) - v \right)^+ \right\} \tag{5.4}$$

and it can be further rewritten as

$$\mathrm{CVaR}_\alpha(x, P) = \min_{v, z_1, \ldots, z_S} \left\{ v + \frac{1}{1 - \alpha} \sum_s p_s z_s : z_s \geq 0, \ z_s + v \geq f\left(x, \omega^s\right) \forall s \right\} \tag{5.5}$$

For the special case $f(x, \omega) = -\omega^T x$, mean-CVaR model is a linear programming problem.

Similarly, *CVaR deviation function* for a discrete probability distribution can be expressed as follows:

$$\mathrm{DCVaR}_\alpha(x, P) = \mathrm{CVaR}_\alpha(x, P_c)$$

$$= \min_{v, z_1, \ldots, z_S} \left\{ v + \frac{1}{1 - \alpha} \sum_s p_s z_s : z_s \geq 0, \ z_s + v \geq f\left(x, \omega^s\right) \forall s \right\}$$

$$- \frac{1}{S} \sum_{s=1}^s f(x, \omega^s).$$

In dual form, CVaR deviation function at level α equals

$$\max_{\beta_1,\dots,\beta_S} \left\{ \sum_s \beta_s f\left(x,\omega^s\right): \sum_s \beta_s = 1, \beta_s \leq \frac{p_s}{1-\alpha}, \beta_s \geq 0 \forall s \right\} - \frac{1}{S}\sum_{s=1}^{S} f(x,\omega^s)$$

what corresponds to risk envelope $\mathcal{A} = \{A \in \mathcal{Q}: A(\omega) \leq 1/(1-\alpha)\}$.

Risk-shaping with CVaR handles several probability thresholds $\alpha_1,\dots,\alpha_J$ and loss tolerances $b_j, j = 1,\dots,J$. For a suitable objective function $G_0(x,P)$ the problem is to minimize $G_0(x,P)$ subject to $x \in X$ and $\text{CVaR}_{\alpha_j}(x,P) \leq b_j$, $j = 1,\dots,J$.

According to Theorem 16 of Rockafellar and Uryasev (2002), this is equivalent to

$$\min_{x,v_1,\dots,v_J} \{G_0(x,P): \ x \in X, \ \Phi_{\alpha_j}(x,v_j,P) \leq b_j, \ j = 1,\dots,J\}, \tag{5.6}$$

that is, to a problem with expectation type constraints.

Expected Utility and Stochastic Dominance

An alternative idea could be to use the expected utility or disutility function as a criterion in portfolio selection problems. Such criterion depends on the choice of investor's utility function; to assume its knowledge is not realistic. In empirical applications, several popular utility functions (power, logarithmic, quadratic, S-type) are often used as an approximation of the unknown investor's utility function. Moreover, following Levy (1992) and references therein, one can compare investments jointly for all considered utility functions using *stochastic dominance* relations. In this case, we shall work with the common choice:

$$h(x,\omega) = \omega^T x \text{ and } f(x,\omega) = -\omega^T x.$$

Having two portfolios x, y, and no assumptions about decision maker's preferences, we say that x dominates y by *the first-order stochastic dominance* (FSD) if no decision maker prefers portfolio y to x; that is, $E_P u(\omega^T x) \geq E_P u(\omega^T y)$ for all nondecreasing utility functions u. Accepting the common assumption of risk aversion, one limits attention to the set of nondecreasing concave utility functions that generates *the second-order stochastic dominance*. That is, portfolio x dominates portfolio y by the second-order stochastic dominance (SSD) if $E_P u(\omega^T x) \geq E_P u(\omega^T y)$ for all nondecreasing concave utility functions u.

Let $H(x,P;z)$ denote the cumulative probability distribution function of returns $h(x,\omega)$. The twice cumulative probability distribution function of returns of portfolio x in point w is defined as:

$$H^{(2)}(x, P; w) = \int_{-\infty}^{w} H(x, P; z)\mathrm{d}z. \tag{5.7}$$

Similarly, for $p, q \in (0, 1]$, we consider a quantile function of returns $h(x, \omega)$:

$$H^{(-1)}(x, P; p) = \min\{v \in \mathbb{R} : H(x, P; v) \geq p\}$$

and the second quantile function (absolute Lorenz curve):

$$H^{(-2)}(x, P; q) = \int_{-\infty}^{q} H^{(-1)}(x, P; p)\mathrm{d}p. \tag{5.8}$$

We summarize the necessary and sufficient conditions for the first and the second-order stochastic dominance relations (see, e.g., Ogryczak and Ruszczyński (2002), Dentcheva and Ruszczyński (2003), Post (2003), Kuosmanen (2004), Kopa and Chovanec (2008)):

Portfolio $x \in X$ dominates portfolio $y \in X$ by the first-order stochastic dominance if and only if:

- $H(x, P; z) \leq H(y, P; z) \; \forall z \in \mathbb{R}$ or
- $H^{(-1)}(x, P; p) \geq H^{(-1)}(y, P; p) \; \forall p \in (0, 1]$ or
- $\mathrm{VaR}_\alpha(x, P) \leq \mathrm{VaR}_\alpha(y, P) \; \forall \alpha \in (0, 1]$, see (5.2).

Similarly, the second-order stochastic dominance relation holds if and only if

- $H^{(2)}(x, P; w) \leq H^{(2)}(y, P; w) \; \forall w \in \mathbb{R}$ or
- $H^{(-2)}(x, P; q) \geq H^{(-2)}(y, P; q) \; \forall q \in (0, 1]$ or
- $\mathrm{CVaR}_\alpha(x, P) \leq \mathrm{CVaR}_\alpha(y, P) \; \forall \alpha \in [0, 1]$, see (5.3), or
- $E_P[\eta - \omega^T x]^+ \leq E_P[\eta - \omega^T y]^+ \; \forall \eta \in \mathbb{R}$ such that both expectations exist, where$[.]^+ = \max(0, .)$.

In general, one can consider any generator $\mathcal{U}$ of stochastic dominance, especially the choice $\mathcal{U}_N = \{u(w) : (-1)^n u^n(w) \leq 0 \; \forall w, \; n = 1, \ldots, N\}$ gives the Nth-order stochastic dominance relation. Since these relations allow only for pairwise comparisons, one needs to have a benchmark for practical applications of stochastic dominance. Having a benchmark, one can enrich the mean-risk model by stochastic dominance constraints (Dentcheva and Ruszczyński, 2003). Another application of stochastic dominance relations leads to a portfolio efficiency testing whether a given portfolio is the optimal choice for at least one of considered decision makers; see Kopa and Post (2009), Post and Kopa (2013).

Mean-Risk Efficiency

For a chosen risk function, $R(x, P)$ ideas of multiobjective optimization (see, e.g., Ehrgott (2005)) lead to the mean-risk formulations

$$\min_{x \in X} \{ \lambda E_P f(x, \omega) + R(x, P) \}, \tag{5.9}$$

or

$$\max_{x \in X} \{ E_P h(x, \omega) - a R(x, P) \}, \tag{5.10}$$

or to inclusion of risk constraints,

$$\min_{x \in X} R(x, P) \text{ subject to } E_P h(x, \omega) \geq k, \tag{5.11}$$

or

$$\max_{x \in X} E_P h(x, \omega) \text{ subject to } R(x, P) \leq v; \tag{5.12}$$

compare with the mean-variance model of Markowitz (1952) with the random return quantified as $h(x, \omega) := \omega^T x$ and risk quantified as the variance or standard deviation of the portfolio yield. See also Krokhmal, Palmquist, and Uryasev (2002) for the risk quantified as the conditional value at risk CVaR, which is known also under the name expected shortfall.

Solutions of any of these problems (for preselected nonnegative parameters λ, a and for k, v such that there exist feasible solutions of (5.11), (5.12)) are *mean-risk efficient*. At least theoretically, the whole mean-risk efficient frontier can be constructed; see Ruszczyński and Vanderbei (2003) for an application of parametric programming in the case of the Markowitz mean-variance efficient frontier. The previous formulations may be extended to deal with multiple risk functions (see, e.g., Roman, Darby-Dowman, and Mitra (2007)) for "mean-variance-CVaR" model.

Formulations (5.9) or (5.10) with a probability independent set of feasible decisions X are convenient for applications of quantitative stability analysis: Sets of parameter values for which a point $x_0 \in X$ is an optimal solution (local stability sets) can be constructed, and on these sets, the optimal value is an explicit function of the parameter in question. We refer to Chapter 5 of Bank et al. (1982) for related theoretical results and to Dupačová (2012) and Dupačová, Hurt, and Štěpán (2002) for an application to stability with respect to the choice of λ in the Markowitz model

$$\min_{x \in X} \left\{ -\lambda E_P \omega^T x + \frac{1}{2} x^T \left[\text{var}_P \omega \right] x \right\}$$

of the type (5.9).

On the other hand, risk management regulations ask frequently for satisfaction of risk constraints with a prescribed limit v displayed in (5.12). Moreover, (5.12) is favored in practice: Using optimal solutions $x(v)$ for various values of v, one obtains directly the corresponding points $[v, E_P\omega^T x(v)]$ on the mean-risk efficient frontier. Then, the purpose of the study indicates the formulation to be tackled.

Comment: Numerical tractability of the mean-risk problems depends on the choice of the risk function R, on the assumed probability distribution P, and on the choice of random objectives $f(x, \omega)$ or $h(x, \omega)$. Programs (5.9) to (5.12) are convex for convex risk functions $R(\bullet, P)$, such as CVaR, see Dupačová (2006), Dupačová and Polívka (2007), and for convex random loss $f(\bullet, \omega)$ and concave random return $h(\bullet, \omega)$. They are equally suitable when the goal is to get a mean-risk efficient decision and/or properties of such decision.

Robustness and Output Analysis (Stress Testing)

As the probability distribution P is fully known only exceptionally, there is a growing interest in robustness of portfolio optimization problems. Since several large financial disasters in the nineties of the last century, observing various risk functions and stress testing has entered the praxis of financial institutions. We shall focus on output analysis and stress testing with respect to uncertainty or perturbations of input data for static risk portfolio optimization problems, which involve risk considerations.

Moreover, for the sake of numerical tractability, various approximation schemes have been proposed to solve the resulting optimization problems. For example, one may approximate P by a discrete probability distribution based on historical data, by a probability distribution belonging to a given parametric family with an estimated parameter, and so on. The popular sample average approximation (SAA) method solves these problems using a sample counterpart of the optimization problem; that is, instead of P it uses an empirical distribution based on independent samples from P, and asymptotic results can support decisions concerning recommended sample sizes. See Shapiro (2003), Wang and Ahmed (2008), and references therein. The choice of a suitable technique depends on the form of the problem, on the available information and data. Anyway, without additional analysis, it will be dangerous to use the obtained output (the optimal value and the optimal investment decision based on the approximate problem) to replace the sought solution of the "true" problem. Indeed, the optimal or efficient portfolios are rather sensitive to the inputs, and it is more demanding to get applicable results concerning the optimal solutions—optimal investment policies—than robustness results for the optimal value.

Besides focused simulation studies (e.g., Kaut et al. (2007)) and backtesting, there are two main tractable ways for analysis of the output regarding changes or perturbation of P—the worst-case analysis with respect to all probability distributions belonging to an uncertainty set $\mathcal{P}$ or quantitative stability analysis with respect to changes of P by stress testing via contamination; see Dupačová (2006, 2009), Dupačová and Polívka (2007), Dupačová and Kopa (2012, 2014). We shall present them in the next two sections.

WORST-CASE ANALYSIS

The worst-case analysis is mostly used in cases when the probability distribution P is not known completely, but it is known to belong to a family $\mathcal{P}$ of probability distributions. It can be identified by known values of some moments, by a known support, by qualitative properties such as unimodality or symmetry, by a list of possible probability distributions, or by scenarios proposed by experts with inexact values of probabilities. The decisions follow the minimax decision rule; accordingly, the investor aims at hedging against the worst possible situation.

The "robust" counterpart of (5.9) is

$$\min_{x \in X} \max_{P \in \mathcal{P}} \{\lambda E_P f(x, \omega) + R(x, P)\} \tag{5.13}$$

whereas for (5.12) we have

$$\max_{x \in X} \min_{P \in \mathcal{P}} E_P h(x, \omega) \text{ s.t. } R(x, P) \leq v \; \forall P \in \mathcal{P} \tag{5.14}$$

or equivalently, subject to the worst-risk constraint

$$\max_{P \in \mathcal{P}} R(x, P) \leq v. \tag{5.15}$$

If $R(x, P)$ is convex in x on X and *linear (in the sense that it is both convex and concave) in P on P*, then for convex, compact classes $\mathcal{P}$ defined by moment conditions and for fixed x, the maxima in (5.13), (5.15) are attained at extremal points of $\mathcal{P}$. It means that the worst-case probability distributions from $\mathcal{P}$ are *discrete*. In general, these discrete distributions depend on x. Under modest assumptions this result holds true also for risk functions $R(x, P)$ that are *convex* in P. Notice that whereas expected utility or disutility functions and the Expected Regret criterion are linear in P, various popular risk functions are not even convex in P: CVaR (x, P) and variance are concave in P; the mean absolute deviation is neither convex nor concave in P.

Worst-Case Analysis for Markowitz Model (1952)

For the Markowitz model, one deals with the set $\mathcal{P}$ of probability distributions characterized by fixed expectations and covariance matrices without distinguishing among distributions belonging to this set. Incomplete knowledge of input data (i.e., of expected returns $\mu = E\omega$ and covariance matrix $V = \text{var}\omega$) may be also approached via the worst-case analysis or robust optimization; see Fabozzi, Huang, and Zhou (2010), Pflug and Wozabal (2007), and Zymler, Kuhn, and Rustem (2013). The idea is to hedge against the worst possible input belonging to a prespecified uncertainty or ambiguity set U. We shall denote M, $\mathcal{V}$ considered uncertainty sets for parameters μ and V and will assume that $U = M \times \mathcal{V}$. This means to solve

$$\min_{x \in X} \max_{(\mu, V) \in U} \left\{ -\lambda \mu^T x + \frac{1}{2} x^T V x \right\} \tag{5.16}$$

or

$$\min_{x \in X} \max_{V \in \mathcal{V}} \ x^T V x \text{ subject to } \min_{\mu \in M} \mu^T x \geq k, \tag{5.17}$$

or

$$\min_{x \in X} \min_{\mu \in M} \mu^T x \text{ subject to } \max_{V \in \mathcal{V}} x^T V x \leq v. \tag{5.18}$$

Consider, for example, U described by box constraints $0 \leq \underline{\mu}_i \leq \mu_i \leq \overline{\mu}_i$, $i = 1, \ldots, I$, $\underline{V} \leq V \leq \overline{V}$ componentwise and such that V is positive definite. With $X = \{x \in \mathbb{R}^I : x_i \geq 0 \ \forall i, \sum_i x_i = 1\}$, the inner maximum in (5.16) is attained for $\mu_i = \underline{\mu}_i \ \forall i$ and $V = \overline{V}$. The robust mean-variance portfolio is the optimal solution of

$$\min_{x \in X} \left\{ -\lambda \underline{\mu}^T x + \frac{1}{2} x^T \overline{V} x \right\}.$$

We refer to Fabozzi, Huang, and Zhou (2010) for a survey of various other choices of uncertainty sets for the Markowitz model.

Comment: For the class of probability distributions P identified by fixed moments μ, V known from Markowitz model and for linear random objective $f(x, \omega)$, explicit formulas for the worst-case CVaR and VaR can be derived (e.g., Čerbáková (2006)), and according to Theorem 2.2 of Zymler, Kuhn, and Rustem (2013), portfolio composition $x \in X$ satisfies the worst-case VaR constraint $\iff$ satisfies the worst-case CVaR constraint.

Worst-Case (Robust) Stochastic Dominance

Applying the worst-case approach to stochastic dominance relation, Dentcheva and Ruszczyński (2010) introduced *robust stochastic dominance* for the set of considered probability distributions $\mathcal{P}$: A portfolio x robustly dominates portfolio y by SSD if $E_P u(\omega^T x) \geq E_P u(\omega^T y)$ for all concave utility functions and all $P \in \mathcal{P}$. Similarly, one can define a robust FSD relation when the expected utility inequality needs to be fulfiled for all utility functions (allowing also nonconcave ones) and for all $P \in \mathcal{P}$. The choice of $\mathcal{P}$ is very important and typically depends on the application of the robust stochastic dominance relation. The larger set $\mathcal{P}$ is, the stronger the relation would be. If the set is too large, then one can hardly find two portfolios being in the robust stochastic dominance relation, and the concept of robust stochastic dominance is useless. Therefore, Dentcheva and Ruszczyński (2010) considered a convexified closed and bounded neighborhood $\mathcal{P}$ of a given P_0. Alternatively, one can follow Zymler, Kuhn, and Rustem (2013) and define $\mathcal{P}$ as the set of all probability distributions having the same first and second moments as a given distribution P_0. Typically, distribution P_0 is derived from data—for example, as an empirical distribution.

Example: Robust Second-Order Stochastic Dominance Consider I investments and a benchmark as the $(I + 1)$-st investment. Let the original probability distribution P_0 of all investments (including the benchmark) be a discrete distribution given by S equiprobable scenarios. They can be collected in scenario matrix:

$$\mathcal{R} = \begin{pmatrix} r^1 \\ r^2 \\ \vdots \\ r^S \end{pmatrix}$$

where $r^s = (r_1^s, r_2^s, \dots, r_{I+1}^s)$ are the returns along the s-th scenario and $r_i = (r_i^1, r_i^2, \dots, r_i^S)^T$ are scenarios for return of the i-th investment. We will use $x = (x_1, x_2, \dots, x_{I+1})^T$ for the vector of portfolio weights and the portfolio possibilities are given by

$$X = \{x \in \mathbb{R}^{I+1} : 1^T x = 1, \ x_i \geq 0, \ i = 1, 2, \dots, I + 1\},$$

that is, the short sales are not allowed. Then, following Kuosmanen (2004) and Luedtke (2008), the necessary and sufficient condition for the second-order stochastic dominance relation between a portfolio x and the benchmark is: $\mathcal{R}x \geq Wr_{I+1}$ for a double stochastic matrix W (i.e., $1^T W = 1^T, W1 = 1, W \geq 0$ componentwise). Hence the classical optimization problem with SSD constraints (Dentcheva and Ruszczyński (2003)): $\min G_0(x, P)$, with respect to all portfolios x that dominate the benchmark by SSD, leads to:

$$\min \ G_0(x, P) \tag{5.19}$$

$$\text{s.t. } \mathcal{R}x \geq Wr_{I+1}$$

$$1^T W = 1^T, \ W1 = 1, \ W \geq 0$$

$$x \in X.$$

Following Kopa (2010), we consider $\mathcal{P}$ containing all discrete probability distributions with S equiprobable scenarios and scenario matrix $\mathcal{R}_P$ from the ε-neighbourhood of P_0, that is, satisfying $d(P, P_0) \leq \varepsilon$. Let matrix $\Upsilon = \{v_{i,j}\}_{i,j=1}^{S,I+1}$ be defined as $\Upsilon = \mathcal{R}_P - \mathcal{R}$ and $v_{I+1} = (v_{1,I+1}, \ldots, v_{S,I+1})^T$. Moreover, if $d(P, P_0) = \max_{i,j} |v_{ij}|$ then a robust counterpart of (5.19) can be formulated as follows:

$$\min G_0(x, P)$$

$$\text{s.t. } (\mathcal{R} + \Upsilon)x \geq W(r_{I+1} + v_{I+1})$$

$$1^T W = 1^T, \ W1 = 1, \ W \geq 0$$

$$-\varepsilon \leq v_{ij} \leq \varepsilon, \ i = 1, \ldots, S, \ j = 1, \ldots, I+1$$

$$x \in X.$$

STRESS TESTING VIA CONTAMINATION

In practice, approximated or simplified stochastic decision problems are solved instead of the true ones, and it could be misleading, even dangerous, to apply the results without any subsequent analysis such as stress testing, output analysis, or backtesting.

Stress testing is used in financial practice without any generally accepted definition, and it differs among institutions. It appears in the context of quantification of losses or risks that may appear under special, mostly extreme, circumstances. It uses

1. Scenarios that come from historical experience (a crisis observed in the past)—historical stress test, or from the worst-case analysis;
2. Scenarios that might be possible in future, given changes of macroeconomic, socioeconomic, or political factors—prospective stress test, and so on;
3. Recommended, stylized scenarios, such as changes in the interest rates, parallel shift of the yield curve for ± 100 bp, changes of the stock index for ± 6 percent, of volatility for ± 20 percent.

Stress testing approaches differ due to the nature of the tested problem and of the stress scenarios. Performance of the obtained optimal decision is frequently evaluated along these stress, possibly dynamic scenarios, or the model is solved with an alternative input. We shall present stress testing via contamination, which puts together both of these ideas.

Stress testing via contamination was originally derived for the minimization type of model (5.1), with the set X independent of P and for expectation type objective $G_0(x, P) := E_P f(x, \omega)$ to be minimized.

Assume that the problem (5.1) was solved for probability distribution P; denote $\varphi(P)$ the optimal value and $X^*(P)$ the set of optimal solutions. Changes in probability distribution P are modeled using contaminated distributions P_t,

$$P_t := (1 - t)P + tQ, \ t \in [0, 1]$$

with Q another *fixed* probability distribution, the alternative or stress distribution. It does not require any specific properties of the probability distribution P. Via contamination, robustness analysis with respect to changes in P gets reduced to much simpler analysis with respect to the scalar parameter t. The objective function in (5.1) is the expectation of the random objective function $f(x, \omega)$ (i.e., is linear in P), and we denote it $G_0(x, P)$ to stress its dependence on P. Hence, $G_0(x, P_t) := E_{P_t} f(x, \omega)$ is linear in t and the optimal value function

$$\varphi(t) := \min_{x \in X} G_0(x, P_t)$$

is concave on $[0, 1]$. This implies continuity and existence of its directional derivatives on $(0, 1)$. Continuity at $t = 0$ is property related with stability for the original problem (5.1). In general, one needs that the set of optimal solutions $X^*(P)$ is nonempty and bounded.

Stress testing and robustness analysis via contamination with respect to changes in probability distribution P is straightforward for expected disutility models (the objective function is again linear in P). When the risk or deviation measures are *concave with respect to probability distribution P*, they are concave with respect to parameter t of the contaminated probability distributions P_t, hence, $\varphi(t)$ is concave and stress testing via contamination can be developed again. The results are contamination bounds for the optimal value function, which quantify the change in the optimal value due to considered perturbations of probability distribution P.

Contamination Bounds

The bounds are a straight consequence of the concavity of the optimal value function $\varphi(t)$:

$$\varphi(0) + t\varphi'(0^+) \geq \varphi(t) \geq (1 - t)\varphi(0) + t\varphi(1), \ t \in [0, 1]. \tag{5.20}$$

For the case of unique optimal solution $x^*(P)$ of (5.1) the directional derivative equals $G_0(x^*(P), Q) - \varphi(0)$. In general, each optimal solution

$x^*(P)$ provides an upper bound

$$\varphi'(0^+) \leq G_0(x^*(P), Q) - \varphi(0)$$

which can be used in (5.20).

Similarly one may construct the upper bound in (5.20) for the optimal value $\varphi(t)$ on the interval $[0, 1]$ starting from the right end $t = 1$ of the interval. This provides the right upperbound marked on Figure 5.1.

The obtained contamination bounds (5.20) are global, valid for all $t \in [0, 1]$. They quantify the change in the optimal value due to considered perturbations of (5.1); see the application to stress testing of CVaR by Dupačová and Polívka (2007) and of multiperiod two-stage bond portfolio management problems by Dupačová, Bertocchi, and Moriggia (1998). Notice that to get the bounds (5.20), one has to solve the portfolio problem with the alternative probability distribution Q to get $\varphi(1)$ and to evaluate the performance $G_0(x^*(P), Q)$ of an optimal solution of the original problem in case that Q applies. Both of these calculations appear in various stress tests.

Also, a specific value of contamination parameter t can be fixed in agreement with the stress testing purpose. For stability studies with respect to small changes in the underlying probability distribution, small values of the

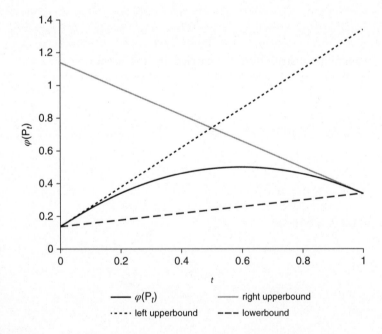

FIGURE 5.1 Lower and upper bound for a concave optimal value function.

contamination parameter t are typical. The choice of t may reflect the degree of confidence in expert opinions represented as the contaminating distribution Q, and so on. Using a contaminating distribution Q carried by additional scenarios, one can study the influence of including these additional "out-of-sample" scenarios; also the response on an increasing importance of a scenario can be quantified, and so on.

Example Consider the problem of investment decisions in the international debt and equity markets. Assume that historical data allow us to construct many scenarios of returns of investments in the considered assets categories. We denote these (in principle equiprobable) scenarios by ω^s, $s = 1, \ldots, S$, and let P be the corresponding discrete probability distribution. Assume that for each of these scenarios, the outcome of a feasible investment strategy x can be evaluated as $f(x, \omega^s)$. Maximization of the expected outcome

$$G_0(x, P) = \frac{1}{S} \sum_{s=1}^{S} f(x, \omega^s) \text{ with respect to } x \in X$$

provides the optimal value $\varphi(P)$ and an optimal investment strategy $x(P)$.

The historical data definitely do not cover all possible extremal situations on the market. Assume that experts suggest an additional scenario ω^*. This is the only atom of the degenerated probability distribution Q, for which the best investment strategy is $x(Q)$—an optimal solution of $\max_{x \in X} f(x, \omega^*)$. The contamination method explained earlier is based on the probability distribution P_t, carried by the scenarios ω^s, $s = 1, \ldots, S$, with probabilities $\frac{1-t}{S}$ and by the experts scenario ω^* with probability t. The probability t assigns a weight to the view of the expert and the bounds (5.20) are valid for all $0 \leq t \leq 1$. They clearly indicate how much the weight t, interpreted as the degree of confidence in the investor's view, affects the outcome of the portfolio allocation.

The impact of a modification of every single scenario according to the investor's views on the performance of each asset class can be studied in a similar way. We use the initial probability distribution P contaminated by Q, which is now carried by equiprobable scenarios $\hat{\omega}^s = \omega^s + \delta^s$, $s = 1, \ldots, S$. The contamination parameter t relates again to the degree of confidence in the expert's view.

Contamination by a distribution Q, which gives the same expectation $E_Q \omega = E_P \omega$, is helpful in studying resistance with respect to changes of the sample in situations when the expectation of random parameters ω is to be preserved.

Comment The introduced contamination technique extends to objective functions $G_0(x, P)$ convex in x and concave in P including the mean-variance objective function; see Dupačová (1996; 1998; 2006) for the related contamination results. To get these generalizations, it is again necessary to analyze persistence and stability properties of the parametrized problems $\min_{x \in X} G_0(x, P_t)$ and to derive the form of the directional derivative. For a fixed set X of feasible solutions, the optimal value function $\varphi(t)$ is again concave on [0,1]. Additional assumptions (e.g., Gol'shtein (1970)) are needed to get the existence of its derivative; the generic form is

$$\varphi'(0^+) = \min_{x \in X^*(P)} \frac{d}{dt} G_0(x, P_t)|_{t=0^+}.$$

Contamination Bounds—Constraints Dependent on *P*

Whereas the stress testing and robustness analysis via contamination with respect to changes in probability distribution P are straightforward when the set X does not depend on P, difficulties appear for models, which contain risk constraints:

$$\min_{x \in X} G_0(x, P)$$

subject to

$$G_j(x, P) \leq 0, \ j = 1, \dots, J; \tag{5.21}$$

such as the risk shaping with CVaR (5.6). Assume the following:

- $X \subset \mathbb{R}^n$ is a fixed nonempty closed convex set.
- Functions $G_j(x, P)$, $j = 0, \dots, J$ are convex in x and linear in P.
- P is the probability distribution of the random vector ω with range $\Omega \subset \mathbb{R}^m$.

Denote $X(t) = \{x \in X : G_j(x, P_t) \leq 0, \ j = 1, \dots, J\}$, $\varphi(t)$, $X^*(t)$ the set of feasible solutions, the optimal value and the set of optimal solutions of the contaminated problem

$$\text{minimize } G_0(x, P_t) \text{ on the set } X(t). \tag{5.22}$$

The task is again to construct computable lower and upper bounds for $\varphi(t)$ and to exploit them for robustness analysis. The difficulty is that the optimal value function $\varphi(t)$ is no more concave in t.

Thanks to the assumed structure of perturbations a *lower bound* for $\varphi(t)$ can be derived under relatively modest assumptions. Consider first only one constraint dependent on probability distribution P and an objective G_0 *independent* of P; that is, the problem is

$$\min_{x \in X} G_0(x) \text{ subject to } G(x, P) \leq 0. \tag{5.23}$$

For probability distribution P contaminated by another fixed probability distribution Q, that is, for $P_t := (1 - t)P + tQ$, $t \in (0, 1)$ we get

$$\min_{x \in X} G_0(x) \text{ subject to } G(x, t) := G(x, P_t) \leq 0. \tag{5.24}$$

Theorem [Dupačová and Kopa (2012)]
Let $G(x, t)$ be a concave function of $t \in [0, 1]$. Then, the optimal value function $\varphi(t)$ of (5.24) is quasiconcave in $t \in [0, 1]$ and

$$\varphi(t) \geq \min\{\varphi(1), \varphi(0)\}. \tag{5.25}$$

When also the objective function *depends* on the probability distribution, that is, on the contamination parameter t, the problem is

$$\min_{x \in X} G_0(x, t) := G_0(x, P_t) \text{ subject to } G(x, t) \leq 0. \tag{5.26}$$

For $G_0(x, P)$ linear or concave in P, a lower bound can be obtained by application of the bound (5.25) separately to $G_0(x, P)$ and $G_0(x, Q)$. The resulting bound

$$\varphi(t) \geq (1 - t) \min \left\{ \varphi(0), \min_{X(Q)} G_0(x, P) \right\} + t \min \left\{ \varphi(1), \min_{X(P)} G_0(x, Q) \right\} \tag{5.27}$$

is more complicated but still computable.

Multiple constraints (5.21) can be reformulated as $G(x, P) := \max_j G_j(x, P) \leq 0$, but the function $G(x, P)$ is convex in P. Still for $G_j(x, P) = E_P f_j(x, \omega)$ and for contaminated distributions, $G(x, t) := \max_j G_j(x, P_t)$ in (5.24) is a convex *piecewise linear* function of t. It means that there exists $\tilde{t} > 0$ such that $G(x, t)$ is a linear function of t on $[0, \tilde{t}]$ and according to Theorem we get the local lower bound $\varphi(t) \geq \min\{\varphi(0), \varphi(\tilde{t})\}$ valid for $t \in [0, \tilde{t}]$. This bound applies also to objective functions $G_0(x, P)$ concave in P similarly as in (5.27). Notice that no convexity assumption with respect to x was required.

Further assumptions are needed for derivation of an *upper bound*: Formulas for directional derivative $\varphi'(0^+)$ based on Lagrange function $L(x, u, t) = G_0(x, P_t) + \sum_j u_j G_j(x, P_t)$ for the contaminated problem follow, for example, from Theorem 17 of Gol'shtein (1970) if the set of optimal solutions $X^*(0)$ and of the corresponding Lagrange multipliers $U^*(x, 0)$ for the original, noncontaminated problem are nonempty and bounded. Their generic form is

$$\varphi'(0^+) = \min_{x \in X^*(0)} \max_{u \in U^*(x, 0)} \frac{\partial}{\partial t} L(x, u, 0). \tag{5.28}$$

Nevertheless, to get at least a local upper bound (5.20) means to get $X(t)$ fixed, that is, $\varphi(t)$ concave, for t small enough. For X convex polyhedral this can be achieved for (5.21) if the optimal solution $x^*(0)$ of the noncontaminated problem is a nondegenerated point in which the strict complementarity conditions hold true. Then, for t small enough, $t \leq t_0$, $t_0 > 0$, the optimal value function $\varphi(t)$ is concave, and its upper bound equals

$$\varphi(t) \leq \varphi(0) + t\varphi'(0^+) \; \forall t \in [0, t_0]. \tag{5.29}$$

For a discussion and general references, see Dupačová and Kopa (2012). Differentiability of $G_j(\bullet, P_t)$ can be exploited, but there are rather limited possibilities to construct local upper contamination bounds when neither convexity nor differentiability is present (e.g., for nonconvex problems with VaR constraints). In some special cases, trivial upper bounds are available— for example, if $x^*(0)$ is a feasible solution of (5.22) with $t = 1$, then

$$\varphi(t) \leq G_0(x^*(0), t) \; \forall t \in [0, 1]. \tag{5.30}$$

See Dupačová and Kopa (2012; 2014).

In the general case, to allow for the stress testing an indirect approach was suggested; see Branda and Dupačová (2012): Apply contamination technique to penalty reformulation of the problem. Then the set of feasible solutions does not depend on P and for approximate problem, global bounds (5.20) follow. See Example 4 of Branda and Dupačová (2012) for numerical results.

Illustrative Examples [Dupačová and Kopa (2012)]

Consider $S = 50$ equiprobable scenarios of monthly returns of $I = 9$ assets (8 European stock market indexes: AEX, ATX, FCHI, GDAXI, OSEAX, OMXSPI, SSMI, FTSE, and a risk-free asset) in period June 2004 to August 2008. The scenarios can be collected in the matrix $\mathcal{R}$ as in the example titled "Robust second-order stochastic dominance"; however, now without a benchmark, that is, a vector of portfolio weights $x = (x_1, x_2, \ldots, x_I)^T$ is taken from the portfolio possibilities set:

$$X = \{x \in \mathbb{R}^I : 1^T x = 1, \; x_i \geq 0, \; i = 1, 2, \ldots, I\}.$$

The historical data come from the precrisis period. The data are contaminated by a scenario r^{S+1} from September 2008 when all indexes strongly fell down. The additional scenario can be understood as a stress scenario or the worst-case scenario. It can be seen in Table 5.1 presenting basic descriptive statistics of the original data and the additional scenario (A.S.).

TABLE 5.1 Descriptive Statistics and the Additional Scenario of Returns of 8 European Stock Indexes and of the Risk-Free Asset

Index	Country	Mean	Max	Min	A.S.
AEX	Netherlands	0.00456	0.07488	−0.14433	−0.19715
ATX	Austria	0.01358	0.13247	−0.14869	−0.23401
FCHI	France	0.0044	0.0615	−0.13258	−0.1005
GDAXI	Germany	0.01014	0.07111	−0.15068	−0.09207
OSEAX	Norway	0.01872	0.12176	−0.19505	−0.23934
OMXSPI	Sweden	0.00651	0.08225	−0.14154	−0.12459
SSMI	Switzerland	0.00563	0.05857	−0.09595	−0.08065
FTSE	England	0.00512	0.06755	−0.08938	−0.13024
Risk-free		0.002	0.002	0.002	0.002

We will apply the contamination bounds to mean-risk models with CVaR as a measure of risk. Two formulations are considered: In the first one, we are searching for a portfolio with minimal CVaR and at least the prescribed expected return. Second, we minimize the expected loss of the portfolio under the condition that CVaR is below a given level.

Minimizing CVaR Mean-CVaR model with CVaR minimization is a special case of the general formulation (5.1) when $G_0(x, P) = \text{CVaR}(x, P)$ and $G_1(x, P) = E_P(-\omega^T x) - \mu(P)$; $\mu(P)$ is the maximal allowable expected loss. We choose

$$\mu(P) = -E_P \omega^T \left(\frac{1}{9}, \frac{1}{9}, \dots, \frac{1}{9} \right)^T = -\frac{1}{50} \sum_{s=1}^{50} r^s \left(\frac{1}{9}, \frac{1}{9}, \dots, \frac{1}{9} \right)^T.$$

It means that the minimal required expected return is equal to the average return of the equally diversified portfolio. The significance level $\alpha = 0.95$ and X is a fixed convex polyhedral set representing constraints that do not depend on P. Since P is a discrete distribution with equiprobable scenarios $r^1, r^2, \dots, r^{50}$, using (5.5), the mean-CVaR model can be formulated as the following linear program:

$$\varphi(0) = \min_{x \in X, v \in \mathbb{R}, z_s \in \mathbb{R}^+} v + \frac{1}{50 * 0.05} \sum_{s=1}^{50} z_s \tag{5.31}$$

$$\text{s.t. } z_s \geq -r^s x - v, \ s = 1, 2, \dots, 50$$

$$-\frac{1}{50} \sum_{s=1}^{50} r^s x - \mu(P) \leq 0.$$

By analogy, for the additional scenario we have:

$$\varphi(1) = \min_{x\in X, v\in\mathbb{R}, z\in\mathbb{R}^+} v + \frac{1}{0.05}z \tag{5.32}$$

$$\text{s.t. } z \geq -r^{51}x - v, \ -r^{51}x - \mu(Q) \leq 0$$

or, equivalently:

$$\varphi(1) = \min_{x\in X}\{-r^{51}x \ : \ -r^{51}x - \mu(Q) \leq 0\} \tag{5.33}$$

where $\mu(Q) = -r^{51}\left(\frac{1}{9}, \frac{1}{9}, \ldots, \frac{1}{9}\right)^T$.

First, we compute for $t \in [0, 1]$ the optimal value function of the contaminated problem.

$$\varphi(t) = \min_{x\in X, v\in\mathbb{R}, z_s\in\mathbb{R}^+} v + \frac{1}{0.05}\left(\sum_{s=1}^{50}\frac{1}{50}(1-t)z_s + tz_{51}\right) \tag{5.34}$$

$$\text{s.t. } z_s \geq -r^sx - v, \ s = 1, 2, \ldots, 51$$

$$-\sum_{s=1}^{50}\frac{1}{50}(1-t)r^sx - tr^{51}x - \mu((1-t)P + tQ) \leq 0$$

where $\mu((1-t)P + tQ) = -\sum_{s=1}^{50}\frac{1}{50}(1-t)r^s\left(\frac{1}{9}, \frac{1}{9}, \ldots, \frac{1}{9}\right)^T - tr^{51}\left(\frac{1}{9}, \frac{1}{9}, \ldots, \frac{1}{9}\right)^T$.

Second, applying (5.27), we derive a *lower bound* for $\varphi(t)$. Note that now

$$\min_{X(Q)} G_0(x, p) = \min_{x\in X, v\in\mathbb{R}, z_s\in\mathbb{R}^+} v + \frac{1}{50 * 0.05}\sum_{s=1}^{50}z_s$$

$$\text{s.t.} z_s \geq -r^sx - v, s = 1, 2, \ldots, 50$$

$$-r^{51}x - \mu(Q) \leq 0$$

and

$$\min_{X(P)} G_0(x, Q) = \min_{x\in X}\left\{-r^{51}x: \frac{1}{50}\sum_{s=1}^{50}-r^sx - \mu(P) \leq 0\right\}.$$

Finally, we construct an *upper bound* for $\varphi(t)$. Since the optimal solution $x^*(0)$ of (5.31) is a feasible solution of (5.32), we can apply (5.30) as a trivial upper bound for all $t \in [0, 1]$:

$$\varphi(t) \leq G_0(x^*(0), t) = \min_{v \in \mathbb{R}, z_s \in \mathbb{R}^+} v + \frac{1}{0.05}\left(\sum_{s=1}^{50} \frac{1}{50}(1-t)z_s + tz_{51}\right)$$

s.t. $z_s \geq -r^s x^* - v$, $s = 1, 2, \ldots, 51$.

The disadvantage of this trivial bound is the fact that it would require evaluation of the CVaR for $x^*(0)$ for each t. Linearity with respect to t does not hold true, but we may apply the upper bound for CVaR derived in Dupačová and Polívka (2007):

$$\text{CVaR}_\alpha(x, (1-t)P + tQ) \leq (1-t)\text{CVaR}_\alpha(x, P) + t\Phi_\alpha(x, v^*(x, P), Q). \quad (5.35)$$

This yields an upper estimate for $G_0(x^*(0), t)$, which is a convex combination of $\varphi(0)$ and $\Phi_\alpha(x^*(0), v^*(x^*(0), P), Q)$. The optimal value $\varphi(0)$ is given by (5.31) and

$$\Phi_\alpha(x^*(0), v^*(x^*(0), P), Q) = v^* + \frac{1}{0.05}(-r^{51}x^* - v^*)^+$$

where v^* and x^* are optimal solutions of (5.31). The graphs of $\varphi(t)$, its lower bound and two upper bounds (trivial one and its upper estimate) for small contamination $t \in [0, 0.1]$ are presented in Figure 5.2. Since all original scenarios have probability 0.02, the performance for $t > 0.1$ is not of much interest. For $t > 0.04$, $\varphi(t)$ in (5.34) coincides with its lower bound because the optimal portfolios consist only of the risk free asset. The upper bound is piecewise linear in t, and for small values of t it coincides with the estimated upper bound.

Minimizing Expected Loss As the second example, consider the mean-CVaR model minimizing the expected loss subject to a constraint on CVaR. This corresponds to (5.21) with $G_0(x, P) = E_P(-\omega^T x)$ and $G_1(x, P) = \text{CVaR}(x, P) - c$ where $c = 0.19$ is the maximal accepted level of CVaR. For simplicity, this level does not depend on the probability distribution. Similar to the previous example, we compute the optimal value $\varphi(t)$ and its lower and upper bound. Using Theorem 16 of Rockafellar and Uryasev (2002), the minimal CVaR-constrained expected loss is obtained for $t \in [0, 1]$ as

$$\varphi(t) = \min_{x \in X, v \in \mathbb{R}} -\sum_{s=1}^{50} \frac{1}{50}(1-t)r^s x - tr^{51}x \quad (5.36)$$

$$\text{s.t.} v + \frac{1}{0.05}\left(-\sum_{s=1}^{50} \frac{1}{50}(1-t)r^s x - tr^{51}x - v\right)^+ - c \leq 0 \quad (5.37)$$

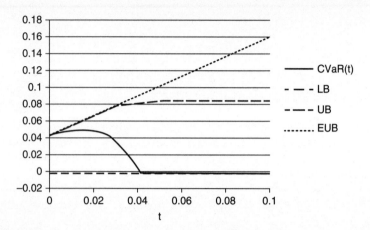

FIGURE 5.2 Comparison of minimal (CVaR(t)) value of mean-CVaR model with lower bound (LB), upper bound (UB) and the estimated upper bound (EUB).

and thus equals the optimal value function of the parametric linear program

$$\varphi(t) = \min_{x \in X, v \in \mathbb{R}, z_s \in \mathbb{R}^+} -\sum_{s=1}^{50} \frac{1}{50}(1-t)r^s x - tr^{51}x \qquad (5.38)$$

$$\text{s.t.} v + \frac{1}{0.05}\left(\sum_{s=1}^{50} \frac{1}{50}(1-t)z_s + tz_{51}\right) - c \leq 0$$

$$z_s \geq -r^s x - v, s = 1, 2, \dots, 51$$

for $t \in [0, 1]$. In particular, for $t = 1$ we have

$$\varphi(1) = \min_{x \in X, v \in \mathbb{R}, z_s \in \mathbb{R}^+} -r^{51}x$$

$$\text{s.t.} v + \frac{1}{0.05}z_{51} - c \leq 0, \ z_{51} + v \geq -r^{51}x,$$

what is equivalent to

$$\varphi(1) = \min_{x \in X}\left\{-r^{51}x: \ -r^{51}x - c \leq 0\right\};$$

compare with (5.33). Using (5.27), we can evaluate the *lower bound* for $\varphi(t)$ with

$$\min_{X(Q)} G_0(x, P) = \min_{x \in X}\left\{-\sum_{s=1}^{50} \frac{1}{50}r^s x: \ -r^{51}x - c \leq 0\right\}$$

and

$$\min_{X(P)} G_0(x, Q) = \min_{x \in X, v \in \mathbb{R}, z_s \in \mathbb{R}^+} -r^{51}x$$

$$\text{s.t.} v + \frac{1}{0.05} \sum_{s=1}^{50} \frac{1}{50} z_s - c \leq 0, \ z_s \geq -r^s x - v, s = 1, 2, \dots, 50.$$

Finally, we compute an ~~upper bound for~~ $\varphi(t)$. Contrary to the previous example, the optimal solution $x^*(0)$ of the noncontaminated problem is not a feasible solution of the fully contaminated problem. Therefore, the trivial global upper bound (5.30) cannot be used. We apply instead the local upper bound (5.29) with the directional derivative

$$\varphi'(0^+) = \frac{\partial}{\partial t} L(x^*(0), u^*(0), 0) = L(x^*(0), u^*(0), Q) - L(x^*(0), u^*(0), P)$$

$$= G_0(x^*(0), Q) + \sum_j u_j^*(0) G_j(x^*(0), Q) - G_0(x^*(0), P), \qquad (5.39)$$

which takes into account the uniqueness of optimal solutions and Lagrange multipliers in (5.28). In this example, the value of multiplier $u^*(0)$ corresponding to (5.37) for $t = 0$ is equal to zero, the CVaR constraint (5.37) is not active, and for sufficiently small t, the upper bound reduces to:

$$\varphi(t) \leq (1 - t)\varphi(0) + t G_0(x^*(0), Q). \qquad (5.40)$$

Figure 5.3 depicts the graph of $\varphi(t)$ given by (5.38) and its lower and upper bound.

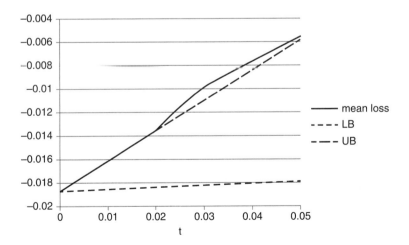

FIGURE 5.3 Comparison of minimal mean loss with its lower bound (LB) and upper bound (UB).

The upper bound coincides with $\varphi(t)$ for $t \leq 0.02$. It illustrates the fact that the local upper bound is meaningful if the probability of the additional scenario is not too large—that is, no more than probabilities of the original scenarios for our example.

CONCLUSIONS AND NEW PROBLEMS

Applicability of output analysis techniques depends on the structure of the model, on assumptions concerning the probability distribution, on available data, hardware, and software facilities. Incorporating risk and deviation measures into the portfolio optimization model, presence of stochastic dominance constraints, or presence of multiple stages makes the model much harder to solve. It means to design suitable stress tests, to compare alternative choices of risk measures, utility functions, and of probability distributions by multimodeling, to develop stability and robustness analysis, and so on. Convexity allows keeping a relatively friendly structure of the problem both for computational and theoretical purposes, and polyhedral property allows to rely on linear programming techniques for scenario-based problems with incorporated polyhedral risk measures, such as CVaR. For static models discussed in this chapter, the outcome is a decision dependent one-dimensional random variable; this does not apply to dynamic multistage stochastic decision problems. Modeling suitable multidimensional risk measures and analyzing their properties was initiated by Artzner et al. (2007). It has become an active area of research. Using them in dynamic portfolio optimization brings along various problems connected with model building, scenario generation, and output analysis that have not been solved satisfactorily yet. We refer to Pflug and Römisch (2007), Shapiro, Dentcheva, and Ruszczyński (2009), and numerous references therein.

Acknowledgment: The research was supported by the project of the Czech Science Foundation P402/12/G097, "DYME-Dynamic Models in Economics."

REFERENCES

Artzner, P., F. Delbaen, J. M. Eber, and D. Heath. 1999. Coherent measures of risk. *Mathematical Finance* 9: 202–228.

Artzner, P., F. Delbaen, J. M. Eber, D. Heath, and H. Ku. 2007. Coherent multiperiod risk adjusted values *and* Bellman's principle. *Annals of Operations Research* 152: 5–22.

Bank, B., J. Guddat, D. Klatte, B. Kummer, and K. Tammer. 1982. *Non-Linear Parametric Optimization*. Berlin: Akademie-Verlag.

Branda, M., and J. Dupačová. 2012. Approximation and contamination bounds for probabilistic programs. *Annals of Operations Research* 193: 3–19.

Čerbáková, J. 2006. Worst-case VaR and CVaR. In *Operations Research Proceedings 2005* edited by H. D. Haasis, H. Kopfer, and J. Schönberger. Berlin: Springer, 817–822.

Dentcheva D., and A. Ruszczyński. 2003. Optimization with Stochastic Dominance Constraints. *SIAM Journal on Optimization* 14: 548–566.

Dentcheva D., and A. Ruszczyński. 2010. Robust stochastic dominance and its application to risk-averse optimization. *Math. Program.* 123: 85–100.

Dupačová, J. 1996. Scenario-based stochastic programs: Resistance with respect to sample. *Annals of Operations Research* 64: 21–38.

Dupačová, J. 1998. Reflections on robust optimization. In *Stochastic Programming Methods and Technical Applications*, edited by K. Marti and P. Kall, LNEMS 437. Berlin: Springer, 111–127.

Dupačová, J. 1999. Portfolio optimization via stochastic programming: Methods of output analysis. *Math. Meth. Oper. Res.* 50: 245–227.

Dupačová, J. 2006. Stress testing via contamination. In *Coping with Uncertainty*, edited by K. Marti, Y. Ermoliev, and M. Makowski, LNEMS 581. New York: Springer, 29–46.

Dupačová J. 2009. *Portfolio Optimization and Risk Management via Stochastic Programming*. Osaka University Press.

Dupačová J. 2012. Output analysis and stress testing for mean-variance efficient portfolios. In *Proc. of 30th International Conference Mathematical Methods in Economics*, edited by J. Ramík and D. Stavárek. Karviná: Silesian University, School of Business Administration, 123–128.

Dupačová, J., M. Bertocchi, and V. Moriggia. 1998. Postoptimality for scenario based financial planning models with an application to bond portfolio management. In *Worldwide Asset and Liability Modeling*, edited by W. T. Ziemba, and J. M. Mulvey. Cambridge University Press, 263–285.

Dupačová, J., J. Hurt, and J. Štěpán. 2002. *Stochastic Modeling in Economics and Finance*, Kluwer, Dordrecht.

Dupačová, J., and M. Kopa. 2012. Robustness in stochastic programs with risk constraints. *Annals of Operations Research* 200: 55–74.

Dupačová, J., and M. Kopa. 2014. Robustness of optimal portfolios under risk and stochastic dominance constraints, *European Journal of Operational Research*, 234: 434–441

Dupačová, J., and J. Polívka. 2007. Stress testing for VaR and CVaR. *Quantitative Finance* 7: 411–421.

Ehrgott, M. 2005. *Multicriteria Optimization*. New York: Springer.

Eichhorn, A., and W. Römisch. 2005. Polyhedral risk measures in stochastic programming. *SIAM Journal on Optimization* 16: 69–95.

Fabozzi, F. J., D. Huang, and G. Zhou. 2010. Robust portfolios: Contributions from operations research and finance. *Annals of Operations Research* 176: 191–220.

Gol'shtein, E. G. 1970. *Vypukloje Programmirovanije. Elementy Teoriji*. Nauka, Moscow. [*Theory of Convex Programming*, Translations of Mathematical Monographs, 36, American Mathematical Society, Providence RI, 1972].

Kaut, M., H. Vladimirou, S. W. Wallace, and S. A. Zenios. 2007. Stability analysis of portfolio management with conditional value-at-risk. *Quantitative Finance* 7: 397–400.

Kopa, M. 2010. Measuring of second-order stochastic dominance portfolio efficiency. *Kybernetika* 46: 488–500.

Kopa, M., and P. Chovanec. 2008. A second-order stochastic dominance portfolio efficiency measure. *Kybernetika* 44: 243–258.

Kopa, M., and T. Post. 2009. A Portfolio Optimality Test Based on the First-Order Stochastic Dominance Criterion. *Journal of Financial and Quantitative Analysis* 44: 1103–1124.

Krokhmal, P., J. Palmquist, and S. Uryasev. 2002. Portfolio optimization with conditional-value-at-risk objective and constraints. *Journal of Risk* 2: 11–27.

Krokhmal, P., S. Uryasev, and M. Zabarankin. 2011. Modeling and Optimization of Risk. *Surveys in Operations Research and Management Science* 16: 49-66.

Kuosmanen, T. 2004. Efficient diversification according to stochastic dominance criteria. *Management Science* 50: 1390–1406.

Levy, H. 1992. Stochastic dominance and expected utility: Survey and analysis. *Management Science* 38: 555–593.

Luedtke, J. 2008. New formulations for optimization under stochastic dominance constraints. *SIAM Journal on Optimization* 19: 1433–1450.

Markowitz, H. 1952. Portfolio selection. *Journal of Finance* 6: 77–91.

Ogryczak, W., and A. Ruszczyński. 2002. Dual stochastic dominance and related mean-risk models. *SIAM Journal on Optimization* 13: 60–78.

Pflug, G. Ch., and W. Römisch. 2007. *Modeling, Measuring and Managing Risk*. Singapore: World Scientific.

Pflug, G. Ch., and D. Wozabal. 2007. Ambiguity in portfolio selection. *Quantitative Finance* 7: 435–442.

Post, T. 2003. Empirical tests for stochastic dominance efficiency. *Journal of Finance* 58: 1905–1932.

Post, T., and M. Kopa. 2013. General Linear Formulations of Stochastic Dominance Criteria. *European Journal of Operational Research* 230: 321–332.

Rockafellar, R. T., and S. Uryasev. 2002. Conditional value-at-risk for general loss distributions. *Journal of Banking and Finance* 26: 1443–1471.

Rockafellar, R. T., S. Uryasev, and M. Zabarankin. 2006. Generalized deviations in risk analysis. *Finance Stochast.* 10: 51–74.

Roman, D., K. Darby-Dowman, and G. Mitra. 2007. Mean-risk models using two risk measures: a multiobjective approach. *Quantitative Finance* 7: 443–458.

Ruszczyński, A., and A. Shapiro, eds. 2003. *Stochastic Programming, Handbooks in OR & MS*, Vol. 10. Amsterdam: Elsevier.

Ruszczyński, A., and R. J. Vanderbei. 2003. Frontiers of stochastically nondominated portfolios. *Econometrica* 71: 1287–1297.

Shapiro, A. 2003. Monte Carlo sampling methods, Ch. 6 in Ruszczyński and Shapiro (2003), pp. 353–425, and Chapter 5 of Shapiro, Dentcheva, and Ruszczyński (2009).

Shapiro, A., D. Dentcheva, and A. Ruszczyński. 2009. *Lectures on Stochastic Programming*. Philadelphia: SIAM and MPS.

Wang, Wei, and S. Ahmed. 2008. Sample average approximation for expected value constrained stochastic programs. *OR Letters* 36: 515–519.

Zymler, S., D. Kuhn, and B. Rustem. 2013. Distributionally robust joint chance constraints with second-order moment information. *Math. Program. A* 137: 167–198.

CHAPTER 6

Risk Measures and Management in the Energy Sector

Marida Bertocchi
Rosella Giacometti
Maria Teresa Vespucci
University of Bergamo[1], Department of Management,
Economics, and Quantitative Methods

INTRODUCTION

As a result of the liberalization of energy markets, energy companies got an increased understanding of the need both of profit maximization and of considering the risks connected with their activities as well as the way of hedging them; they also became aware of their own different level of risk aversion policies. In energy-sector modeling, dealing with uncertainty is a part of the problem, as well as with making decisions in different points in time. These two characteristics bring the energy sector modeling in the stochastic programming framework. The two issues of risks and decisions under uncertainty support the choice of having multistage type stochastic programs (see Ruszczynski and Shapiro, 2003; Shapiro, Dentcheva, and Ruszczynski, 2009).

In this chapter we illustrate two problems in the energy sector where the awareness of risk is fundamental, and we analyze the main advantages of introducing risk management in our models.

---

[1]The work has been developed under Bergamo University grant of Bertocchi, Giacometti, Vespucci 2011–2013.

The first problem is related to power production and electricity trading. There is an extensive literature dealing with optimization of power production and electricity trading. See Alonso-Ayuso, di Domenica, Escudero, and Pizarro (2011), Conejo, Carrion, and Morales (2010), Fleten and Wallace (1998, 2009), Fleten and Kristoffersen (2008), Gröwe-Kuska, Kiwiel, Nowak, Römisch, and Wegner (2002), and Takriti, Krasenbrink, and Wu (2000). In this framework, risk management becomes a significant issue for electricity retailers and producers, and contracts for future delivery of electricity (i.e., forwards contracts) become a tool for hedging risk. Indeed, the retailers are highly constrained by regulated tariff consumers, and they are subject to risk of high electricity price. We show a comparison between deterministic and stochastic models able to optimally solve the problem.

The second problem concerns the incremental selection of power generation capacity, which is of great importance for energy planners. In this chapter, we deal with the case of the single power producer's (GenCo) point of view. That is, we want to determine the optimal mix of different technologies for electricity generation, ranging from coal, nuclear, and combined cycle gas turbine to hydroelectric, wind, and photovoltaic, taking into account the existing plants, the cost of investment in new plants, the maintenance costs, the purchase and sales of CO_2 emission trading certificates, and renewable energy certificates (RECs, or green certificates) to satisfy regulatory requirements over a long-term planning horizon consisting of a set I of years (generally, 30 or more years). Uncertainty of prices (fuels, electricity, CO_2 emission permits, and green certificates) is taken into account. The power producer is assumed to be a price taker; that is, it cannot influence the price of electricity.

We propose various models for maximizing the net present value of the power producer's profit, in order to find an optimal trade-off between the expected profit (should it be the unique term in the objective function to maximize, it is so named risk-neutral strategy) and the risk of getting a negative impact on the solution's profit due to a not-wanted scenario to occur. So this weighted mixture of expected profit maximization and risk minimization undoubtedly may be perceived as a more general model than the levelized cost of energy (LCoE) procedure (Manzhos, 2013). See some similar approaches in Bjorkvoll, Fleten, Nowak, Tomasgard, and Wallace (2001), Eppen, Martin, and Schrage (1989), Genesi, Marannino, Montagna, Rossi, Siviero, Desiata, and Gentile (2009), Cristobal, Escudero, and Monge (2009), and Escudero, Garin, Merino, and Perez (2012), Ehrenmann and Smeers (2011), among others. The main contribution of the proposed model is the provisions of consistent solutions, since for all of them the optimal generation mix mainly consists of conventional thermal power plants for low risk aversion, which are replaced by renewable energy sources plants as risk aversion increases.

UNCERTAINTY CHARACTERIZATION VIA SCENARIOS

Decision-making problems related to electricity markets are characterized by uncertainty. The input data of problems affected by uncertainty are usually described by stochastic processes that can be represented using continuous or discrete random variables.

The most used case is the one of discrete stochastic process that can be represented by a finite set of vectors, named scenarios, obtained by all possible discrete values that the random variables can assume.

If μ is a discrete stochastic process, it can be expressed as μ_ω, with ω the scenario index and Ω the finite number of scenarios. Each scenario has a certain probability p_ω of occurrence with

$$\sum_{\omega \in \Omega} p_\omega = 1.$$

The scenario generation procedure may use time series analysis, statistical, and econometric modeling for the forecasting of future values of the random variables, experts opinion, and simple possible outcomes.

In the problems described in this chapter we study the following sources of uncertainty: the spot price of energy, the forward price of energy, the fuel prices, CO_2 and green certificate prices. Other sources of variability may involve inflows for hydropower plants (see Fleten and Wallace 2009), intensity of wind, demand (see Philpott, Craddock, and Waterer 2000), and many others (see Eppen, Martin, and Schrage 1989, and references therein).

For a general discussion about the procedures for generating scenarios in a multistage stochastic program, see Dupačová, Consigli, and Wallace (2000).

Spot and Forward Prices of Energy

Concerning the spot price of energy, the Italian electricity spot market was opened in 2003, and its activity has been increasing during the last years and it is considered a liquid market with many daily transactions. In our analysis we consider the daily base-load spot prices time series from January 1, 2008, to September 9, 2009. After removing the daily and weekly seasonal components, we analyzed the log prices data and found stationarity but no strong presence of spikes: only four observations are larger then three times the standard deviation on the whole period. The log spot price exhibits autocorrelation and heteroskedasticity but not a dramatic kurtosis. In line with recent findings in literature, we fit a regime-switching model able to capture different market conditions, in terms of changing mean and

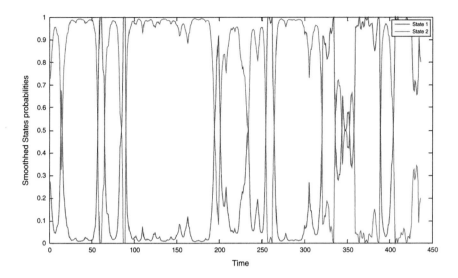

FIGURE 6.1 The spot switching model.

volatilities. For details on the AR(1) model used in fitting the log price process and the Markov chain model used for the switching model, see Giacometti, Vespucci, Bertocchi, and Barone Adesi (2011; 2013).

Using the complete data set, we find the evidence of the presence of two regimes (see Figure 6.1).

We have derived the theoretical dynamics of the forward prices by directly modeling them. The motivation of this approach is that, in reality, the electricity spot and futures prices are not closely related. This is mainly due to the difficulty in storing electricity. Water reservoirs can be used for storing potential energy in limited quantities due to the their physical limited capacity. Often, the spot and futures markets are so dissimilar that the relationship between spot and futures prices breaks down. If we compare, *ex post*, the forward quotations with the realized spot prices, we observe that the difference does not necessarily tend to zero for contracts approaching their maturity; see also Borovkova and Geman (2006; 2006), where they indicate that the futures price is a poor proxy for the electricity spot price. For this reason we have modeled explicitly the dynamics of the forward curve, imposing that the scenarios generated for the spot and forward contracts are correlated and consistent with the currently observed contract quotations.

The procedure used for scenario generation involves two distinct steps. By principal component analysis (PCA) on the daily deseasonalized historical returns of forward key rates, we compute the orthogonal factors: the first three factors explain 92 percent of the forward curve and correspond to a parallel shift (first factor, which explains 61 percent), a tilting (second factor, which explains 17 percent), and a curvature effect (third factor explains 14 percent).

We consider as relevant the first two factors that have an explanatory power of about 80 percent of the variability.

The residuals contain all the information related to the remaining 20 percent of variability and the correlation among the returns of the different maturities. We model the variance of the residuals with a univariate GARCH(1,1) model in order to capture the dependence of returns.

In order to generate correlated scenarios, we combine together the standardized residuals of the GARCH(1,1) model and the residuals from the regime-switching model for the same days. We do not impose any parametric assumption on the marginal distributions and use the empirical cumulative distribution to fit a Gaussian copula of the historical residuals vectors. We simulate a vector of correlated innovations from the Gaussian copula and reconstruct the forecasted scenarios using the estimated principal factors for the forward return scenario and the regime switching for the log spot price, finally adding the seasonal premia.

To build the scenario tree for the three-stage stochastic programming model, we first generate 100 correlated scenarios for spot and forward prices on a time horizon of one year, and then we aggregate them in a recombining tree using the backward scenario reduction technique proposed by Pflug (2001) and Pflug and Hochreiter (2007). In order to maintain consistency with the market, the spot price scenarios were adjusted so that the expected average spot price in a period is equal to the current market price of a forward with delivery in that period. To avoid arbitrage opportunities, we impose that spot price tree satisfies the martingale property in the recombining tree.

Fuel Prices

Tables 6.1 and 6.2 provide six alternative values of the ratio "estimated price over price in year 0" that are considered, together with the associated probabilities for coal and gas, respectively. Analogously, Table 6.3 provides three alternative values and the associated probabilities for nuclear fuel. By combining all alternatives, 108 independent scenarios of fuel prices are obtained.

As the number of scenarios is increased, the 0-1 variables, necessary for modeling the risk measures shortfall probability and first-order stochastic dominance, substantially increase the computing time, and decomposition algorithms have to be used for obtaining the solution in a reasonable computing time. This problem does not arise in the case reported in this chapter using CVaR risk measure.

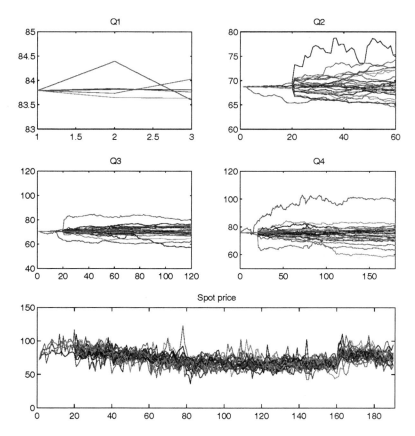

FIGURE 6.2 Multivariate scenarios for spot and forward prices.

TABLE 6.1 Alternative Values of "Estimated Price over Price in Year 0" Ratio (Coal Price in Year 0: 115 €/t (12.3 €/MWh).

ratio	0.786	0.9	1.00	1.246	1.6571	2.0
probability	0.035	0.1	0.565	0.26	0.035	0.005

TABLE 6.2 Alternative Values of "Estimated Price over Price in Year 0" Ratio (Gas Price in Year 0: 0.3 €/Nm³ (31.3 €/MWh).

ratio	0.786	0.9	1.00	1.246	1.6571	2.0
probability	0.035	0.1	0.565	0.26	0.035	0.005

TABLE 6.3 Alternative Values of "Estimated Price over Price in Year 0" Ratio (Nuclear Fuel Price in Year 0: 2100 €/kg (2.21 €/MWh).

ratio	0.8313	1.00	1.28
probability	0.08	0.72	0.2

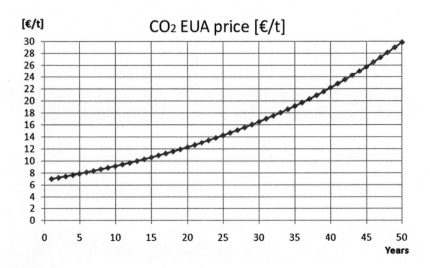

FIGURE 6.3 Scenario for CO_2 price. (EUA).

The price of the CO_2 emission allowances is assumed to increase along the years of the planning horizon. We consider only one scenario; see Figure 6.3.

The ratio "electricity from RES / total electricity produced" is set according to the 20-20-20 European target from year 2011 to year 2020 (i.e., from year 1 to year 8 of the planning period); after 2020, a further increase of 1 percent is assumed.

The GenCo can satisfy the imposed ratio by either producing from RES or buying green certificates.

MEASURES OF RISKS

Being F_ω the value of profit function along scenario $\omega \in \Omega$, the risk-neutral approach determines the values of the decision variables that maximize, over all scenarios, the expected profit $\sum_{\omega \in \Omega} p_\omega F_\omega$ along the planning horizon. This type of modeling does not take into account the variability of the objective function value over the scenarios and, then, the possibility of realizing in some scenarios a very low profit. In the literature, several approaches have been introduced for measuring the profit risk. These measures can be divided into four groups, on the basis of the information the user must provide:

1. A form for the cardinal utility: expected utility approach
2. A confidence level: value-at-risk and conditional-value-at-risk
3. A profit threshold: shortfall probability and expected shortage
4. A benchmark: first-order and second-order stochastic dominance

In this section we consider these risk measures and how they can be used to reduce the risk of having low profits in some scenarios. To see the use of all of them in the power-capacity planning problem, see Vespucci, Bertocchi, Pisciella, and Zigrino (2014).

Risk Aversion Strategy 1: The Expected Utility Approach

The expected utility approach is based on the famous theorem from Von Neumann and Morgenstern (1944). It states that given two probability distributions G_a and G_b of the random variables respectively a and b representing decisions, satisfying axioms of completeness, transitivity, continuity, and independence of preference relation among distributions, there exists a utility function (*the expected utility function*) $U : R \to R$ such that $V(G_a) = \sum_{i=1}^{n} U(x_i) p_{a,i}$, where $V : F \to R$ is the ordinal utility defined on the set F of distributions, and x_i represents the ith realization of random variable a with probability $p_{a,i}$. The argument of function U is quite often the wealth of the individual.

Two further axioms of nonsatiability and risk aversion are usually required on U: the former states that one requires more than less, and the latter states that the utility of the expected value of a random variable is greater than the expected value of the utility function of the same variable. It is easy to show that the risk aversion property is equivalent to require the concavity of function U or that the certainty equivalent is less than the expected value of the random variable.

There are various forms of the utility function that exhibit different characteristics: among them the most famous are the quadratic function that corresponds to having a normal distribution of the random variable, the negative exponential that exhibits constant absolute risk aversion, and the power utility with constant relative risk aversion.

Risk Aversion Strategy 2: Conditional Value at Risk (CVaR)

The CVaR of profits is defined as the expected value of the profits smaller than the α-quantile of the profits distribution—that is, it is the expected profit in the α percentage of the worst scenarios; see Conejo, Carrion, Morales (2010). We observe that increasing value of CVaR means decreasing risk.

Given the confidence level α, the CVaR of profit (see Gaivoronski and Pflug 2005; Rockafellar and Uryasev 2000, 2002; Schultz and Tiedemann, 2006) is defined as

$$\max_V \left[V - \frac{1}{\alpha} \left(\sum_{\omega \in \Omega} p_\omega d_\omega \right) \right]$$

The auxiliary variables V [k€] and d_ω [k€], $\omega \in \Omega$, used for computing the CVaR, are defined by constraints

$$d_\omega \geq V - F_\omega, \quad d_\omega \geq 0, \quad \forall \omega \in \Omega$$

and V is the optimal solution representing the value at risk (VaR).

In order to use the CVaR of profit as a risk-aversion strategy, the objective function can be expressed

$$\max_V \left[(1 - \rho) \left(\sum_{\omega \in \Omega} p_\omega F_\omega \right) + \rho \left[V - \frac{1}{\alpha} \left(\sum_{\omega \in \Omega} p_\omega d_\omega \right) \right] \right]$$

where $\rho \in [0, 1]$ is the CVaR risk-averse weight factor, $\rho = 0$ means to consider the risk-neutral case, $\rho = 1$ means maximum risk aversion. In a different context, see Alonso-Ayuso, di Domenica, Escudero, and Pizarro (2011); Cabero, Ventosa, Cerisola, and Baillo (2010); and Ehrenmann, and Smeers (2011).

Risk Aversion Strategy 3: Shortfall Probability (SP)

Given a profit threshold Φ, the shortfall probability (see Schultz and Tiedemann 2006) is the probability of the scenario to occur having a profit smaller than Φ:

$$\sum_{\omega \in \Omega} p_\omega \mu_\omega$$

where μ_ω is a 0-1 variable defined by the constraint

$$\Phi - F_\omega \leq M_\omega \mu_\omega, \quad \forall \omega \in \Omega \tag{6.1}$$

where variable μ_ω takes value 1 if $F_\omega < \Phi$, that is, if ω is an unwanted scenario, and M_ω is a small enough constant such that it does not prevent any feasible solution to the problem, being this parameter crucial for the computational effort required to obtain the optimal solution.

The profit risk can be hedged by simultaneously pursuing expected profit maximization and shortfall probability minimization: this is done by maximizing the objective function, with $\rho \in [0, 1]$,

$$(1 - \rho)\left(\sum_{\omega \in \Omega} p_\omega F_\omega\right) + \rho\left(\sum_{\omega \in \Omega} p_\omega \mu_\omega\right)$$

subject to constraints related to the modeled problem and constraints (6.1).

Risk Aversion Strategy 4: Expected Shortage (ES)

Given a profit threshold Φ, the expected shortage (see Eppen, Martin, and Schrage 1989) is given by

$$\sum_{\omega \in \Omega} p_\omega d_\omega$$

where d_ω satisfies constraint

$$\Phi - F_\omega \leq d_\omega, \quad d_\omega \geq 0, \quad \forall \omega \in \Omega. \tag{6.2}$$

The profit risk can be hedged by simultaneously pursuing expected profit maximization and expected shortage minimization: This is done by maximizing the objective function, with $\rho \in [0, 1]$,

$$(1 - \rho)\left(\sum_{\omega \in \Omega} p_\omega F_\omega\right) + \rho\left(\sum_{\omega \in \Omega} p_\omega d_\omega\right)$$

subject to constraints related to the modeled problem and constraints (6.2).

Risk Aversion Strategy 5: First-Order Stochastic Dominance (FSD)

A benchmark is given by assigning a set P of profiles (Φ^p, τ^p), $p \in P$, where Φ^p is the threshold to be satisfied by the profit at each scenario and τ^p is the upper bound of its failure probability.

The profit risk is hedged by maximizing the expected value of profit, while satisfying constraints related to the modeled problem, as well as the first-order stochastic dominance constraints; see Carrion, Gotzes, and Schultz (2009) and Gollmer, Neise, and Schultz (2008):

$$\sum_{\omega \in \Omega} p_\omega \mu_\omega^p \leq \tau^p, \quad p \in P \tag{6.3}$$

where the 0-1 variables μ_ω^p by which the shortfall probability with respect to threshold Φ^p is computed are defined by constraints

$$\Phi^p - F_\omega \leq M_\omega \mu_w^p, \quad \forall p \in P, \quad \forall \omega \in \Omega \tag{6.4}$$

with

$$\mu_\omega^p \in \{0, 1\}, \quad \forall p \in P, \quad \omega \in \Omega.$$

Constraints (6.3) and (6.4) belong to the cross-scenario constraint type, and they introduce an additional difficulty in the decomposition algorithms. See in Escudero, Garin, Merino, and Perez (2012) a multistage algorithm for dealing with this type of constraints.

Risk Aversion Strategy 6: Second-Order Stochastic Dominance (SSD)

A benchmark is assigned by defining a set of profiles (Φ^p, e^p), $p \in P$, where Φ^p denotes the threshold to be satisfied by the profit at each scenario and e^p denotes the upper bound of the expected shortage over the scenarios. The profit risk is hedged by maximizing the expected value of profit, while satisfying constraints related to the modeled problem as well as the second-order stochastic dominance constraints (see Gollmer, Gotzes, and Schultz, 2011):

$$\sum_{\omega \in \Omega} p_\omega d_\omega^p \leq e^p, \quad \forall p \in P \tag{6.5}$$

where

$$\Phi^p - F_\omega \leq d_{w_\omega}^p, \quad \forall p \in P, \quad \forall \omega \in \Omega. \tag{6.6}$$

with

$$d_w^p \geq 0, \quad \forall p \in P, \quad \forall \omega \in \Omega.$$

This measure is closely related to the risk measure introduced in Fabian, Mitra, Roman, and Zverovich (2011), where the threshold $p \in P$ is considered as the benchmark. In a different context, see also Cabero, Ventosa, Cerisola, and Baillo (2010).

Notice that constraints (6.5) and (6.6) are also cross-scenario constraints, but the related variables are continuous ones.

It is interesting to point out that the risk-aversion strategies FSD and SSD have the advantage that the expected profit maximization is hedged against a set of unwanted scenarios: The hedging is represented by the requirement of forcing the scenario profit to be not smaller than a set of thresholds, with a bound on failure probability for each of them in strategy FSD and an upper bound on the expected shortage in strategy SSD. The price to be paid is the increase of the number of constraints and variables (being 0-1 variables in strategy FSD).

For large-scale instances, decomposition approaches must be used, like the exact multistage Branch-and-Fix Coordination (BFC-MS) method (Escudero, Garin, Merino, and Perez, 2012), currently being expanded to allow constraint types (FSD) and (SSD) (Escudero, Garin, Merino, and Perez 2012a); multistage metaheuristics, like Stochastic Dynamic Programming (Cristobal, Escudero, and Monge 2009; Escudero, Monge, Romero-Morales, and Wang 2012), for very large scale instances; and Lagrangian heuristic approaches, see (Gollmer, Gotzes, and Schultz 2011).

Notice that both FSD and SSD strategies require the determination of benchmarks, which may require computing time consumption.

CASE STUDIES

Forward Markets Trading for Hydropower Producers

For a hydropower producer, on a yearly horizon, it is very important to identify the optimal scheduling of its production in order to satisfy a production profile that may be particularly difficult to match in some months of the year. The production profile is the forecast of customers' energy demand. The use of derivative contracts may help to optimize the hydro resources.

The hydropower producer's portfolio includes its own production, a set of power contracts for delivery or purchase including derivative contracts, like options, futures or forwards with physical delivery, to hedge against various types of risks. In this subsection, we summarize deterministic and stochastic portfolio models for a hydropower producer operating in a competitive electricity market. For detailed description of the models see Giacometti, Vespucci, Bertocchi, and Barone Adesi (2011; 2013).

The novelty of our approach consists in a more detailed modeling of the electricity derivatives contracts, leading to an effective daily hedging.

The goal of using such a model is to reduce the economic risks connected to the fact that energy spot price may be highly volatile due to various different, unpredictable reasons (i.e., very cold winter) and to the possibility of a scarcity of rain or melting snow. Indeed, the use of forward contracts in a dynamic framework is expensive, but relying on the energy spot market may be extremely risky. See Dentcheva and Römisch (1998), Gröwe-Kuska, Kiwiel, Nowak, Römisch, and Wegner (2002), Wallace, and Fleten (2003), Fleten and Kristoffersen (2008), Conejo, Garcia-Bertrand, Carrion, Caballero, and de Andres (2008) and Nolde, Uhr, and Morari (2008) for discussion on the opportunity of using stochastic programming for such problems and Yamin (2004) for a review of methods for power-generation scheduling.

The basis risk factors include the wholesale spot and forward prices of electric energy, which are supposed to be unaffected by the decision of the utility manager, and the uncertain inflow of hydro reservoirs; see also Fleten and Wallace (2009), Vitoriano, Cerisola, and Ramos (2000), and Latorre, Cerisola, and Ramos (2007). The model we propose differs from the one discussed in Fleten and Wallace (1998; 2009), as we concentrate on the advantage of using derivatives contracts and use both electricity spot prices and forward prices as sources of uncertainties, considering inflows as deterministic. The objective function is the expected utility function of the final wealth, where the cardinal utility is a power function with constant relative risk aversion equal to 0.5.

We report the results of a comparison of deterministic and stochastic approaches in the case of an hydro system composed by one cascade with three basins and three hydro plants, one of these is a pumped storage hydro plant as shown in Figure 6.4 (see Tables 6.4 and 6.5 for input data of the hydro system).

The model has been used on a yearly horizon considering only working days. In order to represent the scenarios we introduce the following notation to indicate the number of days included in the different stages (see also Vespucci, Maggioni, Bertocchi, Innorta, 2012): $T_1 = 1$, $T_2 = \{t : 2 \leq t \leq 20\}$, $T_3 = \{t : 21 \leq t \leq 191\}$, where the subindexes indicate the stage. We have considered 25 scenarios represented by means of a scenario tree

TABLE 6.4 Hydro Basin Data: Capacity, Initial and Minimum Final Storage Volumes.

Hydro Basin	Capacity ($10^3 m^3$)	Initial Storage Volume ($10^3 m^3$)	Final Storage Volume ($10^3 m^3$)
1	1000	100	0
2	2000	1000	500
3	2000	1000	500

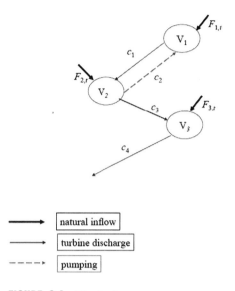

FIGURE 6.4 The hydro system.

TABLE 6.5 Hydro Arc Data: Energy Coefficient and Capacity.

Hydro Arc Data	Capacity ($10^3 \mathrm{m}^3$)	Energy Coefficient ($10^3 \mathrm{m}^3$)
c_1	100	1.0
c_2	50	−1.7
c_3	150	1.1
c_4	200	0.9

where the nodes at different stages are as follows: $N_1 = 1$, $N_2 = \{2, \ldots, 6\}$, $N_3 = \{7, \ldots, 31\}$.

In order to assess the value of modeling uncertainty for our three-stage model, we follow the procedure introduced in the literature by Escudero, Garin, and Perez (2007), and Vespucci, Maggioni, Bertocchi, and Innorta (2012), for evaluating the value of the stochastic solution for three-stage problem, and further deepened in Maggioni, Allevi, and Bertocchi (2012) and Maggioni, Allevi, and Bertocchi (2013).

The procedure is based on the idea of reproducing the decision process as the uncertainty reveals: This procedure is suitable for multistage problems.

The optimal objective value obtained in stage 3 is called *multistage expected value of the reference scenario* (MEVRS), where the reference scenario is the mean value scenario.

Technically, this is computed by the following steps:

1. Scenario tree $S_{(1,mean)}$ is defined by considering the expected value of the uncertainty parameters (spot and forward prices); the stochastic model with this scenario tree is solved and the optimal values of the first-stage variables are stored. In this way, the optimal solution of the *expected mean value* (EV) problem is computed.
2. Scenario tree $S_{(2,mean)}$ is defined by evaluating the expected value of the spot and forward prices on nodes belonging to N_3. The stochastic model with this scenario tree is solved having assigned the value stored at step 1 to the first-stage decision variables. The optimal value of second-stage variables are stored.
3. The stochastic model on benchmark tree $S_{(1,mean)}$ is solved, assigning to the first-stage decision variables the values stored at step 1 and to the second-stage decision variables the values stored at step 2.

We report the results considering all the sources of variability, the spot and the forward prices. The use of forward contracts allows a more efficient use of water pumping with a higher final level of water in the basins.

Overall, the effects of the financial part and the production scheduling lead to an increase in the objective function, from 232,068.61 to 251,308.03 €. We report the certainty equivalent related to the previously mentioned utility function.

We observe in Table 6.6 that the value of the objective function (EV value) using the respective average scenario of spot and forward prices (the deterministic case) is higher than in the stochastic solution. The stochastic approach, even with a limited number of scenarios obtained by a reduction technique (see Heitsch, and Römisch, 2007; 2009a; 2009b), allows the producer to better diversify its consecutive choices along the year, adapting the production and the protection against high energy price (i.e., the decision variables) according to the energy price changes along the different scenarios. In the deterministic approach, one cannot take into account different realizations of the random variables.

TABLE 6.6 Certainty Equivalent with Two Sources of Stochasticity.

Type of models	Certainty equivalent (€)
Deterministic Model (EV)	271,248.62
Stochastic Model (RP)	251,308.03
MEVRS	244,509.78
MVSS=MEVRS-RP	6,798.25

We also compute the multistage expected value of the mean value scenario MEVRS = 244,509.78. The modified value of the stochastic solution (MVSS = MEVRS-RP) is 6,798.25, and it allows us to obtain the goodness of the expected solution value when the expected values are replaced by the random values for the input variables. High values of modified VSS indicate the advantage of using the stochastic approach with respect to the deterministic one.

Capacity Power Production Planning in the Long Run

We present a decision support model for a power producer who wants to determine the optimal planning for investment in power generation capacity in a long-term horizon. The power producer operates in a liberalized electricity market, where rules are issued by the regulatory authorities with the aim of promoting the development of power production systems with reduced CO_2 emissions. Indeed, CO_2 emission allowances have to be bought by the power producer as a payment for the emitted CO_2. Moreover, the green certificate scheme supports power production from renewable energy sources (RES)—that is, by geothermal, wind, biomass and hydropower plants—and penalizes production from conventional power plants such as CCGT, coal, and nuclear power plants. Indeed, every year a prescribed ratio is required between the electricity produced from RES and the total electricity produced. In case the actual ratio, attained in a given year, is less than the prescribed one, the power producer must buy green certificates in order to satisfy the related constraint. On the contrary, when the yearly attained ratio is greater than the prescribed one, the power producer can sell green certificates in the market.

The power producer aims at maximizing its own profit over the planning horizon. Revenues from sale of electricity depend both on the electricity market price and on the amount of electricity sold. The latter is bounded above by the power producer's market share; it also depends on the number of operating hours per year characterizing each power plant in the production system.

Costs greatly differ among the production technologies. Investment costs depend both on the plant-rated power and on the investment costs per power unit. Typically, for thermal power plants, rated powers are higher and unit investment costs are lower than for RES power plants. Variable generation costs for conventional power plants highly depend on fuel pricing.

Revenues and costs associated to the green certificate scheme depend on the green certificate price, as well as on the yearly ratio between production from RES and total annual production of the producer. Finally, costs for emitting CO_2 depend on the price of the emission allowances, as well as on the amount of CO_2 emitted, that greatly varies among the production technologies.

We notice that the evolution of prices along the planning horizon is not known at the time when the investment decisions have to be done. The model takes into account the risk associated with the capacity expansion problem due to the uncertainty of prices, as well as the uncertainty of market share. Uncertainty is included in the model by means of scenarios that represent different hypotheses on the future evolution of the market share and of the prices of electricity, green certificates, CO_2 emission allowances, and fuels.

The proposed decision support model determines the evolution of the production system along the planning horizon, taking into account all scenarios representing the uncertainty. Since construction time and industrial life greatly vary among power plants of different technology, the model determines the number of power plants for each technology to start construction in every year of the planning period. Each new power plant is then available for production when its construction is over and its industrial life is not ended. The annual electricity production of each power plant in the production system, and the corresponding green certificates and CO_2 emission allowances, are determined for each year of the planning horizon under each scenario into consideration.

The two-stage stochastic mixed-integer model determines the optimal generation expansion plan, which is given by the values of the first-stage variables

$$\omega_{j,i} \in Z_+ \quad \forall j \in J, \quad \forall i \in I$$

that represent the number of new power plants of technology $j \in J$ where construction is to start in year $i \in I$ along the planning horizon, being J the set of all candidate technologies, and I the set of years in the planning horizon. The second-stage variables are the continuous operation variables of all power plants along the time horizon.

The optimal generation expansion plan must satisfy the following constraints.

For every candidate technology j, the total number of new power plants constructed along the planning horizon is bounded above by the number of sites ready for construction of new power plants of that technology—that is, sites for which all the necessary administrative permits have been released. The new power plants of technology j available for production in year i are those for which both the construction is over and the industrial life is not ended.

The sum of the present annual debt repayments, corresponding to the number of new power plants of each technology j available for production in every year i, is required not to exceed the available budget.

The annual electricity production obtained by all new power plants of technology j is nonnegative and bounded above by the number of new plants available for production in year i times the maximum annual production of a plant of technology j.

The annual electricity production of power plant $k \in K$ (K the set of all power plants owned in year 0) is nonnegative and bounded above by the maximum annual production in year i. Parameters are introduced to take into account possible plant breakdown and maintenance.

Notice that for some technologies a lower bound to the annual electricity production could be imposed, if it is selected, in order to take into account technical limitations.

The electricity generated in year i cannot exceed the power producer's market share under scenario w.

The amount of electricity $G_{i,w}$ for which the corresponding green certificates are bought, if $G_{i,w} \geq 0$, or sold, if $G_{i,w} \leq 0$, in year i under scenario ω is used to take into account revenue or costs, depending on whether the energy production from renewable sources with respect to the total energy production is greater or less than the quantity β_i fixed by the regulatory authority.

The amount $Q_{i,w}$ of CO_2 emissions the power producer must pay for in year i under scenario ω is computed by adding the emissions obtained by all the thermal plants (original and candidates).

The annual profit F_w under scenario ω is computed taking into account the revenues from sale of electricity, the revenues or costs of green certificates, the costs of CO_2 emission allowances, fixed and variable costs for thermal and RES production, and the annuity of investment costs.

The risk-neutral approach determines the values of the decision variables that maximize, over all scenarios, the expected profit along the planning horizon. It does not take into account the variability of the objective function value over the scenarios and, then, the possibility of realizing in some scenarios a very low profit.

In order to use the CVaR of profit as a risk-aversion strategy, the objective function has to be expressed:

$$\max_V \left[(1 - \rho) \left(\sum_{\omega \in \Omega} p_\omega F_\omega \right) + \rho \left[V - \frac{1}{\alpha} \left(\sum_{\omega \in \Omega} p_\omega d_\omega \right) \right] \right]$$

where $\rho \in [0, 1]$ is the CVaR risk averse weight factor.

We report the results obtained for a power producer who owns in year 0 the medium-size generation system described in Table 6.7, where rated power, residual life, and efficiency are reported for every power plant of the system. The generation system owned initially, with total capacity of

TABLE 6.7 Power Plants Owned by the Power Producer in Year 0.

Power plant	Type	Rated Power	Residual Life	Efficiency
1	CCGT	840	19	0.52
2	CCGT	425	18	0.52
3	CCGT	1,090	16	0.50
4	CCGT	532	15	0.51
5	CCGT	75	9	0.52
6	CCGT	227	7	0.50
7	Coal	600	8	0.40
8	Coal	500	3	0.39
9	Coal	402	12	0.41

8,629 MW, is biased toward the CCGT technology and is therefore highly dependent on the gas price.

Let us consider a market electricity price of 106 €/MWh and two values for the initial budget, in order to show its influence on the technology mix. The confidence level α used to compute the CVaR is 5 percent.

For the case corresponding to the budget B = 3.84 G€, the profit distributions are shown in Figure 6.5.

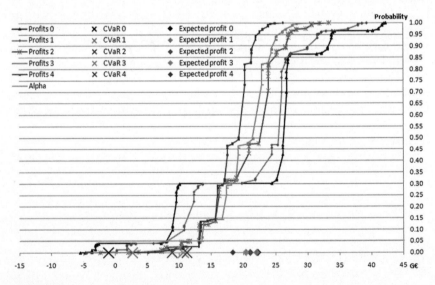

FIGURE 6.5 Profit distribution for different risk aversion parameters using CVaR with α equal to 5 percent, budget = 3.84 G€ and a market electricity price of 106€/MWh.

TABLE 6.8 Technology Mix Obtained with CVaR and Different Risk Aversion Parameters—Budget: 3.84 G€.

Case	0	1	2	3	4
ρ	0	0.1	0.2	0.3	0.8
CCGT	13	9	5	1	0
Coal	0	2	3	6	4
Wind	1	0	0	1	10
Expected profit [G€]	22.173	21.990	21.019	20.367	18.357
CVaR	1.026	2.682	8.910	10.585	11.164

In Table 6.8 we can observe a regular change in the technology mix as the risk aversion parameter increases.

Notice the difference between the case with $\rho = 0$ (risk neutral) and the case with $\rho = 0.2$ (risk averse): The expected profit decreases by only 5 percent (1.154 G€), while the CVaR has grown by 9.926 G€.

By further increasing the risk aversion parameter ($\rho = 0.3$ and $\rho = 0.8$), the corresponding optimal technology mixes have a small growth of the CVaR but have a big decrease in the expected profit.

For the case with a higher budget, say 14.5 G€, the profit distributions are shown in Figure 6.6.

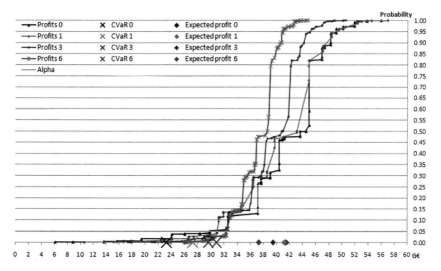

FIGURE 6.6 Profit distribution for different risk aversion parameters using CVaR with α equal to 5 percent, budget = 14.5 G€ and a market electricity price of 106 €/MWh.

TABLE 6.9   Technology Mix Obtained with CVaR and Different Risk Aversion Parameters—Budget: 14.5 G€.

Case	0	1	2	3	4	5	6
ρ	0	0.2	0.4	0.5	0.6	0.8	0.95
CCGT	17	10	8	6	5	4	3
Nuclear	0	0	0	1	1	1	1
Coal	1	6	5	2	1	0	0
Wind	60	60	60	60	60	59	59
Expected profit [G€]	41.484	41.243	40.627	39.496	38.785	37.904	37.347
CVaR		23.234	27.227	28.439	29.584	30.205	30.768	30.824

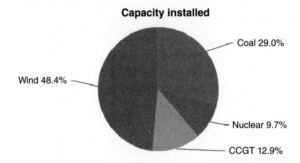

FIGURE 6.7   Percentage of new capacity installed for the case of budget = 14.5 G€, CVaR and $\rho = 0.5$.

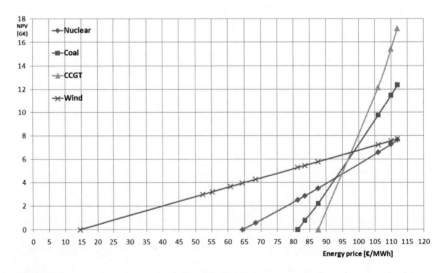

FIGURE 6.8   Net present value of optimal expected profit when investment is in a single technology (only the available technologies are shown).

The nuclear technology appears in the mix (see Table 6.9) only with high risk aversion ($\rho \geq 0.5$), and it represents a low percentage of the new capacity mix (see Figure 6.7).

With a budget lower than 14.5 G€, the nuclear technology is not included in the optimal mix, due to the rated power of nuclear plants.

Moreover, it can be seen in Figure 6.8 that for electricity prices less than 112 €/MWh, the LCoE associated to the nuclear technology is less than the LCoE associated to the wind power technology.

SUMMARY

In this chapter, we have explored the most important notions of risk in the energy sector, as well as the major sources of uncertainty from which risk is originating. We have described how to cope with these uncertainties by two main tools: construction of scenarios and stochastic programming modeling. The former has been achieved by using discrete stochastic processes, mainly GARCH processes. The latter has been attained by implementing a stochastic programming approach and analyzing the behavior of the solutions. Two relevant problems for the energy sector have been discussed:

1. A hydropower producer that wants to use the electricity forward market for hedging against the increase in electricity prices
2. The capacity power production planning in the long run for a single price-taker producer

We point out that one of the most promising research direction in the dynamic energy problems with embedded risk profile is the use of the discussed risk measures in the multistage framework instead of the two-stage one. This stimulating topic, which is at present under analysis within the financial research studies, implies a careful analysis of "consistent" risk measures to be used in energy problems.

REFERENCES

Alonso-Ayuso, A., N. di Domenica N., L.F. Escudero L.F., and C. Pizarro. 2011. Structuring bilateral energy contract portfolios in competitive markets. In Bertocchi M., Consigli G., Dempster M.A.H., *Stochastic Optimization Methods in Finance and Energy*. International Series in Operations Research and Management Science, New York: Springer Science + Business Media 163 (2): 203–226.

Björkvoll, T., S. E. Fleten, M.P. Nowak, A. Tomasgard, and S.W. Wallace. 2001. Power generation planning and risk management in a liberalized market, *IEEE Porto Power Tech Proceeding* 1: 426–431.

Borovkova, S., and H. Geman. 2006. Analysis and Modeling of Electricity Futures Prices Studies. *Studies in Nonlinear Dynamics and Econometrics* 10 (3): 1–14.

Borovkova, S., and H. Geman. 2006a. Seasonal and stochastic effects of commodity forward curve. *Review of Derivatives Research* 9 (2): 167–186.

Cabero, J., M. J. Ventosa, S. Cerisola, and A. Baillo. 2010. Modeling risk management in oligopolistic electricity markets: a Benders decomposition approach. *IEEE Transactions on Power Systems* 25: 263–271.

Carrion, M., U. Gotzes, and R. Schultz. 2009. Risk aversion for an electricity retailer with second-order stochastic dominance constraints. *Computational Management Science* 6: 233–250.

Conejo, A. J., M. Carrion, and J. M. Morales. 2010. *Decision making under uncertainty in electricity market*. International Series in Operations Research and Management Science. New York: Springer Science+Business Media.

Conejo, A. J., R. Garcia-Bertrand, M. Carrion, A. Caballero, and A. de Andres. 2008. Optimal involvement in future markets of a power producer. *IEEE Transactions on Power Systems* 23 (2): 703–711.

Cristobal, M. P., L. F. Escudero, and J. F. Monge. 2009. On stochastic dynamic programming for solving large-scale tactical production planning problems. *Computers and Operations Research* 36: 2418–2428.

Dentcheva, D., and W. Römisch. 1998. Optimal power generation under uncertainty via stochastic programming. *Stochastic Programming Methods and Technical Applications, Lecture Notes in Economics and Mathematical Systems*. New York: Springer 458: 22–56.

Dupačová, J., G. Consigli, and S. W. Wallace. 2000. Scenarios for multistage stochastic programs. *Annals of Operations Research* 100(1–4): 25–53.

Ehrenmann, A., and Y. Smeers. 2011. Stochastic equilibrium models for generation capacity expansion. In *Stochastic Optimization Methods in Finance and Energy*, edited by M. Bertocchi, G. Consigli, and M. A. H. Dempster. International Series in Operations Research and Management Science. New York: Springer Science + Business Media 163(2), 203–226.

Eppen, G. D., R. K. Martin, and L. Schrage. 1989. Scenario approach to capacity planning. *Operations Research* 34: 517–527.

Escudero, L. F., M. A. Garín, M. Merino, and G. Perez. 2012. An algorithmic framework for solving large scale multistage stochastic mixed 0-1 problems with nonsymmetric scenario trees, *Computers and Operations Research* 39: 1133–1144.

Escudero, L. F., M. A. Garín, M. Merino, and G. Perez. 2012a. Risk management for mathematical optimization under uncertainty. Part II: Algorithms for solving multistage mixed 0-1 problems with risk averse stochastic dominance constraints strategies. To be submitted.

Escudero, L. F., M. A. Garín, and G . Perez. 2007. The value of the stochastic solution in multistage problems. *TOP* 15 (1): 48–66.

Escudero L. F., J. F. Monge, D. Romero-Morales, and J. Wang. 2012. Expected future value decomposition based bid price generation for large-scale network revenue management. *Transportation Science* doi:10.1287/trsc.1120.0422

Fabian, C., G. Mitra, D. Roman, and V. Zverovich. 2011. An enhanced model for portfolio choice SSD criteria: a constructive approach. *Quantitative Finance* 11: 1525–1534.

Fleten, S. E., and T. Kristoffersen. 2008. Short-term hydropower production planning by stochastic programming. *Computers and Operations Research* 35: 2656–2671.

Fleten, S. E., and S. W. Wallace. 2009. Delta-hedging a hydropower plant using stochastic programming. In J. Kallrath, P. M. Pardalos, S. Rebennack, M. Scheidt (eds.), *Optimization in the Energy Industry*. Berlin Heidelberg: Springer-Verlag: 507–524.

Fleten, S. E., and S. W. Wallace. 1998. Power scheduling in forward contracts. *Proceedings of the Nordic MPS*. Norway: Molde, May 9–10.

Fleten, S. E., S. W. Wallace, and W. T. Ziemba. 2002. Hedging electricity portfolios via stochastic programming. In *Decision Making under Uncertainty: Energy and Power, IMA Volumes in Mathematics and its Applications*. edited by C. Greengard, A. Ruszczynski. New York: Springer 128: 71–93.

Gaivoronski, A. A., and G. Pflug. 2005.Value-at-risk in portfolio optimization: Properties and computational approach. *Journal of Risk* 7: 11–31.

Genesi, C., P. Marannino P., M. Montagna, S. Rossi, I. Siviero, L. Desiata, and G. Gentile. 2009. Risk management in long-term generation planning. *6th Int. Conference on the European Energy Market* 1–6.

Giacometti, R., M. T. Vespucci, M. Bertocchi, and G. Barone Adesi. 2011. Hedging electricity portfolio for an hydro-energy producer via stochastic programming. In *Stochastic Optimization Methods in Finance and Energy—New Financial Products and Strategies in Liberalized Energy Markets*. edited by M. Bertocchi, G. Consigli, and M. A. H. Dempster. Heidelberg: Springer International Series in Operations Research & Management Science, 163–179.

Giacometti, R., M. T. Vespucci, M. Bertocchi, and G. Barone Adesi. 2013. Deterministic and stochastic models for hedging electricity portfolio of a hydropower producer. *Statistica e Applicazioni* 57–77.

Gollmer R., U. Gotzes, and R. Schultz. 2011. A note on second-order stochastic dominance constraints induced by mixed-integer linear recourse. *Mathematical Programming* A 126: 179–190.

Gollmer, R., F. Neise, and R. Schultz. 2008. Stochastic programs with first-order stochastic dominance constraints induced by mixed-integer linear recourse. *SIAM Journal on Optimization* 19: 552–571.

Gröwe-Kuska, N., K. Kiwiel, M. Nowak, W. Römisch, and I. Wegner. 2002. Power management in a hydro-thermal system under uncertainty by Lagrangian relaxation. In C. Greengard, A. Ruszczyński (eds.), Decision Making under Uncertainty: Energy and Power, *IMA Volumes in Mathematics and its Applications*. New York: Springer, 128: 39–70.

Heitsch, H., and W. Römisch. 2007. Scenario reduction algorithms in stochastic programming. *Computational Optimization and Applications* 24: 187–206.

Heitsch, H., and W. Römisch. 2009a. Scenario tree modelling for multistage stochastic programs. *Mathematical Programming* 118: 371–406.

Heitsch, H., and W. Römisch. 2009b. Scenario tree for multistage stochastic programs. *Computational Management Science* 6: 117–133.

Latorre, J., S. Cerisola, and A. Ramos. 2007. Clustering algorithms for scenario tree generation: application to natural hydro inflows. *European Journal of Operational Research* 181(3): 1339–1353.

Maggioni, F., E. Allevi, and M. Bertocchi. 2012. Measures of information in multistage stochastic programming. In *Stochastic Programming for Implementation and Advanced Applications*, edited by L. Sakaluaskas, A. Tomasgard, and S. Wallace (STOPROG2012), 78–82.

Maggioni, F., E. Allevi, and M. Bertocchi. 2013. Bounds in multistage linear stochastic programming, Journal of Optimization Theory and Applications doi: 10.1007/S10957-013-0450-1.

Manzhos, S. 2013. On the choice of the discount rate and the role of financial variables and physical parameters in estimating the levelized cost of energy. *International Journal of Financial Studies* 1: 54–61.

Nolde, K., M. Uhr, and M. Morari. 2008. Medium term scheduling of a hydro-thermal system using stochastic model predictive control. *Automatica* 44: 1585–1594.

Pflug, G. 2001. Scenario tree generation for multiperiod financial optimization by optimal discretization. *Mathematical Programming* B 89: 251–271.

Pflug, G., and R. Hochreiter. 2007. Financial scenario generation for stochastic multi-stage decision processes as facility location problem. *Annals of Operations Research* 152(1): 257–272.

Philpott, A., M. Craddock, and H. Waterer. 2000. Hydro-electric unit commitment subject to uncertain demand. *European Journal of Operational Research* 125: 410–424.

Rockafellar, R. T., and S. Uryasev. 2000. Optimization of conditional value-at-risk. *Journal of Risk* 2: 21–41.

Rockafellar, R. T., and S. Uryasev. 2002. Conditional value-at-risk for general loss distributions. *Journal of Banking and Finance* 26: 1443–1471.

Ruszczyński, A., and A. Shapiro, eds. 2003. *Stochastic Programming*. 1st ed. *Ser. Handbook in Operations Research and Management Science*, vol. 10. Amsterdam: Elsevier.

Shapiro A., D. Dentcheva, and A. Ruszczyński. 2009. *Lectures on Stochastic Programming. Modeling and Theory*. MPS-SIAM Series on Optimization. Philadelphia: SIAM.

Schultz, R., and S. Tiedemann. 2006. Conditional Value-at-Risk in stochastic programs with mixed-integer recourse. *Mathematical Programming* Ser. B 105: 365–386.

Takriti, S., B. Krasenbrink, and L. S. Y. Wu. 2000. Incorporating fuel constraints and electricity spot prices into the stochastic unit commitment problem. *Operations Research* 48: 268–280.

Vespucci, M. T., M. Bertocchi, M. Innorta, and S. Zigrino. 2013. Deterministic and stochastic models for investment in different technologies for electricity production in the long period, *Central European Journal of Operations Research* 22(2): 407–426.

Vespucci, M. T., F. Maggioni, M. Bertocchi, and M. Innorta. 2012. A stochastic model for the daily coordination of pumped storage hydro plants and wind power plants. In G. Pflug and R. Hochreither, eds., *Annals of Operations* 193: 191–105.

Vespucci, M. T., M. Bertocchi, P. Pisciella, and S. Zigrino. 2014. Two-stage mixed integer stochastic optimization model for power generation capacity expansion with risk measures, submitted to *Optimization Methods and Software*.

Vitoriano, B., S. Cerisola, and A. Ramos. 2000. Generating scenario trees for hydro inflows. *6th International Conference on Probabilistic Methods Applied to Power Systems PSP3-106*, Portugal: Madeira.

Von Neumann, J., and O. Morgenstern. 1944. *Theory of games and economic behaviour*, Princeton: Princeton University Press.

Wallace, S. W., and S. E. Fleten. 2003. Stochastic programming models in energy. In *Stochastic programming, Handbooks in Operations Research and Management Science*, edited by A. Ruszczyński and A. Shapiro. Amsterdam: Elsevier, 637–677.

Yamin, H. 2004. Review on methods of generation scheduling in electric power systems. *Electric Power Systems Research* 69 (2–3): 227–248.

Portfolio Management

CHAPTER 7

Portfolio Optimization: Theory and Practice

William T. Ziemba
Alumni Professor of Financial Modeling and
Stochastic Optimization (Emeritus),
University of British Columbia

Distinguished Visiting Research Associate
Systemic Risk Center, London School of Economics

STATIC PORTFOLIO THEORY

In the static portfolio theory case, suppose there are n assets, $i = 1, \dots, n$, with random returns $\xi_1, \dots, \xi_n$. The return on asset i, namely ξ_i, is the capital appreciation plus dividends in the next investment period such as monthly, quarterly, or yearly or some other time period. The n assets have the distribution $F(\xi_1, \dots, \xi_n)$ with known mean vector $\bar{\xi} = (\bar{\xi}_1, \dots, \bar{\xi}_n)$ and known $n \times n$ variance-covariance matrix Σ with typical covariance σ_{ij} for $i \neq j$ and variance σ_i^2 for $i = j$. A basic assumption (relaxed in section 6) is that the return distributions are independent of the asset weight choices, so $F \neq \varphi(x)$.

A mean-variance frontier is

$$\phi(\delta) = \text{Maximize } \bar{\xi}' x$$
$$s.t. \quad x' \Sigma x \leq \delta$$
$$e' x = w_0$$
$$x \in K$$

where e is a vector of ones, $x = (x_1, \dots, x_n)$ are the asset weights, K represents other constraints on the x, and w_0 is the investor's initial wealth.

When variance is parameterized with $\delta > 0$, it yields a concave curve, as in Figure 7.1(a). This is a Markowitz (1952, 1987, 2006) mean-variance efficient frontier and optimally trades off mean, which is desirable, with variance, which is undesirable. Tobin (1958) extended the Markowitz model to include a risk-free asset with mean ξ_0 and no variance. Then the efficient frontier concave curve becomes the straight line as shown in Figure 7.1(b). The standard deviation here is plotted rather than the variance to make the line straight. An investor will pick an optimal portfolio in the Markowitz model by using a utility function that trades off mean for variance or, equivalently, standard deviation, as shown in Figure 7.1(a), to yield portfolio A. For the Tobin model, one does a simpler calculation to find the optimal portfolio that will be on the straight line in Figure 7.1(b) between the risk-free asset and the market index M. Here, the investor picks portfolio B that is two-thirds cash (risk-free asset) and one-third market index. The market index may be proxied by the S&P500 or Wilshire 5000 value weighted indices. Since all investors choose between cash and the market index, this separation of the investor's problem into finding the market index independent of the investor's assumed concave utility function and then where to be on the line for a given utility function is called Tobin's separation theorem. Ziemba, Parkan, and Brooks-Hill (1974) discuss this and show how to compute the market index and optimal weights of cash and the market index for various utility functions and constraints. They show how to calculate the straight-line efficient frontier in Figure 1 with a simple n variable deterministic linear complementary problem or a quadratic program. That calculation of Tobin's separation theorem means that for every concave, nondecreasing utility function u, the solution of the optimal ratio of risky assets, $i = 1, \ldots, n$, is the same. Hence, x_i^*/x_j^*, $i, j = 1, \ldots, n, i \neq j$ is the same for all $u \in U_2 = [u|u' \geq 0, u'' \leq 0]$.

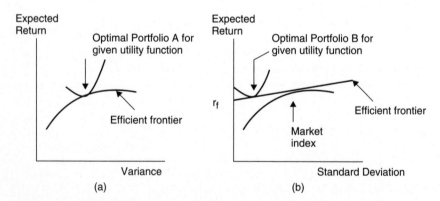

FIGURE 7.1 Two efficient frontiers: (a) Markowitz mean-variance efficient frontier; (b) Tobin's risk-free asset and separation theorem.

The portfolio problem is

$$\max_{x \geq 0} \quad E_\xi u(\xi' x)$$
$$e'x = 1 \tag{7.1}$$

where $\hat{\xi} = (\xi_0, \xi_1, \ldots, \xi_n) = (\xi_0, \xi)$, ξ_0 is the risk-free asset, and $\xi \sim N(\bar{\xi}, \Sigma)$ with initial wealth $w_0 = 1$.

In step 1, one solves the n-variable deterministic linear complementary problem (LCP),

$$w = Mz - \bar{\xi}, \quad w^t z = 0, \quad w \geq 0, \quad z \geq 0$$

where $\bar{\bar{\xi}} = \bar{\xi}_i - \xi_0, i = i, \ldots, m$ or the quadratic program min $-\bar{\bar{\xi}}'z + \frac{1}{2}z'z$ s.t. $z \geq 0$ for the optimal risky asset weights, which are

$$x_i^* = \frac{z_i^*}{e^* z^*}, \quad i = 1, \ldots, n.$$

This LCP is derived as follows. The slope of the efficient frontier line in Figure 7.1 is found by

Maximizing $\quad \dfrac{\bar{\xi}'x - \xi_0}{(x'\Sigma x)^{1/2}} \quad$ s.t. $\quad e'x = 1, \ x \in K,$

which is equivalent to

Max $g(x) = \dfrac{\bar{\bar{\xi}}'x}{(x'\Sigma x)^{1/2}} \quad$ s.t. $\quad e'x = 1, x \in K$

where $\bar{\bar{\xi}}_i = \bar{\xi}_i - \xi_0$.

Since $g(x)$ is linear homogeneous and assuming $\lambda x \in K$, where $g(\lambda x) = g(x)$ for $\lambda \geq 0$, then the Kuhn–Tucker conditions can be written as the LCP problem above, where $w_i = -\bar{\bar{\xi}}_i + \Sigma_i z$, and Σ_i is the ith row of Σ. From the theory of the LCP, see, for example, Murty (1972); there is a unique solution, since Σ is positive definite.

This gives the market index $M = \sum_{i=1}^n \xi_i' x_i^*$ independent of u. Then in step 2, one determines the optimal ratio of M and the risk-free asset. So for a given $u \in U_2$ from the single variable $\alpha \in (-\infty, 1]$, in Figure 7.1(b), $\alpha = 1$ is M, $\alpha = 1/2$ if half M and half ξ_0, and $\alpha = -3$ means that three of the risk-free asset ξ_0 is borrowed to invest four in M. The optimal allocation in the risk-free asset is α^*, and the optimal allocation in risky asset $i, i = 1, \ldots, n$ is $(1 - \alpha^*)x_i^*, i = 1, \ldots, n$, which are obtained by solving

$$\max_{-\infty \leq \alpha \leq 1} E_M u(\alpha \xi_0 + (1 - \alpha)M) \qquad (7.2)$$

where $M = \xi'x^* \sim N(\overline{\xi'}x^*, x^{*'}\Sigma x^*)$, and $\xi = (\xi_1, \ldots, \xi_n)$.

One may solve (7.2) using a search algorithm such as golden sections or a bisecting search; see Zangwill (1969). Examples with data and specific utility functions appear in Ziemba, Parkan, and Brooks-Hill (1974). Ziemba (1974) generalized this to certain classes of infinite variance stable distributions. That analysis, though more complex, follows the normal distribution case. In place of variances, dispersions are used. Under the assumptions one has the convexity of the risk measure property that is analogous to Figure 7.1. That paper, as well as many other important classic papers, discussions, and extensive problems, are reprinted in Ziemba and Vickson (1975, 2006).

Figure 7.1(b) illustrates the Sharpe (1964)–Lintner (1965)–Mossin (1966) capital asset pricing model, which has $E(R_i) = \alpha_i + \beta_i E(R_M)$, where $E(R_i)$ and $E(R_M)$ are the mean return of the asset and the market, respectively, α_i is the excess return from this asset, and β_i is the asset's correlation with the market, M.

Referring to Figure 7.1(a), the point A is determined through a trade-off of expected return and variance. This trade-off is determined through risk aversion. The standard way to measure absolute risk aversion is via the Arrow (1965)–Pratt (1964) absolute risk aversion index

$$R_A(w) = \frac{-u''(w)}{u'(w)}.$$

Risk tolerance as used in the investment world is

$$R_T(w) = \frac{100}{\frac{1}{2}R_A(w)}.$$

$R_A = 4$, represents the standard pension fund strategy 60–40 stock bond mix corresponds to $R_T = 50$ (independent of wealth).

$R_A(w)$ represents all the essential information about the investor's utility function $u(w)$, which is only defined up to a linear transformation, while eliminating everything arbitrary about u, since

$$u(w) \sim \int e^{\int R_A(w)}$$

The major theoretical reasons for the use of R_A is

$$R_A^1(w) \geq R_A^2(w) \quad \Longleftrightarrow \quad \pi_1(w, z) \geq \pi_2(w, z) \quad \text{for all } w, z$$

$$\Longleftrightarrow \quad p_1(w, h) \geq p_2(w, h) \quad \text{for all } w, h$$

$\underbrace{\qquad\qquad\qquad\qquad}_{\text{formula replicates behavior}}$ $\underbrace{\qquad\qquad\qquad\qquad\qquad\qquad}_{\text{behavior}}$

where the risk premium $\pi(w, z)$ is defined so that the decision maker is indifferent to receiving the random risk z and the nonrandom amount $\bar{z} - \pi = -\pi$, where $\bar{z} = 0$ and $u[w - \pi] = E_z u(w + z)$ (this defines π). When u is concave, $\pi \geq 0$.

For σ_z^2 small, a Taylor series approximation yields

$$\pi(w, z) = \frac{1}{2}\sigma_z^2 R_A(w) + \text{small errors}$$

and for the special risk

$$z = \begin{cases} +h & pr = \frac{1}{2} \\ \\ -h & pr = \frac{1}{2} \end{cases}$$

where $p(w, h) = $ probability premium $= P(z = h) - P(z + h)$ such that the decision maker is indifferent between status quo and the risk z.

$$u(w) = E_z u(w + z) = \frac{1}{2}[1 + p(w, h)]u(w + h) + \frac{1}{2}[1 - p(w, h)]u(x - h).$$

$$(7.3)$$

Equation 7.3 defines p.

By a Taylor series approximation, $p(w, h) = \frac{1}{2}h R_A(w) + \text{small errors}$.

So risk premiums and probability premiums rise when risk aversion rises and vice versa.

Good utility functions, such as those in the general class of decreasing risk aversion functions $u'(w) = (w^a + b)^{-c}$, $a > 0$, $c > 0$, contain log, power, negative power, arctan, and so on. Decreasing absolute risk aversion utility functions are preferred because they are the class where a decision maker attaches a positive risk premium to any risk ($\pi(w, z) > 0$), but a smaller premium to any given risk the larger his wealth

$$\left(\frac{\partial \pi(w, z)}{\partial w} \leq 0 \right).$$

A key result is

$$\underbrace{\frac{\partial R_A(w)}{\partial w} \le 0}_{\text{formula replicates behavior}} \iff \underbrace{\frac{\partial \pi(w,z)}{\partial w} \le 0 \iff \frac{\partial p(w,h)}{\partial w} \le 0}_{\text{behavior}} \quad \text{for all } w, z, h > 0.$$

So decreasing absolute risk-aversion utility functions replicates those where the risk premium and probability premium are decreasing in wealth.

An individual's utility function and risk aversion index can be estimated using the double exponential utility function

$$u(w) = -e^{-aw} - be^{-cw}$$

where a, b, and c are constants. An example using the certainty-equivalent and gain-and-loss equivalent methods is in Figure 7.2 for Donald Hausch (my coauthor of various horse-racing books and articles) when he was a

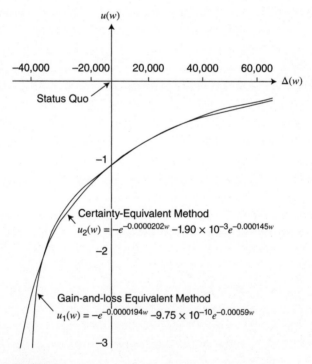

FIGURE 7.2 Utility of wealth function for Donald Hausch.

student. See the appendix, which describes these estimation methods. This function is strictly concave and strictly increasing and has decreasing absolute risk aversion.

Hausch's utility function was fit by least squares, and both methods provide similar curves. His absolute risk aversion is decreasing, see Figure 7.3(a,b), and nearly constant in his investment range where initial wealth w_0 changes by $\pm 10,000$ corresponding to R_A between 2.0 and 2.5.

$$-w \left[\frac{u''(w)}{u'(w)} \right]$$

His relative risk aversion is increasing and linear in his investment range.

The Arrow–Pratt risk aversion index is the standard way to measure risk aversion, but the little-known Rubinstein risk aversion measure is actually optimal, assuming normal (discussed here) or symmetric distributions. Indeed, Kallberg and Ziemba (1983) showed that given utility functions u_1 and u_2, initial wealth w_1 and w_2, and assets $(\xi_1, \ldots, \xi_n) \sim N(\bar{\xi}, \Sigma)$, and then if

$$-\frac{E_\xi u_1''(w_1 \xi' x^*)}{E_\xi u_1'(w_1 \xi' x^*)} = \frac{E_\xi u_2''(w_2 \xi' x^*)}{E_\xi u_2'(w_2 \xi' x^*)}$$

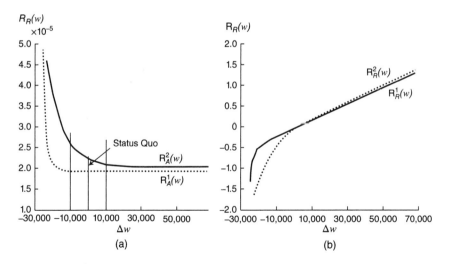

FIGURE 7.3 Risk aversion functions for Donald Hausch (a) absolute risk aversion function estimated by the certainly equivalent method (1) and gain and loss equivalent method; (b) relative risk aversion function estimated by the certainly equivalent method (1) and gain and loss equivalent method (2).

where x^* solves

$$\max_{\substack{s.t.\ x \in K, e'x=w}} E_\xi u_1(w_1 \xi' x),$$

then x^* solves

$$\max_{\substack{s.t.\ x \in K, e'x=1}} E_\xi u_2(w_2 \xi' x).$$

Hence, if two investors have the same Rubinstein risk aversion measure, they will then have the same optimal portfolio weights. As shown in Figure 7.4a,b,c,d, special exponential and negative power with the same average risk aversion have very similar mean, variance, expected utility, and portfolio weights and these are very different than with quadratic or exponential utility. When two utility functions have the same average risk aversion, then they have very similar optimal portfolio weights. Here $u_4(w) = e^{-\beta_4/w}$ and $u_6(w) = (w - w_0)^{-\beta_6}$ are different utility functions but their average risk aversions have similar ranges, and these are very different than the quadratic and exponential utilities in Figure 7.4a,b. The size of the errors is shown in Table 7.1 for fixed risk aversion of $R_A = 4$.

The basic theory of Markowitz, Sharpe, and Tobin assumes that the parameters are known. The real world, of course, does not have constant parameters. So let's look first at the errors associated with parameter errors and later at models (stochastic programming) where the probability distribution of asset returns is explicitly considered.

TABLE 7.1 Optimal Portfolio Weights for Alternative Utility Functions and $\overline{R}_A = 4$.

Security/ Static	Exponential 4.0	Quadratic (0.351447)	Log (−0.832954)	Special Exponential (2.884400)	Negative Power (1.443557)
1	0.088219	0.082991	0.046975	0.021224	0.047611
2	0.169455	0.165982	0.116220	0.185274	0.112794
3	0.106894	0.106663	0.080160	0.104064	0.079600
4	0.194026	0.198830	0.161247	0.048522	0.154474
5	0.441385	0.445533	0.343318	0.441182	0.328958
6					
7					
8					
9					
10			0.252077	0.199733	0.258232
Mean	1.186170	1.185175	1.151634	1.158397	1.149527
Variance	0.037743	0.037247	0.024382	0.027802	0.023756
Expected utility	0.988236	0.988236	0.987863	0.987589	0.987821
Percent error	—	0	0.703000	0.709900	0.782700

Source: Kallberg and Ziemba, 1983

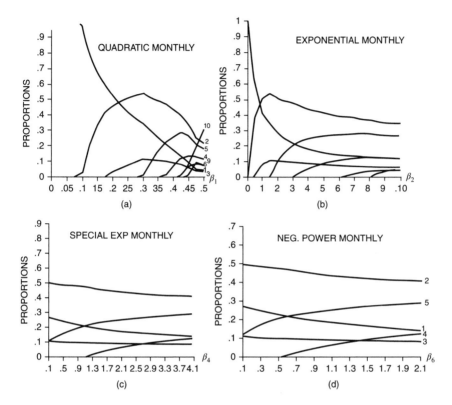

FIGURE 7.4 Functional forms asset weights: (a) Quadratic monthly $U_1(w) = w - \beta_1 w^2$; (b) Exp monthly $U_2(w) = 1 - e^{-\beta_2 w}$; (c) Special exp monthly $U_4(w) = -e^{\frac{\beta_4}{w}}$; (d) Neg power monthly $U_6(w) = (w - W_0)^{-\beta_6}$.
Source: Kallberg and Ziemba, 1983

IMPORTANCE OF MEANS

Means are by far the most important part of any return distribution for actual portfolio results. If you are to have good results in any portfolio problem, you must have good mean estimates for future returns:

> If asset X has cumulative distribution $F(\cdot)$ and asset Y has $G(\cdot)$ and these cumulative distribution functions cross only once, then asset X dominates asset Y for all increasing concave utility functions, that is, has higher expected utility, if and only if the mean of X exceeds the mean of Y.

This useful result of Hanoch and Levy (1969) implies that the variance and other moments are unimportant for single crossing distributions.

Only the means count. With normal distributions, X and Y will cross only once if and only if the standard deviation of asset X is less than the standard deviation of asset Y. This is the basic equivalence of mean-variance analysis and expected utility analysis via second-order (concave, nondecreasing) stochastic dominance. This is shown in Figure 7.5, where the second-degree and mean-variance dominance is on the left. There is no dominance on the right because there are two crosses. This F has a higher mean but also higher variance than G. The densities f and g are plotted here for convenience and give the same results as if the cumulative distribution functions F and G were plotted.

Errors in inputs can lead to significant losses (Figure 7.6) and larger turnover (Figure 7.7). Additional calculations appear in Kallberg and Ziemba (1981, 1984) and Chopra and Ziemba (1993).

The error depends on the risk tolerance, the reciprocal of the Arrow–Pratt risk aversion $\left(R_T = \frac{100}{\frac{1}{2} R_A} \right)$. However See Table 7.2, errors in means, variances, and covariances are roughly 20:2:1 times as important, respectively. But with low risk aversion, like log, the ratios can be 100:2:1. So good estimates are by far the most crucial aspect for successful application of a mean-variance analysis, and we will see that in all other stochastic modeling approaches.

The sensitivity of the mean carries into multiperiod models. There the effect is strongest in period 1, then less and less in future periods; see Geyer and Ziemba (2008). This is illustrated in Figures 7.8 and 7.9 for a five-period, 10-year model designed for the Siemen's Austria pension fund

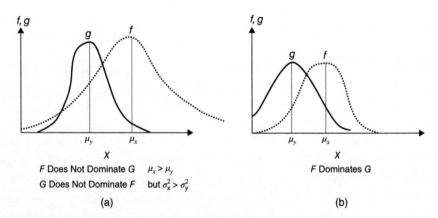

FIGURE 7.5 Mean variance and second order stochastic dominance: (a) Dominance does not exist; (b) Dominance exists.

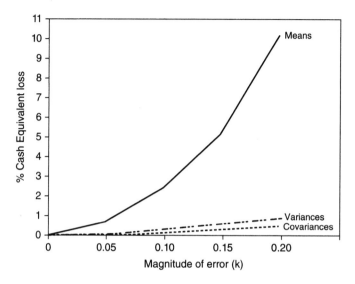

FIGURE 7.6 Mean percentage cash equivalent loss due to errors in inputs.
Source: Chopra-Ziemba, 1993

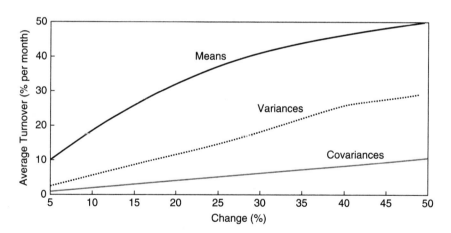

FIGURE 7.7 Average turnover for different percentage changes in means, variances, and covariances.
Source: Chopra, 1993

TABLE 7.2 Average Ratio of CEL for Errors in Means, Variances, and Covariances.

Risk Tolerance	Errors in Means vs. Covariances	Errors in Means vs. Variances	Errors in Variances vs. Covariances
25	5.38	3.22	1.67
50	22.50	10.98	2.05
75	56.84	21.42	2.68
	↓	↓	↓
	20	10	2
	Error Mean	Error Var	Error Covar
	20	2	1

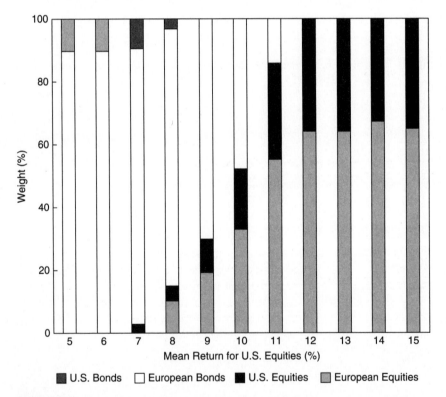

FIGURE 7.8 Optimal equity and bond allocations in period 1 of the InnoALM model.
Source: Geyer and Ziemba 2008

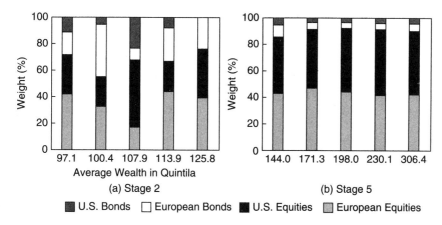

FIGURE 7.9 The effects of state-dependent correlations: optimal weights conditional on quintiles of portfolio weights in periods 2 and 5 of the InnoALM model: (a) Stage 2; (b) Stage 5.
Source: Geyer and Ziemba 2008

that is discussed later in this chapter. There it is seen that in period 1, with bond means for the U.S. and Europe in the 6 to 7 percent area, the optimal allocation to European and U.S. equity can be fully 100 percent.

STOCHASTIC PROGRAMMING APPROACH TO ASSET LIABILITY MANAGEMENT

I now discuss my approach using scenarios and optimization to model asset-liability decisions for pension funds, insurance companies, individuals, retirement, bank trading departments, hedge funds, and so on. It includes the essential problem elements: uncertainties, constraints, risks, transactions costs, liquidity, and preferences over time, to provide good results in normal times and avoid or limit disaster when extreme scenarios occur. The stochastic programming approach, while complex, is a practical way to include key problem elements that other approaches are not able to model.

Other approaches (static mean variance, fixed mix, stochastic control, capital growth, continuous time finance, etc.) are useful for the microanalysis of decisions, and the SP approach is useful for the aggregated macro (overall) analysis of relevant decisions and activities. They yield good results most of the time, but frequently lead to the recipe for disaster: overbetting and not being truly diversified at a time when an extreme scenario occurs. It pays to make a complex stochastic programming model when a lot is at stake and the essential problem has many complications.

The accuracy of the actual scenarios chosen and their probabilities contribute greatly to model success. However, the scenario approach generally leads to superior investment performance, even if there are errors in the estimations of both the actual scenario outcomes and their probabilities. It is not possible to include all scenarios, or even some that may actually occur. The modeling effort attempts to cover well the range of possible future evolution of the economic environment. The predominant view is that such models do not exist, are impossible to successfully implement, or are prohibitively expensive. I argue that given modern computer power, better large-scale stochastic linear programming codes, and better modeling skills, such models can be widely used in many applications and are very cost effective.

We know from Harry Markowitz's work and that of others that mean-variance models are useful in an assets-only situation. From my consulting at Frank Russell, I know that professionals adjust means (mean-reversion, James-Stein, etc.) and constrain output weights.

They do not change asset positions unless the advantage of the change is significant. Also, they do not use mean-variance analysis with liabilities and other major market imperfections except as a first test analysis. Mean-variance models can be modified and applied in various ways to analyze many problems; see Markowitz (1987) and Grinold and Khan (1999) for examples. Masters of this have used Barra Risk Factor Analysis, which analyzes any question via a simple mean-variance model. But mean-variance models define risk as a terminal wealth surprise, regardless of direction, and make no allowance for skewness preference. Moreover, they treat assets with option features inappropriately, as shown in Figure 7.10.

But we will use in my models a relative of variance—namely, the convex risk measure weighted downside target violations—and that will avoid such objections.

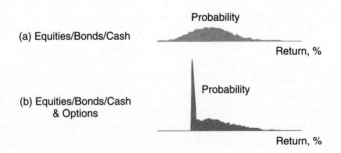

FIGURE 7.10 Two distributions with the same mean and variance.

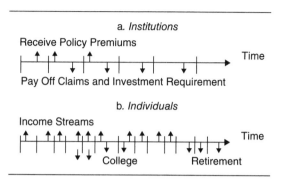

FIGURE 7.11 Time and events in institutional and individual ALM models.

Asset-liability problems can be for institutions or individuals (Figure 7.11). My experience is that the latter is much more difficult because one must make models useful for many individuals, and people change their assets, goals, and preferences, and hide assets. Basic references are Ziemba and Mulvey (1998), Zenios and Ziemba (2006, 2007), and Gassman and Ziemba (2013) that contain theory, computations, and many case studies. See also Wallace and Ziemba (2005), which has descriptions of computer codes as well as applications.

Possible approaches to model ALM situations include:

- **Simulation:** There is usually too much output to understand, but it is very useful as check.
- **Mean variance:** This is okay for one period but hard to use in multi-period problems and with liabilities. It assumes means and variances are known.
- **Expected log:** Very risky strategies that do not diversify well; fractional Kelly with downside constraints are excellent for multiperiod risky investment betting (see Section 6).
- **Stochastic control:** Bang-bang policies; see the Brennan-Schwartz paper in Ziemba and Mulvey (1998) on how to constrain to be practical.
- **Stochastic programming/stochastic control:** Mulvey—see Mulvey (1996), Mulvey and Pauling (2002), and Mulvey et al. (2007)—uses this approach, which is a form of volatility pumping, discussed in general by Luenberger (1998).
- **Stochastic programming:** This is my approach.

Continuous time modeling, though popular in the academic world, seems to be impractical in the real world, as Figure 7.12 shows. Here, the

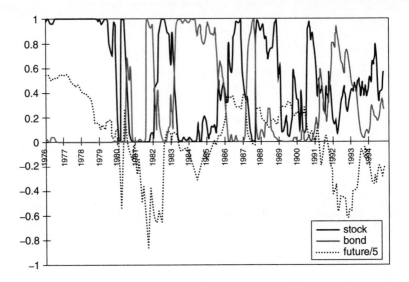

FIGURE 7.12 Asset weights over time with a stochastic control continuous time Merton type model.
Source: Brennan and Schwartz (1998)

asset proportions from a Merton (1992) stochastic control type model are stocks, bonds, and interest rate futures representing spot and future interest rates.

The stochastic programming approach is ideally suited to analyze such problems with the following features:

- Multiple time periods; end effects—steady state after decision horizon adds one more decision period to the model
- Consistency with economic and financial theory for interest rates, bond prices, etc.
- Discrete scenarios for random elements—returns, liability costs, currency movements
- Utilization of various forecasting models, handle fat tails
- Institutional, legal, and policy constraints
- Model derivatives, illiquid assets, and transactions costs
- Expressions of risk in terms understandable to decision makers (the more you lose, the more is the penalty for losing)
- Maximize long-run expected profits net of expected discounted convex penalty costs for shortfalls, paying more and more penalty for shortfalls as they increase
- Model as constraints or penalty costs in the objective to maintain adequate reserves and cash levels and meet regularity requirements

We can now solve very realistic multiperiod problems on PCs. If the current situation has never occurred before, then use one that's similar to add scenarios. For a crisis in Brazil, use Russian crisis data, for example. The results of the SP will give you good advice when times are normal and keep you out of severe trouble when times are bad.

Those using SP models may lose 5, 10, or even 15 percent, but they will not lose 50, 70, or even 95 percent, like some investors and hedge funds. If the scenarios are more or less accurate and the problem elements reasonably modeled, the SP will give good advice. You might slightly underperform in normal markets but you will greatly overperform in bad markets when other approaches may blow up.

These models make you diversify, which is the key for keeping out of trouble. My work in stochastic programming began in my Ph.D. work at Berkeley. In 1974, I taught my first stochastic programming class and that led to early papers with my students Jarl Kallberg and Martin Kusy; see Kallberg, White and Ziemba (1982) and Kusy and Ziemba (1986). Table 7.3 illustrates the models we built at Frank Russell in the 1990s.

In Cariño, Myers, and Ziemba (1998), we showed that stochastic programming models usually beat fix-mix models. The latter are basically volatility pumping models (buy low, sell high); see Luenberger (1998). Figure 7.13 illustrates how the optimal weights change, depending on previous periods' results. Despite good results, fixed-mix and buy-and-hold

TABLE 7.3 Russell Business Engineering Models.

Model	Type of Application	Year Delivered	Number of Scenarios	Computer Hardware
Russell-Yasuda (Tokyo)	Property and Casualty Insurance	1991	256	IBM RISC 6000
Mitsubishi Trust (Tokyo)	Pension Consulting	1994	2000	IBM RISC 6000 with Parallel Processors
Swiss Bank Corp (Basle)	Pension Consulting	1996	8000	IBM UNIX2
Daido Life Insurance Company (Tokyo)	Life Insurance	1997	25,600	IBM PC
Banca Fideuram (Rome)	Assets Only Personal	1997	10,000	IBM UNIX2 and PC
Consulting Clients	Assets Only Institutional	1998	various	IBM UNIX2 and PC

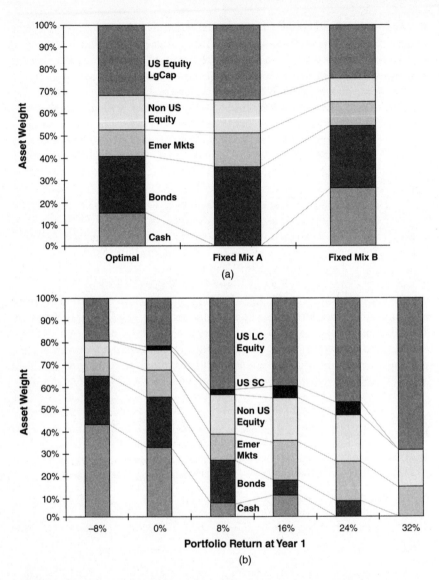

FIGURE 7.13 Example portfolios: (a) Initial portfolios of the three strategies; (b) Contingent allocations at year one.

strategies do not utilize new information from return occurrences in their construction. By making the strategy scenario dependent using a multiperiod stochastic programming model, a better outcome is possible.

We compare two strategies:

1. The dynamic stochastic programming strategy, which is the full optimization of the multiperiod model; and
2. The fixed mix in which the portfolios from the mean-variance frontier have allocations rebalanced back to that mix at each stage; buy when low and sell when high. This is like covered calls, which is the opposite of portfolio insurance.

Consider fixed mix strategies A (64–36 stock–bond mix) and B (46–54 stock–bond mix). The optimal stochastic programming strategy dominates as shown in Figure 7.14.

A further study of the performance of stochastic dynamic and fixed-mix portfolio models was made by Fleten, Høyland, and Wallace (2002). They compared two alternative versions of a portfolio model for the Norwegian life insurance company Gjensidige NOR, namely multistage stochastic linear programming and the fixed-mix constant rebalancing study. They found that the multiperiod stochastic programming model dominated the fixed-mix approach but the degree of dominance is much

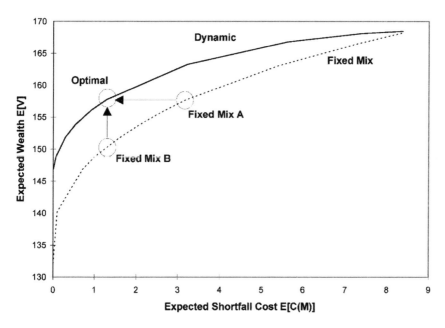

FIGURE 7.14 The optimal stochastic strategy dominates fixed mix.

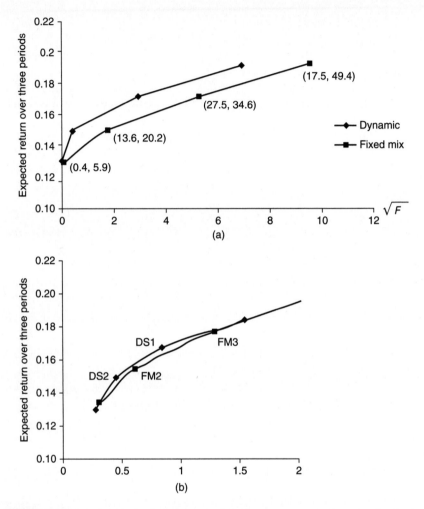

FIGURE 7.15 Comparison of advantage of stochastic programming over fixed mix model in and out of sample: (a) In-sample; (b) Out-of-sample.
Source: Fleten et al. (2002)

smaller out-of-sample than in-sample; see Figure 7.15. This is because out-of-sample, the random input data are structurally different from in-sample, so the stochastic programming model loses its advantage in optimally adapting to the information available in the scenario tree. Also, the performance of the fixed-mix approach improves because the asset mix is updated at each stage.

The Russell-Yasuda Kasai was the first large-scale multiperiod stochastic programming model implemented for a major financial institution; see Henriques (1991). As a consultant to the Frank Russell Company during 1989 to 1991, I designed the model. The team of David Cariño, Taka Eguchi, David Myers, Celine Stacy, and Mike Sylvanus at Russell in Tacoma, Washington, implemented the model for the Yasuda Fire and Marine Insurance Co., Ltd. in Tokyo under the direction of research head Andy Turner. Roger Wets and my former UBC Ph.D. student Chanaka Edirishinghe helped as consultants in Tacoma, and Kats Sawaki was a consultant to Yasuda Kasai in Japan to advise them on our work. Kats, a member of my 1974 UBC class in stochastic programming where we started to work on ALM models, was then a professor at Nanzan University in Nagoya and acted independently of our Tacoma group. Kouji Watanabe headed the group in Tokyo, which included Y. Tayama, Y. Yazawa, Y. Ohtani, T. Amaki, I. Harada, M. Harima, T. Morozumi, and N. Ueda.

Experience has shown that we should not be concerned with getting all the scenarios exactly right when using stochastic programming models. You cannot do this, and it does not matter much, anyway. Rather, you should worry that you have the problem periods laid out reasonably and that the scenarios basically cover the means, the tails, and the chance of what could happen.

Back in 1990/1991, computations were a major focus of concern. I knew how to formulate the model, which was an outgrowth of Kallberg, White, and Ziemba (1982) and Kusy and Ziemba (1986). David Cariño did much of the formulation details. Originally, we had 10 periods and 2,048 scenarios. It was too big to solve at that time and became an intellectual challenge for the stochastic programming community. Bob Entriken, D. Jensen, R. Clark, and Alan King of IBM Research worked on its solution but never quite cracked it. We quickly realized that 10 periods made the model far too difficult to solve and also too cumbersome to collect the data and interpret the results, and the 2,048 scenarios were at that time too large a number to deal with. About two years later, Hercules Vladimirou, working with Alan King at IBM Research, was able to effectively solve the original model using parallel processing on several workstations.

The Russell-Yasuda model was designed to satisfy the following need as articulated by Kunihiko Sasamoto, director and deputy president of Yasuda Kasai:

> The liability structure of the property and casualty insurance business has become very complex, and the insurance industry has various restrictions in terms of asset management. We concluded that existing models, such as Markowitz mean variance, would not function well and that we needed to develop a new asset/liability management model.

The Russell-Yasuda Kasai model is now at the core of all asset/liability work for the firm. We can define our risks in concrete terms, rather than through an abstract measure like, in business terms, standard deviation. The model has provided an important side benefit by pushing the technology and efficiency of other models in Yasuda forward to complement it. The model has assisted Yasuda in determining when and how human judgment is best used in the asset/liability process (Cariño et al., 1994). The model was a big success and of great interest both in the academic and institutional investment asset-liability communities.

The Yasuda Fire and Marine Insurance Company

The Yasuda Fire and Marine Insurance Company called Yasuda Kasai (meaning fire) is based in Tokyo. It began operations in 1888 and was the second largest Japanese property and casualty insurer and seventh largest in the world by revenue in 1989. Its main business was voluntary automobile (43.0 percent), personal accident (14.4 percent), compulsory automobile (13.7 percent), fire and allied (14.4 percent), and other (14.5 percent). The firm had assets of 3.47 trillion yen (US$26.2 billion) at the end of fiscal 1991 (March 31, 1992). In 1988, Yasuda Kasai and Russell signed an agreement to deliver a dynamic stochastic asset allocation model by April 1, 1991. Work began in September 1989. The goal was to implement a model of Yasuda Kasai's financial planning process to improve its investment and liability payment decisions and overall risk management. In 1989, after Russell could not determine how to do this, I proposed a stochastic programming model, which we then built at Russell in Tacoma.

The business goals were to:

1. Maximize long run expected wealth.
2. Pay enough on the insurance policies to be competitive in current yield.
3. Maintain adequate current and future reserves and cash levels.
4. Meet regulatory requirements, especially with the increasing number of saving-oriented policies being sold that were generating new types of liabilities.

The following is a summary of the Russell Yasuda model and its results. See, also, the original papers by Cariño Ziemba et al. (1994, 1998ab) and the survey by Ziemba (2006):

- The model needed to have more realistic definitions of operational risks and business constraints than the return variance used in previous mean-variance models used at Yasuda Kasai.

- The implemented model determines an optimal multiperiod investment strategy that enables decision makers to define risks in tangible operational terms such as cash shortfalls.
- The risk measure used is convex and penalizes target violations more and more as the violations of various kinds and in various periods increase.
- The objective is to maximize the discounted expected wealth at the horizon net of expected discounted penalty costs incurred during the five periods of the model.
- This objective is similar to a mean-variance model, except that it is over five periods and only counts downside risk through target violations.
- I greatly prefer this approach to VaR or CVaR and its variants for ALM applications because for most people and organizations, the nonattainment of goals is more and more damaging, not linear in the nonattainment (as in CVaR) or not considering the size of the nonattainment at all (as in VaR); see Ziemba (2013).
- A reference on VaR and CVaR as risk measures is Artzner et al. (1999). They argue that good risk measures should be coherent and satisfy a set of axioms.

The convex risk measure I use is coherent. Rockafellar and Ziemba (2013) define a set of axioms that justify these convex risk measures:

- The model formulates and meets the complex set of regulations imposed by Japanese insurance laws and practices.
- The most important of the intermediate horizon commitments is the need to produce income sufficiently high to pay the required annual interest in the savings type insurance policies without sacrificing the goal of maximizing long-run expected wealth.
- During the first two years of use, fiscal 1991 and 1992, the investment strategy recommended by the model yielded a superior income return of 42 basis points (US$79 million) over what a mean-variance model would have produced. Simulation tests also show the superiority of the stochastic programming scenario–based model over a mean-variance approach.
- In addition to the revenue gains, there have been considerable organizational and informational benefits.
- The model had 256 scenarios over four periods, plus a fifth end-effects period.
- The model is flexible regarding the time horizon and length of decision periods, which are multiples of quarters.

- A typical application has initialization, plus period 1 to the end of the first quarter; period 2 the remainder of fiscal year 1; period 3 the entire fiscal year 2, period 4 fiscal years 3, 4, and 5; and period 5, the end effects years 6 on to forever.

Figure 7.16 shows the multistage stochastic linear programming structure of the Russell-Yasuda Kasai model.

The basic formulation of the model is as follows. The objective of the model is to allocate discounted fund value among asset classes to maximize the expected wealth at the end of the planning horizon T less expected penalized shortfalls accumulated throughout the planning horizon:

$$\text{Maximize } E\left[W_T - \sum_{t=1}^{T} c_i\left(w_t\right)\right]$$

subject to budget constraints

$$\sum_n X_{nt} - V_t = 0,$$

asset accumulation relations

$$V_{t+1} - \sum_n (1 + RP_{nt+1} + RI_{nt+1})X_{nt} = F_{t+1} - P_{t+1} - I_{t+1},$$

income shortfall constraints

$$\sum_n RI_{nt+1}X_{nt} + w_{t+1} + -v_{t+1} = g_t + L_t$$

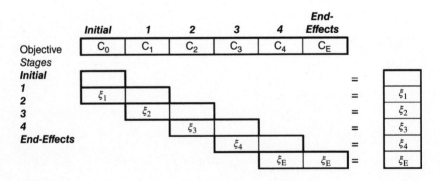

FIGURE 7.16 Layout of the Russell-Yasuda Kasai model.

and non-negativity constraints

$$x_{nt} \geq 0, \quad v_{t+1} \geq 0, \quad w_{t+1} \geq 0,$$

for $t = 0, 1, 2, \ldots, T - 1$. Liability balances and cash flows are computed to satisfy the liability accumulation relations

$$L_{t+1} = (1 + g_{t+1})L_t + F_{t+1} - P_{t+1} - I_{t+1}, \quad t = 0, \ldots, T - 1.$$

Publicly available codes to solve such models are discussed in Wallace and Ziemba (2005); see also Gonzio and Kouwenberg (2001). The Russell–Yasuda model is small by 2015 standards, but in 1991, it was a challenge. The dimensions of a typical implemented problem are shown in Table 7.4.

Figure 7.17 shows Yasuda Kasai's asset liability decision making process.

Yasuda Fire and Marine faced the following situation:

- An increasing number of savings-oriented policies were being sold, which had new types of liabilities.
- The Japanese Ministry of Finance imposed many restrictions through insurance law that led to complex constraints.
- The firm's goals included both current yield and long-run total return, and that led to multidimensional risks and objectives.

The insurance policies were complex, with a part being actual insurance and another part an investment with a fixed guaranteed amount, plus a bonus dependent on general business conditions in the industry. The insurance contracts are of varying length—maturing, being renewed or starting in various time periods—and subject to random returns on assets managed,

TABLE 7.4 Dimensions of a Typical Implemented Problem.

Per	BrPar	Scen	Assets	Alloc Var	Rows	Cols	Coeff	GLP: Rows	Cols	Coeff
INI	1	1	7	59	22	60	257	22	60	257
Q01	8	8	7	59	48	85	573	384	680	4584
Y01	4	32	7	59	54	96	706	1728	3072	22592
Y02	4	128	7	29	52	66	557	6656	8448	71296
Y05	2	256	7	29	52	66	407	13312	16896	104192
YFF	1	256	5	21	35	58	450	8960	14848	115200

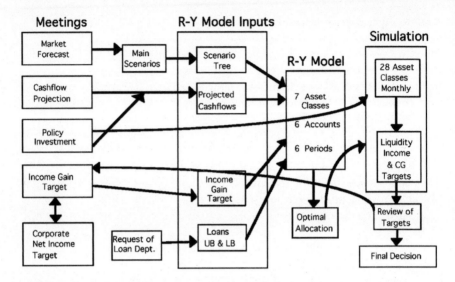

FIGURE 7.17 Yasuda Kasai's asset liability decision process.

insurance claims paid, and bonus payments made. There are many regulations on assets, including restrictions on equity, loans, real estate, foreign investment by account, foreign subsidiaries, and tokkin (pooled accounts). The asset classes were:

Asset	Associated Index
Cash bonds	Nomura bond performance index
Convertible bonds	Nikko research convertible bond index
Domestic equities	TOPIX
Hedged foreign bonds	Salomon Brothers world bond index (or hedged equivalent)
Hedged foreign equities	Morgan Stanley world equity index (or hedged equivalent)
Unhedged foreign bonds	Salomon Brothers world bond index
Unhedged foreign equities	Morgan Stanley world equity index
Loans	Average lending rates (trust/long-term credit (or long-term prime rates)
Money trusts, etc.	Call rates (overnight with collateral)
Life insurance company general accounts	

To divide the universe of available investments into a manageable number of asset classes involves a trade-off between detail and complexity. A large number of asset classes would increase detail at the cost of increasing size. Therefore, the model allows the number and definition of asset classes to be specified by the user. There can be different asset classes in different periods. For example, asset classes in earlier periods can be collapsed into aggregate classes in later periods.

A major part of the information from the model is in the terms of reports consisting of tables and figures of model output. Actual asset allocation results from the model are confidential. But we have the following expected allocations in the initialization (Table 7.5) and end effects periods (Table 7.6). These are averages across scenarios in 100 million yen units and percentages by account.

TABLE 7.5 Expected Allocations for Initialization Period: INI (100 million yen: percentages by account).

	Total	Percentage
Cash	2053	9
Loans—f1	5598	26
Loans—fx	5674	26
Bonds	2898	13
Equity	1426	7
Foreign bonds	3277	15
Foreign equity	875	4
Total	21800	100
Total book value 1: 22510		
Total book value 2: 34875		

TABLE 7.6 Expected Allocations in the End Effects Period.

	General	Savings	Spec Savings 1	Spec Savings 2	Exogenous	Total	%
Cash	0	44	0	36	0	80	0.1
Bonds	5945	17	14846	1311	0	22119	40.1
Equity	0	0	4	0	18588	18592	33.7
For bonds	2837	1094	0	0	0	3931	7.1
For equity	0	4650	6022	562	0	11234	20.4
Total	8782	5804	20072	1908	18588	55154	
Total book value 1: 28566							
Total book value 2: 50547							

In summary:

- The 1991, Russell Yasuda Kasai Model was then the largest known application of stochastic programming in financial services.
- There was a significant ongoing contribution to Yasuda Kasai's financial performance—US$79 million and US$9 million in income and total return, respectively, over FY1991–1992—and it has been in use since then.
- The basic structure is portable to other applications because of flexible model generation. Indeed, the other models in Table 7.3 are modified versions of the Russell-Yasuda Kasai model.
- There is substantial potential impact in performance of financial services companies.
- The top 200 insurers worldwide have in excess of $10 trillion in assets.
- Worldwide pension assets are also about $7.5 trillion, with a $2.5 trillion deficit.
- The industry is also moving toward more complex products and liabilities and risk-based capital requirements.

SIEMENS INNOALM PENSION FUND MODEL

I made this model with Alois Geyer in 2000 for the Siemens Austria pension fund. The model has been in constant use since then and is described in Geyer and Ziemba (2008). I begin by discussing the pension situation in Europe.

There is rapid aging of the developed world's populations—the retiree group, those 65 and older, will roughly double from about 20 percent to about 40 percent of the worker group, those 15–64:

- Better living conditions, more effective medical systems, a decline in fertility rates, and low immigration into the Western world contribute to this aging phenomenon.
- By 2030, two workers will have to support each pensioner, compared with four now.
- Contribution rates will rise.
- Rules to make pensions less desirable will be made. For example, the United Kingdom, France, Italy, and Greece have raised or are considering raising the retirement age.
- Many pension funds worldwide are greatly underfunded.

Historically, stocks have greatly outperformed bonds and other assets; see Figure 7.18 which shows the relative returns in nominal terms.

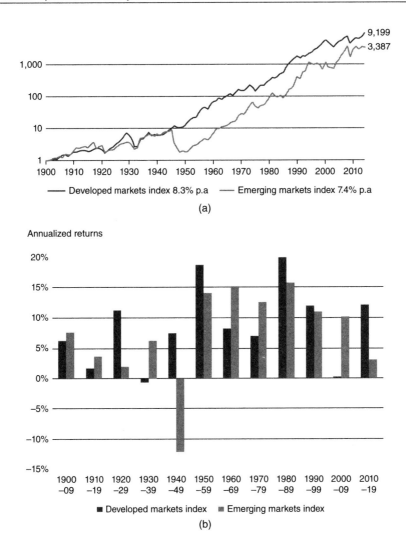

FIGURE 7.18 Emerging and developed market returns, 1900–2013
(*Source:* Credit Suisse Global Investment Returns Yearbook 2014)

Long horizons have produced very high returns from stocks. However, the wealth ride is very rocky and in short periods, the stock market is risky. There can be long periods of underperformance. There have been four periods where equities have had essentially zero gains in nominal terms (not counting dividends): 1899 to 1919, 1929 to 1954, 1964 to 1981, and 2000 to 2009.

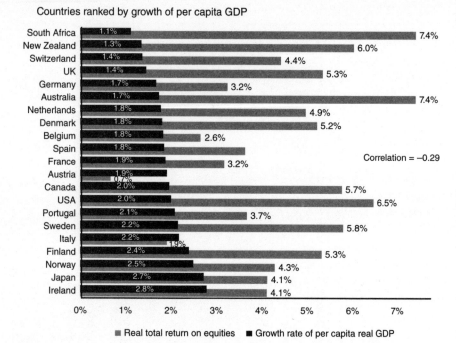

Countries ranked by growth of per capita GDP

■ Real total return on equities   ■ Growth rate of per capita real GDP

FIGURE 7.19   Real equity returns and per capita GDP, 1900–2013
(*Source:* Credit Suisse Global Investment Returns Yearbook 2014)

Seen another way, since 1900, there have only been four periods with nominal gains: 1919 to 1929, 1954 to 1964, 1981 to 2000, and March 2009 to February 2015. Figure 7.19 shows the Dow Jones 30 stock price weighted index, real and nominal, from 1802 to 2006. This index does not include dividends, so it is very bumpy.

Among other things, European pension funds, including those in Austria, have greatly underperformed those in the United States and the United Kingdom and Ireland largely because they greatly underweight equity. For example, Table 7.7 shows with the asset structure of European pension funds with Austria at 4.1 percent.

InnoALM is a multi-period stochastic linear programming model designed by Ziemba and implemented by Geyer with input from Herold and Kontriner for Innovest to use for Austrian pension funds (Figure 7.20). It is a tool to analyze Tier 2 pension fund investment decisions. It was developed in response to the growing worldwide challenges of aging populations and increased number of pensioners who put pressure on

TABLE 7.7 Asset Structure of European Pension Funds.

Countries	Equity	Fixed Income	Real Estate	Cash STP	Other
Austria	4.1	82.4	1.8	1.6	10.0
Belgium	47.3	41.3	5.2	5.6	0.6
Denmark	23.2	58.6	5.3	1.8	11.1
Finland	13.8	55.0	13.0	18.2	0.0
France	12.6	43.1	7.9	6.5	29.9
Germany	9.0	75.0	13.0	3.0	0.0
Greece	7.0	62.9	8.3	21.8	0.0
Ireland	58.6	27.1	6.0	8.0	0.4
Italy	4.8	76.4	16.7	2.0	0.0
Luxembourg	23.7	59.0	0.0	6.4	11.0
Netherlands	36.8	51.3	5.2	1.5	5.2
Portugal	28.1	55.8	4.6	8.8	2.7
Spain	11.3	60.0	3.7	11.5	13.5
Sweden	40.3	53.5	5.4	0.8	0.1
United Kingdom	72.9	15.1	5.0	7.0	0.0
Total EU	53.6	32.8	5.8	5.2	2.7
United States*	52	36	4	8	n.a.
Japan*	29	63	3	5	n.a.

*European Federation for Retirement Provision (EFRP) (1996), Table 4

government services such as health care and Tier 1 national pensions to keep Innovest competitive in their high level fund management activities.

Siemens AG Österreich is the largest privately owned industrial company in Austria. Turnover (EUR 2.4 Bn. in 1999) is generated in a wide range of business lines including information and communication networks, information and communication products, business services, energy and traveling technology, and medical equipment.

■ The Siemens Pension fund, established in 1998, is the largest corporate pension plan in Austria and follows the defined contribution principle.

■ More than 15,000 employees and 5,000 pensioners are members of the pension plan with about EUR 500 million in assets under management.

■ Innovest Finanzdienstleistungs AG, which was founded in 1998, acts as the investment manager for the Siemens AG Österreich, the Siemens Pension Plan, as well as for other institutional investors in Austria.

■ With EUR 2.2 billion in assets under management, Innovest focuses on asset management for institutional money and pension funds.

■ The fund was rated the first of 19 pension funds in Austria for the two-year 1999/2000 period.

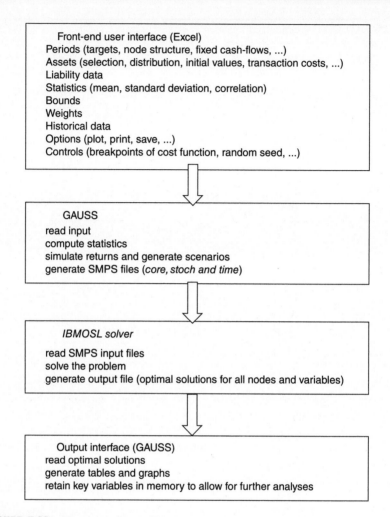

FIGURE 7.20   Elements of InnoALM.
Source: Geyer et al. (2002)

Features of InnoALM.

- A multiperiod stochastic linear programming framework with a flexible number of time periods of varying length.
- Generation and aggregation of multiperiod discrete probability scenarios for random return and other parameters.
- Various forecasting models.
- Scenario dependent correlations across asset classes.

- Multiple covariance matrices corresponding to differing market conditions.
- Constraints reflect Austrian pension law and policy.

As in the Russell-Yasuda Kasai models, the objective function is a

- Concave risk-averse preference function that maximizes the expected present value of terminal wealth net of expected convex (piecewise linear) penalty costs for wealth and benchmark targets in each decision period.
- InnoALM user interface allows for visualization of key model outputs, the effect of input changes, growing pension benefits from increased deterministic wealth target violations, stochastic benchmark targets, security reserves, policy changes, and so on.
- The solution process using the IBM OSL stochastic programming code is fast enough to generate virtually online decisions and results and allows for easy interaction of the user with the model to improve pension fund performance.

The model has deterministic wealth targets that grow 7.5 percent per year; in a typical application the model also has stochastic benchmark targets on asset returns:

$$\tilde{R}_B B + \tilde{R}_S S + \tilde{R}_C C + \tilde{R}_{RE} RE + M_{it}$$
$$\geq \tilde{R}_{BBM} BBM + \tilde{R}_{SBM} SBM + \tilde{R}_{CBM} CBM + \tilde{R}_{REBM} REBM.$$

Bonds, stocks, cash, and real estate have stochastic benchmark returns with asset weights B, S, C, RE, M, with the shortfall to be penalized.

Examples of national investment restrictions on pension plans are as follows.

Country	Investment Restrictions
Germany	Max. 30% equities, max. 5% foreign bonds
Austria	Max. 40% equities, max. 45% foreign securities, min. 40% EURO bonds
France	Min. 50% EURO bonds
Portugal	Max. 35% equities
Sweden	Max. 25% equities
UK, U.S.	Prudent man rule

The model gives insight into the wisdom of such rules, and portfolios can be structured around the risks:

- An Excel™ spreadsheet is the user interface.
- The spreadsheet is used to select assets, define the number of periods, and choose the scenario node-structure.
- The user specifies the wealth targets, cash inflows and outflows, and the asset weights that define the benchmark portfolio (if any).
- The input-file contains a sheet with historical data and sheets to specify expected returns, standard deviations, correlation matrices, and steering parameters.
- A typical application with 10,000 scenarios takes about 7 to 8 minutes for simulation, generating SMPS files and solving and producing output on a 1.2 Ghz Pentium III notebook with 376 MB RAM. For some problems, execution times can be 15 to 20 minutes.

When there is trouble in the stock market, the positive correlation between stocks and bonds fails and they become negatively correlated (Figures 7.21, 7.22). When the mean of the stock market is negative, bonds are most attractive, as is cash (See Table 7.8).

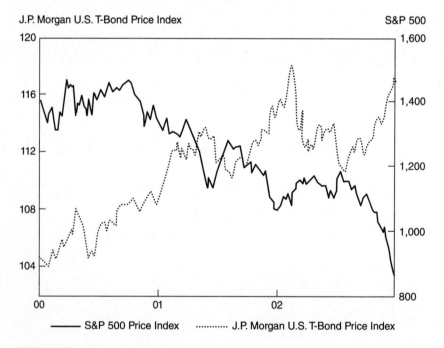

FIGURE 7.21   S&P500 index and U.S. government bond returns, 2000–2002.
Source: Schroder Investment Management Ltd. 2002

TABLE 7.8 Means, Standard Deviations, and Correlations Assumptions Based on 1970–2000 Data.

		Stocks Europe	Stocks U.S.	Bonds Europe	Bonds U.S.
normal periods	Stocks U.S.	.755			
(70% of the time)	Bonds Europe	.334	.286		
	Bonds U.S.	.514	.780	.333	
	Standard deviation	14.6	17.3	3.3	10.9
high volatility	Stocks U.S.	.786			
(20% of the time)	Bonds Europe	.171	.100		
	Bonds U.S.	.435	.715	.159	
	Standard deviation	19.2	21.1	4.1	12.4
extreme periods	Stocks U.S.	.832			
(10% of the time)	Bonds Europe	−.075	−.182		
	Bonds U.S.	.315	.618	−.104	
	Standard deviation	21.7	27.1	4.4	12.9
average period	Stocks U.S.	.769			
	Bonds Europe	.261	.202		
	Bonds U.S.	.478	.751	.255	
	Standard deviation	16.4	19.3	3.6	11.4
all periods	Mean	10.6	10.7	6.5	7.2

Source: Geyer and Ziemba (2008)

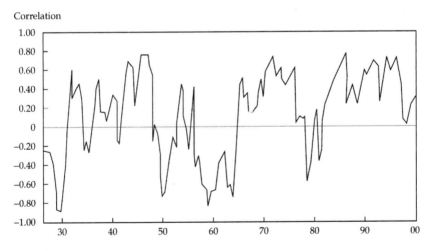

FIGURE 7.22 Rolling correlations between U.S. equity and government bond returns.
Source: Schroder Investment Management Ltd. 2002

Assumptions about the statistical properties of returns measured in nominal euros are based on a sample of monthly data from January 1970 for stocks and 1986 for bonds to September 2000. Summary statistics for monthly and annual log returns are in Table 7.9. The U.S. and European equity means for the longer period 1970–2000 are much lower than for 1986–2000 and slightly less volatile. The monthly stock returns are non-normal and negatively skewed. Monthly stock returns are fat tailed, whereas monthly bond returns are close to normal (the critical value of the Jarque-Bera test for $a = .01$ is 9.2).

We calculate optimal portfolios for seven cases: cases with and without mixing of correlations and consider normal, t-, and historical distributions. Cases NM, HM, and TM use mixing correlations. Case NM assumes normal distributions for all assets. Case HM uses the historical distributions of each asset. Case TM assumes t-distributions with five degrees of freedom for stock returns, whereas bond returns are assumed to have normal distributions. Cases NA, HA, and TA are based on the same distribution assumptions with no mixing of correlations matrices. Instead the correlations and standard deviations used in these cases correspond to an *average period* where 10 percent, 20 percent, and 70 percent weights are used to compute averages of correlations and standard deviations used in the three different regimes.

Comparisons of the average (A) cases and mixing (M) cases are mainly intended to investigate the effect of mixing correlations. Finally, in the case,

TABLE 7.9   Statistical Properties of Asset Returns.

	Stocks Europe		Stocks U.S.		Bonds Europe	Bonds U.S.
	1/70	1/86	1/70	1/86	1/86	1/86
monthly returns	−9/00	−9/00	−9/00	−9/00	−9/00	−9/00
mean (% p.a.)	10.6	13.3	10.7	14.8	6.5	7.2
std.dev (% p.a.)	16.1	17.4	19.0	20.2	3.7	11.3
skewness	−0.90	−1.43	−0.72	−1.04	−0.50	0.52
kurtosis	7.05	8.43	5.79	7.09	3.25	3.30
Jarque-Bera test	302.6	277.3	151.9	155.6	7.7	8.5
annual returns						
mean (%)	11.1	13.3	11.0	15.2	6.5	6.9
std.dev (%)	17.2	16.2	20.1	18.4	4.8	12.1
skewness	−0.53	−0.10	−0.23	−0.28	−0.20	−0.42
kurtosis	3.23	2.28	2.56	2.45	2.25	2.26
Jarque-Bera test	17.4	3.9	6.2	4.2	5.0	8.7

Source: Geyer et al. (2002)

TMC, we maintain all assumptions of case TM but use Austria's constraints on asset weights. Eurobonds must be at least 40 percent and equity at most 40 percent, and these constraints are binding.

A distinct pattern emerges:

- The mixing correlation cases initially assign a much lower weight to European bonds than the average period cases.
- Single-period, mean-variance optimization, and the average period cases (NA, HA, and TA) suggest an approximate 45–55 mix between equities and bonds.
- The mixing correlation cases (NM, HM, and TM) imply a 65–35 mix. Investing in U.S. bonds is not optimal at stage 1 in any of the cases, which seems due to the relatively high volatility of US bonds.

Optimal initial asset weights at Stage 1 by case are shown in Table 7.10.

If the level of portfolio wealth exceeds the target, the surplus is allocated to a reserve account and a portion used to increase (10 percent usually) wealth targets.

Table 7.11 has the expected terminal wealth levels, expected reserves, and probabilities of shortfall. TMC has the poorest results showing that

TABLE 7.10   Optimal Initial Asset Weights at Stage 1 (in %).

	Stocks Europe	Stocks U.S.	Bonds Europe	Bonds U.S.
Single-period, mean-variance optimal weights (average periods)	34.8	9.6	55.6	0.0
Case NA: no mixing (average periods) Normal distributions	27.2	10.5	62.3	0.0
Case HA: no mixing (average periods) Historical distributions	40.0	4.1	55.9	0.0
Case TA: no mixing (average periods) T-distributions for stocks	44.2	1.1	54.7	0.0
Case NM: mixing correlations Normal distributions	47.0	27.6	25.4	0.0
Case HM: mixing correlations historical distributions	37.9	25.2	36.8	0.0
Case TM: mixing correlations t-distributions for stocks	53.4	11.1	35.5	0.0
Case TMC: mixing correlations historical distributions constraints on asset weights	35.1	4.9	60.0	0.0

TABLE 7.11 Expected Terminal Wealth, Expected Reserves, and Probabilities of Shortfalls with a Target Wealth, $W_t = 206.1$.

	Stocks Europe	Stocks U.S.	Bonds	Bonds U.S.	Expected Terminal Wealth	Expected Reserves at Stage 6	Probability of Target Shortfall	Probability Shortfall >10%
NA	34.3	49.6	11.7	4.4	328.9	202.8	11.2	2.7
HA	33.5	48.1	13.6	4.8	328.9	205.2	13.7	3.7
TA	35.5	50.2	11.4	2.9	327.9	202.2	10.9	2.8
NM	38.0	49.7	8.3	4.0	349.8	240.1	9.3	2.2
HM	39.3	46.9	10.1	3.7	349.1	235.2	10.0	2.0
TM	38.1	51.5	7.4	2.9	342.8	226.6	8.3	1.9
TMC	20.4	20.8	46.3	12.4	253.1	86.9	16.1	2.9

the arbitrary constraints hurt performance. The mixing strategies NM, HM, and, especially, TM have the best results with the highest expected terminal wealthy, expected reserves and the lowest shortfall probabilities.

In summary: optimal allocations, expected wealth, and shortfall probabilities are mainly affected by considering mixing correlations while the type of distribution chosen has a smaller impact. This distinction is mainly due to the higher proportion allocated to equities if different market conditions are taken into account by mixing correlations.

Geyer and I ran an out-of-sample test to see if the scenario-dependent correlation matrix idea adds value (Figure 7.23). It was assumed that in the first month wealth is allocated according to the optimal solution for stage 1. In subsequent months, the portfolio is rebalanced as follows:

- Identify the current volatility regime (extreme, highly volatile, or normal) based on the observed U.S. stock return volatility. It is assumed that the driving variable is U.S. volatility.
- Search the scenario tree to find a node that corresponds to the current volatility regime and has the same or a similar level of wealth.
- The optimal weights from that node determine the rebalancing decision.
- For the no-mixing cases NA, TA, and HA, the information about the current volatility regime cannot be used to identify optimal weights. In those cases, we use the weights from a node with a level of wealth as close as possible to the current level of wealth.

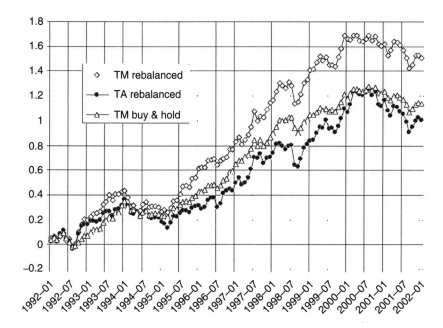

FIGURE 7.23 Cumulative monthly returns for different strategies.
Source: Geyer and Ziemba (2008)

The following quote by Konrad Kontriner (member of the board) and Wolfgang Herold (senior risk strategist) of Innovest emphasizes the practical importance of InnoALM:

> The InnoALM model has been in use by Innovest, an Austrian Siemens subsidiary, since its first draft versions in 2000. Meanwhile it has become the only consistently implemented and fully integrated proprietary tool for assessing pension allocation issues within Siemens AG worldwide. Apart from this, consulting projects for various European corporations and pensions funds outside of Siemens have been performed on the basis of the concepts of InnoALM.
>
> The key elements that make InnoALM superior to other consulting models are the flexibility to adopt individual constraints and target functions in combination with the broad and deep array of results, which allows to investigate individual, path dependent behavior of assets and liabilities as well as scenario-based and Monte-Carlo-like risk assessment of both sides.

In light of recent changes in Austrian pension regulation the latter even gained additional importance, as the rather rigid asset-based limits were relaxed for institutions that could prove sufficient risk management expertise for both assets and liabilities of the plan. Thus, the implementation of a scenario-based asset allocation model will lead to more flexible allocation restraints that will allow for more risk tolerance and will ultimately result in better long-term investment performance.

Furthermore, some results of the model have been used by the Austrian regulatory authorities to assess the potential risk stemming from less constrained pension plans.

DYNAMIC PORTFOLIO THEORY AND PRACTICE: THE KELLY CAPITAL GROWTH APPROACH

The first category of multiperiod models are those reducable to static models. Part IV of Ziemba and Vickson (1975; 2006) reprints key papers and discusses important results of such models.

It is well known in stochastic programming that n-period concave stochastic programs are theoretically equivalent to concave static problems; see Dantzig (1955). In the theory of optimal investment over time, it is not quadratic (the utility function behind the Sharpe ratio) but log that yields the most long-term growth. But the elegant results on the Kelly (1956) criterion, as it is known in the gambling literature, and the capital growth theory, as it is known in the investments literature, are long-run asymptotic results; see the surveys by Hakansson and Ziemba (1995) and MacLean and Ziemba (2006) and Thorp (2006) that were proved rigorously by Breiman (1961) and generalized by Algoet and Cover (1988).

However, the Arrow–Pratt absolute risk aversion of the log utility criterion, namely $1/\omega$, is essentially zero. Hence, in the short run, log can be an exceedingly risky utility function with wide swings in wealth values (Figure 7.24). And fractional, Kelly strategies are not much safer as their risk aversion indices are $1/\gamma\omega$ where the negative power utility function αW^α, $\alpha < 0$. This formula

$$\gamma = \frac{1}{1 - \alpha}$$

is exact for lognormal assets and approximately correct otherwise; see MacLean, Ziemba, and Li (2005).

The myopic property of log utility (optimality is secured with today's data and you do not need to consider the past or future) is derived as follows in the simplest Bernoulli trials ($p =$ probability you win, $q = 1 - p =$ probability you lose a fixed amount).

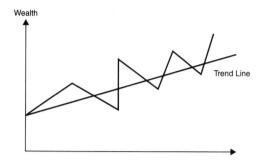

FIGURE 7.24 A typical full Kelly wealth path.

Final wealth after N trials is

$$X_N = (1 + f)^M (1 - f)^{N-M} X_0$$

where f = fraction bet, X_0 =initial wealth and you win M of N trials.
The exponential rate of growth is

$$G = \lim_{N \to \infty} \log \left(\frac{X_N}{X_0} \right)^{1/N}$$

$$G = \lim_{N \to \infty} \left[\frac{M}{N} \log (1 + f) + \frac{N - M}{N} \log(1 - f) \right]$$

$$= p \log(1 + f) + q \log(1 - f) \quad \text{by the strong law of large numbers}$$

$$= E \log W.$$

Thus, the criterion of maximizing the long-run exponential rate of asset growth is equivalent to maximizing the one period expected logarithm of wealth. So an optimal policy is myopic. See Hakansson (1972) for generalizations of this myopic policy.

$$\text{Max}G(f) = p \ \log(1 + f) + q \ \log(1 - f) \to f^* = p - q.$$

The optimal fraction to bet is the edge $p - q$. The bets can be large:
$$-\frac{u''}{u'} = \frac{1}{w} \approx 0$$

p	.5	.51	.6	.99
q	.5	.49	.4	.01
f^*	0	.02	.2	.98

$$f^* = \frac{\text{edge}}{\text{odds}} = \frac{\text{edge}}{10} \quad \text{with } 10 - 1 \text{ situation.}$$

The key to the size of the bet is not the edge, it is the risk.

An example was the bet to place and show on Slew O'Gold in the inaugural Breeders' Cup Classic in 1984: $f^* = 64$ percent for place/show suggests fractional Kelly (that is, a lower bet where you blend the Kelly full expected log bet with cash). See the discussion of the Thorp-Ziemba bets on that day in Ziemba and Hausch (1986) and an expanded version in Ziemba (2015).

In continuous time,

$$f^* = \frac{\mu - r}{\sigma^2} - \frac{\text{edge}}{\text{risk(odds)}}$$

$$g^* = \frac{1}{2}\left(\frac{(\mu - r)^2}{\sigma^2}\right) + r$$

$$= \frac{1}{2}(\text{Sharpe Ratio})^2 + \text{risk free asset.}$$

The classic Breiman (1960; 1961) results are: in each period $t = 1, 2, \ldots$ there are K investment opportunities with returns per unit invested $X_{N_1}, \ldots, X_{N_k}$, intertemporally independent with finitely many distinct values.

$$X_N = \sum_{i=1}^{K} \lambda_i X_{N_i}$$

$$\text{Max E log } X_N$$

Property 1: Maximizing E log X_N asymptotically maximizes the rate of asset growth.

If in each time period, two portfolio managers have the same family of investment opportunities and one uses a Λ^* maximizing

$$\text{E log } X_N = \sum_{i=1}^{K} \lambda_i X_{N_i}$$

whereas the other uses an *essentially different* strategy; for example:

$$\text{Max E log } X_N(\Lambda^*) - \text{E log } X_N(\Lambda) \to \infty$$

then

$$\lim_{N \to \infty} \log \frac{X_N(\Lambda^*)}{X_N(\Lambda)} \to \infty$$

as essentially different means they differ infinitely often. So the actual amount of the fortune exceeds that with any other strategy by more and more as the horizon becomes more distant.

Property 2: The expected time to reach a preassigned goal is, asymptotically as X increases, least with a strategy maximizing $E \log X_N$.

We learn a lot from the following Kelly and half Kelly medium time simulations from Ziemba and Hausch (1986). This simulation had 700 independent investments, all with a 14 percent advantage, with 1,000 simulated runs and $w_0 = \$1,000$.

	Final Wealth			Number of Times the Final Wealth out of 1000 Trials Was				
Strategy	Min	Max	Mean	Median	>500	>1,000	>10,000	>50,000	>100,000
Kelly	18	483,883	48,135	17,269	916	870	598	302	166
Half Kelly	145	111,770	13,069	8,043	990	954	480	30	1

The power of the Kelly criterion is shown when 16.6 percent of the time final wealth is 100 times the initial wealth with full Kelly but only once with half Kelly. Thirty percent of the time, final wealth exceeds 50 times initial wealth. But the probability of being ahead is higher with half Kelly 87 percent versus 95.4 percent. So Kelly is much riskier than half Kelly. However, the minimum wealth is 18, and it is only 145 with half Kelly. So with 700 bets all independent with a 14 percent edge, the result is that you can still lose over 98 percent of your fortune with bad scenarios, and half Kelly is not much better with a minimum of 145 or a 85.5 percent loss. Here, financial engineering is important to avoid such bad outcomes.

Figures 7.25(a), (b) from MacLean, Thorp, Zhao, and Ziemba (2012) show the highest and lowest final wealth trajectories for full, $3/4$, $1/2$, $1/4$, and $1/8$ Kelly strategies for this example. Most of the gain is in the final 100 of the 700 decision points. Even with these maximum graphs, there is much volatility in the final wealth with the amount of volatility generally higher with higher Kelly fractions. Indeed with $3/4$ Kelly, there were losses from about decision points 610 to 670.

The final wealth levels are much higher on average, the higher the Kelly fraction. As you approach full Kelly, the typical final wealth escalates dramatically. This is shown also in the maximum wealth levels in Table 7.12.

There is a chance of loss (final wealth is less than the initial $1,000) in all cases, even with 700 independent bets each with an edge of 14 percent. The size of the losses can be large as shown in the >50, >100, and >500 and columns of Table 7.12. Figure 7.25(b) shows these minimum wealth paths.

If capital is infinitely divisible and there is no leveraging, then the Kelly bettor cannot go bankrupt, since one never bets everything (unless the probability of losing anything at all is zero and the probability of winning is positive). If capital is discrete, then presumably Kelly bets are rounded down

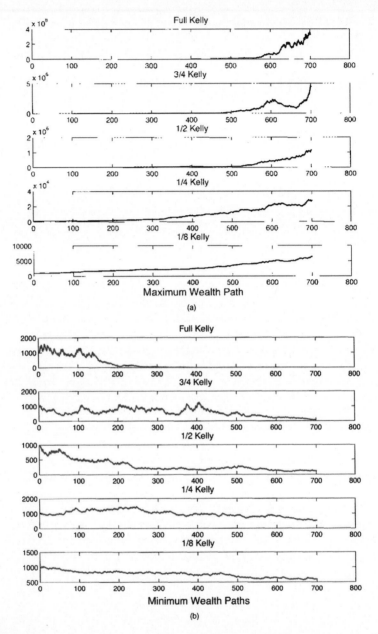

FIGURE 7.25   Final wealth trajectories: Ziemba-Hausch (1986) Model: (a) Highest; (b) Lowest.
Source: MacLean, Thorp, Zhao, and Ziemba (2011)

TABLE 7.12 Final Wealth Statistics by Kelly Fraction: Ziemba-Hausch (1986) Model Kelly Fractions.

Statistic	1.0k	0.75k	0.50k	0.25k	0.125k
Max	318854673	4370619	1117424	27067	6330
Mean	524195	70991	19005	4339	2072
Min	4	56	111	513	587
St. Dev.	8033178	242313	41289	2951	650
Skewness	35	11	13	2	1
Kurtosis	1299	155	278	9	2
$>5 \times 10$	1981	2000	2000	2000	2000
10^2	1965	1996	2000	2000	2000
$>5 \times 10^2$	1854	1936	1985	2000	2000
$>10^3$	1752	1855	1930	1957	1978
$>10^4$	1175	1185	912	104	0
$>10^5$	479	284	50	0	0
$>10^6$	111	17	1	0	0

to avoid overbetting—in which case, at least one unit is never bet. Hence, the worst case with Kelly is to be reduced to one unit, at which point betting stops. Since fractional Kelly bets less, the result follows for all such strategies. For levered wagers, that is, betting more than one's wealth with borrowed money, the investor can lose much more than their initial wealth and become bankrupt. See MacLean, Thorp, Zhao, and Ziemba (2011) for examples.

TRANSACTIONS COSTS

The effect of transactions costs, which is called slippage in commodity trading, is illustrated with the following place/show horseracing formulation; see Hausch, Ziemba, and Rubinstein (1981). Here, q_i is the probability that i wins, and the Harville probability of an ij finish is $\frac{q_i q_j}{1-q_i}$, and so on. Q, the track payback, is about 0.82 (but is about 0.90 with professional rebates). The players' bets are to place p_j and show s_k for each of the about 10 horses in the race out of the players' wealth w_0. The bets by the crowd are P_i with $\sum_{i=1}^{n} P_i = P$ and S_k with $\sum_{k=1}^{n} S_k = S$. The payoffs are computed so that for place, the first two finishers, say i and j, in either order share the net pool profits once each P_i and p_i bets cost of say \$1 is returned. The show payoffs are computed similarly. The model is

$$
\max_{p_i s_i} \sum_{i=1}^{n} \sum_{\substack{j=i \\ j\neq i}}^{n} \sum_{\substack{k=i \\ k\neq i,j}}^{n} \frac{q_i q_j q_k}{(1-q_i)(1-q_i-q_j)} \log \left[\frac{Q\left(P+\sum_{l=1}^{n} p_l\right)-(p_i+p_j+P_{ij})}{2} \times \left[\frac{p_i}{p_i+P_i} + \frac{p_j}{p_j+P_j} \right] + \frac{Q\left(S+\sum_{l=1}^{n} s_l\right)-(s_i+s_j+s_k+S_{ijk})}{3} \times \left[\frac{s_i}{s_i+S_i} + \frac{s_j}{s_j+S_j} + \frac{s_k}{s_k+S_k} \right] + w_0 - \sum_{\substack{l=i \\ l\neq i,j,k}}^{n} s_l - \sum_{\substack{l=i \\ l\neq i,j}}^{n} p_l \right]
$$

$$
\text{s.t.} \sum_{l=1}^{n} (p_l + s_l) \le w_0, \quad p_l \ge 0, \quad s_l \ge 0, \quad l = 1, \dots, n,
$$

While the Harville formulas make sense, the data indicate that they are biased. To correct for this, professional bettors adjust the Harville formulas, using for example discounted Harville formulas, to lower the place and show probabilities for favorites and raise them for the longshots; see papers in Hausch, Lo, and Ziemba (2008) and Hausch and Ziemba (2008).

This is a nonconcave program but it seems to converge when nonlinear programming algorithms are used to solve such problems. But a simpler way is via expected value approximation equations using thousands of sample calculations of the NLP model:

$$
\text{Ex Place}_i = 0.319 + 0.559 \left(\frac{w_i/w}{p_i/p} \right)
$$

$$
\text{Ex Show}_i = 0.543 + 0.369 \left(\frac{w_i/w}{s_i/s} \right).
$$

The expected value (and optimal wager) are functions of only four numbers—the totals to win and place for the horse in question. These equations approximate the full optimized optimal growth model. See Hausch and Ziemba (1985). This is used in calculators. See the discussion in Ziemba (2015).

An example is the 1983 Kentucky Derby (Figure 7.26).

	Totals	#8 Sunny's Halo	Expected Value Per Dollar Bet	Optimal Bet $(W_0 = 1000)$
Odds		5-2		
Win	3,143,669	745,524		
Show	1,099,990	179,758	1.14	52

Sunny's Halo won the race

Win	Place	Show
7.00	4.80	(4.00)

$\Pi = \$52$

15 second bet!

Watch board in lineup
while everyone is at the TV

FIGURE 7.26 Mutuel pools for 1983 Kentucky Derby.

Here, Sunny's Halo has about one-sixth of the show pool versus a quarter of the win pool, so the expected value is 1.14 and the optimal Kelly bet is 5.2 percent of one's wealth.

SOME GREAT INVESTORS

This portfolio optimization survey now shows the wealth plots of a number of great investors who have successfully used the Kelly and fractional Kelly strategies. These include John Maynard Keynes at King's College, University of Cambridge, Warren Buffett of Berkshire Hathaway, Bill Benter, the top racetrack bettor in Hong Kong, Ed Thorp, Princeton Newport, and Jim Simons of Renaissance Medallion (Figure 7.27).

Ziemba (2005) argues that a modification of the Sharpe ratio is needed to evaluate properly the great investors, as the ordinary Sharpe ratio,

$$S = \frac{\overline{R}_P - R_F}{\sigma_P}$$

penalizes gains. See also the updated paper by Gergaud and Ziemba (2012). The modified measure uses only losses in the calculation of σ_P; namely,

$$\sigma_p = \frac{\sum_{i=1}^{n} (r_i - \overline{r})^2}{n - 1},$$

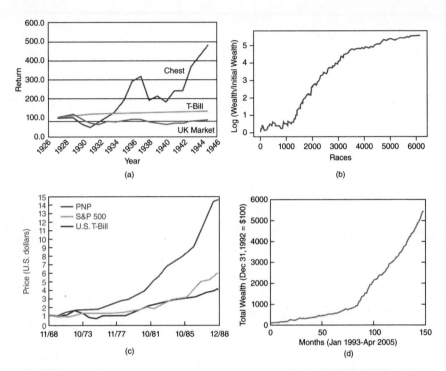

FIGURE 7.27 Four Great Investors: (a) John Maynard Keynes, King's College, Cambridge, 1927–1945; (b) Bill Benter, 1989–1991; (c) Ed Thorp, Princeton Newport Hedge Fund 1969–1988; (d) Jim Simons, Renaissance Medallion Hedge Fund, 1993–2005.

where $\bar{r} = 0$ and ( )—means only the losses are counted. Using this measure, only Buffett improves on his Sharpe ratio as shown in Table 7.13. But Buffett is still below the Ford Foundation and the Harvard endowment with DSSRs near 1.00. The reason for that can be seen in Figure 7.28 where Berkshire has the highest monthly gains but also the largest monthly losses of the funds studies. It is clear that Warren Buffett is a long-term Kelly type investor who does not care about monthly losses, just high final wealth. The great hedge fund investors Thorp at DSSR = 13.8 and Simons at 26.4 dominate dramatically. In their cases, the ordinary Sharpe ratio does not show their brilliance. For Simons, his Sharpe was only 1.68.

Simons's wealth graph is one of the best I have seen (see Figure 7.14 and Table 7.14 for the distribution of his gains and losses). Renaissance Medallion has had a remarkable record: a net of 5 percent management fees and 44 percent incentive fees, so the gross returns are about double

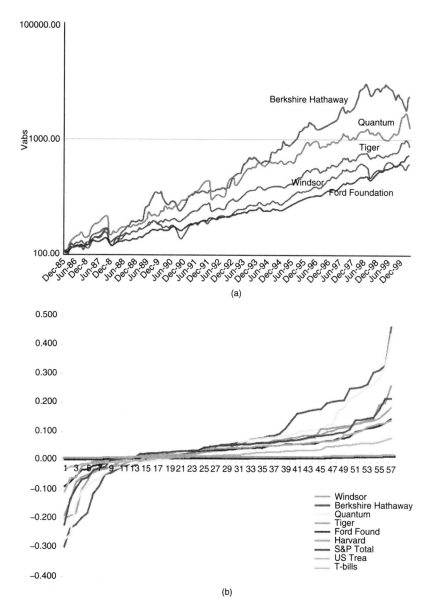

(a)

(b)

FIGURE 7.28 The wealth paths and return distributions of Berkshire Hathaway, Quantum, Tiger, Windsor, the Ford Foundation, and the S&P500, 1985–2000: (a) Growth of assets, log scale, various high performing funds, 1985–2000. *Source:* Ziemba (2003); (b) Return distributions of all the funds, quarterly returns distribution, December 1985 to March 2000. *Source:* Ziemba (2005)

TABLE 7.13 Comparison of Ordinary and Symmetric Downside Sharpe Yearly Performance Measures, Monthly Data, and Arithmetic Means.

	Ordinary	Downside
Ford Foundation	0.970	0.920
Tiger Fund	0.879	0.865
S&P500	0.797	0.696
Berkshire Hathaway	0.773	0.917
Quantum	0.622	0.458
Windsor	0.543	0.495

Source: Ziemba (2005)

TABLE 7.14 Medallion Fund Net Returns, %, January 1993 to April 2005.

Yearly	1993	1994	1995	1996	1997	1998	1999	2000	2001	2002	2003	2004	2005
	39.06	70.69	38.33	31.49	21.21	41.50	24.54	98.53	31.12	29.14	25.28	27.77	
Quarterly													
Q1	78.1	14.69	22.06	7.88	3.51	7.30	(0.25)	25.44	12.62	5.90	4.29	9.03	8.30
Q2	25.06	35.48	4.84	1.40	6.60	7.60	6.70	20.51	5.64	7.20	6.59	3.88	
Q3	4.04	11.19	3.62	10.82	8.37	9.69	6.88	8.58	7.60	8.91	8.77	5.71	
Q4	(0.86)	(1.20)	4.31	8.44	1.41	11.73	9.48	20.93	2.42	4.44	3.62	6.72	
Monthly													
January	1.27	4.68	7.4	3.25	1.16	5.02	3.79	10.5	4.67	1.65	2.07	3.76	2.26
February	3.08	5.16	7.54	1.67	2.03	1.96	(2.44)	9.37	2.13	3.03	2.53	1.97	2.86
March	3.28	4.19	5.68	2.77	0.29	0.21	(1.49)	3.8	5.36	1.12	(0.35)	3.05	2.96
April	6.89	2.42	4.10	0.44	1.01	0.61	3.22	9.78	2.97	3.81	1.78	0.86	0.95
May	3.74	5.66	5.53	0.22	4.08	4.56	1.64	7.24	2.44	1.11	3.44	2.61	
June	12.78	25.19	(4.57)	0.73	1.36	2.28	1.71	2.37	0.15	2.13	1.24	0.37	
July	3.15	6.59	(1.28)	4.24	5.45	(1.10)	4.39	5.97	1.00	5.92	1.98	2.20	
August	(0.67)	7.96	5.91	2.97	1.9	4.31	1.22	3.52	3.05	1.68	2.38	2.08	
September	1.54	(3.38)	(0.89)	3.25	0.85	6.33	1.15	(1.02)	3.38	1.13	4.18	1.33	
October	1.88	(2.05)	0.3	6.37	(1.11)	5.33	2.76	6.71	1.89	1.15	0.35	2.39	
November	(1.51)	(0.74)	2.45	5.93	(0.22)	2.26	5.42	8.66	0.17	1.42	1.42	3.03	
December	(1.20)	1.62	1.52	(3.74)	2.77	3.73	1.06	4.30	0.35	1.81	1.81	1.16	

Source: Ziemba and Ziemba 2007

these net returns (Figure 7.29). Thorp's returns (Figure 7.27c) are with 2+20 fees and are a model for successful hedge fund performance with no yearly or quarterly losses and only three monthly losses in 20 years. See Gergaud and Ziemba (2012) for some funds with even higher DSSRs and one whose results are too good to be true with an infinity DSSR. That one turned out to be a Madoff-type fraud!

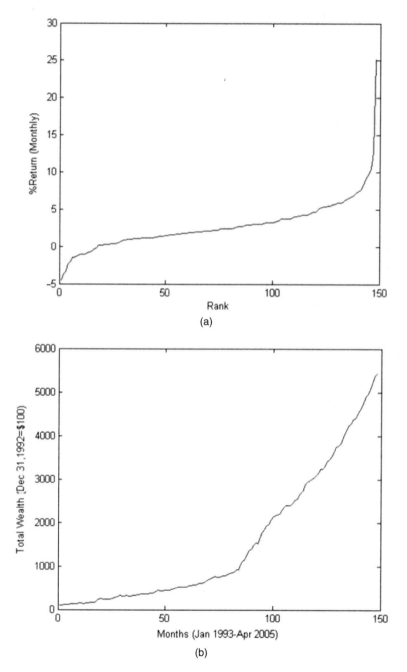

FIGURE 7.29 Medallion Fund, January 1993 to April 2005: (a) Rates of return in increasing order by month, %; (b) Wealth over time.

APPENDIX 7.1: ESTIMATING UTILITY FUNCTIONS AND RISK AVERSION

Certainty Equivalent Method

Set $\quad u(w_L) = 0, u(w_U) = 1$

Find $\quad w_{0.5}$

$$u(w_{0.5}) = \frac{1}{2}u(w_L) + \frac{1}{2}u(w_U)$$

Find $\quad w_{0.25}, w_{0.75}$

$$u(w_{0.25}) = \frac{1}{2}u(w_{0.5}) + \frac{1}{2}u(w_L)$$

$$u(w_{0.75}) = \frac{1}{2}u(w_U) + \frac{1}{2}u(w_{0.5})$$

The three points plus the 0, 1 point generate u

$$u(w_{0.25}) = .25$$

$$u(w_{0.5}) = .5$$

$$u(w_{0.75}) = .75$$

Split each range one more to generate nine points.
For Donald Hausch, see Figure 2 these values were

w	−30,000	−26,000	−20,000	−14,000	−5,000	+5,000	20,000	28,000	70,000
$u_2(w)$	0.000	0.125	0.250	0.375	0.500	0.625	0.750	0.875	1.000

$\quad\quad\quad\uparrow$ $\qquad\qquad\qquad\qquad\qquad\qquad\qquad\qquad\qquad\qquad\qquad\qquad\qquad\qquad\qquad\uparrow$

$\quad\quad u(w_L)$ $\qquad\qquad\qquad\qquad\qquad\qquad\qquad\qquad\qquad\qquad\qquad\qquad\qquad\qquad\quad u(w_U)$

Gain and Loss Equivalent Method

1. Consider the gambles

$$A \begin{cases} \text{lose } \frac{1}{2} \text{ wealth} & \text{pr} = \frac{1}{2} \\ \text{gain x} & \text{pr} = \frac{1}{2} \end{cases}$$

or

$$B \left\{ \text{gain } \$5000 \quad \text{pr} = 1 \right.$$

x_0 is the gain that would make the subject indifferent to a choice between A and B (gain equivalence)

$$u(5000 + w_0) = \frac{1}{2}u(w_0 + x_0) + \frac{1}{2}u\left(\frac{w_0}{2}\right).$$

Set $u\left(\frac{w_0}{2}\right) = a, u(w_0 + 5000) = b$.

Hence this yields $u(w^0 + x_0)$.

2. Repeat with probability of winning $= 0.2, 0.3, 0.4, 0.6,$ and 0.8.
3. Consider the gambles

$$A \begin{cases} \text{lose fraction } y \text{ of wealth} \quad pr = \frac{1}{2} \\ \\ \text{gain } x^1 \quad\quad\quad\quad\quad\quad\quad pr = \frac{1}{2} \end{cases}$$

or

$$B \left\{ \text{gain } \$5000 \quad pr = 1 \right.$$

$\rightarrow y_0$ (loss equivalence)

$$u(5000 + w^2) = \frac{1}{2}u(w_0 + x_0) + \frac{1}{2}u(w^0(1 - y^0)).$$

Set $u\left(\frac{w_0}{2}\right) = a$, and $u(w_0 + 5000) = b$

4. Repeat with probability of winning $= 0.2, 0.3, 0.4, 0.6,$ and 0.8.
   For Donald Hausch, these values were

W	−35,000	−25,000	−15,000	−7,500	+2,500	10,000	14,000	18,000	20,000	39,000	70,000
ul(w)	−15.0	−5.00	−3.00	−1.67	0.00	1.00	1.25	1.67	2.00	2.50	5.00

$\quad\quad\quad\quad\quad\quad\quad\quad\quad\quad\quad\quad\quad\quad\uparrow\quad\quad\quad\uparrow$

$\quad\quad\quad\quad\quad\quad\quad\quad\quad\quad\quad\quad u(.5\,w_0)\; u(w_0 + 5000)$

Points determined by 1, 2 are above $(w_0 + 5000)$ and by 3, 4 are below; see Figure 7.2.

Kallberg and Ziemba (1983) Method

Kallberg and Ziemba showed that the average Arrow Pratt risk aversion approximates closely the optimal Rubinstein measure under normality assumptions. So a consequence is that one can devise risk attitude questions to determine if a particular investor is a $R_A = 4$ (pension fund investor 60–40 mix type) or a risk taker $R_A = 2$ or a conservative investor $R_A = 6$. Kallberg and Ziemba show that the accuracy of such questions is most

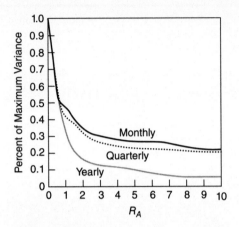

FIGURE 7.30 Riskiness as a percentage of maximum variance versus R_A.
Source: Kallberg and Ziemba, 1983

crucial when R_A is low; see Figure 7.30. The Chopra and Ziemba (1993) results discussed above are consistent with this.

REFERENCES

Algoet, P. H., and T. Cover. 1988. Asymptotic optimality and asymptotic equipartition properties of log-optimum investment. *Annals of Probability* 16 (2): 876–898.

Arrow, K. J. 1965. Aspects of the theory of risk bearing. Technical report. Helsinki: Yrjo Jahnsson Foundation.

Breiman, L. 1961. Optimal gambling system for favorable games. *Proceedings of the 4th Berkeley Symposium on Mathematical Statistics and Probability* 1: 63–8.

Brennan, M. J., and E. S. Schwartz 2008. The use of treasury bill futures in strategic asset allocation programs, in: W. T. Ziemba, and J. M. Mulvey. 2008, *Worldwide Asset and Liability Modeling.* Cambridge University Press, Cambridge, UK: 205–228.

Chopra, V. K. 1993. Improving optimization. *Journal of Investing,* 51–59.

Chopra, V. K., and W. T. Ziemba. 1993. The effect of errors in mean, variance and covariance estimates on optimal portfolio choice. *Journal of Portfolio Management* 19: 6–11.

Dantzig, G. 1955. Linear programming under uncertainty. *Management Science* 1: 197–206.

Fleten, S.-E., K. Høyland, and S. Wallace. 2002. The performance of stochastic dynamic and fixed mix portfolio models. *European Journal of Operational Research* 140 (1): 37–49.

Gassman, H. I., and W. T. Ziemba, eds. 2012. *Stochastic Programming Applications in Finance, Energy and Production.* Singapore: World Scientific.

Gergaud, O., and W. T. Ziemba. 2012. Evaluating great traders. *Journal of Portfolio Management,* Summer: 128–147.

Geyer, A., Herold, K. Kontriner, and W. T. Ziemba. 2002. The Innovest Austrian pension fund financial planning model InnoALM. Working paper, UBC.

Geyer, A., and W. T. Ziemba. 2008. The Innovest Austrian pension fund planning model InnoALM. *Operations Research* 56: 797–810.

Gondzio, J., and R. Kouwenberg. 2001. High performance computing for asset liability management. *Operations Research* 49: 879–891.

Grinold, R. C., and R. N. Khan. 1999. *Active Portfolio Management: Quantitative Theory and Applications.* New York: McGraw-Hill.

Guerard, J., ed. 2010. *Ideas in Asset Liability Management in the Tradition of H.M. Markowitz in Essays in Honor of H.M. Markowitz.* New York: Springer.

Hakansson, N. H. 1972. On optimal myopic portfolio policies with and without serial correlation. *Journal of Business* 44: 324–334.

Hakansson, N. H., and W. T. Ziemba. 1995. Capital growth theory. In *Finance Handbook*, edited by R. A. Jarrow, V. Maksimovic, and W. T. Ziemba, pp. 123–144. Amsterdam: North Holland.

Hanoch, G., and H. Levy. 1969. The efficiency analysis of choices involving risk. *Review of Economic Studies* 36: 335–346.

Hausch, D. B., V. Lo, and W. T. Ziemba, eds. 2008. *Efficiency of Racetrack Betting Markets,* 2nd ed. Academic Press, World Scientific.

Hausch, D. B., and W. T. Ziemba. 1985. Transactions costs, entries, and extent of inefficiencies in a racetrack betting model. *Management Science* XXXI: 381–394.

————. (2008). *Handbook of Sports and Lottery Markets.* Amsterdam: North Holland

Hausch, D. B., W. T. Ziemba, and M. E. Rubinstein. 1981. Efficiency of the market for racetrack betting. *Management Science* XXVII: 1435–1452.

Kallberg, J. G., and W. T. Ziemba. 1981. Remarks on optimal portfolio selection. In *Methods of Operations Research, Oelgeschlager,* edited by G. Bamberg and O. Opitz, Vol. 44, pp. 507–520. Cambridge, MA: Gunn and Hain.

————. 1983. Comparison of alternative utility functions in portfolio selection problems. *Management Science* 29 (11): 1257–1276.

————. 1984. Mis-specifications in portfolio selection problems. In *Risk and Capital,* edited by G. Bamberg and K. Spremann, pp. 74–87. New York: Springer Verlag.

Lintner, J. 1965. The valuation of risk assets and the selection of risky investment in stock portfolios and capital budgets. *Review of Economics and Statistics* 47: 13–37.

Luenberger, D. G. 1993. A preference foundation for log mean-variance criteria in portfolio choice problems. *Journal of Economic Dynamics and Control* 17: 887–906.

————. 1998. *Investment Science.* Oxford University Press.

MacLean, L., R. Sanegre, Y. Zhao, and W. T. Ziemba. 2004. Capital growth with security. *Journal of Economic Dynamics and Control* 38 (5): 937–954.

MacLean, L., W. T. Ziemba, and Li. 2005. Time to wealth goals in capital accumulation and the optimal trade-off of growth versus securities. *Quantitative Finance* 5 (4): 343–357.

MacLean, L. C., E. O. Thorp, Y. Zhao, and W. T. Ziemba. 2012. How does the Fortunes Formula-Kelly capital growth model perform? *Journal of Portfolio Management* 37 (4): 96–111.

MacLean, L. C., and W. T. Ziemba. 2006. Capital growth theory and practice. In S. A. Zenios and W. T. Ziemba (eds.), *Handbook of asset and liability management, Volume 1, Handbooks in Finance*, pp. 139–197. North Holland.

MacLean, L. C., and W. T. Ziemba, eds. 2013. *Handbook of the Fundamentals of Financial Decision Making*. Singapore: World Scientific.

Mangasarian, O. L. 1969. *Nonlinear programming*. New York: McGraw-Hill.

Markowitz, H. M. 1952. Portfolio selection. *Journal of Finance* 7 (1): 77–91.

————. 1976. Investment for the long run: New evidence for an old rule. *Journal of Finance* 31 (5): 1273–1286.

————. 1987. *Mean-variance analysis in portfolio choice and capital markets*. Cambridge, MA: Basil Blackwell.

Markowitz, H. M., and E. van Dijk. 2006. Risk-return analysis. In S. A. Zenios and W. T. Ziemba (Eds.), *Handbook of asset and liability management, Volume 1, Handbooks in Finance*. Amsterdam: North Holland, 139–197.

Merton, R. C., and P. A. Samuelson. 1974. Fallacy of the log-normal approximation to optimal portfolio decision-making over many periods. *Journal of Financial Economics* 1: 67–94.

Mossin, J. 1966. Equilibrium in a capital asset market. *Econometrica* 34 (October): 768–783.

————. 1968. Optimal multiperiod portfolio policies. *Journal of Business* 41: 215–229.

Mulvey, J. M. 1996. Generating scenarios for the Towers Perrin investment system. *Interfaces* 26: 1–13.

Mulvey, J. M., and B. Pauling. 2002. Advantages of multi-period portfolio models. *Journal of Portfolio Management* 29: 35–45.

Mulvey, J. M., B. Pauling, S. Britt, and F. Morin. 2007. Dynamic financial analysis for multinations insurance companies. In *Handbook of asset and liability management, Volume 2, Handbooks in Finance* edited by S. A. Zenios and W. T. Ziemba. Amsterdam: North Holland, 543–590.

Murty, K. G. 1972. On the number of solutions to the complementarity problem and spanning properties of complementarity cones. *Linear Algebra* 5: 65–108.

Pratt, J. W. 1964. Risk aversion in the small and in the large. *Econometrica* 32: 122–136.

Rockafellar, T., and W. T. Ziemba. 2013, July. Modified risk measures and acceptance sets. in *The Handbook of the Fundamentals of Financial Decision Making* edited by L. C. MacLean and W. T Ziemba, Vol. II: 505–506.

Samuelson, P. A. 1969. Lifetime portfolio selection by dynamic stochastic programming. *Review of Economics and Statistics* 51: 239–246.

_____. 1971. The fallacy of maximizing the geometric mean in long sequences of investing or gambling. *Proceedings National Academy of Science* 68: 2493–2496.

_____. 2006. Letter to W. T. Ziemba, December 13.

_____. 2007. Letter to W. T. Ziemba, May 7.

Sharpe, W. F. 1964. Capital asset prices: A theory of market equilibrium under conditions of risk. *Journal of Finance* 19: 425–442.

Siegel, J. 2008. *Stocks for the Long Run*, 4th ed. New York: McGraw-Hill.

Thorp, E. O. 2006. The Kelly criterion in blackjack, sports betting and the stock market. In *Handbook of asset and liability management, Handbooks in Finance*, edited by S. A. Zenios and W.T. Ziemba, pp. 385–428. Amsterdam: North Holland.

Tobin, J. 1958. Liquidity preference as behavior towards risk. *Review of Economic Studies* 25 (2): 65–86.

Wallace, S. W., and W. T. Ziemba, eds. 2005. *Applications of Stochastic Programming*. SIAM—Mathematical Programming Society Series on Optimization.

Zangwill, W. I. 1969. *Nonlinear Programming: A Unified Approach*. Englewood Cliffs, NJ: Prentice Hall.

Ziemba, R. E. S., and W. T. Ziemba. 2007. *Scenarios for Risk Management and Global Investment Strategies*. New York: John Wiley & Sons.

Ziemba, W. T. 2015. *Exotic betting at the racetrack*. Singapore: World Scientific.

Ziemba, W. T. 1974. Calculating investment portfolios when the returns have stable distributions. In *Mathematical Programming in Theory and Practice*, edited by P. L. Hammer and G. Zoutendijk, pp. 443–482. Amsterdam: North Holland.

_____. 2003. *The stochastic programming approach to asset liability and wealth management*. Charlottesville, VA: AIMR.

_____. 2005. The symmetric downside risk Sharpe ratio and the evaluation of great investors and speculators. *Journal of Portfolio Management*, Fall: 108–122.

_____. 2007. The Russell–Yasuda Kasai InnoALM and related models for pensions, insurance companies and high net worth individuals. In *Handbook of asset and liability management, Volume 2, Handbooks in Finance*, edited by S. A. Zenios and W. T. Ziemba, pp. 861–962. Amsterdam: North Holland.

_____. 2013. The case for convex risk measures and scenario dependent correlation matrices, *Quantitative Finance Letters* 1: 47–54.

Ziemba, W. T., and D. B. Hausch. 1986. *Betting at the Racetrack*. Dr. Z Investments, Inc., San Luis Obispo, CA.

Ziemba, W. T., and J. M. Mulvey. 2008. *Worldwide Asset and Liability Modeling*. Cambridge University Press, Cambridge, UK.

Ziemba, W. T., C. Parkan, and F. J. Brooks-Hill. 1974. Calculation of investment portfolios with risk free borrowing and lending. *Management Science XXI*: 209–222.

Ziemba, W. T., and R. G. Vickson, eds. 1975. *Stochastic Optimization Models in Finance*. New York: Academic Press. Reprinted (2006) with a new preface. Singapore: World Scientific.

CHAPTER 8

Portfolio Optimization and Transaction Costs

Renata Mansini
University of Brescia,
Department of Information Engineering

Wlodzimierz Ogryczak
Warsaw University of Technology,
Institute of Control and Computation Engineering

M. Grazia Speranza
University of Brescia,
Department of Economics and Management

INTRODUCTION

In financial markets, expenses incurred when buying or selling securities are commonly defined as *transaction costs* and usually include brokers' commissions and spreads (i.e., the difference between the price the dealer paid for a security and the price the buyer pays). Broadly speaking, the transaction costs are the payments that banks and brokers receive for performing transactions (buying or selling securities). In addition to brokerage fees/commissions, the transaction costs may represent capital gain taxes and thus be considered in portfolio rebalancing. Transaction costs are important to investors because they are one of the key determinants of their net returns. Transaction costs diminish returns and reduce the amount of capital available to future investments. Investors, in particular individual ones, are thus interested to the amount and structure of transaction costs and to how they will impact their portfolios.

The portfolio optimization problem we consider is based on a single-period model of investment, which is based on a single decision at the beginning of the investment horizon (buy and hold strategy). This model has played a crucial role in stock investment and has served as basis for the development of modern portfolio financial theory (Markowitz 1952 and 1959).

We consider the situation of an investor who allots her/his capital among various securities, assigning a share of the capital to each one. During the investment period, the portfolio generates a random rate of return. At the end of the period, the value of the capital will be increased or decreased with respect to the invested capital by the average portfolio return. Let $N = \{1, 2, \ldots, n\}$ denote a set of securities considered for an investment. For each security $j \in N$, the rate of return is represented by a random variable R_j with a given mean $\mu_j = \mathbb{E}\{R_j\}$. Further, let $x = (x_j)_{j=1,\ldots,n}$ denote a vector of decision variables x_j expressing the shares of capital in terms of amounts defining a portfolio. Each portfolio x defines a corresponding random variable $R_x = \sum_{j=1}^{n} R_j x_j$ that represents the portfolio return. The mean return for portfolio x is given as $\mu(x) = \mathbb{E}\{R_x\} = \sum_{j=1}^{n} \mu_j x_j$. To represent a portfolio, the shares must satisfy a set P of constraints that form a feasible set of linear inequalities. This basic set of constraints is defined by the requirement that the amount invested (shares of the capital) must sum to the capital invested $\overline{C}$, and that short selling is not allowed:

$$\sum_{j=1}^{n} x_j = \overline{C}$$

$$x_j \geq 0 \ \text{ for } \ j \in N.$$

We use the notation $\overline{C}$ to denote the capital available, when it is a constant. Later we will use the notation C to denote the capital investment, when it is a problem variable.

An investor usually needs to consider some other requirements expressed as a set of additional side constraints (e.g. thresholds on the investment). Most of them can be expressed as linear equations and inequalities (see Mansini et al. 2014).

Following the seminal work by Markowitz (1952), we model the portfolio optimization problem as a mean-risk bicriteria optimization problem

$$\max\{[\mu(x), -\varrho(x)]: \quad x \in P\} \tag{8.1}$$

where the mean $\mu(x)$ is maximized and the risk measure $\varrho(x)$ is minimized. We will say that a risk measure is *LP computable* if the portfolio optimization model takes a linear form in the case of discretized returns (see Mansini et al. 2003a). We will consider as risk measure the mean semi-absolute deviation (semi-MAD) that is an LP computable risk measure.

One of the most basic results in traditional portfolio optimization theory is that small investors choose well-diversified portfolios to minimize risk. However, in contrast to theory, noninstitutional investors usually hold relatively undiversified portfolios. While there may be specific motivations for this behavior, it is recognized both in the literature and by practitioners that this is also due to the presence of transaction costs and, in particular, of fixed transaction costs. The introduction of fixed transaction costs may require the use of binary variables. It is known that finding a feasible solution to a portfolio optimization problem with fixed costs is an NP-complete problem (see Kellerer et al. 2000). This implies that, even with an LP computable risk function, a portfolio optimization problem which includes transaction costs may turn out to be a complex problem to solve.

The objective of this work is the analysis of the impact of transaction costs on portfolio optimization. We overview the most commonly used transaction cost structures and discuss how the transaction costs are modeled and embedded in a portfolio optimization model.

This chapter is organized as follows. In the second section the literature on portfolio optimization with transaction costs is surveyed. The focus is on transaction costs incurred by small investors with a buy and hold strategy, but we also briefly analyze contributions on transaction costs in portfolio rebalancing. Essentially, with respect to the single-period problem, in the portfolio rebalancing problem, the investor makes investment decisions starting with a portfolio rather than cash, and consequently some assets must be liquidated to permit investment in others. In the third section, we introduce some portfolio optimization models based on LP computable risk measures. In the fourth section, we discuss the main structures of transaction costs, their mathematical formulations, and how they can be incorporated in a portfolio optimization model. Following the most traditional financial literature on portfolio optimization, we classify transaction costs as *fixed* and *variable*. While convex piecewise linear cost functions can be dealt with using linear constraints in a continuous setting, concave piecewise linear cost functions require the introduction of binary variables to be modeled using linear constraints. In the fifth section, we provide an example that shows how the portfolio optimization with transaction costs may lead to a discontinuous efficient frontier and therefore to a nonunique solution when minimizing the risk under a required expected return (a similar result for portfolio optimization with cardinality constraint can be found in Chang et al. 2000). This result motivates the introduction of a regularization term in the objective function in order to guarantee the selection of an efficient portfolio. This modified model has been used in the computational testing. Finally, the last section is devoted to the experimental analysis. We provide a comparison of three simplified cost structures on a small set of securities taken from a benchmark data set. The experiments show that the impact of the transaction costs is significant, confirming the findings of the recent work by Chen et al. (2010) on the mean–variance framework and those of the well-known work by Chen et al. (1971) showing that lower revision frequency may reduce the magnitude of transaction costs in a rebalancing context.

LITERATURE REVIEW ON TRANSACTION COSTS

The impact of the introduction of real features in a portfolio optimization model has been largely discussed in the literature (see the recent survey by Mansini et al. 2014). The focus of this section will be on transaction costs that are among the most relevant real features. In financial markets, transaction costs are entailed by purchases and sales of securities and are paid both in case of portfolio revision and in case of buy and hold investments. Contributions from the literature are analyzed in chronological order, specifying if referring to a single-period portfolio optimization problem or to a rebalancing problem. Moreover, for each analyzed reference we specify which type of cost (fixed and/or variable) is considered and how costs are embedded into a portfolio optimization model. We summarize the contributions in Table 8.1, where the references are classified according to the way in which the transaction costs are modeled. As we will see later in more detail, the transaction costs may be deducted from the return (second column of Table 8.1), reduce the capital available for the investment (third column), be bounded (fourth column), or be considered in the objective function, typically the risk function (last column).

It is well known that excluding transaction costs may generate inefficient portfolios (see Arnott and Wagner 1990). An interesting question is whether the performance of a buy and hold strategy may be improved by a periodic revision of the portfolio (see Chen et al. 2010). A first study in this direction is a model due to Chen et al. (1971), which is a portfolio revision model where transaction costs are included in Markowitz model as a constant proportion of the transacted amount. The costs, incurred to change the old portfolio to the new one, are deduced from the ending value of the old portfolio. Afterward, Johnson and Shannon (1974) showed experimentally that a quarterly portfolio revision may outperform a buy and hold policy. Their findings, however, do not consider transaction costs.

TABLE 8.1 State of the Art on Portfolio Optimization with Transaction Costs.

	Return	Capital	UpperBound on Cost	Objective Function
Variable costs	Kellerer et al. (2000), Chiodi et al. (2003), Konno, Yamamoto (2005), Konno et al. (2005), Lobo et al. (2007), Angelelli et al. (2008), Guastaroba et al. (2009), Krejić et al. (2011), Angelelli et al. (2012)	Young (1998), Beasley et al. (2003), Lobo et al. (2007), Woodside-Oriakhi et al. (2013)	Beasley et al. (2003), Woodside-Oriakhi et al. (2013)	Adcock, Meade (1994), Yoshimoto (1996), Young (1998), Beasley et al. (2003), Konno, Wijayanayake (2001), Konno, Yamamoto (2005), Konno et al. (2005), Xue et al. (2006), Lobo et al. (2007), Bertsimas, Shioda (2009), Angelelli et al. (2008), Guastaroba et al. (2009), Angelelli et al. (2012), Woodside-Oriakhi et al. (2013),
Fixed Costs	Kellerer et al. (2000), Chiodi et al. (2003), Mansini, Speranza (2005), Angelelli et al. (2008), Guastaroba et al. (2009), Krejić et al. (2011), Angelelli et al. (2012)	Young (1998), Woodside-Oriakhi et al. (2013)	Woodside-Oriakhi et al. (2013)	Young (1998), Mansini, Speranza (2005), Angelelli et al. (2008), Le Thi et al. (2009), Guastaroba et al. (2009), Angelelli et al. (2012), Woodside-Oriakhi et al. (2013)

While variable transaction costs make individual securities less attractive, fixed transaction costs are usually a reason for holding undiversified portfolios. The first detailed analysis on portfolio selection with fixed costs can be attributed to Brennan (1975). The author introduced a model for determining the optimal number of securities in the portfolio. Earlier, Mao (1970), Jacob (1974), and Levy (1978) considered the fixed transaction cost problem, avoiding, however, a direct modeling but placing instead restrictions on the number of securities. Afterward, Patel and Subrahmanyam (1982) criticized Brennan's approach as based on the capital asset pricing theory when it is well known that this pricing relationship is affected if trading costs are taken into account (see Levy (1978) for a theoretical proof). They introduced transaction costs by placing restrictions on the variance-covariance matrix.

Adcock and Meade (1994) considered the problem of rebalancing a tracking portfolio over time, where transaction costs are incurred at each rebalancing. They introduced the costs in the objective function by adding a linear term to the risk term of the mean-variance model. Yoshimoto (1996) introduced instead a V-shaped function representing a proportional cost applied to the absolute difference between an existing and a new portfolio. The proposed model considered the transaction costs in the portfolio return that was optimized in a mean-variance approach. The author examined the effect of transaction costs on portfolio performance.

Young (1998) extended his linear minimax model to include for each security both a fixed cost and a variable cost for unit purchased. This is one of the first papers directly accounting for fixed transaction costs. The author underlined the importance of the investment horizon when computing the net expected return. In particular, he made an explicit assumption on the number of periods P in which the portfolio would be held. The net expected return was then computed by multiplying the portfolio return by P and then subtracting the transaction costs. The solved problem maximized the net return and considered the costs also in the capital constraint.

Mansini and Speranza (1999) dealt with a portfolio optimization problem with minimum transaction lots where the risk was measured by means of the mean semi-absolute deviation. They also considered proportional transaction costs modifying directly the securities price. Also, Crama and Schyns (2003) did not incorporate transaction costs in the objective function or in the constraints, but imposed upper bounds on the variation of the holdings from one period to the next in a mean-variance model.

In Kellerer et al. (2000) the authors studied a problem with fixed and proportional costs, and possibly with minimum transaction lots. They formulated different mixed-integer linear programming models for portfolio optimization using the mean semi-absolute deviation as risk measure. The first model considered the case in which the investor pays for each selected security a fixed sum plus a proportional cost as a percentage of the amount invested. The second model dealt with the case where along with proportional costs a fixed cost for each security is taken into account that is charged only if the sum of money invested in the individual security exceeds a predefined bound. In the models, the costs were introduced only in the return constraint. In computational experiments, the authors showed that fixed costs influence portfolio diversification and that the introduction of costs, much more than their amount, had a relevant impact on portfolio diversification. Such an impact was strengthened by the introduction of minimum lots.

Konno and Wijayanayake (2001) analyzed a portfolio construction/rebalancing problem under concave transaction costs and minimal transaction unit constraints. The concave transaction cost for each security was assumed to be a nonlinear function of the investment (a nondecreasing concave function up to certain invested amount). This modeled the situation where the unit transaction cost is relatively large when the amount invested is small, and gradually decreases as amount increases. In fact, the unit transaction cost may increase beyond some point, due to illiquidity effects, and become convex. The authors, however, assumed that the amount of investment (disinvestment) is below that point and that the transaction cost was defined by a well specified concave function. They adopted the absolute deviation of the rate of return of the portfolio as risk measure. The net return, after payment of the transaction costs, was maximized while the risk was bounded in the constraints. A branch and bound algorithm was proposed to compute an optimal solution.

Chiodi et al. (2003) considered mutual funds as assets on which to build a portfolio. They proposed a mixed-integer linear programming model for a buy-and-hold strategy, with the mean semi-absolute deviation as risk measure where variable (commissions to enter/leave the funds) and fixed (management fees) costs were included. In particular, they analyzed a classical type of entering commissions where the applied commission rate decreases when the capital invested increases and assuming as null the leaving commission, which is the case of an investor who does not leave the fund as long as leaving commissions are charged. The entering cost function was a concave piecewise linear function, and binary variables were introduced to correctly model the problem. The costs were considered only in the expected return constraint.

Beasley et al. (2003) analyzed the index tracking problem (i.e., the problem of reproducing the performance of a stock market index without purchasing all of the stocks that make up the index), and explicitly included transaction costs for buying or selling stocks. They suggested a new way of dealing with transaction costs by directly imposing a limit on the total transaction costs that could be incurred. This was a way to prevent the costs to become excessive. Costs were then introduced in the capital constraint to reduce the amount of cash available for the reinvestment. As stated by the authors, the majority of the work on index tracking presented in the literature does not consider transaction costs.

In Mansini and Speranza (2005) the authors considered a single-period mean-safety portfolio optimization problem using the mean downside underachievement as performance measure (i.e., the safety measure corresponding to the mean semi-absolute deviation). The problem considered integer constraints on the amounts invested in the securities (rounds) and fixed transaction costs enclosed in both the constraint on the expected return and the objective function. The paper presented one of the first exact approaches to the solution of a portfolio optimization model with real features.

In Konno and Yamamoto (2005) the authors analyzed a portfolio optimization problem under concave and piecewise constant transaction cost. They formulated the problem as non-concave maximization problem under linear constraints using the absolute deviation as a measure of risk. Konno et al. (2005) proposed a branch and bound algorithm for solving a class of long-short portfolio optimization problems with concave and d.c. (difference of two convex functions) transaction cost and complementary conditions on the variables. They maximized the return subject to a bound on the absolute deviation value of the portfolio.

Xue et al. (2006) studied the classical mean-variance model modified to include a nondecreasing concave function to approximate the original transaction cost function, as described by Konno and Wijayanayake (2001). In the resulting model, costs were treated only in the objective function. A branch-and-bound algorithm was proposed to solve the problem.

Best and Hlouskova (2005) considered the problem of maximizing an expected utility function of a given number of assets, such as the mean-variance or power-utility function. Associated with a change in an asset holding from its current or target value, the authors considered a transaction cost. They accounted for the transaction costs implicitly rather than explicitly.

Lobo et al. (2007) dealt with a single-period portfolio optimization by assuming a reoptimization of a current portfolio. They considered the maximization of expected return, taking transaction costs into account in the capital constraints or as an alternative, minimizing the transaction costs subject to a minimum expected return requirement.

Angelelli et al. (2008) considered two different mixed-integer linear programming models for solving the single-period portfolio optimization problem, taking into account integer stock units, transaction costs, and a cardinality constraint. The first model was formulated using the maximization of the worst conditional expectation. The second model was based on the maximization of the safety measure associated with the mean absolute deviation. In both models, proportional and fixed costs had to be paid if any positive amount was invested in a security. Costs were deducted from the expected return and the net returns were also considered in the objective function.

In Bertsimas and Shioda (2009) the authors focused on the traditional mean-variance portfolio optimization model with cardinality constraint. They also considered some costs reflecting the stock price impact derived from purchase or sale orders. The magnitude of the costs depended on the particular stock and on the trade sizes: large purchase orders increased the price whereas large sale orders decreased the price of the stock. Assuming symmetric impact for purchases and sales, the authors modeled this effect by a quadratic function included only in the objective function.

Le Thi et al. (2009) addressed the portfolio optimization under step-increasing transaction costs. The step-increasing functions were approximated, as closely as desired, by a difference of polyhedral convex functions. They maximized the net expected return.

Guastaroba et al. (2009) modified the single-period portfolio optimization model to introduce portfolio rebalancing. They used the conditional value at risk (CVaR) as measure of risk and studied the optimal portfolio selection problem considering fixed and proportional transaction costs in both the return constraint and the objective function.

Baule (2010) studied a direct application of classical portfolio selection theory for the small investor, taking into account transaction costs in the form of bank and broker fees. In particular, the problem maximized the single-period expected utility and introduced cost in the form of proportional cost with minimum charge, that is cost was constant up to a defined amount. Above this amount, cost was assumed to increase linearly. The analysis was made in terms of tangent portfolio.

Krejić et al. (2011) considered the problem of portfolio optimization under value at risk (VaR) risk measure, taking into account transaction costs. Fixed costs as well as impact costs as a nonlinear function of trading activity were incorporated in the optimal portfolio model that resulted to be a nonlinear optimization problem with nonsmooth objective function. The model was solved by an iterative method based on a smoothing VaR technique. The authors proved the convergence of the considered iterative procedure and demonstrated the nontrivial influence of transaction costs on the optimal portfolio weights. More recently, Woodside-Oriakhi et al. (2013) considered the problem of rebalancing an existing portfolio, where transaction costs had to be paid if the amount held of any asset was varied. The transaction costs may be fixed and/or variable. The problem was modeled as a mixed-integer quadratic program with an explicit constraint on the amount to pay as transaction costs.

Angelelli et al. (2012) proposed a new heuristic framework, called Kernel Search, to solve the complex problem of portfolio selection with real features such as cardinality constraint. They considered fixed and proportional transaction costs inserted in both return constraint and objective function represented by CVaR maximization.

AN LP COMPUTABLE RISK MEASURE: THE SEMI-MAD

While the classical risk measure, from the original Markowitz model (1952), is the standard deviation or variance, several other performance measures have been later considered, giving rise to an entire family of portfolio optimization models (see Mansini et al. 2003b and 2014). It is beyond the scope of this chapter to discuss the different measures. In order to have a complete modeling framework and also in view of the computational testing, we choose one of the most popular LP computable risk measures, the semi-mean absolute deviation (semi-MAD). To make this chapter self-contained, we briefly recall the basic portfolio optimization model with the semi-MAD as risk function.

We consider T scenarios with probabilities $p_t, t = 1, \ldots, T$, and assume that for each random variable R_j its realization r_{jt} under the scenario t is known and $\mu_j = \sum_{t=1}^{T} r_{jt}/T$. Typically, the realizations are derived from historical data. Similar to the mean $\mu(x)$, the realizations of the portfolio returns R_x are given by $y_t = \sum_{j=1}^{n} r_{jt}x_j, t = 1, \ldots, T$.

The mean absolute deviation (MAD) model was first introduced by Konno and Yamazaki (1991) with the mean absolute deviation $\delta(x)$ as risk measure. The MAD is the mean of the differences between the average portfolio return (or rate of return in case the investments are expressed in shares and not in amounts) and the portfolio return in the scenarios, where the differences are taken in absolute value. The semi-MAD was introduced in Speranza (1993) as the mean absolute downside deviation, where the mean is taken only over the scenarios where the return is below the average portfolio return. The mean absolute downside deviation is equal to the mean upside deviation and equal to half the MAD. The measure is simply referred to as semi-MAD and indicated as $\bar{\delta}(x)$, with

$$\delta(x) = \mathbb{E}\{|R_x - \mu(x)|\} = 2\bar{\delta}(x).$$

Adopting the semi-MAD as risk measure gives rise to portfolio optimization models that are equivalent to those adopting the MAD. For discrete random variables, the semi-MAD is LP computable as follows (see Mansini et al. 2003b for details):

$$\min \sum_{t=1}^{T} p_t \overline{d}_t \tag{8.2}$$

$$\overline{d}_t + \sum_{j \in N} (r_{jt} - \mu_j) x_j \geq 0 \quad t = 1, \ldots, T \tag{8.3}$$

$$\sum_{j \in N} \mu_j x_j \geq \mu_0 \tag{8.4}$$

$$\sum_{j \in N} x_j = \overline{C} \tag{8.5}$$

$$x_j \geq 0 \quad j \in N \tag{8.6}$$

$$\overline{d}_t \geq 0 \quad t = 1, \ldots, T, \tag{8.7}$$

where variable $\overline{d}_t, t = 1, \ldots, T$, represents the portfolio semi-deviation under scenario t that is, the difference between the average portfolio return and the portfolio return under scenario t. We refer to this model as the basic semi-MAD model.

In order to guarantee the mean-risk efficiency of the optimal solution even in the case of discontinuous efficient frontier, we consider the regularized MAD model:

$$\min \sum_{t=1}^{T} p_t \overline{d}_t - \varepsilon \sum_{j=1}^{n} \mu_j x_j \tag{8.8}$$

s.t. $(8.3) - (8.7)$,

thus differing from the basic semi-MAD model (8.2) to (8.7) only due to the objective function combining the original risk measure with the expected return discounted by an arbitrary small positive number ε.

Note that the SSD consistent (Ogryczak and Ruszczyński 1999) and coherent MAD model with complementary safety measure, $\mu_\delta(x) = \mu(x) - \overline{\delta}(x) = \mathbb{E}\{\min\{\mu(x), R_x\}\}$ (Mansini et al. 2003a), leads to the following LP minimization problem:

$$\min \sum_{t=1}^{T} p_t \overline{d}_t - \sum_{j=1}^{n} \mu_j x_j \tag{8.9}$$

s.t. $(8.3) - (8.7)$

which is a special case of (8.8).

MODELING TRANSACTION COSTS

We define *available capital* as the total amount of money that is available to an investor, both for the investment in securities and possible additional costs. In general, part of this money may be left uninvested. The *invested capital* is the capital strictly used for the investment and that yields a return.

Frequently, in portfolio optimization models the invested capital coincides with the available capital and is a constant, which is the case in the basic semi-MAD model (8.2)–(8.7). Being a constant, capital $\overline{C}$ can be normalized to 1, while the amount invested in each security can be expressed as share by the linear transformation $w_j = x_j/\overline{C}$. Although in many cases the modeling of the investment in a security as amount or share is irrelevant, there are cases, as when transaction lots are considered, where the use of amounts instead of shares, is necessary (see Mansini and Speranza 1999). This is the reason why from the beginning of this paper we have used the value $\overline{C}$ of the available capital, and the amounts x_j as variables in the portfolio optimization.

When considering transaction costs in portfolio optimization models, two main modeling issues have to be analyzed:

- the structure of the transaction costs;
- how the transaction costs are incorporated into a portfolio optimization model.

In the following, we will develop these two issues. For the sake of simplicity, we will restrict the presentation to a buy-and-hold strategy of the kind considered in the Markowitz model, where a portfolio is constructed and not rebalanced.

Structure of the Transaction Costs

Transaction costs are commonly classified as fixed and variable. For each of these two classes, we will analyze the most common cost functions. General cost functions may not be linear; see, for instance, the concave cost function dealt with in Konno and Wijayanayake (2001). With concave transaction costs, the portfolio optimization problem becomes nonlinear and hard to solve, even without binary or integer variables. For this reason, concave functions are often approximated by piecewise linear functions.

Let us indicate with $K(x)$ the transaction cost function for portfolio x. We will assume that transaction costs are charged on each security, independently of the investment in the others. Thus, we restrict our analysis to functions that are separable, such that

$$K(x) = \sum_{j \in N} K_j(x_j).$$ (8.10)

Fixed Costs A *fixed transaction cost* is a cost that is paid for handling a security independently of the amount of money invested. The total transaction cost for security j can be expressed as:

$$K_j(x_j) := \begin{cases} f_j & \text{if } x_j > 0, \\ 0 & \text{otherwise,} \end{cases}$$

where f_j is the transaction cost paid if security j is included in the portfolio.

To include fixed costs in a mathematical programming model we need binary variables z_j, one for each security $j, j \in N$. Variable z_j must be equal to 1 when security j is selected in the portfolio, and to 0 otherwise. Constraints need to be added that impose that z_j is equal to 1 if $x_j > 0$ and 0 otherwise. Typical linear constraints are

$$l_j z_j \leq x_j \leq u_j z_j,$$ (8.11)

where l_j, u_j are positive lower and upper bounds on the amount invested on security j, with u_j possibly equal to $\overline{C}$. These constraints impose that if $x_j > 0$ then $z_j = 1$, and that if $x_j = 0$ then $z_j = 0$.

From now on, we identify the above cost structure imposing a fixed cost f_j for each selected security j as *pure fixed cost* (PFC) (see Figure 8.1, left-hand side). This is one of the most common cost structures applied by financial institutions to investors.

Variable Costs Variable transaction costs depend on the capital invested in the securities and may have different structures. We divide variable transaction cost functions into linear (proportional) cost functions, convex and concave piecewise linear cost functions. In all cases the transactions costs $K_j(x)$ are introduced through variables $k_j (j \in N)$ defined by appropriate relations to other model variables.

Linear Cost Function Proportional transaction costs are the most used in practice and the most frequently analyzed in the literature. In this case, a rate c_j is specified for each security $j \in N$ as a percentage of the invested amount in the security:

$$k_j = c_j x_j$$ (8.12)

and $K(x) = \sum_{j=1}^{n} k_j$. We call this cost structure pure proportional cost (PPC).

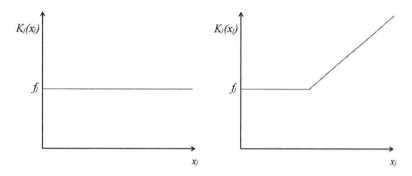

FIGURE 8.1 Pure fixed cost structure (left-hand figure) and proportional cost with minimum charge structure (right-hand figure).

Convex Piecewise Linear Cost Function We consider here the case where each $K_j(x_j), j \in N$, is a convex piecewise linear function. Convex piecewise linear costs are not frequently used in practice, but can be encountered as leaving commissions for mutual funds and model some cost components as taxes. A different rate c_{ji} is applied to each, nonoverlapping with others, interval $i \in I$ of capital invested in security $j, j \in N$, that is:

$$
K_j(x_j) := \begin{cases}
c_{j1}x_j & \text{if } 0 \le x_j \le M_1, \\
c_{j2}(x_j - M_1) + c_{j1}M_1 & \text{if } M_1 \le x_j \le M_2, \\
\begin{aligned}&c_{j3}(x_j - M_2) + c_{j1}M_1 \\ &+ c_{j2}(M_2 - M_1)\end{aligned} & \text{if } M_2 \le x_j \le M_3, \\
\dots \\
\begin{aligned}&c_{j|I|}(x_j - M_{|I|-1}) + c_{j1}M_1 \\ &+ c_{j2}(M_2 - M_1) + \dots + c_{j,|I|-1}(M_{|I|-1} - M_{|I|-2})\end{aligned} & \text{if } x_j \ge M_{|I|-1},
\end{cases}
$$

where $M_1, \dots, M_{|I|-1}$ are the extremes defining the intervals into which the capital is divided. Note that, without loss of generality, we can always assume that also the last interval $(M_{|I|-1}, \infty)$ has a finite upper bound $M_{|I|}$ corresponding to the maximum amount that can be invested in a security, that is, the whole capital $\overline{C}$.

As $K_j(x_j)$ is convex, the rates c_{ji} are increasing, that is, $c_{j1} < c_{j2} < c_{j3} < \dots < c_{j|I|}$. In Figure 8.2, we show an example of a three intervals convex piecewise linear function.

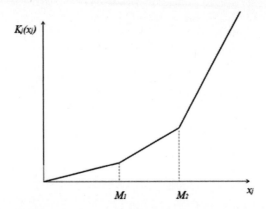

FIGURE 8.2 A convex piecewise linear cost function.

This case is easy to model in terms of linear constraints and continuous variables when the costs are minimized within the optimization model (Williams 2013). Namely, introducing one continuous variable x_{ji} for each interval $i \in I$, the investment x_j in security j can be expressed as the sum of all auxiliary variables x_{ji} as:

$$x_j = \sum_{i \in I} x_{ji} \tag{8.13}$$

and the transaction cost function as:

$$k_j = \sum_{i \in I} c_{ji} x_{ji} \tag{8.14}$$

with the additional constraints:

$$0 \le x_{j1} \le M_1 \tag{8.15}$$

$$0 \le x_{j2} \le (M_2 - M_1) \tag{8.16}$$

$$\ldots \tag{8.17}$$

$$0 \le x_{j,|I|-1} \le (M_{|I|-1} - M_{|I|-2}) \tag{8.18}$$

$$0 \le x_{j,|I|} \le \overline{C} - M_{|I|-1}. \tag{8.19}$$

This LP model guarantees only inequalities $k_j \ge K_j(x_j)$, which is enough when relying on optimization model to enforce minimal costs if possible.

In fact, due to the increasing cost rates, a sensible complete optimization model should be such that it is not beneficial to activate variable x_{ji} unless all variables with a smaller cost rate are saturated. Unfortunately, as demonstrated further, it is not always the case in portfolio optimization where a risk measure is minimized.

Therefore, to represent equations not relying on optimization process, we should also include constraints that impose that, if variable x_{ji} takes a positive value, all variables $x_{jk}, k = 1, \ldots, i - 1$, are set to their upper bounds. For this purpose, one needs to implement implications by binary variables replacing (8.15)–(8.19) with the following:

$$M_1 y_{j2} \leq x_{j1} \leq M_1 \tag{8.20}$$

$$(M_2 - M_1)y_{j3} \leq x_{j2} \leq (M_2 - M_1)y_{j2} \tag{8.21}$$

$$\ldots$$

$$(M_{|I|-1} - M_{|I|-2})y_{j,|I|} \leq x_{j,|I|-1} \leq (M_{|I|-1} - M_{|I|-2})y_{j,|I|-1} \tag{8.22}$$

$$0 \leq x_{j,|I|} \leq (\overline{C} - M_{|I|-1})y_{j,|I|} \tag{8.23}$$

where $y_{j2}, \ldots, y_{j,|I|}$ are binary variables.

Concave Piecewise Linear Cost Function Each cost function $K_j(x_j), j \in N$ is here a piecewise linear concave function. In this case, the rates c_{ji} are decreasing, that is, $c_{j1} > c_{j2} > c_{j3} > \ldots > c_{j|I|}$. This structure of transaction costs is commonly applied by financial institutions and frequently appears as entering commission for mutual funds. These costs are also studied in the literature for the market illiquidity effect described in Konno and Wijayanayake (2001). In Figure 8.3, we show an example of a four intervals concave piecewise linear function, where $M_4 = \overline{C}$.

Contrary to the case of convex functions, in a "sensible" complete model, the variable x_{ji} has a smaller rate and thus is more convenient than all variables $x_{jk}, k = 1, \ldots, i - 1$ associated with the preceding intervals. Then, we always need here additional binary variables, one for each interval, as in (8.20) – (8.23).

Another model can be built when having available the list of all breaking points for the cost function. In addition to the r breaking points $(M_1, K_j(M_1)), \ldots, (M_r, K_j(M_r))$, we have the starting point $(M_0, K_j(M_0))$ corresponding to the origin $(0, 0)$. Again, we can assume that the last breaking point is $M_r = \overline{C}$. For example, in Figure 8.3 we have four breaking

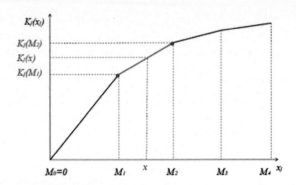

FIGURE 8.3 A concave piecewise linear cost function.

points, plus the origin. We know that each line segment can be expressed as the convex combination of its extremes. Then, if $M_i \leq x \leq M_{i+1}$, x can be expressed as $x = \lambda_i M_i + \lambda_{i+1} M_{i+1}$ with $\lambda_i + \lambda_{i+1} = 1, \lambda_i, \lambda_{i+1} \geq 0$, we correctly obtain $K_j(x) = \lambda_i K_j(M_i) + \lambda_{i+1} K_j(M_{i+1})$ (see, for instance, the line segment between $(M_1, K_j(M_1))$ and $(M_2, K_j(M_2))$ in Figure 8.3). Thus, we have to consider each single line segment connecting two consecutive breaking points and use additional binary variables $y_i, i = 0, \ldots, r-1$, where $y_i = 1$ if $M_i \leq x \leq M_{i+1}$ and $y_i = 0$ otherwise. The resulting linear constraints are (see Williams 2013):

$$x_j = \sum_{i=0}^{r} \lambda_i M_i, \tag{8.24}$$

and

$$K_j(x_j) = \sum_{i=0}^{r} \lambda_i K_j(M_i), \tag{8.25}$$

with constraints on variables as follows:

$$0 \leq \lambda_0 \leq y_0 \tag{8.26}$$

$$0 \leq \lambda_i \leq y_{i-1} + y_i, \quad i = 1, \ldots, r-1 \tag{8.27}$$

$$\lambda_r \leq y_{r-1} \tag{8.28}$$

$$\sum_{i=0}^{r-1} y_i = 1. \tag{8.29}$$

Note that, thanks to these constraints, only pairs of adjacent coefficients λ_i are allowed to be strictly positive.

Linear Function with Minimum Charge In practice, a common piecewise linear cost function frequently used by financial institutions has the structure shown in Figure 8.1 (right-hand side). This structure models a situation where a fixed cost f_j is charged for any invested amount lower than or equal to a given threshold $M = f_j/c_j$ and then, for an investment greater than M, a proportional cost c_j is charged:

$$K_j(x_j) := \begin{cases} 0 & \text{if } x_j = 0, \\ f_j & \text{if } 0 < x_j \leq M, \\ c_j x_j & \text{if } x_j \geq M. \end{cases}$$

We call this cost structure proportional cost with minimum charge (PCMC). This cost structure is convex piecewise linear with a discontinuity at $x_j = 0$. The inequality $k_j \geq K_j(x_j)$ with, thus, the model relying on optimization of transaction costs can be easily built with inequalities:

$$k_j \geq f_j y_j, \quad k_j \geq c_j x_j, \quad 0 \leq x_j \leq \overline{C} y_j, \tag{8.30}$$

where y_j are binary variables.

In order to get a model not relying on the optimization (and thus imposing equality $k_j = K_j(x_j)$), one needs to build the corresponding model (8.20)–(8.23), together with a defined minimal investment level l_j and corresponding fixed charge inequalities:

$$x_j = x_{j1} + x_{j2} \tag{8.31}$$

$$l_j y_{j1} \leq x_{j1} \tag{8.32}$$

$$M y_{j2} \leq x_{j1} \leq M y_{j1} \tag{8.33}$$

$$0 \leq x_{j2} \leq (\overline{C} - M) y_{j2} \tag{8.34}$$

with the cost formula:

$$k_j = f_j y_{j1} + c_j x_{j2}, \tag{8.35}$$

where y_{j1} and y_{j2} are binary variables.

Transaction Costs in Portfolio Optimization

Now, we will discuss the most common ways to embed transaction costs in a complete portfolio optimization model:

1. Costs in the return constraint: Transaction costs are considered as a sum (or a percentage, in case of shares instead of amounts) directly deducted from the average portfolio return (rate of return, in case of shares instead of amounts). This assumption is reasonable in a single-period investment, provided that the investor has a clear idea of the length of his/her investment period when deducting such an amount from the return. We will clarify this concept later.
2. Costs in the capital constraint: Transaction costs reduce the capital available. In this case, the invested capital is different from the initial capital and is not a constant but depends on the transaction costs paid, that is, on the portfolio. This way of dealing with transaction costs is more frequent in rebalancing problems.

In addition to the two main ways of considering transaction costs, one may also impose an upper bound on the total transaction costs paid (see, e.g., Beasley et al. 2003).

Let us now consider each of the two aforementioned main cases separately.

Costs in the Return Constraint In this case, the classical constraint on the expected return on the portfolio is modified as follows:

$$\sum_{j \in N} \mu_j x_j - \sum_{j \in N} K_j(x_j) \geq \mu_0 \overline{C}. \tag{8.36}$$

This models the situation where the transaction costs are charged at the end of the investment period.

As mentioned earlier, the introduction of the transaction costs in the return constraint correctly models the problem if the investor has an investment horizon in mind (see also Young 1998). To clarify the concept, we consider an example. Let us assume that a proportional cost equal to 0.20 percent for each transaction is charged. If the investment horizon is one year, a percentage 0.20 percent will have to be deducted from each return rate μ_j, computed on a yearly basis, in constraint (8.36). If, on the contrary, the horizon is of one month only, then the percentage 0.20 percent will have to be deducted from the return rate μ_j computed this time on a monthly basis. In the last case, the impact of the transaction costs is much higher. Obviously, the portfolios generated will be different.

This approach essentially depends on the assumption that the transaction costs only decrease the final return. This means we are focused on the net return $\overline{R}_x = R_x - K(x)$. Hence, in comparison to the original distribution of returns, the net returns are represented with a distribution shifted by the transaction costs. Such a shift directly affects the expected value $\overline{\mu}(x) = \mathbb{E}\{\overline{R}_x\} = \mathbb{E}\{R_x\} - K(x) = \mu(x) - K(x)$. On the other hand, for shift-independent risk measures like the MAD, we get for the net returns the same value of risk measure as for the original returns $\mathbb{E}\{|\overline{R}_x - \mathbb{E}\{\overline{R}_x\}|\} = \mathbb{E}\{|R_x - \mathbb{E}\{R_x\}|\}$. This means such a risk measure minimization is neutral with respect to the transaction costs, and it does not support the cost minimization. When using this risk minimization, one needs to use exact models for transactions cost calculation, models that do not rely on optimization to charge the correct amount of the transaction costs. In addition, one may face another difficulty related to discontinuous efficient frontier and non-unique optimal solution (possibly inefficient). All these problems can be solved, if the risk minimization is regularized with the introduction of an additional term on mean net return. Actually, there is no such problem when coherent (safety) forms of risk measures are used. Optimization based on such measures supports costs minimization and therefore allows us for simpler cost models while guaranteeing efficient solutions.

Costs in the Capital Constraint If the transaction costs are accounted for in the capital constraint, the invested capital becomes a variable C, in general different from the initial available capital $\overline{C}$. The invested capital will be

$$C = \overline{C} - \sum_{j=1}^{n} K_j(x_j),$$

when the initial capital is entirely used, either in investment or in transaction costs, which is the most common case and the natural extension of the classical Markowitz model. In this case, when using amounts (with respect to shares), risk decreases due to decreased invested capital. This means that higher transaction costs result in lower absolute risk measure value (Woodside-Oriakhi et al. 2013). Such an absolute risk minimization may be simply achieved due to increasing transaction costs. Transaction costs must be then modeled exactly (with equality relations). This applies also to the coherent (safety) measures. To get better results, one should use rather relative risk measurement dividing by the invested capital. However, the invested capital is a variable thus leading to the ratio criteria, which creates further complications. For instance, in Mitchell and Braun (2013) the authors considered convex transaction costs incurred when rebalancing an investment portfolio in a mean-variance framework. In order to properly represent the variance of the resulting portfolio, they suggested rescaling by the funds available after paying the transaction costs.

In our computational analysis, we have focused on the costs in the return constraint approach as more popular and better suited for risk-minimization models with amounts as decision variables, rather than shares.

NON-UNIQUE MINIMUM RISK PORTFOLIO

The problem of non-unique minimum risk portfolios with bounded (required) expected return may arise also when transaction costs are ignored. As a very naive example, one may consider a case where two risk-free assets are available with different returns but both meeting the required expected return.

In the following we show a nontrivial example of non-unique solution for the case of proportional transaction costs with minimum charge.

Example

Let us consider the case of proportional transaction costs with minimum charge (see Figure 8.1, right-hand side). Let us assume $f_j = 50$ while the proportional cost is on the level of 1 percent; that is, $c_j = 0.01$.

$$K_j(x_j) = \begin{cases} 0 & \text{if } x_j = 0 \\ \max\{50, 0.01x_j\} & \text{if } x_j > 0. \end{cases}$$

Consider a simplified portfolio optimization problem having three assets available with rates of return represented by r.v. $R_1, R_2,$ and R_3, respectively. They are defined by realizations r_{jt} under three equally probable scenarios S_t, $t = 1, 2, 3$, as presented in Table 8.2. Thus, the expected rates of return are given as $0.1567, 0.1507,$ and 0.1492, respectively. The capital to be invested is $\overline{C} = 10,000$.

Consider a portfolio (x_1, x_2, x_3) defined by the shares of capital in terms of amounts defining a portfolio, $x_1 + x_2 + x_3 = \overline{C}$, thus generating rate of return represented by r.v. $R_x = x_1 R_1 + x_2 R_2 + x_3 R_3$. The expected net return of the portfolio taking into account the transaction costs is given by the following formula:

$$\overline{\mu}(x) = (0.1567x_1 + 0.1507x_2 + 0.1492x_3) - K_1(x_1) - K_2(x_2) - K_3(x_3).$$
$$(8.37)$$

TABLE 8.2 Rates of Return (in %) for Three Assets under Three Scenarios.

	Scenarios		
Assets	S1	S2	S3
R_1	14.67	14.67	17.67
R_2	15.07	16.07	14.07
R_3	15.92	14.92	13.92

Assume we are looking for minimum risk portfolio meeting the specified lower bound on the expected net return, say 14 percent—that is,

$$\overline{\mu}(x) \geq 0.14\overline{C}. \tag{8.38}$$

We focus our analysis on the risk measured with the mean absolute deviation. Note that our absolute risk measure is defined on distributions of returns not reduced by the transaction costs. However, the transaction costs are deterministic; this causes the same risk measure to remain valid for the net returns.

Finally, our problem of minimizing risk under the required return takes the following form:

$$\min\{\overline{\delta}(x): \ x_1 + x_2 + x_3 = \overline{C}, \ x_j \geq 0 \ \forall j, \ \overline{\mu}(x) \geq 0.14\overline{C}\}. \tag{8.39}$$

One can find out that the required return bound may be satisfied by two single asset portfolios $(\overline{C}, 0, 0)$ and $(0, \overline{C}, 0)$, as well as by some two-asset portfolios with large enough share of the first asset, that is, portfolios $(x_1, x_2, 0)$ built on R_1 and R_2 with $x_1 \geq 43/160\overline{C}$, and portfolios $(x_1, 0, x_3)$ built on R_1 and R_3 with $x_1 \geq 58/175\overline{C}$. On the other hand, no two-asset portfolio built on R_2 and R_3 and no three-asset portfolio fulfills the required return bound.

While minimizing the MAD measure, one can see that $\delta(\overline{C}, 0, 0) = 0.04\overline{C}/3$ and $\delta(0, \overline{C}, 0) = 0.02\overline{C}/3$. Among portfolios $(x_1, x_2, 0)$ built on R_1 and R_2, the minimum MAD measure is achieved for $\delta(\overline{C}/3, 2\overline{C}/3, 0) = 0.02\overline{C}/9$. Similarly, among portfolios $(x_1, 0, x_3)$ built on R_1 and R_3, the minimum MAD measure is achieved for $\delta(\overline{C}/3, 0, 2\overline{C}/3) = 0.02\overline{C}/9$. Thus, finally, while minimizing the MAD measure, one has two alternative optimal portfolios $(\overline{C}/3, 2\overline{C}/3, 0)$ and $(\overline{C}/3, 0, 2\overline{C}/3)$. Both portfolios have the same MAD value, but they are quite different with respect to the expected return.

Expected return of portfolio $(\overline{C}/3, 0, 2\overline{C}/3)$ is smaller than that of portfolio $(\overline{C}/3, 2\overline{C}/3, 0)$. Therefore, portfolio $(\overline{C}/3, 0, 2\overline{C}/3)$ is clearly dominated (inefficient) in terms of mean-risk analysis. While solving problem (8.39), one may receive any of the two min risk portfolios. It may be just the dominated one. Therefore, a regularized risk minimization must be used to guarantee selection of an efficient portfolio:

$$\min\{\delta(x) - \varepsilon\overline{\mu}(x): \ x_1 + x_2 + x_3 = \overline{C}, \ x_j \geq 0 \ \forall j, \overline{\mu}(x) \geq 0.14\overline{C}\}. \quad (8.40)$$

Note that such a regularization is not necessary if the corresponding safety measure is maximized instead of the risk measure minimization.

Details on the supporting calculations for the example presented in this section can be found in the Appendix.

EXPERIMENTAL ANALYSIS

In this section, we revisit the portfolio optimization problem with transaction costs, exploring the impact of transaction costs incurred in portfolio optimization using real data. We consider a capital invested equal to 100,000 euros, a unique set of 20 securities from Italian Stock Exchange with weekly rates of returns over a period of two years ($T = 104$), and three different values for the required rate of return, $\mu_0 = 0, 5, 10$ percent (on a yearly basis), respectively. The data set is available on the website of the book. We test and compare the three cost structures identified as pure fixed cost (PFC), pure proportional cost (PPC), and proportional cost with minimum charge (PCMC). As objective function, we consider the semi-MAD as risk measure (see (8.2)), the regularized semi-MAD (see (8.8)) and the semi-MAD as safety measure (see (8.9)), respectively. This means we solved $3 \times 3 \times 3 = 27$ portfolio optimization instances altogether. Models were implemented in C++ using Concert Technology with CPLEX10.

In the Italian market, a small investor who wants to allocate her/his capital buying online a portfolio usually incurs in costs as shown in Table 8.3 (source is online information brochure provided by banks). These costs are applied by banks for reception and transmission of orders on behalf of the customers through online trading. Assets are from the Italian Stock Exchange. Dealing with foreign assets implies larger costs. Not all banks apply pure fixed costs. However, when available, the option implies a cost that varies from a minimum of 9 euros for transaction to a maximum of 12.

In the following experimental results, we assume that the proportional cost is equal to $c_j = 0.25$ percent for all the securities in both the PPC and the

TABLE 8.3 Transaction Costs Applied by Banks Operating in Italy.

	ITALY				
Bank	%	min	max	>	<
Unicredit	0.21%	€ 11.50	–	€ 5,476	–
Fineco	0.19%	€ 2.95	€ 19.00	€ 1,553	€ 10,000
Webank	0.19%	€ 2.75	€ 19.50	€ 1,447	€ 10,263
Intesas.p.	0.24%	€ 3.50	–	€ 1,458	–
INGdirect	0.19%	€ 8.00	€ 18.00	€ 4,211	€ 9,474
CheBanca	0.18%	€ 3.00	–	€ 1,667	–
MonteP.S.	0.25%	€ 12.00	–	€ 4,800	–
Barclays	0.40%	€ 5.00	–	€ 1,250	–

PCMC cases. This value corresponds to the average percentage imposed by the banks. In particular, in PCMC the value M corresponding to the capital threshold under which a fixed charge is applied is set to 4,000 euros. This implies $f_j = 10$ for all the securities. Finally, in case of a PFC structure, we assume $f_j = 10$ euros for all the assets. Again, the value corresponds to the average value applied in practice.

In Table 8.4, we provide the results obtained when applying the PPC structure. The table is divided in three parts, one for each objective function, namely the semi-MAD (in the risk form), semi-MAD regularized with the introduction of an adjustment coefficient ($\epsilon = 0.05$) (8.8), and the semi-MAD formulated as a coherent (safety) measure (8.9). For the first two parts the three columns correspond to three different required rates of return (on a yearly basis) set to 0 percent, 5 percent, and 10 percent, respectively. For the safety measure, we only provide the MSP (maximum safety portfolio) since for any μ_0 lower than the expected net return of the MSP, the MSP is the optimal solution to the problem. Table 8.4 consists of six lines. Line "#" indicates the number of selected securities, while lines "min" and "max" provide the minimum (positive) and the maximum amounts per security invested in the portfolio; line "cost" shows the total cost paid in the transaction costs whereas line "net return" provides the portfolio return net of the transaction costs. Finally, "obj" reports the value of the objective function.

Tables 8.5 and 8.6 provide the same results shown in Table 8.4 for the PFC and the PCMC structures, respectively.

One may notice that the semi-MAD model in the coherent (safety) form, even with proportional transaction costs, builds portfolios with an

TABLE 8.4 Computational Results: Pure Proportional Cost Structure with $c_j = 0.25$ percent for all $j \in N$.

μ_0	Semi-MAD			Regularized Semi-MAD			Safety Semi-MAD
	0%	5%	10%	0%	5%	10%	MSP
#	14	16	17	16	16	17	3
min	156.895	595.122	75.275	124.179	595.122	75.2747	12864.6
max	29536.3	25930.5	20427.8	25161	25930.5	20427.8	49861.3
cost	250	250	250	250	250	250	250
net return	0	93.871	183.457	65.0415	93.8713	183.457	2014.62
obj	588.802	596.485	608.555	574.449	574.598	577.71	−1938.07

TABLE 8.5 Computational Results: Pure Fixed Cost Structure with $f_j = 10$ euros for all $j \in N$.

μ_0	Semi-MAD			Regularized Semi-MAD			Safety Semi-MAD
	0	5%	10%	0	5%	10%	MSP
#	14	14	11	12	12	12	3
min	189.887	189.887	1254.94	1201.91	1201.91	1201.91	12864.6
max	30245.3	30245.3	31503.2	28104.3	28104.3	28104.3	49861.3
cost	140	140	110	120	120	120	30
net return	94.401	94.401	183.457	188.616	188.616	188.616	2234.62
obj	587.995	587.995	593.014	568.706	568.706	568.706	−2158.07

extremely low level of diversification and high expected return. Therefore, the introduction of fixed transaction costs or minimum charge transaction costs does not affect results of this model. On the other hand, in the standard semi-MAD model and its regularized version, introducing fixed (minimum) charges into the transaction costs schemes decreases the portfolio diversification while still keeping it at a reasonable level. Moreover, in comparison to the standard semi-MAD model, the regularized semi-MAD model even for low net return requirements generates higher expected returns, while not increasing remarkably the risk level. This model seems to be very attractive for portfolio optimization with transaction costs including fixed or minimum charges.

TABLE 8.6 Computational Results: Proportional Cost with Minimum Charge Structure with Fixed Cost Equal to 10 euros for a Minimum Charge up to 4,000 euros and 0.25% Proportional Cost for Larger Values of Capital.

μ_0	Semi-MAD			Regularized Semi-MAD			Safety Semi-MAD
	0	5%	10%	0	5%	10%	MSP
#	13	14	13	13	14	13	7
min	680.71	1126.04	1647.63	680.71	1126.04	1647.63	4000
max	28479.8	26595	21336.9	28479.8	26595	21336.9	48456.4
cost	275.002	274.57	266.201	275.002	274.57	266.201	250
net return	0	93.8713	183.457	0	93.8713	183.457	1231.73
obj	590.431	599.304	613.068	590.431	594.61	603.895	−12.9708

CONCLUSIONS

In this chapter, we analyze the portfolio optimization problem with transaction costs by classifying them in variable and fixed costs. Past and recent literature on the topic has been surveyed. We analyze in detail the most common structures of transaction costs and the different manners to model them in portfolio optimization. The introduction of transaction costs may require the use of binary variables. For this reason, we focus on a risk measure that gives rise to a linear model, namely the mean semi-absolute deviation (semi-MAD).

We provide an example that shows how the portfolio optimization with transaction costs may lead to discontinuous efficient frontier and therefore a non-unique solution when minimizing the risk under a required expected return. This result motivates the introduction of a regularization term in the objective function in order to guarantee the selection of an efficient portfolio (regularized semi-MAD).

Finally, we run some simple computational results on a small set of securities to compare three simplified cost structures (pure proportional cost, pure fixed cost, proportional cost with minimum charge) when using three different objective functions: the semi-MAD in both the risk and safety form and the regularized semi-MAD. In the experimental analysis, we focus on costs inserted in the return constraint as more popular and better suited for absolute risk-minimization models. Results show how the regularized semi-MAD model even for low net return requirements generates higher expected returns while not increasing remarkably the risk level, thus resulting as an attractive model for portfolio optimization with transaction costs including fixed or minimum charges.

APPENDIX

In the following we show the main calculations behind the example reported in the fifth section of the chapter, "Non-unique Minimum Risk Portfolio." The example shows how the portfolio optimization considering proportional transaction costs with minimum charge may lead to a discontinuous efficient frontier and therefore to a non-unique solution when minimizing the risk under a required expected return.

Feasibility of Portfolios (x_1, x_2, 0)

If $x_1 \leq 5000 = 0.5\overline{C}$, then $\overline{\mu}(x_1, x_2, 0)100 = 15.67x_1 + 15.07(\overline{C} - x_1) - 0.5\overline{C} - 1.0(\overline{C} - x_1) = 1.60x_1 + 13.57\overline{C}$. Hence, $\overline{\mu}(x_1, x_2, 0)100 \geq 14\overline{C}$ for any $43/160\overline{C} \leq x_1 \leq 0.5\overline{C}$.

If $x_1 \geq 5000 = 0.5\overline{C}$, then $\overline{\mu}(x_1, x_2, 0)100 = 15.67x_1 + 15.07(\overline{C} - x_1) - 1.0x_1 - 0.5\overline{C} = -0.40x_1 + 14.57\overline{C}$. Hence, $\overline{\mu}(x_1, x_2, 0)100 \geq 14\overline{C}$ for any $0.5\overline{C} \leq x_1 \leq \overline{C}$.

Finally, feasibility for $43/160\overline{C} \leq x_1 \leq \overline{C}$.

Feasibility of Portfolios (x_1, 0, x_3)

If $x_1 \leq 5000 = 0.5\overline{C}$, then $\overline{\mu}(x_1, 0, x_3)100 = 15.67x_1 + 14.92(\overline{C} - x_1) - 0.5\overline{C} - 1.0(\overline{C} - x_1) = 1.75x_1 + 13.42\overline{C}$. Hence, $\overline{\mu}(x_1, 0, x_3)100 \geq 14\overline{C}$ for any $58/175\overline{C} \leq x_1 \leq 0.5\overline{C}$.

If $x_1 \geq 5000 = 0.5\overline{C}$, then $\overline{\mu}(x_1, 0, x_3)100 = 15.67x_1 + 14.92(\overline{C} - x_1) - 1.0x_1 - 0.5\overline{C} = -0.25x_1 + 14.42\overline{C}$. Hence, $\overline{\mu}(x_1, 0, x_3)100 \geq 14\overline{C}$ for any $0.5\overline{C} \leq x_1 \leq \overline{C}$.

Finally, feasibility for $58/175\overline{C} \leq x_1 \leq \overline{C}$.

Infeasibility of Portfolios (0, x_2, x_3)

If $x_2 \leq 5000 = 0.5\overline{C}$, then $\overline{\mu}(0, x_2, x_3)100 = 15.07x_2 + 14.92(\overline{C} - x_2) - 0.5\overline{C} - 1.0(\overline{C} - x_2) = -13.85x_2 + 13.42\overline{C}$. Hence, $\overline{\mu}(0, x_2, x_3)100 \geq 14\overline{C}$ for no $x_2 \leq 0.5\overline{C}$.

If $x_2 \geq 5000 = 0.5\overline{C}$, then $\overline{\mu}(0, x_2, x_3)100 = 15.07x_2 + 14.92(\overline{C} - x_2) - 1.0x_2 - 0.5\overline{C} = -0.85x_2 + 14.42\overline{C}$. Hence, $\overline{\mu}(0, x_2, x_3)100 \geq 14\overline{C}$ needs $0.5\overline{C} \leq x_2 \leq 42/85\overline{C}$ and there is no such x_2.

Finally, no feasibility for any $0 \leq x_2 \leq \overline{C}$.

Infeasibility of Portfolios (x_1, x_2, x_3)

If $x_1 \leq 5000 = 0.5\overline{C}$, then $\overline{\mu}(x_1, x_2, x_3)100 < 15.67x_1 + 15.07(\overline{C} - x_1) - 1.5\overline{C} = 0.60x_1 + 13.57\overline{C}$. Hence, $\overline{\mu}(x_1, x_2, x_3)100 \geq 14\overline{C}$ for no $x_1 \leq 0.5\overline{C}$.

If $x_1 \geq 5000 = 0.5\overline{C}$, then $\overline{\mu}(x_1, x_2, x_3)100 < 15.67x_1 + 15.07(\overline{C} - x_1) - 1.0x_1 - 1.0\overline{C} = -0.40x_1 + 14.07\overline{C}$. Hence, $\overline{\mu}(x_1, x_2, x_3)100 \geq 14\overline{C}$ for no $x_1 \geq 0.5\overline{C}$.

Finally, no feasibility for any $0 \leq x_1 \leq \overline{C}$.

REFERENCES

Adcock, C. J., and N. Meade, 1994. A simple algorithm to incorporate transactions costs in quadratic optimisation. *European Journal of Operational Research* 79: 85–94.

Angelelli, E., R. Mansini, and M. G. Speranza, 2008. A comparison of MAD and CVaR models with real features. *Journal of Banking and Finance* 32: 1188–1197.

_____. 2012. Kernel Search: A new heuristic framework for portfolio selection. *Computational Optimization and Applications* 51: 345–361.

Arnott, R. D., and W. H. Wagner. 1990. The measurement and control of trading costs. *Financial Analysts Journal* 46: 73–80.

Baule, R. 2010. Optimal portfolio selection for the small investor considering risk and transaction costs. *OR Spectrum* 32: 61–76.

Beasley, J. E., N. Meade, and T.-J. Chang. 2003. An evolutionary heuristic for the index tracking problem. *European Journal of Operational Research* 148: 621–643.

Bertsimas, D., and R. Shioda. 2009. Algorithm for cardinality-constrained quadratic optimization. *Computational Optimization and Applications* 43: 1–22.

Best, M. J., and J. Hlouskova. 2005. An algorithm for portfolio optimization with transaction costs. *Management Science* 51: 1676–1688.

Brennan, M. J. 1975. The optimal number of securities in a risky asset portfolio when there are fixed costs of transacting: Theory and some empirical results. *Journal of Financial and Quantitative Analysis* 10: 483–496.

Chang, T.-J., N. Meade, J. E Beasley, and Y. M. Sharaia. 2000. Heuristics for cardinality constraint portfolio optimisation. *Computers and Operations Research* 27: 1271–1302.

Chen, A. H., F. J. Fabozzi, and D. Huang. 2010. Models for portfolio revision with transaction costs in the mean-variance framework. Chapter 6 in *Handbook of Portfolio Construction*, John B. Guerard, Jr., Ed., Springer: 133–151.

Chen, A. H., F. C. Jen, and S. Zionts. 1971. The optimal portfolio revision policy. *Journal of Business* 44: 51–61.

Chiodi, L., R. Mansini, and M. G. Speranza. 2003. Semi-absolute deviation rule for mutual funds portfolio selection. *Annals of Operations Research* 124: 245–265.

Crama, Y., and M. Schyns. 2003. Simulated annealing for complex portfolio selection problems. *European Journal of Operational Research* 150: 546–571.

Guastaroba, G., R. Mansini, and M. G. Speranza. 2009. Models and simulations for portfolio rebalancing. *Computational Economics* 33: 237–262.

Jacob, N. L. 1974. A limited-diversification portfolio selection model for the small investor. *Journal of Finance* 29: 847–856.

Johnson, K. H., and D. S. Shannon. 1974. A note on diversification and the reduction of dispersion. *Journal of Financial Economics* 1: 365–372.

Kellerer, H., R. Mansini, and M. G. Speranza. 2000. Selecting portfolios with fixed cost and minimum transaction lots. *Annals of Operations Research* 99: 287–304.

Konno, H., K. Akishino, and R. Yamamoto. 2005. Optimization of a long-short portfolio under non convex transaction cost. *Computational Optimization and Applications* 32: 115–132.

Konno H., and R. Yamamoto 2005. Global optimization versus integer programming in portfolio optimization under nonconvex transaction costs. *Journal of Global Optimization* 32: 207–219.

Konno, H., and H. Yamazaki. 1991. Mean–absolute deviation portfolio optimization model and its application to Tokyo stock market. *Management Science* 37: 519–531.

Konno, H., and A. Wijayanayake. 2001. Portfolio optimization problem under concave transaction costs and minimal transaction unit constraints. *Mathematical Programming* 89: 233–250.

Krejić, N., M. Kumaresan, and A. Roznjik. 2011. VaR optimal portfolio with transaction costs. *Applied Mathematics and Computation* 218: 4626–4637.

Le Thi, H. A., M. Moeini, and T. Pham Dinh. 2009. DC programming approach for portfolio optimization under step increasing transaction costs. *Optimization: A Journal of Mathematical Programming and Operations Research* 58: 267–289.

Levy, H. 1978. Equilibrium in an imperfect market: A constraint on the number of securities in the portfolio. *American Economic Revue* 68: 643–658.

Lobo, M. S., M. Fazel, and S. Boyd. 2007. Portfolio optimization with linear and fixed transaction costs. *Annals of Operations Research* 152: 341–365.

Mansini, R., W. Ogryczak, and M. G. Speranza. 2003a. LP solvable models for portfolio optimization: A classification and computational comparison. *IMA Journal of Management Mathematics* 14: 187–220.

_____. 2003b. On LP solvable models for portfolio selection. *Informatica* 14: 37–62.

_____. 2007. Conditional value at risk and related linear programming models for portfolio optimization. *Annals of Operations Research* 152: 227–256.

_____. 2014. Twenty years of linear programming based portfolio optimization. *European Journal of Operational Research* 234 (2): 518–535.

Mansini, R., and M. G. Speranza. 1999. Heuristic algorithms for the portfolio selection problem with minimum transaction lots. *European Journal of Operational Research* 114: 219–233.

_____. 2005. An exact approach for portfolio selection with transaction costs and rounds. *IIE Transactions* 37: 919–929.

Markowitz, H. M. 1952. Portfolio selection, *Journal of Finance* 7: 77–91.

_____. 1959. Portfolio selection: Efficient diversification of investments. New York: John Wiley & Sons.

Mao, J. C. T. 1970. Essentials of portfolio diversification strategy. *Journal of Finance* 25: 1109–1121.

Mitchell J. E., and S. Braun. 2013. Rebalancing an investment portfolio in the presence of convex transaction costs, including market impact costs. *Optimization Methods and Software* 28: 523–542.

Ogryczak, W., and A. Ruszczyński. 1999. From stochastic dominance to mean–risk models: Semideviations as risk measures. *European Journal of Operational Research* 116: 33–50.

Patel, N. R., and M. G. Subrahmanyam. 1982. A simple algorithm for optimal portfolio selection with fixed transaction costs. *Management Science* 38: 303–314.

Speranza, M. G. 1993. Linear programming models for portfolio optimization. *Finance* 14: 107–123.

Williams, H. P. 2013. Model building in mathematical programming. 5th ed. Chichester: Wiley,

Woodside-Oriakhi, M., C., Lucas, and J. E. Beasley. 2013. Portfolio rebalancing with an investment horizon and transaction costs. *Omega* 41: 406–420.

Xue, H.-G., C.-X. Xu, and Z.-X. Feng. 2006. Mean-variance portfolio optimal problem under concave transaction cost. *Applied Mathematics and Computation* 174: 1–12.

Yoshimoto, A. 1996. The mean-variance approach to portfolio optimization subject to transaction costs. *Journal of Operations Research Society of Japan* 39: 99–117.

Young, M. R. 1998. A minimax portfolio selection rule with linear programming solution. *Management Science* 44: 173–183.

CHAPTER 9

Statistical Properties and Tests of Efficient Frontier Portfolios

C J Adcock

Sheffield University Management School, Sheffield, UK

INTRODUCTION

The standard theory of portfolio selection due to Markowitz (1952) makes an implicit assumption that asset returns follow a multivariate normal distribution. The original concept of minimizing portfolio variance subject to achieving a target expected return is equivalent to assuming that investors maximize the expected value of a utility function that is quadratic in portfolio returns. Stein's lemma (1981) means that Markowitz's efficient frontier arises under normally distributed returns for any suitable utility function, subject only to relatively undemanding regularity conditions. Recent developments of the lemma (e.g., Liu, 1994; Landsman and Nešlehová, 2008) show that the efficient frontier arises under multivariate probability distributions that are members of the elliptically symmetric class (Fang, Kotz and Ng, 1990). There is a direct extension to a mean-variance-skewness efficient surface for some classes of multivariate distributions that incorporate asymmetry (Adcock, 2014a).

The literature that addresses the theory and application of Markowitzian portfolio selection is very large. Much of this published work assumes that the parameters of the underlying distributions, most commonly the vector of expected returns and the covariance matrix, are known. In reality, they are not known and all practical portfolio selection is based on estimated parameters. There is also often at least an implicit assumption made about the appropriate probability distribution. Practitioners, in particular, are well aware that the effect of estimation error is almost always to ensure that the *ex post* performance of a portfolio is inferior to that expected *ex ante*. Notwithstanding that the effects of estimation error can be serious, the literature that deals formally with the effect of estimated parameters is still relatively small. Furthermore, the number of papers in the area that can be regarded as well-known is even smaller.

Investigations of the sensitivity of portfolio performance are due to the well-known works of Best and Grauer (1991) and Chopra and Ziemba (1993). The latter paper, in particular, is considered by some to be the source of the rule of thumb that errors in the estimated expected return are 10 times more serious than errors in the estimate of variance. There is an early monograph that addresses parameter uncertainty; see Bawa, Brown, and Klein (1979). There are also works that provide tests of the efficiency (in Markowitz's sense) of a given portfolio. These works include papers by Jobson and Korkie (1980), Gibbons, Ross and Shanken (1989), Britten-Jones (1999), and Huberman and Kandel (1987), among others. Huberman and Kandel, in particular, present likelihood ratio type tests for efficiency, thus continuing a theme of research due to Ross (1980) and Kandel (1983, 1984). There is a recent survey in Sentana (2009).

In addition to these works, there is a more recent stream of literature that is concerned with the effect of estimated parameters on the properties of the weights of an efficient portfolio and on the components of the equation of the efficient frontier itself. Most of this literature considers the case where the vector time series of asset returns is IID normally distributed and the only restriction in portfolio selection is the budget constraint. Even under the IID normal and budget constraint assumptions, the majority of results that have appeared in recent literature are complicated mathematically. As several authors point out, actual computations are today relatively easy to undertake because of the wide availability of suitable software. However, understanding the derivations in sufficient detail to allow a reader to make further advances is a more demanding task. This surely acts to inhibit use of these methods, if not further technical development, by researchers.

It is helpful to classify the areas in which new methods have been developed. Inevitably, there is some overlap, but nonetheless it is useful to consider three areas: First, there are papers that are concerned with the properties of the vector of portfolio weights. At a general level, there are three distinct sets of weights to consider that correspond to different maximization criteria. These are: (1) the tangency portfolio, which arises when a position in the risk-free asset is allowed; (2) the maximum Sharpe ratio or market portfolio, which is the point on the efficient frontier that is the tangent to the risk-free rate; (3) the portfolio that arises from Markowitz's original criterion or from maximizing the expected value of a quadratic utility function. Second, there are papers that present results concerning the distribution of the three scalar parameters that determine the location, scale, and slope of the equation of the efficient frontier. As is well known, there are analytic expressions for these in terms of the mean vector and covariance matrix (see Merton, 1972). The majority of the extant literature in the area is concerned with these two sets, both of which address the behavior of a portfolio *ex ante*. Third, there is a small literature that is concerned with *ex post* performance.

Even though the total number of papers that address the effect of parameter uncertainty is small, the technical nature of the subject means that it is impractical to consider all three areas of research in a single article. This paper is therefore concerned with the first topic—namely, the distribution of portfolio weights. The second topic, the properties of the parameters of the efficient frontier, is described in Adcock (2014b). The third area is discussed briefly in the conclusions to this article. The article contains a summary of the state of the art and presents some new results. The article is not a complete survey of all works in the area. In the manner of Smith (1976) and quoting Adcock (1997), "Ideas are interpreted from a personal point of view and no attempt is made to be completely comprehensive ... any review could only address a subset of approaches and application areas." Furthermore and quoting Smith (1976) himself, "No review can ever replace a thorough reading of a fundamental paper since what is left out is often just as important as what is included."

As the title indicates, the following sections present statistical tests for portfolio weights. As is clear from the literature, the probability distribution of portfolio weights is often confounded by nuisance parameters. Development of suitable test statistics thus requires either approximations or perhaps some ingenuity. However, as is shown next, it is possible to develop likelihood ratio tests, thus continuing the research first reported by Ross (1980) and Kandel (1983, 1984). These avoid the nuisance parameters and the difficulties of using exact distributions. Likelihood ratio tests employ a standard distribution, but rely on asymptotics for their properties. They may therefore be unsuitable for portfolio selection in which only a small number of observations are used. They also depend on the IID normal assumption, which implies that they are more likely to be useful for low-frequency returns, when it is possible to rely to an extent on the central limit theorem. However, given that even IID normality leads to mathematically complex results, the case for a simple approach, which depends on a standard distribution, is a strong one.

The structure is of this chapter is as follows. The first section below presents notation and summarizes the standard formulae for portfolio weights. This is followed by the main methodological content of the article. This contains both the review of relevant literature and the presentation of new tests. To contain the length of the article, technical details of development of the tests are omitted, but are in Adcock (2014b). The penultimate section presents an empirical study in which the results are exemplified. The last section contains concluding remarks and a short description of outstanding research issues. Notation not explicitly defined in the next section is that in common use.

NOTATION AND SETUP

The notation used in this article is that in widespread use in this area of financial economics. It follows Okhrin and Schmid (2006) and related papers, such as Bodnar and Schmid (2008a, 2008b), Adcock (2013), and several others.

It is assumed that there are n assets and observations for T time periods. The time subscript t is omitted unless needed explicitly. The n-vector of asset returns is denoted by R. It is assumed that the vector time series is IID multivariate normal, $N(\mu, \Sigma)$ in the usual notation, and that the covariance matrix Σ is nonsingular. The inverse of the covariance matrix is denoted by Ψ. The n-vector of portfolio weights and the budget constraint are denoted by w and 1 respectively. Portfolio return $w^T R$ is denoted by R_p. Given the assumptions, this has the normal distribution $N(\mu_p, \sigma_p^2)$, with $\mu_p = w^T \mu$ and $\sigma_p^2 = w^T \Sigma w$. The risk free rate is R_f. Excess returns are denoted by $\tilde{R}$ and $\tilde{R}_p$ with corresponding notation for expected returns. Parameter estimates are denoted with the symbol $\wedge$, for example $\hat{\mu}$. In the results described below it should be assumed that T is always big enough for relevant moments to exist. Restrictions on both T and n will be clear from the context. It is assumed that parameters are estimated by the sample moments, that is

$$\hat{\mu} = \overline{R} = \sum_{t=1}^{T} R_t / T, \quad \hat{\Sigma} = \sum_{t=1}^{T} (R_t - \overline{R})(R_t - \overline{R})^T / (T - 1).$$

In this case $\hat{\mu} \sim N(\mu, \Sigma/T)$ and $\hat{\Sigma}$ has the independent Wishart distribution $W_n(q, \Sigma/q)$ with $q = T - 1$.

The standard approach to portfolio selection is to maximize the expected value of the quadratic utility function

$$U(R_p) = \theta R_p - (R_p - \mu_p)^2 / 2,$$

where $\theta \geq 0$ measures the investor's appetite for risk. Expectations are taken over the distribution of R_p in the standard frequentist manner, assuming that the parameters are given. As noted in the introduction, a consequence of Stein's lemma (Stein, 1981), is that under normally distributed returns, the quadratic utility function may be used without loss of generality; subject to regularity conditions all utility functions will lead to Markowitz's efficient frontier. The objective function to be maximized is

$$\phi(w) = \theta w^T \mu - w^T \Sigma w / 2,$$

subject to the budget constraint $w^T 1 = 1$. The solution is

$$w_\theta = w_0 + \theta w_1 \quad w_0 = \Sigma^{-1} 1 / 1^T \Sigma^{-1} 1, \quad w_1 = \Pi \mu,$$

where

$$\Pi = \Sigma^{-1} - \Sigma^{-1} 1 1^T \Sigma^{-1} / 1^T \Sigma^{-1} 1.$$

The vector w_0 is the minimum variance portfolio, and w_1 is a self-financing portfolio. The expected return and variance of the portfolio are respectively

$$\mu_p = \alpha_0 + \theta \alpha_1, \quad \sigma_p^2 = \alpha_2 + \theta^2 \alpha_1,$$

where the standard constants are

$$\alpha_2 = 1 / 1^T \Sigma^{-1} 1, \quad \alpha_0 = \mu^T \Sigma^{-1} 1 / 1^T \Sigma^{-1} 1,$$

$$\alpha_1 = \mu^T \left(\Sigma^{-1} - \Sigma^{-1} 1 1^T \Sigma^{-1} / 1^T \Sigma^{-1} 1 \right) \mu.$$

Note that these are not quite the same as the standard constants as defined in Merton (1972) but are more convenient for the current purpose.

In this formulation, the parameter θ is given even when μ and Σ are replaced by estimates. An important variation is to specify a target expected return τ. In this case $\theta = (\tau - \alpha_0) / \alpha_1$, which then also becomes an estimated value. As next described, this can make a material difference to the distribution of the estimated portfolio weights. A third formulation is to maximize the Sharpe ratio. In this case, the vector of portfolio weights is

$$w_S = \Sigma^{-1} \tilde{\mu} / 1^T \Sigma^{-1} \tilde{\mu}.$$

The final formulation is to assume the availability of the risk-free rate. An amount $w^T 1$ is invested in risky assets and $1 - w^T 1$ in the risk-free asset.

This setup generates the security market line, which is the tangent to the efficient frontier. The vector of portfolio weights is

$$w_T = \theta \Sigma^{-1} \widetilde{\mu}.$$

As above, a variation is to specify a target expected return τ. In this case, $\theta = \tau / \widetilde{\mu}^T \Sigma^{-1} \widetilde{\mu}$. Consistent with these notations, the vectors of estimated portfolio weights are denoted $\widehat{w}_X$ where the subscript takes values $\theta, 0, S$ and T and the above estimators of μ and Σ are used. Note that the notation T plays three roles in the paper, but no confusion arises.

DISTRIBUTION OF PORTFOLIO WEIGHTS

The substantial paper by Okhrin and Schmid (2006), O&S henceforth, presents expressions for the vector of expected values of the portfolio weights and for their covariance matrices. These are accompanied by numerous results for the portfolio selection approaches described previously. This section contains a summary of the results in O&S as well as results from other authors. New results, which overcome some of the difficulties posed by the nuisance parameters problems referred to in the introduction, are from Adcock (2014b). The results presented are illustrated with an empirical study, which is reported in the next section.

Tangency Portfolio with One Risky Asset

O&S consider the tangency portfolio, with estimated weights

$$\widehat{w}_T = \theta \widehat{\Sigma}^{-1} \widehat{\widetilde{\mu}}.$$

Since this depends on risk appetite θ, in what follows it is assumed that $\theta = 1$. As O&S note, the scalar case in which there is one risky asset is of importance. This is because it is relevant to the basic asset allocation decision between risky and nonrisky assets. In this case,

$$\widehat{w}_T = \widehat{\widetilde{\mu}} / \widehat{\sigma}^2,$$

with $\widehat{\widetilde{\mu}}$ and $\widehat{\sigma}^2$ independently distributed as, respectively

$$N(\widetilde{\mu}, \sigma^2 / T), \quad (\sigma^2 / q) \chi^2_{(q)}.$$

The mean and variance of $\hat{w}_T$ are respectively

$$E(\hat{w}_T) = (T - 1)w_T/(T - 3),$$

$$\text{var}(\hat{w}_T) = 2\{E(\hat{w}_T)\}^2/(T - 5) \; + (T - 1)^2/T(T - 3)(T - 5)\sigma^2.$$

These results illustrate that $\hat{w}_T$ is a biased estimator of w_T and that the variance may be materially affected if the tangency weight is of comparable magnitude to $1/\sigma$ or larger. The probability density function of $\hat{w}_T$ may be obtained by standard methods. In the notation of this article, it is

$$f_{\hat{w}_T}(x) = Ke^{-T\tilde{\mu}^2/2\sigma^2}|x|^{-p/2}\sum_{k=0}^{\infty}\Gamma\{p/4 + k/2\}y^k/k!,$$

where $\Gamma(v)$ with $v > 0$ is Euler's gamma function and

$$p = T + 1, \;\; K^{-1} = \sqrt{2\pi}\Gamma(q/2)\sigma^{q/2}2^{p/4}T^{q/4}q^{-q/2},$$

$$y = \sigma\sqrt{2}\{Txw_T - q/2\sigma^2\}/\sqrt{T}|x|.$$

This expression is proportional to the hypergeometric function $_1F_1$. O&S show that it may also be expressed as the difference of two such functions and note that it may be computed using routines that are readily available. The probability density function provides an illustration of the fact, already noted in the introduction, that the statistical properties of the efficient frontier are confounded by the nuisance parameter, in this case σ. Inference is therefore complicated, and within the standard frequentist approach it is necessary to consider approximations. A practical test of the null hypothesis $H_0 : w_T = w_T^0$ against both one- and two-sided alternatives is provided by the statistic

$$Z_T = (\hat{w}_T - w_T^0)/\sqrt{k_1\hat{w}_1^2 + k_2\hat{\sigma}^{-2}},$$

$$k_1 = 2(T - 1)^2/(T - 3)^2(T - 5), k_2 = (T - 1)^2/T(T - 3)(T - 5).$$

This is assumed to have a standard normal distribution. The accuracy of this test procedure may be computed as follows. First note that, conditional on the estimated variance

$$\hat{w}_T \sim N\{w_T/U, 1/(T\sigma^2U^2)\},$$

where $(T-1)U \sim \chi^2_{(T-1)}$. Hence,

$$Pr(\hat{w}_T \leq w^*) = \int_0^\infty \Phi\left\{\sigma u \sqrt{T}\left\{w^* - w_T/u\right\}\right\} f_U(u)du,$$

where $f_U()$ is the probability density function of U and $\Phi(x)$ is the standard normal distribution function evaluated at x. This integral may be used to compute the exact distribution function of $\hat{w}_T$ and hence evaluate the accuracy of the test statistic Z_T. Since the probability density function of U has a single mode and vanishes at the end points, this integral may be may computed to any desired degree of accuracy using the trapezoidal rule. For some exercises in portfolio selection, the sample size T will be large. In such cases, the test is supported by a result reported in Adcock (2014b), which shows that the asymptotic distribution of Z_T is N(0, 1). An alternative approach is to use a likelihood ratio test. For this, the null hypothesis is that a given investment weight is a tangency portfolio, that is

$$H_0 : \mu/\sigma^2 = \overline{w}.$$

The alternate hypothesis is that there is no restriction on either μ or σ^2. Under the null hypothesis, the maximum likelihood estimator (MLE) of σ^2, which is now the sole free parameter, is

$$\hat{\sigma}_T^2 = \left(\sqrt{1 + 4\overline{w}^2 S} - 1\right)/2\overline{w}^2, S = T^{-1}\sum_{t=1}^T R_t^2.$$

The resulting likelihood ratio test statistic, which is computed in the usual way, is distributed as $\chi^2_{(1)}$ under the null hypothesis. The sensitivity of estimates of w_T may be investigated using the exact or approximate distributions reported above. The normal approximation, for example, may be used to compute confidence limits for w_T. It is also interesting to note that the partial derivatives of w_T with respect to μ and σ^2 are

$$\partial w/\partial \mu = 1/\sigma^2, \partial w/\partial \sigma^2 = -w/\sigma^2,$$

and that the ratio of these is equal to $-w^{-1}$. Thus, for small values of the absolute value of w_T, the weight is more sensitive to changes in w_T itself. For large values, the opposite is true.

Tangency Portfolio with *n* Risky Assets

For the general case with n risky assets, the estimated weights of the tangency portfolio (and with $\theta = 1$) are

$$\hat{w}_T = \hat{\Sigma}^{-1}\hat{\mu}.$$

O&S opine that it is difficult to generalize the results from the case $n = 1$. To some extent this is true, although there are recent results in Bodnar and Okhrin (2011). The expected value of $\hat{w}_T$ is however straightforward to compute. Using the independence property of $\hat{\mu}$ and $\hat{\Sigma}$, and a result from Muirhead (1982, p. 97), it follows that

$$E(\hat{w}_T) = r_1 w_T, \quad r_1 = (T - 1)/(T - n - 2).$$

Using Siskind (1972), who reprises an earlier result from Das Gupta (1968), the covariance matrix is

$$cov(\hat{w}_T) = (r_3 + r_5 w_T^T \Psi w_T) \Psi + r_4 w_T w_T^T = \Sigma_T,$$

with the constants r_i given by

$$r_2 = r_1^2/(T - n - 1)(T - n - 4), r_3 = r_1^2/T + r_2\{(T - n)(n + 1) - 2n\}/T,$$

$$r_4 = r_2(T - n), \quad r_5 = r_2(T - n - 2).$$

The distribution of $\hat{w}_T$ is not straightforward to compute and would in any case depend on nuisance parameters. In the spirit of the results for the univariate case, the null hypothesis $H_0 : w_T = w_T^0$ against suitable alternatives can be tested by the statistic

$$X^2 = (\hat{w}_T - w_T^0)^T \hat{\Sigma}_T^{-1} (\hat{w}_T - w_T^0),$$

and comparing the computed value with percentage points of the Chi-squared distribution with n degrees of freedom. A procedure that avoids the nuisance parameter more formally is based on the likelihood ratio test. For a given portfolio w_T the null hypothesis is $H_0 : \Sigma^{-1}\tilde{\mu} = w_T^0$. The MLEs of $\tilde{\mu}$ and Σ may be computed numerically and the resulting likelihood ratio test also has n degrees of freedom. As noted in the introduction, details of this and other likelihood ratio tests are in Adcock (2014b). A variation on the tangency portfolio is in Ross (1980). In this, the expected return is specified to be equal to τ, in which case the degree of risk is estimated as $\tau/\hat{\tilde{\mu}}^T \hat{\Sigma}^{-1} \hat{\mu}$.

Maximum Sharpe Ratio Portfolio

In Proposition 2, O&S show that the moments of the elements of $\hat{w}_S$, the vector of estimated weights that maximizes the Sharpe ratio, do not exist. Additional results are reported in Bodnar and Schmid (2008a) concerning the distribution of the estimated return and variance of the maximum Sharpe ratio portfolio. As they report, moments of order one and, hence, greater do not exist for the estimated return. For the estimated variance, moments of order greater than one half do not exist. These results are for estimated *ex ante* returns. There is also a related result in Proposition 8 of Adcock (2013), which is concerned with *ex post* properties of efficient portfolios.

The implication of these results is both serious and noteworthy. Maximizing the Sharpe ratio is an important component of finance theory because of its connections to the CAPM and to the market portfolio. The Sharpe ratio is a widely used practical measure of portfolio performance. That the estimated weights and return have undefined moments implies that a maximum Sharpe ratio portfolio may be a dangerous point on the efficient frontier both *ex ante* and *ex post*. It is interesting, however, to note that the paper by Jobson and Korkie (1980) presents tests for the maximum Sharpe ratio portfolio based on the delta method. These thus avoid problems of nonexistence of moments. They also serve to remind that the assumption of normality is of course a convenient mathematical fiction. It seems clear, though, that it is safe to say the maximum Sharpe ratio portfolios are likely to be volatile in the presence of estimation error. This is supported by the study by Britten-Jones (1999), who presents a regression-based test of maximum Sharpe ratio portfolios. He reports the results of a study of 11 international stock indices and writes, "The sampling error in the weights of a global efficient portfolio is large."

As reported in O&S, the probability distribution of the weights involves nuisance parameters. Notwithstanding the properties reported in the preceding paragraphs, a likelihood ratio test is available. For a given portfolio with weights w_S the null hypothesis is

$$H_0 : \Sigma^{-1}\widetilde{\mu} = (1^T\Sigma^{-1}\widetilde{\mu})w_S.$$

As shown earlier, the MLEs of $\widetilde{\mu}$ and Σ might be computed numerically, and the resulting likelihood ratio test has n degrees of freedom. Bodnar and Okhrin (2011) present a test for a linear combination of weights in the maximum Sharpe ratio portfolio based on Student's t-distribution. They also describe more general tests that are based on expression for the distribution of $\Sigma^{-1}\widehat{\widetilde{\mu}}$. As they note, these are complicated to evaluate in general.

Expected Utility with Set Risk Appetite

Using the notation defined in the previous section, in Theorem 1 of O&S the expected value of $\widehat{w}_\theta$ is

$$E(\widehat{w}_\theta) = w_0 + \theta p w_1, \quad p = (T-1)/(T-n-1),$$

and the corresponding covariance matrix is

$$cov(\widehat{w}_\theta) = \{\alpha_2/(T-n-1)\}\Pi$$
$$+ p^2\theta^2(q_1 w_1 w_1^T + [q_2\alpha_1 + T^{-1}\{q_1 + (n-1)q_2 + 1\}]\Pi),$$

where

$$q_1 = (T-n+1)/(T-n)(T-n-3), \quad q_2 = (T-n-1)/(T-n)(T-n-3).$$

As O&S remark, the estimated weights are biased estimators of the population values. The biases may be removed, but at the expense of an increase in variability. However, an alternative interpretation is that, after allowing for the effect of estimation error, the weights are unbiased for a point on the efficient frontier corresponding to the higher risk appetite $p\theta$. Thus, an investor may construct a portfolio with risk appetite θ in an expected value sense by using $p^{-1}\theta$. A more worrying aspect is that if the number of observations is not large relative to the number of assets, the effective point on the frontier may be materially different from that intended. For example, an asset allocation portfolio with ten assets based on a sample of 36 months results in $p = 1.4$, loosely speaking, 40 percent further up the frontier than intended.

In their Theorem 1, O&S show that the vector of weights has an asymptotic multivariate normal distribution. Indeed for large T the covariance matrix is well approximated by

$$Tvar(\widehat{w}_\theta) = \alpha_2\Pi + \theta^2(w_1 w_1^T + \{\alpha_1 + 1\}\Pi) = \theta^2 w_1 w_1^T + (\theta^2 + \sigma_p^2)\Pi,$$

This expression demonstrates that the penalty of uncertainty in the covariance matrix is substantial, at least in algebraic terms. Assume that the covariance matrix is given and that only the vector of expected returns in estimated. In this case, the covariance matrix of $\widehat{w}_\theta$ is $\theta^2\Pi/T$. It may also be noted that the two components of $\widehat{w}_\theta$, the minimum variance and self-financing portfolios, are uncorrelated.

Bodnar and Schmid (2008b) provide the distribution for affine transformations of $\widehat{w}_0$, the estimated minimum variance portfolio. This is a multivariate Student distribution, but is confounded by nuisance parameters. They provide a test statistic, in which the nuisance parameters are replaced by their estimators. This is similar in spirit to the tests reported in the two previous sections. Under suitable null hypotheses this statistic has an F-distribution. Computations of power require integration of the product of an F density with the hypergeometric function $_2F_1$.

For a likelihood ratio test, the null hypothesis is

$$H_0 : \Sigma^{-1}1/1^T\Sigma^{-1}1 = w_0; \quad \Pi\mu = w_1,$$

The resulting likelihood ratio test has $2n$ degrees of freedom. The test for the minimum variance portfolio omits the second component and has n degrees of freedom. This may be contrasted with the test based on regression that is reported in Gibbons, Ross, and Shanken (1989) and which results in a F-test based on n and $T - n - 1$ degrees of freedom. There are also related tests in Huberman and Kandel (1987) that are concerned with mean-variance spanning and in Jobson and Korkie (1989).

Expected Utility Portfolio with Expected Return Target

A common extension to the expected utility approach is to specify an expected return target τ. In this case, risk appetite is given by

$$\theta = (\tau - \alpha_0)/\alpha_1,$$

and the portfolio weights are denoted by w_τ. Computation of portfolio weights, expected return and variance then employs $\hat{\theta}$ in which $\alpha_{0,1}$ are replaced by their estimated values. Kandel (1984) presents a likelihood ratio test. A stochastic representation of the distribution of the weights is reported in Kan and Smith (2008), which is another substantial paper in this area of financial economics. They use this to derive the expected value and covariance matrix. Their results provide a clear illustration of the complexity of this area. The expected value of the weights is

$$E(\hat{w}_\tau) = w_0 + \beta(w_\tau - w_0),$$

where β is a nonnegative constant defined in their equation (39). In the notation of this paper it is

$$\beta = \lambda e^{-\lambda/2} \sum_{j=0}^{\infty} (\lambda/2)^j/j!(n - 1 + 2j), \quad \lambda = T\alpha_1.$$

The covariance matrix is reported in equations (56) to (58) of Kan and Smith (2008). To simplify the presentation here, the following notation is used

$$b = 1 + \gamma, \quad \gamma = T(\tau - \alpha_0)^2/\alpha_2, \quad \overline{\mu} = \mu - \alpha_0 1, \quad \Gamma = \Psi\overline{\mu\mu}^T\Psi/\overline{\mu}^T\Psi\overline{\mu},$$

along with a random variable W, which is defined as

$$W = \alpha_2(1 + U/V),$$

where U and V are independent random variables distributed as $\chi^2_{(1)}(\gamma)$ and $\chi^2_{(n-1)}(\lambda)$, respectively. The notation $\chi^2_{(v)}(\lambda)$ denotes a noncentral Chi-squared variable with v degrees of freedom and noncentrality parameter λ and follows the definitions in Johnson and Kotz (1970, p. 132). Using this notation, the covariance matrix is

$$\text{cov}(\widehat{\boldsymbol{w}}_\tau) = s_1\boldsymbol{\Pi} + s_2\boldsymbol{\Gamma} - (\beta\theta)^2\boldsymbol{w}_1\boldsymbol{w}_1^T,$$

where

$$s_1 = \frac{(T-n-1)}{(T-n)}h\alpha_2\left\{\frac{(1-\beta)}{2(n-3)} - \frac{\beta}{2\lambda}\right\} + \frac{1}{(T-n)}\left\{E(W) - \frac{\alpha_2\beta}{\lambda}\right\},$$

and

$$s_2 = \frac{(T-n-1)}{2(T-n)}h\alpha_2\left\{\frac{(n-1)\beta}{\lambda} - (1-\beta)\right\} - \frac{\alpha_2}{(T-n)}\left\{1 - \frac{(n-1)\beta}{\lambda}\right\}.$$

In Proposition 1, Kan and Smith (2008) present results for the distribution of the estimated values of the standard constants. In the present notation, these are as follows:

$$\widehat{\alpha}_1 = R, \quad \widehat{\alpha}_2 = \alpha_2 Q/T, \quad \widehat{\alpha}_0 = \alpha_0 + \sqrt{\alpha_2(1+R)/T}Z,$$

where Q, R, and Z are independent random variables distributed as follows:

$$Q \sim \chi^2_{(T-n)}, \quad R \sim \chi^2_{(n-1)}(\lambda)/\chi^2_{(T-n+1)}, \quad Z \sim N(0,1).$$

In this notation, the estimated risk appetite is

$$\widehat{\theta} = R^{-1}\left\{(\tau - \alpha_0) - \sqrt{\alpha_2(1+R)/T}Z,\right\}.$$

As shown in Adcock (2014b), the mean and variance of $\widehat{\theta}$ are

$$E(\widehat{\theta}) = (\tau - \alpha_0)E(R^{-1}),$$
$$var(\widehat{\theta}) = (\tau - \alpha_0)^2 \; var(R^{-1}) + (\alpha_2/T)\left\{E(R^{-2}) + E(R^{-1})\right\}.$$

It is possible to compute the mean and variance analytically for the unusual case in which $\alpha_1 = 0$. For other cases, the mean and variance of R^{-1} are evaluated numerically. The distribution function $\hat{\theta}$ may be written as

$$Pr(\hat{\theta} \leq \theta^*) = \int_0^\infty \Phi\left\{ \sqrt{T}\left(r\theta^* - \tau + \alpha_0\right) / \sqrt{\alpha_2(1+r)} \right\} f_R(r)dr,$$

where $f_R(.)$ denotes the probability density function of R. As above, this integral may be evaluated using the trapezoidal rule. In the following section, it is shown that, at least for the assets considered, confidence limits for θ are wide. That is, it is possible for a portfolio to be at a point on the efficient frontier that is materially different from that expected. This is further discussed in the concluding section.

EMPIRICAL STUDY

This section contains examples of tests described in the previous section. It is based on returns computed from 608 weekly values of 11 FTSE indices from June 10, 2000, to January 28, 2012. These indices are chosen for illustrative purposes to exemplify the tests. These indices were also used as exemplars in Adcock et al. (2012). The text in this paragraph and Tables 9.1 and 9.2 are taken with minor modifications from that paper. Weekly returns were computed by taking logarithms. The means, variances, and covariances were

TABLE 9.1 Descriptive Statistics.

Index	Avg	Vol	Skew	Kurt	Min	Median	Max
FTSE100	−0.0002	0.0260	−1.1690	16.3306	−0.2363	0.0019	0.1258
FTSE250	0.0008	0.0271	−0.9205	7.6078	−0.1652	0.0039	0.1040
FTS250-ex-Inv	0.0009	0.0279	−0.8383	7.1382	−0.1571	0.0037	0.1097
FTSE350	0.0000	0.0262	−1.0815	14.7323	−0.2275	0.0024	0.1235
FTSE350-ex-inv	0.0000	0.0256	−1.3236	15.5683	−0.2276	0.0023	0.1244
FTSE350-HY	0.0001	0.0249	−1.5336	18.1964	−0.2350	0.0021	0.1213
FTSE350-LY	−0.0004	0.0283	−0.8166	10.0377	−0.2172	0.0021	0.1245
FTSE-SC	−0.0002	0.0227	−1.0794	12.2159	−0.1556	0.0026	0.1374
FTSE-All-Share	−0.0001	0.0254	−1.2929	15.3090	−0.2255	0.0022	0.1211
FTSE-AS-ex-inv	−0.0001	0.0255	−1.3033	15.2954	−0.2261	0.0020	0.1229
FTSE-AS-ex-mult	−0.0004	0.0267	−1.4628	15.1637	−0.2399	0.0024	0.1062

Based on weekly returns for 13 FTSE indices from June 10, 2000, to January 28, 2012. This table has been reproduced with minor amendments from Adcock et al. (2012).
The indices are used solely for illustrative purposes. The statistics, *Avg, Vol, Min, Median* and *Max*, are computed in the usual way. *Skew* and *Kurt* are standardized values.

TABLE 9.2   Covariance/Correlation Matrix.

	100	250	250-ex-Inv	350	350-ex-inv	350-HY
FTSE100	0.0007	0.0006	0.0006	0.0007	0.0006	0.0006
FTSE250	0.844	0.0007	0.0008	0.0006	0.0006	0.0005
FTS250-ex-Inv	0.8271	0.9954	0.0008	0.0006	0.0006	0.0005
FTSE350	0.9774	0.8649	0.8501	0.0007	0.0006	0.0006
FTSE350-ex-inv	0.9627	0.8478	0.8347	0.967	0.0007	0.0006
FTSE350-HY	0.8848	0.7628	0.7467	0.8698	0.8762	0.0006
FTSE350-LY	0.9176	0.843	0.8312	0.9089	0.9271	0.7598
FTSE-SC	0.6515	0.7884	0.7809	0.6736	0.6872	0.6093
FTSE-AS	0.9617	0.8493	0.8354	0.9544	0.9791	0.8755
FTSE-AS-ex-inv	0.9559	0.8454	0.8323	0.9459	0.9716	0.8667
FTSE-AS-ex-mult	0.8747	0.8703	0.8652	0.8739	0.895	0.8206

	350-LY	SC	AS	AS-ex-inv	AS-ex-mult
FTSE100	0.0007	0.0004	0.0006	0.0006	0.0006
FTSE250	0.0006	0.0005	0.0006	0.0006	0.0006
FTS250-ex-Inv	0.0007	0.0005	0.0006	0.0006	0.0006
FTSE350	0.0007	0.0004	0.0006	0.0006	0.0006
FTSE350-ex-inv	0.0007	0.0004	0.0006	0.0006	0.0006
FTSE350-HY	0.0005	0.0003	0.0006	0.0006	0.0005
FTSE350-LY	0.0008	0.0004	0.0007	0.0007	0.0006
FTSE-SC	0.6714	0.0005	0.0004	0.0004	0.0004
FTSE-AS	0.9327	0.6966	0.0006	0.0006	0.0006
FTSE-AS-ex-inv	0.9254	0.6903	0.9701	0.0007	0.0006
FTSE-AS-ex-mult	0.8403	0.7181	0.8943	0.8896	0.0007

Values on or above the leading diagonal are sample variances and covariances. Values below are correlations.

Based on weekly returns for 13 FTSE indices from June 10, 2000, to January 28, 2012. This table has been reproduced with minor amendments from Adcock et al. (2012).

estimated using the sample data. Descriptive statistics for the 11 indices are shown in Table 9.1. This table indicates that the weekly returns on these indices are not normally distributed. The risk-free rate is taken to be equal to zero.

Table 9.2 shows variances, covariances, and correlations for returns on the indices. Covariances are shown above the leading diagonal and correlations below.

Table 9.3 shows the results of the Z-test for the univariate tangency portfolio weights for each of the 11 indices. Table 9.3 shows that estimated

TABLE 9.3 Univariate Confidence Limits for Tangency Portfolio Weights.

	LL[99%]	UL[99%]	$\hat{w}$	LL[95%]	UL[95%]
FTSE100	−4.3129	3.7833	−0.2648	−3.3401	2.8105
FTSE250	−2.7600	5.0214	1.1307	−1.8250	4.0865
FTS250-ex-Inv	−2.6131	4.9519	1.1694	−1.7041	4.0429
FTSE350	−4.0920	3.9537	−0.0691	−3.1252	2.9870
FTSE350-ex-inv	−4.1878	4.0399	−0.0739	−3.1992	3.0513
FTSE350-HY	−4.0748	4.3876	0.1564	−3.0580	3.3708
FTSE350-LY	−4.1768	3.2693	−0.4538	−3.2821	2.3746
FTSE-SC	−5.0945	4.1835	−0.4555	−3.9797	3.0687
FTSE-All-Share	−4.2390	4.0679	−0.0855	−3.2409	3.0698
FTSE-AS-ex-inv	−4.2194	4.0366	−0.0914	−3.2274	3.0446
FTSE-AS-ex-mult	−4.5213	3.3687	−0.5763	−3.5733	2.4207

The table shows the results of the Z-test for the univariate tangency portfolio weights for each of the 11 indices. The table shows estimated weights, 99% and 95% confidence limits. Based on weekly returns for 13 FTSE indices from June 10, 2000, to January 28, 2012. Computations are shown to four decimal places.

weight, together with 99 percent and 95 percent confidence limits. As the table clearly demonstrates, the limits are wide.

Panel (1) of Table 9.4 shows the likelihood ratio test probabilities for univariate tangency weights. The value of the weight under the null hypothesis is shown at the head of each column. The results in Panel (1) confirm the results in Table 9.3, namely that the univariate tangency portfolio weights are volatile. For example the absolute value of the tangency weight for the FTSE100 index has to be greater than 2.5 before the null hypothesis is rejected. Panel (2) of Table 9.4 shows the p-values for the corresponding Z-test. As Table 9.4 shows, these are very similar to the corresponding cells in panel (1) and, when displayed to four decimal places, are the same in many cases.

Table 9.5 shows lower and upper 99 percent confidence limits for the FTSE100 index for a range of values of expected return and variance. In the table, these ranges are shown as percentages of the sample estimates used in preceding tables, as reported in Table 9.1. The columns of Table 9.5 show variation in the expected return and rows show variation in variance. As the table shows, the confidence limits are relatively robust to changes in expected return, but not to changes in variance. The two numbers reported in boldface type correspond to the values shown for the FTSE100 in Table 9.3. The corresponding tables for the other indices are available on request.

TABLE 9.4 Likelihood Ratio and Z-tests for Univariate Tangency Portfolio Weights.

	−5	−2.5	−1	−0.5	0.5	1	2.5	5
(1) Likelihood ratio test probabilities								
FTSE100	0.0025	0.1528	0.6378	0.8803	0.6242	0.4179	0.0768	0.0008
FTSE250	0.0000	0.0155	0.1552	0.2767	0.6741	0.9306	0.3622	0.0104
FTS250-ex-Inv	0.0000	0.0118	0.1366	0.2520	0.6462	0.9075	0.3625	0.0091
FTSE350	0.0016	0.1176	0.5486	0.7812	0.7138	0.4908	0.0981	0.0011
FTSE350-ex-inv	0.0020	0.1267	0.5595	0.7883	0.7175	0.4985	0.1051	0.0014
FTSE350-HY	0.0016	0.1038	0.4786	0.6875	0.8332	0.6053	0.1514	0.0031
FTSE350-LY	0.0016	0.1548	0.7037	0.9743	0.5065	0.3113	0.0398	0.0002
FTSE-SC	0.0114	0.2536	0.7609	0.9802	0.5933	0.4159	0.0987	0.0024
FTSE-All-Share	0.0022	0.1322	0.5682	0.7958	0.7147	0.4980	0.1068	0.0016
FTSE-AS-ex-inv	0.0021	0.1307	0.5683	0.7975	0.7103	0.4931	0.1039	0.0014
FTSE-AS-ex-mult	0.0038	0.2068	0.7807	0.9600	0.4792	0.3001	0.0433	0.0003
(2) Z-test probabilities								
FTSE100	0.0025	0.1543	0.6394	0.8809	0.6259	0.4202	0.0781	0.0008
FTSE250	0.0000	0.0161	0.1577	0.2795	0.6758	0.9309	0.3639	0.0103
FTS250-ex-Inv	0.0000	0.0123	0.1389	0.2548	0.6480	0.9080	0.3641	0.0090
FTSE350	0.0016	0.1190	0.5505	0.7823	0.7151	0.4929	0.0994	0.0011
FTSE350-ex-inv	0.0020	0.1281	0.5614	0.7893	0.7189	0.5006	0.1065	0.0015
FTSE350-HY	0.0017	0.1053	0.4807	0.6890	0.8341	0.6070	0.1530	0.0031
FTSE350-LY	0.0016	0.1562	0.7050	0.9744	0.5086	0.3137	0.0407	0.0002
FTSE-SC	0.0115	0.2555	0.7620	0.9803	0.5951	0.4182	0.1002	0.0024
FTSE-All-Share	0.0023	0.1337	0.5700	0.7968	0.7161	0.5001	0.1083	0.0016
FTSE-AS-ex-inv	0.0022	0.1322	0.5701	0.7984	0.7117	0.4952	0.1053	0.0015
FTSE-AS-ex-mult	0.0038	0.2084	0.7817	0.9602	0.4815	0.3026	0.0442	0.0003

Panel (1) shows the likelihood ratio test probabilities for univariate tangency weights. The null hypothesis value is shown at the head of each column. Panel (2) shows the p-values for the corresponding Z-test.
Based on weekly returns for 13 FTSE indices from June 10, 2000, to January 28, 2012. Computations are shown to four decimal places.

Table 9.6 shows simultaneous confidence intervals for each of the weights in the (multivariate) tangency portfolio based on Scheffé's method (Scheffé 1959, p. 406). Also shown in the table are the estimated tangency portfolio weights. As the table makes clear, the weights are very different from those estimated using univariate methods. This is due to the high sample correlations between the returns on these FTSE indices as shown in Table 9.2. The multivariate confidence limits are also wide.

TABLE 9.5 Robustness of 99% Confidence Intervals for the Univariate Tangency Portfolio Weights.

				μ			
	50%	75%	90%	100%	110%	125%	150%
(1) Lower							
50%	−2.9972	−3.0679	−3.1103	−3.1385	−3.1668	−3.2092	−3.2799
75%	−3.6474	−3.7181	−3.7605	−3.7888	−3.8171	−3.8595	−3.9160
90%	−3.9867	−4.0574	−4.0998	−4.1139	−4.1422	−4.1846	−4.2553
σ^2 100%	−4.1987	−4.2553	−4.2977	**−4.3129**	−4.3542	−4.3966	−4.4673
110%	−4.3966	−4.4532	−4.4956	−4.5239	−4.5521	−4.5945	−4.6652
125%	−4.6794	−4.7359	−4.7783	−4.8066	−4.8349	−4.8773	−4.9479
150%	−5.1034	−5.1741	−5.2165	−5.2448	−5.2731	−5.3155	−5.3720
(2) Upper							
50%	2.7420	2.6855	2.6431	2.6148	2.5865	2.5441	2.4734
75%	3.3923	3.3216	3.2792	3.2509	3.2368	3.1944	3.1237
90%	3.7315	3.6609	3.6184	3.5902	3.5619	3.5195	3.4629
σ^2 100%	3.9436	3.8729	3.8305	**3.7833**	3.7739	3.7315	3.6609
110%	4.1415	4.0708	4.0284	4.0001	3.9718	3.9294	3.8588
125%	4.4242	4.3535	4.3111	4.2828	4.2546	4.2122	4.1415
150%	4.8483	4.7776	4.7493	4.7210	4.6928	4.6504	4.5797

This table shows lower and upper 99% confidence limits for the FTSE100 index for a range of values of expected return and variance, which are shown as percentages of the sample estimates used in preceding tables and reported in Table 9.1. The columns of Table 5 show variation in the expected return, and rows show variation in variance. The confidence limits are relatively robust to changes in expected return, but not to changes in variance. The two numbers reported in bold face type correspond to the values shown for the FTSE100 in Table 9.1.
Based on weekly returns for 13 FTSE indices from June 10, 2000, to January 28, 2012. Computations are shown to four decimal places.

Table 9.7 shows likelihood ratio and Chi-squared tests for a multivariate tangency portfolio. For this purpose an equally weighted portfolio of the 11 FTSE indices is considered. The null hypothesis is that the equally weighted portfolio is a (multivariate) tangency portfolio with a specified risk appetite. That is

$$H_0 : \theta \Sigma^{-1} \widetilde{\mu} = 1/n.$$

For the purpose of illustration, risk appetite takes values from 0.063 to 160. The columns of Table 9.7 show the values of the Chi-squared test statistics and twice the likelihood ratio test statistic. Not surprisingly, the

TABLE 9.6 Simultaneous 95 and 99% Confidence Intervals for Tangency Portfolio Weights.

	LL[1%]	UL[1%]	$\hat{w}$	LL[5%]	UL[5%]
FTSE100	−53.5615	46.4261	−3.5677	−48.8177	41.6823
FTSE250	−87.2690	100.9888	6.8599	−78.3373	92.0571
FTS250-ex-Inv	−82.1923	90.5355	4.1716	−73.9975	82.3406
FTSE350	−51.6197	44.6272	−3.4963	−47.0534	40.0609
FTSE350-ex-inv	−50.1437	60.4370	5.1467	−44.8973	55.1906
FTSE350-HY	−21.5282	22.1066	0.2892	−19.4580	20.0364
FTSE350-LY	−31.9379	19.9970	−5.9704	−29.4739	17.5330
FTSE-SC	−20.4873	12.1094	−4.1890	−18.9408	10.5629
FTSE-All-Share	−45.3132	55.1740	4.9304	−40.5457	50.4065
FTSE-AS-ex-inv	−39.2493	43.6743	2.2125	−35.3151	39.7401
FTSE-AS-ex-mult	−28.9815	14.5894	−7.1960	−26.9143	12.5222

The table shows simultaneous confidence intervals for each of the weights in the (multivariate) tangency portfolio based on Scheffé's method. Also shown in the table are the estimated tangency portfolio weights.
Based on weekly returns for 13 FTSE indices from June 10, 2000, to January 28, 2012. Computations are shown to four decimal places.

TABLE 9.7 Likelihood Ratio and Chi-Squared Tests for a Multivariate Tangency Portfolio.

Risk θ	χ^2	p-value	2*LR	p-value
0.063	92.6575	0.0000	97.4332	0.0000
0.125	29.5344	0.0019	31.8358	0.0008
0.250	13.8415	0.2419	15.0047	0.1823
0.500	9.9622	0.5338	10.8300	0.4576
0.750	9.2569	0.5982	10.0710	0.5240
1.000	9.0144	0.6206	9.8101	0.5475
1.333	8.8807	0.6329	9.6664	0.5606
2.000	8.7884	0.6414	9.5672	0.5697
4.000	8.7374	0.6461	9.5124	0.5747
8.000	8.7274	0.6470	9.5018	0.5757
16.000	8.7263	0.6471	9.5006	0.5758
32.000	8.7267	0.6471	9.5011	0.5757
64.000	8.7271	0.6471	9.5016	0.5757
96.000	8.7273	0.6470	9.5018	0.5757
128.000	8.7274	0.6470	9.5019	0.5757
160.000	8.7275	0.6470	9.5019	0.5757

Risk appetite is shown in the first column. The other columns show the values of the Chi-squared test statistics, twice the likelihood ratio test statistic and corresponding p-values. The null hypothesis is $H_0 : \theta \Sigma^{-1} \tilde{\mu} = 1/n$.
Based on weekly returns for 13 FTSE indices from June 10, 2000, to January 28, 2012. Computations are shown to four decimal places.

values, and hence the computed p-values, are very similar. The implication is that, in practice, the Chi-squared test, which is simpler to compute, may be used. The table shows that for very small values of risk appetite, the null hypothesis that an equally weighted portfolio is a tangency portfolio is rejected. However, as risk appetite increases, it is impossible to reject the null hypothesis.

No empirical results are presented for the maximum Sharpe ratio portfolio. This is in keeping with the theoretical results described earlier, which is that maximum Sharpe ratio portfolio has infinite variance. In addition to being a volatile point on the efficient frontier, it is clear that tests of the type described in this chapter would often not lead to rejection of the null hypothesis. That is, many portfolios would not be statistically distinct from the maximum Sharpe ratio portfolio.

Tests of the minimum variance portfolio are reported in Table 9.8. For this, the null hypothesis is $H_0 : \Sigma^{-1}1/1^T\Sigma^{-1}1 = w_0$, where w_0 is specified portfolio. The results shown in Panel (1) of Table 9.8 were constructed as follows. Five values of risk appetite were used, ranging from 0 to 0.1. Efficient portfolios were constructed in the usual way, using the sample means and covariance matrix. The null hypothesis that each portfolio was a minimum variance portfolio was tested using the likelihood ratio test. As Panel (1) of Table 9.8 shows, at zero risk and risk equal to 0.001 and 0.01, the null hypothesis is not rejected. At higher levels of risk, it is rejected. In Panel (2) of Table 9.8, the same exercise is carried out with the additional restriction that no short positions are allowed. In this case, one can take a position higher up the frontier and still hold a portfolio that is not statistically distinguishable from the minimum variance portfolio. Panel (3) shows a number of minimum variance portfolios constructed by imposing a selection of lower and upper limits. As the panel shows, when the upper limit is unity, the null hypothesis is not rejected. There is a similar set of results that tests efficient frontier portfolios—that is, for the case where the null hypothesis is $H_0 : \Sigma^{-1}1/1^T\Sigma^{-1}1 = w_0; \; \Pi\mu = w_1$. This table is omitted, but is available on request.

The final part of this empirical study is to examine the properties of the estimated risk appetite when an expected return target τ is set. Table 9.9 shows results for range of values of estimated expected excess return $\tau - \hat{\alpha}_0$ from -0.0014 to 0.0014. Table 9.9 shows the corresponding values of estimated risk appetite $\hat{\theta}$, its expected value, and volatility. These are computed using the estimated values of the standard constants. The expected value column indicates that $\hat{\theta}$ is a biased estimator of θ. The volatility column shows

TABLE 9.8   Likelihood Ratio Tests for Minimum Variance Portfolios.

	Risk	l0	l1	lr	Prob
(1) Tests of MV portfolio—Efficient Frontier					
	0	22676.50	22676.50	0.00	1.00
	0.001	22676.49	22676.50	0.01	1.00
	0.01	22675.42	22676.50	1.08	1.00
	0.05	22649.46	22676.50	27.03	0.00
	0.1	22568.37	22676.50	108.13	0.00
(2) Tests of MV portfolio—Efficient Frontier + No short positions					
	0	2958.54	2958.54	0.00	1.00
	0.001	2958.54	2958.54	0.00	1.00
	0.01	2958.52	2958.54	0.02	0.98
	0.05	2958.12	2958.54	0.41	0.66
	0.1	4674.57	4706.80	32.23	0.00
(3) Tests of MV portfolio—MV + various constraints					
lower	upper				
−1.000	1.000	22676.50	22676.50	0.00	1.00
−0.750	0.750	22676.50	22676.50	0.00	1.00
−0.625	0.625	22674.11	22676.50	2.38	0.94
−0.500	0.500	22666.29	22676.50	10.21	0.04
−0.475	0.475	22664.05	22676.50	12.45	0.01
−0.450	0.450	22661.58	22676.50	14.92	0.00
−0.425	0.425	22658.80	22676.50	17.70	0.00
−0.375	0.375	22652.04	22676.50	24.46	0.00
−0.250	0.250	22628.32	22676.50	48.18	0.00
−0.125	0.125	22589.43	22676.50	87.07	0.00
0.000	0.125	15368.58	15455.69	87.10	0.00
0.000	0.250	10750.61	10801.29	50.68	0.00
0.000	0.500	4798.34	4802.55	4.21	0.04
0.000	1.000	2958.54	2958.54	0.00	1.00

The null hypothesis is $H_0 : \Sigma^{-1}1/1^T\Sigma^{-1}1 = w_0$ where w_0 is a specified portfolio. Five values of risk appetite were used, ranging from 0 to 0.1. In Panel (1) efficient portfolios were constructed in the usual way using the sample means and covariance matrix. The null hypothesis that each portfolio was a minimum variance portfolio was tested using the likelihood ratio test. In Panel (2), the same exercise is carried out with the additional restriction of no short positions. Panel (3) shows a selection of minimum variance portfolios constructed by imposing a selection of lower and upper limits.
Based on weekly returns for 13 FTSE indices from June 10, 2000, to January 28, 2012. Computations are shown to two decimal places.

TABLE 9.9 Properties of Estimate Risk Appetite Corresponding to a Target Expected Return.

$\tau - \hat{a}_0$	$\hat{\theta}$	$E(\hat{\theta})$	$vol(\hat{\theta})$	L1%CL	U1%CL	L5%CL	U5%CL	L25%CL	U25%CL
-0.0014	-0.0681	-0.0385	0.0399	-0.7394	0.1119	-0.3706	0.0431	-0.1681	-0.0031
-0.0011	-0.0454	-0.0256	0.0372	-0.5969	0.1756	-0.2969	0.0769	-0.1306	0.0169
-0.0007	-0.0227	-0.0128	0.0355	-0.4669	0.2556	-0.2294	0.1194	-0.0956	0.0406
-0.0004	0.0000	0.0000	0.0349	-0.3519	0.3544	-0.1694	0.1719	-0.0656	0.0681
0.0000	0.0227	0.0128	0.0355	-0.2531	0.4694	-0.1169	0.2319	-0.0381	0.0981
0.0004	0.0454	0.0256	0.0372	-0.1731	0.5994	-0.0744	0.2994	-0.0144	0.1331
0.0007	0.0681	0.0385	0.0399	-0.1094	0.7419	-0.0406	0.3731	0.0056	0.1706
0.0011	0.0909	0.0513	0.0434	-0.0619	0.8931	-0.0144	0.4519	0.0219	0.2106
0.0014	0.1136	0.0641	0.0475	-0.0281	1.0544	0.0056	0.5344	0.0381	0.2519

The table shows results for range of values of estimated expected excess return $\tau - \hat{a}_0$ from -0.0014 to 0.0014 and corresponding values of estimated risk appetite $\hat{\theta}$, its expected value, and volatility. These are computed using the estimated values of the standard constants. The remaining columns in Table 9.9 show lower and upper confidence limits at 99%, 95%, and 25%. These were computed using the integral representation of the distribution of $\hat{\theta}$.
Based on weekly returns for 13 FTSE indices from June 10, 2000, to January 28, 2012. Computations are shown to four decimal places.

that its effect is substantial for values of $\hat{\theta}$, which are small in magnitude. The remaining columns in Table 9.9 show lower and upper confidence limits at 99 percent, 95 percent, and 25 percent. These were computed using the integral representation of the distribution of $\hat{\theta}$. These three sets of limits show that the range of variability in $\hat{\theta}$ is often large. For example, if the expected return target is set to $-\hat{a}_0$, the overall estimated expected return on the portfolio is zero and the estimated risk appetite is equal to 0.0227. In this case, the chance that the true risk appetite is larger than 0.098 is 12.5 percent. There is also a 12.5 percent chance that it is less than −0.038. In short, the effect of estimation error on risk appetite may lead to a different position on the efficient frontier from that desired. The implications of this are discussed in the concluding section. It may also be noted that the distribution of $\hat{\theta}$ is not normal and is skewed to the right (left) if θ is positive (negative).

Variability in risk appetite will have an effect on estimated portfolio weights. This is illustrated in Table 9.10 for the case where the estimated expected return on the portfolio is zero. Table 9.10 has three vertical panels, headed A, B, and C. Panel A reports weights for efficient set portfolios—that is, portfolios constructed using only the budget constraint. Panel B includes the non−negativity constraint. Panel C seeks to achieve a degree of diversification by requiring that no weight exceed 0.2. In each of the three panels, there are four columns headed 1, 2, 3, and 4. These correspond to risk appetites −0.0381, 0.0227, 0, and 0.0981. These are, respectively, the lower 25 percent limit of $\hat{\theta}$, the estimated value, zero for the minimum variance portfolio, and the upper 25 percent limit. The horizontal panel numbered (1) shows the portfolio weights constructed using sample data. Panel (2) shows summary statistics for the absolute weight changes compared to the minimum variance portfolio. As panels (1) and (2) indicate, some weights are stable across the range of risk appetites, but many exhibit substantial variability. For comparison purposes, horizontal panels (3) and (4) show results when the sample covariance matrix is replaced with a shrinkage estimator. In this comparison, the shrinkage covariance matrix is

$$0.5(\hat{\Sigma} + \overline{\sigma^2}I_n),$$

where $\overline{\sigma^2}$ denotes the average sample variance. Panels (3) and (4) show that the degree of instability in the portfolio weights is reduced, but that there are still significant changes for some assets.

TABLE 9.10 Effect of Variability in Risk Appetite on Portfolio Weights.

	A				B				C			
	1	2	3	4	1	2	3	4	1	2	3	4
(1) Sample												
FTSE100	0.315	0.134	0.107	−0.149	0.007	0.000	0.000	0.000	0.093	0.010	0.000	0.000
FTSE250	0.064	0.336	0.498	1.000	0.000	0.000	0.000	0.228	0.000	0.099	0.200	0.200
FTS250-ex-Inv	−0.694	−0.552	−0.467	−0.155	0.000	0.000	0.000	0.000	0.000	0.000	0.000	0.200
FTSE350	0.048	−0.088	−0.169	−0.437	0.000	0.000	0.000	0.000	0.000	0.000	0.000	0.000
FTSE350-ex-inv	−0.193	0.003	0.120	0.507	0.000	0.000	0.000	0.000	0.000	0.041	0.000	0.000
FTSE350-HY	0.378	0.402	0.416	0.463	0.349	0.383	0.400	0.354	0.200	0.200	0.200	0.200
FTSE350-LY	0.181	−0.048	−0.184	−0.637	0.000	0.000	0.000	0.000	0.000	0.000	0.000	0.000
FTSE-SC	0.882	0.746	0.664	0.395	0.643	0.617	0.600	0.418	0.200	0.200	0.200	0.200
FTSE-All-Share	−0.197	−0.009	0.103	0.474	0.000	0.000	0.000	0.000	0.174	0.200	0.200	0.127
FTSE-AS-ex-inv	−0.005	0.081	0.133	0.305	0.000	0.000	0.000	0.000	0.145	0.200	0.200	0.073
FTSE-AS-ex-mult	0.221	−0.055	−0.220	−0.766	0.000	0.000	0.000	0.000	0.188	0.051	0.000	0.000
(2) Summary												
Minimum	0.037	0.014	0.000	0.047	0.000	0.000	0.000	0.000	0.000	0.000	0.000	0.000
Mean	0.263	0.098	0.000	0.326	0.009	0.003	0.000	0.042	0.051	0.018	0.000	0.036
Maximum	0.440	0.164	0.000	0.546	0.051	0.017	0.000	0.228	0.200	0.101	0.000	0.200
Stan. Devn.	0.122	0.046	0.000	0.147	0.019	0.007	0.000	0.083	0.077	0.033	0.000	0.068

(Continued)

TABLE 9.10 (*Continued*).

	A				B				C			
	1	2	3	4	1	2	3	4	1	2	3	4
(3) Shrinkage												
FTSE100	0.092	0.073	0.063	0.027	0.088	0.073	0.063	0.013	0.095	0.077	0.065	0.018
FTSE250	−0.009	0.058	0.098	0.230	0.000	0.058	0.098	0.217	0.003	0.068	0.105	0.200
FTS250-ex-Inv	−0.029	0.044	0.088	0.233	0.000	0.044	0.088	0.221	0.000	0.055	0.095	0.200
FTSE350	0.071	0.065	0.061	0.048	0.067	0.065	0.061	0.035	0.076	0.069	0.064	0.041
FTSE350-ex-inv	0.078	0.076	0.074	0.069	0.075	0.076	0.074	0.055	0.085	0.081	0.078	0.060
FTSE350-HY	0.144	0.154	0.160	0.180	0.141	0.154	0.160	0.172	0.153	0.160	0.165	0.176
FTSE350-LY	0.073	0.035	0.012	−0.062	0.068	0.035	0.012	0.000	0.078	0.039	0.015	0.000
FTSE-SC	0.293	0.262	0.243	0.180	0.286	0.262	0.243	0.171	0.200	0.200	0.200	0.179
FTSE-All-Share	0.085	0.082	0.080	0.075	0.082	0.082	0.080	0.059	0.093	0.088	0.084	0.064
FTSE-AS-ex-inv	0.086	0.082	0.080	0.073	0.083	0.082	0.080	0.058	0.093	0.088	0.084	0.063
FTSE-AS-ex-mult	0.116	0.069	0.041	−0.053	0.110	0.069	0.041	0.000	0.125	0.076	0.046	0.000
(4) Summary												
Minimum	0.004	0.001	0.000	0.005	0.001	0.001	0.000	0.011	0.000	0.000	0.000	0.011
Mean	0.044	0.016	0.000	0.054	0.037	0.016	0.000	0.048	0.038	0.015	0.000	0.038
Maximum	0.117	0.044	0.000	0.145	0.098	0.044	0.000	0.132	0.102	0.041	0.000	0.105
Stan. Devn.	0.042	0.016	0.000	0.052	0.036	0.016	0.000	0.043	0.039	0.015	0.000	0.033

Based on weekly returns for 13 FTSE indices from June 10, 2000, to January 28, 2012. Computations are shown to four decimal places.

DISCUSSION AND CONCLUDING REMARKS

This chapter is concerned with the vectors of estimated portfolio weights. It presents a synthesis of recent research and a summary of some new results. One objective of this article is to present a summary of the state of the art in a style and notation that is accessible. A second is to present some tests of efficiency that are straightforward to compute.

There is a closely related set of research that is concerned with the properties of the location, scale, and slope of the efficient frontier—that is, with the properties of the standard constants denoted collectively by α. Bodnar and Schmid (2008a) provide expressions for the probability distribution of the estimated return and estimated variance of an efficient frontier portfolio. They also provide expressions for moments up to order four. The corresponding distributions for the minimum variance portfolio are special cases. Essentially, the same results are given in the major paper by Kan and Smith (2008). The distributions typically involve nuisance parameters and are expressible as convolutions involving noncentral F distributions and the hyper geometric function $_1F_1$. Nonetheless, there is a test for the curvature or slope of the efficient frontier that uses the noncentral F-distribution. There is a similar result for the slope of the efficient frontier when a risk-free asset is available. Building on their previous work, Bodnar and Schmid (2009) provide confidence sets for the efficient frontier.

Two notable results emerge from research in this area. First, when the effect of estimated parameters is taken into account, the maximum Sharpe ratio portfolio should probably be avoided in practice. This is because its moments are infinite. Second, using an estimated value of risk appetite, which is a consequence of setting an expected return target, leads to additional variability, both in portfolio weights and performance. It is difficult not to adhere to advice heard on more than one occasion: "Pick a point on the frontier that is suitable." In other words, treat a suitable value of risk appetite as given.

The likelihood ratio tests described in this chapter are straightforward to compute. However, as they are asymptotic tests, they assume that the sample size is large. Construction of tests for small sample sizes may use exact distributions when these are available. These may be confounded by nuisance parameters. Furthermore, all results in this work and the majority of results reported in other papers make the standard IID normal assumptions. Bodnar and Schmid (2008a; 2008b) present results for elliptical distributions and for ARMA processes. Bodnar and Gupta (2011) study the effects of skewness on tests for the minimum variance portfolio, assuming that returns follow Azzalini multivariate skew-normal distributions. Overall, however, the tests reported here and elsewhere are appropriate for low-frequency applications based on large samples. For other types of portfolio selection, notably high-frequency applications, the tests may be computed but should probably be regarded only as rules of thumb for general guidance.

The third area of work mentioned in the introduction is that of the *ex post* performance of efficient portfolios. This has so far attracted relatively little attention. There are results in Kan and Smith (2008) and in Adcock (2013). Both sets of results indicate why *ex post* performance can be different from that expected *ex ante*, but also demonstrate the reliance of the results on standard assumptions about the distribution of asset returns.

Overall, many outstanding research challenges warrant further study.

REFERENCES

Adcock, C. J. 1997. Sample size determination: A review. *Journal of the Royal Statistical Society*. Series D (The Statistician) 46 (2): 261–283.
_____. 2013. Ex post efficient set mathematics. *The Journal of Mathematical Finance* 3 (1A): 201–210.
_____. 2014a. Mean-variance-skewness efficient surfaces, Stein's lemma and the multivariate extended skew-student distribution. *The European Journal of Operational Research* 234 (2): 392–401.
_____. 2014b. Likelihood Ratio Tests for Efficient Portfolios, *Working Paper*.
Adcock, C., N. Areal, M. R. Armada, M. C. Cortez, B. Oliveira, and F. Silva. 2012. Tests of the correlation between portfolio performance measures. *Journal of Financial Transformation* 35: 123–132.
Bawa, V., S. J. Brown, and R. Klein. 1979. *Estimation Risk and Optimal Portfolio Choice, Studies in Bayesian Econometrics*, Vol. 3. Amsterdam, North Holland.
Best, M. J., and R. R. Grauer. 1991. On the sensitivity of mean-variance-efficient portfolios to changes in asset means: Some analytical and computational results. *Review of Financial Studies* 4 (2): 315–342.
Britten-Jones, M. 1999. The sampling error in estimates of mean-variance efficient portfolio weights. *Journal of Finance* 54 (2): 655–672.
Bodnar, T., and A. K. Gupta. 2011. Robustness of the Inference Procedures for the Global Minimum Variance Portfolio Weights in a Skew Normal Model. *The European Journal of Finance*.
Bodnar, T., and Y. Okhrin. 2011. On the product of inverse wishart and normal distributions with applications to discriminant analysis and portfolio theory. *Scandinavian Journal of Statistics* 38 (2): 311–331.
Bodnar, T., and W. Schmid. 2008a. A test for the weights of the global minimum variance portfolio in an elliptical model. *Metrika* 67 (2): 127–143.
_____. 2008b. Estimation of optimal portfolio compositions for Gaussian returns. *Statistics & Decisions* 26 (3):179–201.
_____. 2009. Econometrical analysis of the sample efficient frontier. *The European Journal of Finance* 15 (3): 317–335.

Chopra, V., and W. T. Ziemba. 1993, Winter. The effect of errors in means, variances and covariances on optimal portfolio choice. *Journal of Portfolio Management*: 6–11.

Das Gupta, S. 1968. Some aspects of discrimination function coefficients. *Sankhya A* 30: 387–400.

Fang, K.-T., S. Kotz, and K.-W. Ng. 1990. *Symmetric multivariate and related distributions*. Monographs on Statistics and Applied Probability, Vol. 36. London: Chapman & Hall, Ltd.

Gibbons, M. R., S. A. Ross, and J. Shanken. 1989. A test of the efficiency of a given portfolio. *Econometrica* 57 (5): 1121–1152.

Huberman, G., and S. Kandel. 1987. Mean-variance spanning, *The Journal of Finance*, 42(4): 873–888.

Jobson, J. D., and B. Korkie. 1980. Estimation for Markowitz efficient portfolios, *Journal of the American Statistical Association* 75 (371): 544–554.

_____. 1989. A performance interpretation of multivariate tests of asset set intersection, spanning, and mean-variance efficiency. *Journal of Financial and Quantitative Analysis* 24 (2): 185–204.

Johnson, N., and S. Kotz. 1970. *Continuous Univariate Distributions 2*. Boston: John Wiley and Sons.

Kan, R., and D. R. Smith. 2008. The distribution of the sample minimum-variance frontier, *Management Science* 54 (7): 1364–1360.

Kandel, S. 1983. Essay no. I: *A Likelihood Ratio Test of Mean Variance Efficiency in the Absence of a Riskless Asset, Essays in Portfolio Theory*. Ph.D. dissertation (Yale University), New Haven, CT.

_____. 1984. The likelihood ratio test statistic of mean-variance efficiency without a riskless asset. *Journal of Financial Economics* 13 (X): 575–592.

Landsman, Z., and J. Nešlehová. 2008. Stein's Lemma for elliptical random vectors. *Journal of Multivariate Analysis* 99 (5): 912–927.

Liu, J. S. 1994. Siegel's Formula via Stein's Identities. *Statistics and Probability Letters*, 21(3): 247–251.

Markowitz, H. 1952. Portfolio selection. *Journal of Finance* 7 (1): 77–91.

Merton, R. 1972. An analytical derivation of the efficient portfolio frontier, *Journal of Financial and Quantitative Analysis* 7 (4): 1851–1872.

Muirhead, R. J. 1982. *Aspects of Multivariate Statistical Theory*. New York: John Wiley and Sons.

Okhrin, Y., and W. Schmid. 2006. Distributional properties of portfolio weights, *Journal of Econometrics* 134 (1): 235–256.

Ross, S. A. 1980. A test of the efficiency of a given portfolio, Paper prepared for the World Econometrics Meetings, Aix-en-Provence.

Scheffé, H. 1959. *The Analysis of Variance*. New York: John Wiley & Sons.

Sentana, E. 2009. The econometrics of mean-variance efficiency tests: A survey. *The Econometrics Journal* 12 (3): 65–101.

Siskind, V. 1972. Second moments of inverse Wishart-matrix elements. *Biometrika* 59 (3): 690.

Smith, T. M. F. 1976. The foundations of survey sampling: a review. *Journal of the Royal Statistical Society, Series A* 139 (2): 183–195.

Stein, C. M. 1981. Estimation of the mean of a multivariate normal distribution. *Annals of Statistics* 9 (6): 1135–1151.

Credit Risk Modelling

Stress Testing for Portfolio Credit Risk: Supervisory Expectations and Practices

Michael Jacobs Jr.[1]
Pricewaterhouse Cooper Advisory LLP

INTRODUCTION AND MOTIVATION

Modern credit risk modeling (e.g., Merton 1974) increasingly relies on advanced mathematical, statistical, and numerical techniques to measure and manage risk in credit portfolios. This gives rise to model risk (OCC/BOG-FRB 2011) and the possibility of understating inherent dangers stemming from very rare yet plausible occurrences not in our reference data sets. In the wake of the financial crisis (Demirguc-Kunt, Detragiache, and Merrouche 2010; Acharya and Schnabl 2009), international supervisors have recognized the importance of *stress testing* (ST), especially in the realm of credit risk, as can be seen in the revised Basel framework (Basel Committee on Banking Supervision 2005; 2006; 2009a–e; 2010a; 2010b) and the Federal Reserve's Comprehensive Capital Analysis and Review (CCAR) program. It can be and has been argued that the art and science of stress testing has lagged in the domain of credit, as opposed to other types of risk (e.g., market risk), and our objective is to help fill this vacuum.

---

[1] The views expressed herein are those of the author and do not necessarily represent a position taken by Deloitte & Touche, Pricewaterhouse Cooper Advisory LLP.

We aim to present classifications and established techniques that will help practitioners formulate robust credit risk stress tests.

We have approached the topic of ST from the point of view of a typical credit portfolio, such as one managed by a typical medium- or large-sized commercial bank. We take this point of view for two main reasons. First, for financial institutions that are exposed to credit risk, it remains their predominant risk. Second, this significance is accentuated for medium- as opposed to large-sized banks, and new supervisory requirements under the CCAR will now be focusing on the smaller banks that were exempt from the previous exercise. To this end, we will survey the supervisory expectations with respect to ST, discuss in detail the credit risk parameters underlying a quantitative component of ST, develop a typology of ST programs, and finally, present a simple and stylized example of an ST model. The latter "toy" example is meant to illustrate the feasibility of building a model for ST that can be implemented even by less sophisticated banking institutions. The only requirements are the existence of an obligor rating system, associate default rate data, access to macroeconomic drives, and a framework for estimating economic capital. While we use the CreditMetrics[2] model for estimating economic capital,[2] we show how this could be accomplished in a simplified framework such as the Basel II IRB model.

Figure 10.1 plots net charge-off rates for the top 50 banks in the United States. This is reproduced from a working paper by Inanoglu, Jacobs, Liu, and Sickles (2013) on the efficiency of the banking system, which concludes that over the last two decades the largest financial institutions with credit portfolios have become not only larger, but also riskier and less efficient. As we can see here, bank losses in the recent financial crisis exceed levels observed in recent history. This illustrates the inherent limitations of backward-looking models and the fact that in robust risk modeling we must anticipate risk, and not merely mimic history.

Figure 10.2 shows a plot from Inanoglu and Jacobs (2009), the bootstrap resample (Efron and Tibshirani 1986) distribution of the 99.97th percentile value at risk (VaR) for the top 200 banks in a Gaussian copula model combining five risk types (credit, market, liquidity, operational, and interest rate risk), as proxied for by the supervisory call report data. This shows that sampling variation in VaR inputs leads to huge confidence bounds for risk estimates, with a coefficient of variation of 35.4 percent, illustrating the

---

[2]We implement the basic CreditMetrics model in the R programming language (R Development Core Team, 2013) using a package by the same name. In Inanoglu, Jacobs, and Karagozoglu (2013), we implement a multifactor version of this in R through a proprietary package. A spreadsheet implementation of this can be found at: http://michaeljacobsjr.com/CreditMetrics_6-20-12_V1.xls.

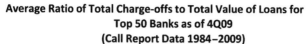

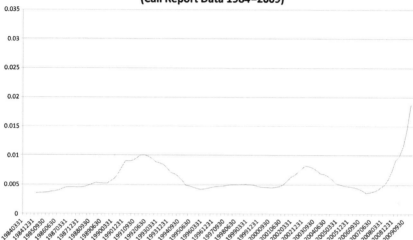

FIGURE 10.1 Historical charge-off rates. Reprinted by permission from Inanoglu, Jacobs, Liu, and Sickles (2013).

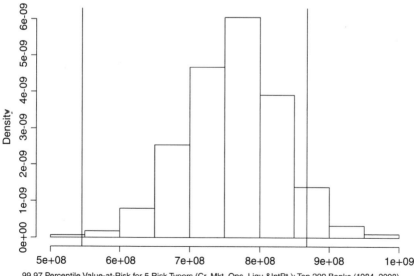

FIGURE 10.2 Distribution of VaR. Reprinted by permission from Inanoglu and Jacobs (2009).

significant uncertainty introduced as sampling variation in parameter estimates flows through to the risk estimate. This is even assuming we have the correct model!

This chapter shall proceed as follows. The second section discusses conceptual considerations. The following sections cover the function of stress testing; supervisory requirements and expectations; an ST example; and finally, conclusions and discussions of future directions.

CONCEPTUAL ISSUES IN STRESS TESTING: RISK VERSUS UNCERTAINTY

In this section we will consider and survey some of the thoughts regarding the concept of risk. A classical dichotomy exists in the literature, the earliest exposition of which is credited to Knight (1921). He defined *uncertainty* as the state in which a probability distribution is unknown or cannot be measured. This is contrasted with the situation in which the probability distribution is known or knowable through repeated experimentation. Arguably, in economics and finance (and more broadly in the social or natural as opposed to the physical or mathematical sciences), uncertainty is the more realistic scenario that we are contending with (e.g., a fair vs. loaded die, or a die with an unknown number of sides). We are forced to rely on empirical data to estimate loss distributions, which is complicated by changing economic conditions that invalidate the forecasts our econometric models generate.

Popper (1945) postulated that situations of uncertainty are closely associated with, and inherent with respect to, changes in knowledge and behavior. This is also known as the rebuttal of the *historicism* concept, that our actions and their outcomes have a predetermined path. He emphasized that the growth of knowledge and freedom implies that we cannot perfectly predict the course of history. For example, a statement that the U.S. currency is inevitably going to depreciate if the United States does not control its debt, is not refutable and therefore not a valid scientific statement, according to Popper.

Shackle (1990) argued that predictions are reliable only for the immediate future. He argues that such predictions affect the decisions of economic agents, and this has an effect on the outcomes under question, changing the validity of the prediction (a feedback effect). This recognition of the role of human behavior in economic theory was a key impetus behind rational expectations and behavioral finance. While it is valuable to estimate loss distributions that help explicate sources of uncertainty, risk managers must be aware of the model limitation that a stress testing regime itself changes behavior (e.g., banks "gaming" the regulators' CCAR process). The conclusion is that the inherent limitations of this practice is a key factor in supporting the use of stress testing in order to supplement other risk measures. Finally, Artzner and others (1999) postulate some desirable features of a risk measure, collectively known as *coherence*. They argue that VaR measures often fail to satisfy such properties.

THE FUNCTION OF STRESS TESTING

There are various possible definitions of ST. One common one is the investigation of *unexpected loss* (UL) under conditions outside our ordinary realm of experience (e.g., extreme events not in our reference data sets). There are numerous reasons for conducting periodic ST, which are largely due to the relationship between UL and measures of risk, examples of the latter being *economic capital* (EC) or *regulatory capital* (RC). Key examples of such exercises are compliance with supervisory guidance on model risk management such as the OCC/BOG-FRB (2011) Bulletin 2011–2012 on managing model risk, or bank stress test and capital plan requirements outlined by the Federal Reserve's CCAR program to gauge the resiliency of the banking system to adverse scenarios.

EC is generally thought of as the difference between a value-at-risk measure—an extreme loss at some confidence level (e.g., a high quantile of a loss distribution)—and an *expected loss* (EL) measure—generally thought of as a likely loss measure over some time horizon (e.g., an allowance for loan losses amount set aside by a bank). Figure 10.3 presents a stylized representation of a loss distribution and the associated EL and VaR measures.

This purpose for ST hinges on our definition of UL. While it is commonly thought that EC should cover EL, it may be the case that UL might not only be unexpected but also not credible, as it is a statistical concept. Therefore, some argue that results of a stress test should be used for EC purposes in lieu of UL. However, this practice is rare, as we usually do not have probability distributions associated with stress events. Nevertheless, ST can be and commonly has been used to challenge the adequacy of RC or EC as an input into the derivation of a buffer for losses exceeding the VaR, especially for new products or portfolios.

ST has an advantage over EC measures in that it can often better address the *risk aggregation problem* that arises when correlations among different risk types are in many cases large and cannot be ignored. As risks are modeled very differently, it is challenging to aggregate these into an EC measure. An advantage to ST in determining capital is that it can easily

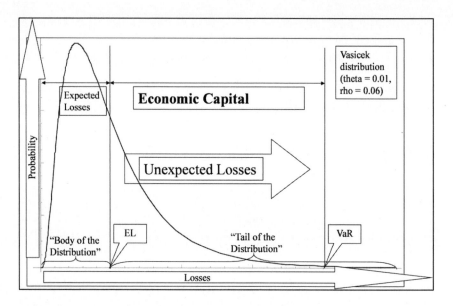

FIGURE 10.3 Stylized representation of economic capital.

aggregate different risk types (e.g., credit, market, and operational), which is problematic under standard EC methodologies (e.g., different horizons and confidence levels for market vs. credit risk). Figure 10.4 presents the pair-wise correlations for a composite of the top 200 banks for five risk types (credit, market, liquidity, operational, and interest rate risk) as proxies of the call report data. This is evidence of powerful long-run dependencies across risk types. Even more compelling is that such dependencies between risk types are accentuated during periods of stress. See Embrechts, McNeil, and Straumann (2001) and Frey and McNeil (2003) for detailed discussions of correlation and dependency modeling in risk management and various relevant caveats.

Apart from risk measurement or quantification, ST can be a risk management tool, used several ways when analyzing portfolio composition and resilience with respect to disturbances. ST can help to identify potential uncertainties and locate the portfolio vulnerabilities such as incurred but not realized losses in value, or weaknesses in structures that have not been tested. ST can also aid in analyzing the effects of new complex structures and credit products for which we may have a limited understanding. ST can also guide discussions on unfavorable developments such as crises and abnormal market conditions, which may be very rare but cannot be excluded from consideration. Finally, ST can be instrumental in monitoring important

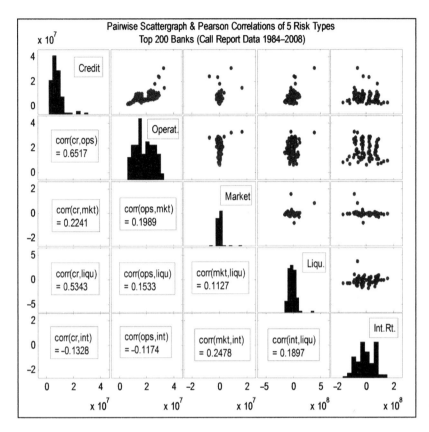

FIGURE 10.4 Correlations among risk types. Reprinted with permission from Inanoglu and Jacobs 2009.

subportfolios exhibiting large exposures or extreme vulnerability to changes in market conditions.

Quantification of ST appears, and can be deployed, across several aspects of risk management with respect to extreme losses. Primarily, ST can be used to establish or test risk buffers. Furthermore, ST is a tool for helping to determine the risk capacity of a financial institution. Another use of ST is in setting subportfolio limits, especially in low-default situation. ST can also be deployed to inform risk policy, tolerance, and appetite. ST can provide impetus to derive some need for action to reduce the risk of extreme losses and, hence, EC, and it can mitigate the vulnerability to important risk-relevant effects. ST is potentially a means to test portfolio diversification by introducing (implicit) correlations. Finally, ST can help us to question a bank's attitude toward risk.

SUPERVISORY REQUIREMENTS AND EXPECTATIONS

ST appears in the Basel II framework (BCBS 2006), under both Pillar 1 (i.e., minimum capital requirements) and Pillar 2 (i.e., the supervisory review process), with the common aim in both facets of improving risk management. Every bank subject to the advanced internal ratings-based (AIRB) approach to RC has to conduct sound, significant, and meaningful stress testing to assess the capital adequacy in a reasonably conservative way. Furthermore, major credit risk concentrations have to undergo periodic stress tests. It is also the supervisory expectation that ST should be integrated into the internal capital adequacy assessment process (i.e., risk management strategies to respond to the outcome of ST and the internal capital adequacy assessment process).

The bottom line is that banks shall ensure that they dispose of enough capital to meet the regulatory capital requirements even in the case of stress. This requires that banks should be able to identify possible future events and changes in economic conditions with potentially adverse effects on credit exposures and assess their ability to withstand adverse negative credit events.

One means of doing this quantifies the impact on the parameters of *probability of default* (PD), *loss given default* (LGD), and *exposure at default* (EAD), as well as ratings migrations. Special notes on how to implement these requirements—meaning the scenarios that might impact the risk parameters—include the use of scenarios that take into consideration the following:

- Economic or industry downturns
- Market-risk events
- Liquidity shortages
- Recession scenarios (worst case not required)

Banks should use their own data for estimating ratings migrations and integrate the insight of such for external ratings. Banks should also build their stress testing on the study of the impact of smaller deteriorations in the credit environment.

Shocking credit risk parameters can give us an idea of what kind of buffer we may need to add to an EC estimate. Although this type of ST is mainly contained in Pillar 1, it is a fundamental part of Pillar 2, an important way of assessing capital adequacy. To some degree, this explains the nonprescriptiveness for ST in Pillar 2, as the latter recognizes that banks are competent to assess and measure their credit risk appropriately. This also implies that ST should focus on EC as well as RC, as these represent the bank's internal and supervisory views on portfolio credit risk, respectively. ST has been addressed regarding the stability of the financial system by regulators or central banks beyond the Basel II framework in published supplements, including now Basel III (BCBS, 2010a; 2010b).

ST should consider extreme deviations from normal situations that involve unrealistic yet still plausible scenarios (i.e., situations with a low probability of occurrence). ST should also consider joint events that are plausible but may not yet have been observed in reference data sets. Financial institutions should also use ST to become aware of their risk profile and to challenge their business plans, target portfolios, risk politics, and so on.

Figure 10.5 presents a stylized representation of ST for regulatory credit risk, using a version of the Basel IRB formula for stressed PD (see Gordy 2003) through the shocking of the IRB parameters. The solid curve represents the 99.97th percentile regulatory credit capital under the base case of a 1 percent PD, a 40 percent LGD, and credit correlation of 10 percent (ballpark parameters for a typical middle-market exposure or a B+ corporate exposure), which has capital of 6.68 percent of EAD (normalized to unity). Under stressed conditions (PD, LGD, and correlation each increased by 50 percent to 1.5 percent, 60 percent, and 15 percent, respectively), regulatory capital more than doubles to 15.79 percent of EAD.

ST should not only be deployed to address the adequacy of RC or EC, but also be used to determine and question credit limits. ST should not be treated only as an amendment to the VaR evaluations for credit portfolios but as a complementary method, which contrasts with the purely statistical approach of VaR methods by including causally determined considerations for UL. In particular, it can be used to specify extreme losses both qualitatively and quantitatively.

EMPIRICAL METHODOLOGY: A SIMPLE ST EXAMPLE

We present an illustration of one possible approach to ST, which may be feasible in a typical credit portfolio. We calculate the risk of this portfolio in the CreditMetrics model, which has the following inputs:

- Correlation matrix of asset returns
- Ratings transition matrix and PDs
- Credit risk parameters of LGD and EAD
- Term structure of interest rates

In order to implement this methodology, we calculate a correlation matrix from daily logarithmic bond returns. The daily bond indices are sourced from Bank of America Merrill Lynch in the Datastream database

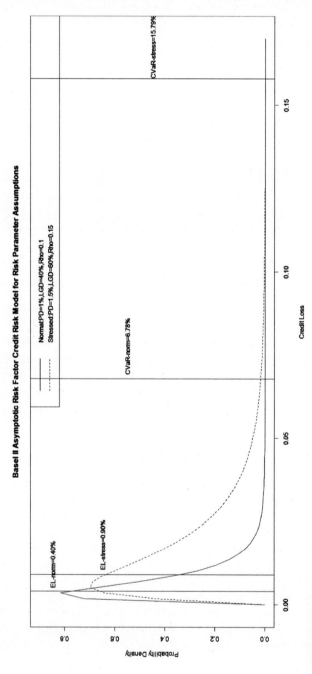

FIGURE 10.5 Stressed regulatory capital example.

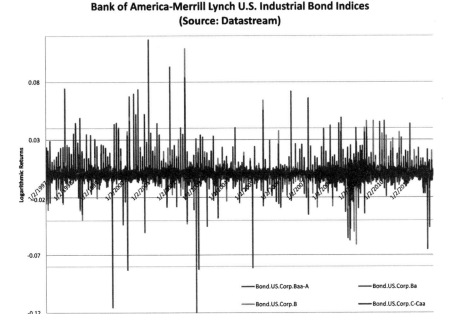

FIGURE 10.6   Bond return index return—Time series (January 2, 1997, to December 19, 2011).

from the period 2 January 1997 to 19 December 2011, and include all US-domiciled industrial companies in four ratings classes (Baa-A, Ba, B, and C-CCC). Time series and summary statistics are shown in Figures 10.6 and Table 10.1, respectively. Note that higher-rated bonds actually return and vary more than lower-rated bonds, but the coefficient of variation (CV) is U-shaped. The highest correlations are between adjacent ratings at the high and low ends. Note, also, that some of the correlations are lower and others somewhat higher than the Basel II prescriptions.

A ratings transition matrix among the rating classes is sourced from Moody's Default Risk Service, shown in Table 10.2. We collapse the best ratings due to paucity of defaults. Note that as ratings worsen, default risks (DRs) increase exponentially, and the diagonals shrink, which is indicative of both higher default risk and greater volatility of ratings for inferior credits. Correlations are also higher between adjacent than separated ratings. Figure 10.7 shows the time series of these default rates, in which the cyclicality of DRs is evident. Table 10.3 shows the summary statistics of the DRs, where we note the high variability relative to the mean of these as ratings worsen.

TABLE 10.1 Bond Return Index Return—Summary Statistics and Correlations (January 2, 1997, to December 19, 2011).

Sector	Rating	Mean	Median	Standard Deviation	Coefficient of Variation	Minimum	Maximum	Correlations			
Portfolio 1-Industrials	Aa-Aaa	0.0377%	0.0274%	0.7167%	18.99	−12.3977%	11.6545%	100.00%	36.07%	8.84%	8.26%
	Baa-A	0.0433%	0.0331%	0.5247%	12.11	−11.5403%	7.4375%		100.00%	8.68%	16.46%
	B-Ba	0.0372%	0.0418%	0.5308%	14.27	−6.0864%	10.8899%			100.00%	78.83%
	C-Caa	0.0194%	0.0425%	0.4478%	23.12	−4.7283%	8.3753%				100.00%

Source: Datastream

TABLE 10.2 Moody's Credit Ratings Migration Matrix.

	Baa-A	Ba	B	Caa-C	Default
Baa-A	97.94%	1.62%	0.36%	0.04%	0.04%
Ba	1.29%	87.23%	9.52%	0.62%	1.34%
B	0.13%	5.11%	83.82%	5.25%	5.69%
Caa-C	0.23%	1.44%	8.10%	68.34%	21.89%

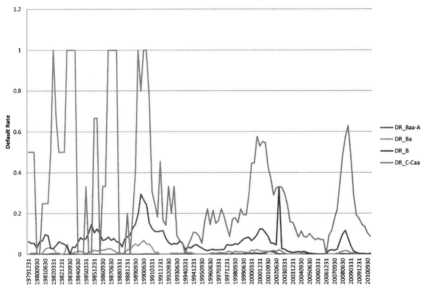

U.S. Industrial Annual Default Rates (Moody's Default Rate Service Database 1980–2010)

FIGURE 10.7 Default rate data—Time series.

In order to compute stressed risk, we build regression models for DRs in the ratings classes and stress values of the independent variables to compute stressed PDs. The remainder of the correlation matrix is rescaled so that it is still valid, and this is inputted in the CreditMetrics algorithm.

A search through a large set of variables available from Wharton Research Data Services yielded a set of final explanatory variables that we choose for our model. These variables are all significantly correlated to the Moody's DR and are summarized in Table 10.4. Figure 10.8 shows the VIX measure of volatility or fear in the equity markets and the C&I charge-off rate, the latter being a credit cycle variable found to work well. Figure 10.9

TABLE 10.3 Default Rate Data—Summary Statistics.

Rating	Mean	Median	Standard Deviation	Coefficient of Variation	Minimum	Maximum	Correlations			
Baa-A	0.0930%	0.0000%	0.2140%	2.30	0.0000%	1.2926%	100.00%	15.88%	10.73%	13.90%
Ba	1.1341%	0.7246%	1.3265%	1.17	0.0000%	6.7460%		100.00%	70.88%	55.35%
B	6.1652%	5.2326%	5.7116%	0.93	0.0000%	33.0645%			100.00%	39.81%
Caa-C	31.1884%	20.0000%	29.1442%	0.93	0.0000%	100.0000%				100.00%

TABLE 10.4 Risk Factor Data—Summary Statistics

Variable	Mean	Median	Standard Deviation	Coefficient of Variation	Minimum	Maximum	Correlations										
							VIX Volatility Index	Fama-French Size	Fama-French Value	Fama-French Market	French Risk-Free Rate	Fama French Momentum	C&I Charge-off Rates	GDP-Level	GDP-Annual Change	CPI-Annual Change	Oil Price-Annual Change
VIX Volatility index	2.39%	2.18%	1.12%	46.73%	1.00%	6.19%	100.00%	-1.12%	4.23%	-14.52%	23.93%	-10.78%	22.08%	-26.08%	-2.75%	34.05%	-11.97%
Fama-French Size	0.00%	0.00%	0.08%	38.12	-0.20%	0.17%	—	100.00%	15.47%	-16.29%	-9.67%	13.13%	11.84%	6.22%	-10.40%	7.25%	6.42%
Fama-French Value	0.02%	0.01%	0.10%	6.30	-0.29%	0.35%	—	—	100.00%	-37.86%	10.34%	-16.99%	3.10%	-5.09%	12.23%	6.41%	-10.96%
Fama-French Market	0.03%	0.04%	0.13%	5.32	-0.37%	0.28%	—	—	—	100.00%	-5.18%	-18.71%	-3.40%	-7.86%	-13.48%	0.54%	-8.92%
Fama-French Risk-Free Rate	0.02%	0.02%	0.01%	0.64	0.00%	0.06%	—	—	—	—	100.00%	15.54%	-25.52%	-79.15%	14.88%	77.91%	0.83%
Fama-French Momentum	0.03%	0.03%	0.12%	3.93	-0.58%	0.34%	—	—	—	—	—	100.00%	-9.98%	-8.24%	11.39%	3.17%	8.67%
C&I Chargeoff Rates	0.01%	0.91%	0.58%	62.84	0.10%	2.54%	—	—	—	—	—	—	100.00%	-9.98%	-27.66%	5.28%	-11.74%
GDP - Annual Change	0.03%	3.00%	2.32%	88.46	-5.03%	8.48%	—	—	—	—	—	—	—	—	100.00%	-23.86%	1.79%
CPI - Annual Change	0.04%	3.00%	2.65%	66.04	1.15%	12.96%	—	—	—	—	—	—	—	—	—	100.00%	-7.12%
Oil Price - Annual Change	0.10%	3.33%	34.71%	364.94	-56.14%	130.93%	—	—	—	—	—	—	—	—	—	—	100.00%

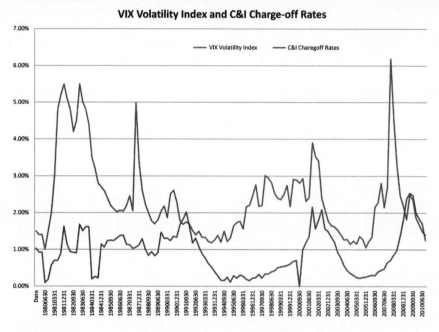

FIGURE 10.8 VIX and C&I charge-off rate—Time series.

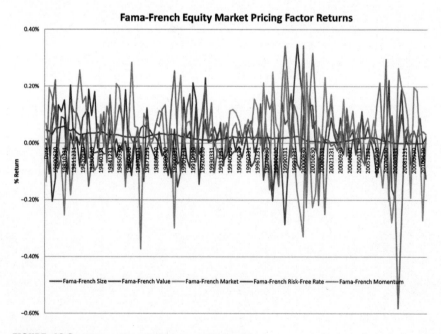

FIGURE 10.9 Fama–French factors—Time series.

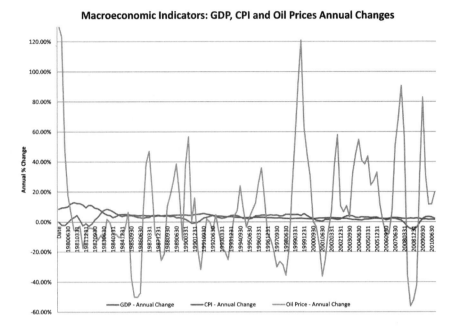

FIGURE 10.10 GDP, CPI, and oil prices—Time series.

shows the four Fama–French pricing indices (returns on small stocks, value stocks, the broad index, and a momentum strategy), which are also found to be good predictors of DR. Finally, for the factors, Figure 10.10 plots the year-over-year changes in GDP, oil prices, and CPI inflation, which are all macro factors found to be predictive of DRs as well.

Table 10.5 shows the regression results. All models are highly significant. Estimates are statistically significant across ratings (at least the 5 percent level), and signs on coefficient estimates are all economically sensible.

The regression results shown in Figure 10.11 show that the five Fama–French equity market factors indicate that default rates are lower if broad-market, small, or value stocks are doing better and with higher momentum. Higher market volatility, interest rates, charge-offs, or oil prices increase DRs. DRs are lower if GDP growth or inflation rates are increasing. The magnitude of coefficients varies across ratings, generally greater and more precisely estimated for lower ratings.

Table 10.6 shows the results of the ST for various hypothetical scenarios for our hypothetical portfolio of four bonds. In the base case, expected loss is a normalized 2.63 percent (i.e., EAD is 1), with CreditMetrics EC of 7.17 percent and Basel II IRB RC of 9.29 percent. Note that over most

TABLE 10.5 Stress Testing Example Regression Results.

Default Rate		VIX Volatility Index	Fama-French Size	Fama-French Value	Fama-French Market	Fama-French Risk-Free Rate	Fama-French Momentum	C&I Charge-off Rates	GDP-Annual Change	CPI-Annual Change	Oil Price-Annual Change	R-Squared Statistic	F Statistic P-Value
Baa-A	Coefficient Estimate	0.0665***	0.118**	−0.3047*	−0.2055*	0.9276**	−0.2872**	0.02354**	−0.01956**	−0.01936*	0.1654**	37.19%	4.47E-04
	P-Value	2.98E-04	6.42E-03	1.53E-02	1.90E-02	7.74E-03	7.17E-03	5.26E-03	5.69E-03	2.29E-01	7.62E-03		
Ba	Coefficient Estimate	0.1973*	−1.047**	−1.055**	−1.64**	0.8095***	−0.6578*	0.7042***	−0.2123***	−0.4336***	0.1351**	38.80%	2.59E-08
	P-Value	5.00E-03	4.61E-03	3.75E-03	6.25E-03	1.78E-05	4.58E-02	9.25E-04	2.95E-04	4.14E-06	6.59E-03		
B	Coefficient Estimate	0.2129**	−2.249**	−5.488**	−4.443*	1.706**	−5.184*	1.5415***	−0.7663**	−1.396**	0.1267**	42.28%	5.79E-05
	P-Value	6.48E-03	7.34E-03	3.23E-03	2.77E-02	4.53E-03	2.11E-02	1.83E-03	4.63E-03	1.14E-03	3.75E-02		
Caa-C	Coefficient Estimate	1.041***	−5.332**	3.242*	−8.875**	3.208**	−5.797**	8.58***	−3.246**	−4.908**	0.1743**	44.78%	1.19E-12
	P-Value	7.27E-07	6.10E-03	1.72E-02	3.09E-03	3.75-03	7.42E-03	6.18E-05	4.95E-03	6.95E-03	4.92E-03		

***,**,*denotes statistical significance at the 0.1%, 1%, and 5% confidence levels, respectively. (Moody's DRS 1980-2011)

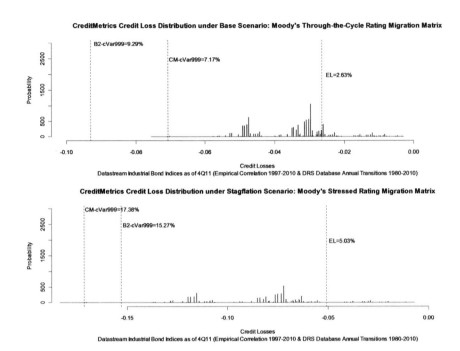

CreditMetrics Credit Loss Distribution under Base Scenario: Moody's Through-the-Cycle Rating Migration Matrix

Credit Losses
Datastream Industrial Bond Indices as of 4Q11 (Empirical Correlation 1997-2010 & DRS Database Annual Transitions 1980-2010)

CreditMetrics Credit Loss Distribution under Stagflation Scenario: Moody's Stressed Rating Migration Matrix

Credit Losses
Datastream Industrial Bond Indices as of 4Q11 (Empirical Correlation 1997-2010 & DRS Database Annual Transitions 1980-2010)

FIGURE 10.11 Stress test results—Graphs of unexpected vs. expected loss in stagflation scenario.

scenarios, RC is bigger, but there are important exceptions; generally, economic scenarios have a bigger stressed EC than RC. In the Uniform ST, the stressing PD/LGD, correlation, and systematic factor shocks have greatest effects. The most severe of the hypothetical scenarios are a spike in market volatility due to a geopolitical disaster, and the "stagflation redux" where we see EC and RC increase by over 100 percent (25 and 30 percent) to 15.27 percent and 17.4 percent (11.9 and 15.3 percent), respectively. We also show the stagflation scenario graphically in Figure 5.6 through plotted loss distributions.

CONCLUSION AND FUTURE DIRECTIONS

We have approached the topic of ST from the point of view of a typical credit portfolio such as one managed by a typical medium- or large-sized commercial bank. We have taken this point of view for two main reasons. First, for financial institutions that are exposed to credit risk, it remains their predominant risk. Second, this importance is accentuated for medium- as

TABLE 10.6 Stress Test Results of Alternative Scenarios.

	Expected Loss—Credit Metrics	Economic Credit Capital— Credit Metrics	Regulatory Credit Capital— Basel 2 IRB
Base case	2.63%	7.17%	9.29%
Uniform 10% increase in LGD	3.16%	8.62%	11.23%
Uniform 50% increase in PD	4.05%	10.80%	11.35%
Uniform 10% & 10% increase in LGD & PD	6.33%	17.10%	13.72%
50% decrease in credits metrics systematic factor	2.63%	13.21%	9.29%
Uniform rating downgrade by 1 notch	3.05%	8.30%	10.54%
Uniform 20% increase in empirical correlations	3.35%	15.21%	9.29%
Equity market crash: 50% decline across pricing factors	3.68%	10.29%	10.97%
Oil price spike: 50% increase in crude index	3.35%	8.94%	10.48%
Extreme recession scenario: 10% decline in GDP	3.92%	10.02%	11.27%
Geopolitical disaster: 30% spike in VIX	4.46%	15.74%	11.90%
Credit crunch: doubling of C&I charge-off rates	4.13%	10.86%	11.61%
1970s stagflation redux: 10% decline (increase) GDP (inflation)	5.03%	17.38%	15.27%

opposed to large-sized banks, and new supervisory requirements under the Federal Reserve's CCAR program will now be extended to smaller banks that were exempt from the previous exercise.

To this end, we have surveyed the supervisory expectations with respect to ST, discussed in detail the credit risk parameters underlying a quantitative component of ST, developed a typology of ST programs, and finally, presented a simple and stylized example of an ST model. The latter "toy" example is meant to illustrate the feasibility of building a model for ST that can be implemented even by less sophisticated banking institutions. The only requirements are the existence of an obligor rating system, associate default rate data, access to macroeconomic drives, and a framework for estimating economic capital. While we used the CreditMetrics model for the latter, we showed how this could be accomplished in a simplified framework such as the Basel II IRB model.

There are various fruitful avenues along which we could extend this research program. We could consider alternative risk types in addition to credit, such as market or operational risk, in order to develop a more general framework, which could be applicable to different types of financial institutions (e.g., insurance companies). This would necessarily involve investigating risk aggregation considerations, as discussed by Jacobs and Inanoglu (2009). Second, we could look at this topic from a more international framework, by comparing and contrasting other supervisory frameworks. Third, we could consider frameworks for validating ST modeling frameworks, research analogous to the validation of EC models as addressed by Jacobs (2010). Fourth, we could expand our example of an ST modeling framework to alternative frameworks, such as a top-down approach that models portfolio-level losses and utilizes ARIMA time series techniques. Finally, we could examine the effect of ST on the financial sector as a whole, contributing to the dialogue and debate on the systemic effect of higher capital requirements (Kashyap, Stein, and Hanson 2010).

REFERENCES

Acharya, V. V., and P. Schnabl, 2009, How banks played the leverage game. In *Restoring Financial Stability*, edited by V. V. Acharya and M. Richardson, Hoboken, NJ: Wiley Finance, pp. 44–78.

Artzner, P., F. Delbaen, J. M. Eber, and D. Heath. 1999. Coherent measures of risk. *Mathematical Finance* 9 (3): 203–228.

The Basel Committee on Banking Supervision, 2005, July, An explanatory note on the Basel II IRB risk weight functions. Bank for International Settlements, Basel, Switzerland.

_____. 2006, June. International convergence of capital measurement and capital standards: A revised framework. Bank for International Settlements, Basel, Switzerland.

_____. 2009a, May. Principles for sound stress testing practices and supervision, Consultative Paper No. 155. Bank for International Settlements, Basel, Switzerland.

_____. 2009b, July. Guidelines for computing capital for incremental risk in the trading book. Bank for International Settlements, Basel, Switzerland.

_____. 2009c, July. Revisions to the Basel II market risk framework. Bank for International Settlements, Basel, Switzerland.

_____. 2009d, October. Analysis of the trading book quantitative impact study, Consultative Document. Bank for International Settlements, Basel, Switzerland.

_____. 2009e, December. Strengthening the resilience of the banking sector. Consultative Document, Bank for International Settlements, Basel, Switzerland.

_____. 2010a, December. Basel III: A global regulatory framework for more resilient banks and banking systems. Bank for International Settlements, Basel, Switzerland.

_____. 2010b, August. An assessment of the long-term economic impact of stronger capital and liquidity requirements. Bank for International Settlements, Basel, Switzerland.

Demirguc-Kunt, A., E. Detragiache, and O. Merrouche. 2010. Bank capital: Lessons from the financial crisis. International Monetary Fund Working Paper No. WP/10/286.

Efron, B., and R. Tibshirani. 1986. Bootstrap methods for standard errors, confidence intervals, and other measures of statistical accuracy. *Statistical Science* 1 (1): 54–75.

Embrechts, P., A. McNeil, and D. Straumann. 2001. Correlation and dependency in risk management: Properties and pitfalls. In *Risk Management: Value at Risk and Beyond*. edited by M. Dempster and H. Moffatt, Cambridge, UK: Cambridge University Press, pp. 87–112,

Frey, R., and A. J. McNeil. 2003. Dependent defaults in models of portfolio credit risk. *Journal of Risk* 6: 59–62.

Gordy, M. 2003. A risk-factor model foundation for ratings-based bank capital rules. *Journal of Financial Intermediation* 12 (3): 199–232.

Inanoglu, H., and M. Jacobs Jr., 2009. Models for risk aggregation and sensitivity analysis: An application to bank economic capital. *The Journal of Risk and Financial Management* 2: 118–189.

Inanoglu, H., M. Jacobs Jr., and A. K. Karagozoglu. 2014, Winter. Bank Capital and New Regulatory Requirements for Risks in Trading Portfolios. *The Journal of Fixed Income*.

Inanoglu, H., M. Jacobs, Jr., J. Liu, and R. Sickles, 2013 (March), Analyzing bank efficiency: Are "too-big-to-fail" banks efficient?, Working Paper, Rice University, U.S.A.

Jacobs, M. Jr., 2010. Validation of economic capital models: State of the practice, supervisory expectations and results from a bank study. *Journal of Risk Management in Financial Institutions* 3 (4): 334–365.

Inanoglu, H., and M. Jacobs Jr., 2009. Models for risk aggregation and sensitivity analysis: an application to bank economic capital. *Journal of Risk and Financial Management* 2: 118–189.

Kashyap, A. K., J. C. Stein, and S. G. Hanson. 2010. An analysis of the impact of "substantially heightened" capital requirements on large financial institutions. Working paper.

Knight, F. H. 1921. *Risk, Uncertainty and Profit*, Boston, MA: Hart, Schaffner and Marx.

Merton, R. 1974. On the pricing of corporate debt: The risk structure of interest rates, *Journal of Finance* 29 (2): 449–470.

Moody's Investors Service. 2010. Corporate Default and Recovery Rates, 1920–2010, Special Report, February.

Popper, K. R. 1945. *The Open Society and Its Enemies*, New York: Routledge and Kegan.

R Development Core Team. 2013. *R: A Language and Environment for Statistical Computing*, R Foundation for Statistical Computing, Vienna, Austria, ISBN 3–900051–07–0.

Shackle, G. L. S., and J. L. Ford. 1990. "Uncertainty in Economics: Selected Essays," ed. E.E. Aldershot.

U.S. Office of the Comptroller of the Currency (OCC) and the Board of Governors of the Federal Reserve System (BOG-FRB). 2011. Supervisory Guidance on Model Risk Management (OCC 2011–12), April 4, 2011.

CHAPTER 11

A Critique of Credit Risk Models with Evidence from Mid-Cap Firms

David E. Allen
Centre for Applied Financial Studies, University of South Australia
and School of Mathematics and Statistics, University of Sydney

Robert J. Powell
School of Business, Edith Cowan University

Abhay K. Singh
School of Business, Edith Cowan University

INTRODUCTION

High bank failures and the significant credit problems faced by banks during the global financial crisis (GFC) are a stark reminder of the importance of accurately measuring and providing for a credit risk. There are a variety of available credit modeling techniques, leaving banks faced with the dilemma of deciding which model to choose. This article examines three widely used categories of models across a 10-year period spanning the global financial crisis (GFC) as well as pre-GFC and post-GFC in order to determine their relative advantages and disadvantages over different economic conditions. The comparison includes ratings-based models, accounting models, and structural models.

Ratings-based models incorporate external ratings models like Moody's, Standard & Poor's (S&P), or Fitch, and transition-based models such as

CreditMetrics and CreditPortfolioView, which measure value at risk (VaR) based on the probability of loans within a portfolio transitioning from one ratings category to another. Accounting-based models provide a rating from the analysis of financial statements of individual borrowers, such as the Altman z-score and Moody's RiskCalc. Structural models such as the Merton and KMV models measure distant to default (DD) and probability of default (PD) based on the firm's balance sheet debt to equity structure and also fluctuations in the market value of assets of a firm. These structural models are based on option-pricing methodologies and obtain information from market data. A default event is triggered by the capital structure when the value of the obligor falls below its financial obligation.

All of the three categories of models were developed well before the GFC. The GFC provided an opportunity to examine them in extreme circumstances. This is the only study we have identified that compares these three model categories using U.S. empirical data across the pre-GFC, GFC, and post-GFC periods, benchmarked to default and delinquency data. The analysis can assist lenders in their understanding and choice of the most appropriate model in dynamic market conditions.

In summary, the study finds that there is no one best model, with each category of model having both advantages and disadvantages. Dual use of models is indicated: a ratings- or accounting-based model to provide a comprehensive analysis of the initial borrower default risk, and a structural model on an ongoing basis to respond quickly to dynamic economic and market conditions.

SUMMARY OF CREDIT MODEL METHODOLOGIES

This section provides an overview of each of the three categories of credit models: ratings-based models; financial statement analysis models; and structural credit models.

Category 1: Ratings-Based Models

External Ratings Services The most prominent of the ratings services are Standard & Poor's (S&P), Moody's, and Fitch. The ratings provide a measure of the relative creditworthiness of the entity, taking into account a wide range of factors such as environmental conditions, competitive position, management quality, and the financial strength of the borrower. Table 11.1 provides a calibration between the well-known rating agencies. This calibration is important when loan portfolios comprise entities with ratings from

TABLE 11.1 Mapping Ratings.

S & P	AAA	AA+	AA	AA−	A+	A−	BBB+	BBB	BBB−	BB+	BB−	B+	B−	CCC+	CCC−	CC	C	D
Moody's	Aaa	Aa1	Aa2	Aa3	A1	A3	Baa1	Baa2	Baa3	Ba1	Ba3	B1	B3	Caa1	Caa3	Ca	C	
Fitch	AAA	AA+	AA	AA−	A+	A−	BBB+	BBB	BBB−	BB+	BB−	B+	B−	CCC+	CCC−	CC	C	D

Source of Calibrations: Bank for International Settlements (2014)

different ratings services. The following definitions are summarized from Standard & Poor's (2014) definitions:

AAA: Extremely strong capacity to meet financial commitments; highest rating.

AA: Very strong capacity to meet financial commitments.

A: Strong capacity to meet financial commitments, but somewhat more susceptible to changes in economic conditions and changes in circumstances than higher rated categories.

BBB: Has adequate protection parameters; however, adverse economic conditions will lead to weakened capacity to meet financial commitments; considered lowest investment grade by market participants.

BB: Less vulnerable to nonpayment than other speculative issues; however, has ongoing exposure to adverse conditions, which could lead to inadequate capacity to meet financial commitments; all ratings BB and lower are considered to have significant speculative characteristics.

B: More vulnerable to nonpayment, but currently has the capacity to meet financial commitments.

CCC: Currently vulnerable to nonpayment.

CC: Currently highly vulnerable to nonpayment.

C: Currently highly vulnerable to nonpayment; is expected to have lower seniority or recovery than higher-rated obligations.

D: Payment default or in breach of promise.

In addition to providing lenders with a tool that measures credit risk, ratings are also used by Basel II and III for allocating capital under the standardized model. The commercial standardized model requires that banks calculate capital as 8% of risk weighted assets (in addition to specified capital buffers, which are not ratings dependent), with the weightings per rating being S&P AAA to AA− (Moody's Aaa to Aa3) at 20%, S&P A+ to A− (Moody's A1 to A3) at 50%, S&P BBB+ to BB− (Moody's Baa1 to Ba3) (or unrated) at 100%, and below S&P BB− (Ba3) at 150%.

Transition Ratings Models Transition models are ratings-based models that measure the probability of a borrower transitioning from their existing grade to a different grade. Two of the most well-known are CreditMetrics and CreditPortfolioView.

CreditMetrics (Gupton, Finger and Bhatia 1997) incorporates a transition matrix showing the probability (ρ) of a borrower moving from one credit grade to another, based on historical data. For a BBB-rated asset:

$$\text{BBB} \quad \rho_{\text{AAA}} \quad \rho_{\text{AA}} \quad \rho_{\text{A}} \quad \rho_{\text{BBB}} \quad \rho_{\text{BB}} \quad \rho_{\text{B}} \quad \rho_{\text{CCC/C}} \quad \rho_{\text{D}}$$

To capture all probability states, the sum of probabilities in each row must equal 1. Transition probability tables are provided by raters such as Moody's and Standard & Poor's. The CreditMetrics model obtains forward zero curves for each category (based on risk-free rates) expected to exist in a year's time. Using the zero curves, the model calculates the loan market value (V), including the coupon, at the one-year risk horizon. Probabilities in the table are multiplied by V to obtain a weighted probability. Based on the revised table, VaR is obtained by calculating the probability weighted portfolio variance and standard deviation (σ), then calculating VaR using a normal distribution (e.g., 1.645σ for a 95 percent confidence level).

To calculate joint probabilities, CreditMetrics (Gupton, Finger and Bhatia 1997) requires that the mean values and standard deviations are calculated for each issue. Each two-asset subportfolio needs to be identified, and the following equation (using a three-asset example) applied:

$$\sigma_p^2 = \sigma^2(V_1 + V_2) + \sigma^2(V_1 + V_3) + \sigma^2(V_2 + V_3) - \sigma^2(V_1) - \sigma^2(V_2) - \sigma^2(V_3) \tag{11.1}$$

CreditMetrics (Gupton, Finger and Bhatia 1997) also provide a Monte Carlo option as an alternative method of calculating VaR. The model maintains that there is a series of asset values that determine a company's rating. If a company's asset value falls or increases to a certain level, at the end of that period, its new asset value will determine the new rating at that point in time. These bands of asset values are referred to by CreditMetrics as asset thresholds. The percentage changes in assets (or *asset returns*) are assumed to be normally distributed and, using the probabilities from the transition matrix table, probabilities (*Pr*) of asset thresholds Z_{Def}, Z_{CCC}, and so on, can be calculated as follows:

$$\Pr_{(\text{Default})} = \Phi(Z_{\text{Def}}/\sigma)$$

$$\Pr_{(\text{CCC})} = \Phi(Z_{\text{CCC}}/\sigma) - \Phi(Z_{\text{Def}}/\sigma)$$

and so on, where Φ denotes the cumulative normal distribution, and

$$Z_{Def} = \Phi^{-1}\sigma \qquad (11.2)$$

CreditMetrics apply the asset thresholds to Monte Carlo modeling using three steps. First, asset return thresholds, as discussed earlier, need to be generated for each rating category. Second, scenarios of asset returns need to be generated using a normal distribution. The third step is to map the asset returns in step 2 with the credit scenarios in step 1. A return falling between ratings will be allocated to the rating in the threshold above it. Thousands of scenarios are normally generated, from which a portfolio distribution and VaR are calculated.

The CreditPortfolioView (CPV) model is described by various sources, including Wilson (1998), Saunders and Allen (2002), Pesaran, Schuermann, Treutler and Weiner (2003), and Crouhy, Galai, and Mark (2000). CPV uses a similar transition matrix approach to CreditMetrics, but it is based on the premise that there is not equal transition probability among borrowers of the same grade, as is assumed by CreditMetrics. CreditPortfolioView creates different migration adjustment ratios for different industries by linking macroeconomic factors to migration probability, such as GDP growth, unemployment rates, and interest rates. CPV provides standard values that can be chosen should the user not want to calculate all of the individual shifts. The migration adjustment ratios (denoted by i) are then incorporated into the transition matrix to calculate an adjusted VaR figure:

$$\text{BBB} \quad \rho_{AAAi} \quad \rho_{AAi} \quad \rho_{Ai} \quad \rho_{BBBi} \quad \rho_{BBi} \quad \rho_{Bi} \quad \rho_{CCC/Ci} \quad \rho_{Di}$$

Category 2: Financial Statement Analysis (Accounting) Models

These models provide a rating based on the analysis of various financial statement items and ratios of individual borrowers. Examples include Moody's RiskCalc and the z-score. Moody's KMV Company (2003) RiskCalc model provides an estimated default frequency (EDF) for private firms. EDF is calculated from 11 financial measures, which measure various aspects of profitability, leverage, debt coverage, liquidity, activity, growth, and size. The z-score by Altman (1968) predicts bankruptcy by applying weightings to five financial measures: working capital / total assets; retained earnings / total assets; earnings before interest and taxes / total assets; market value of equity / book value of total liabilities; and sales / total assets. Variants of these financial models have been introduced by researchers, including among others, Ohlson (1980), who uses eight ratios, and Zmijewski (1984), who uses three ratios. As financial statements are generally produced annually, borrowers are generally rerated on an annual basis.

Category 3: Structural Credit Models

Structural models are so named because they are largely based on the debt to equity structure of a firm. The model measures the distance to default (DD) of a firm per equation 11.8, which is a combination of asset values, debt, and the standard deviation of asset value fluctuations, from which probabilities of default (PD) can be calculated per equation 11.9. The point of default is considered to be where debt exceeds assets, and the greater the volatility of the assets, the closer the entity moves to default. Equity and the market value of the firm's assets are related as follows:

$$E = VN(d_1) - e^{-rT}FN(d_2) \tag{11.3}$$

Where E = market value of firms equity, F = face value of firm's debt, r = risk-free rate, N = cumulative standard normal distribution function:

$$d_1 = \frac{\ln(V/F) + (r + 0.5\sigma_v^2)T}{\sigma v \sqrt{T}} \tag{11.4}$$

$$d_2 = d_1 - \sigma_v \sqrt{T} \tag{11.5}$$

Volatility and equity are related under the Merton model as follows:

$$\sigma_E = \left(\frac{V}{E}\right) N(d_1)\sigma_V \tag{11.6}$$

KMV takes debt as the value of all current liabilities plus half the book value of all long-term debt outstanding. T is commonly set at one year. Per the approach outlined by KMV (Crosbie and Bohn 2003) and Bharath and Shumway (2008), initial asset returns are estimated from historical equity data using the following formula:

$$\sigma_V = \sigma_E \left(\frac{E}{E+F}\right) \tag{11.7}$$

Daily log equity returns and their standard deviations are calculated for each asset for the historical period. These asset returns derived above are applied to equation (11.3) to estimate the market value of assets every day. The daily log asset return is calculated and new asset values estimated.

Following KMV, this process is repeated until asset returns converge. These figures are used to calculate DD and PD:

$$DD = \frac{\ln(V/F) + (\mu - 0.5_v^2)T}{\sigma_V \sqrt{T}}$$

(11.8)

$$PD = N(-DD)$$

(11.9)

Correlation can be calculated through producing a time series of returns for each firm and then calculating a correlation between each pair of assets. KMV has instead adopted a factor modeling approach to their correlation calculation. KMV produces country and industry returns from its database of publicly traded firms, and its correlation model uses these indices to create a composite factor index for each firm, depending on the industry and country (D'Vari, Yalamanchili, and Bai 2003; Kealhofer and Bohn 1993).

OUR EMPIRICAL METHODOLOGY

Our data set comprises the S&P 400 mid-cap companies, which provide a better spread of high and low ratings than large-cap or small-cap loans. We only include companies that have credit ratings and data spanning our 12-year period (2003–2012), which yields 177 companies. Our credit ratings and default data are obtained from Moody's default and recovery database. All other data are obtained from Datastream. Each of the three credit modeling categories contains a range of different models, making it impractical to model all of them in this study. Our empirical analysis will therefore include one model as an example from each category, and this includes external ratings models (also incorporating the Basel standardized credit model), Altman's z-score model (in its original format), and Merton's structural model. We also calculate a beta (β) score for each model for each of the 12 years in the analysis. This score shows the relative credit risk for that year, as compared to the average 12-year credit risk score for that particular model. Thus, a rating of 1.0 would indicate that risk for that year is equal to the 12-year average, a $\beta > 1$ indicates a higher risk than the average, and a $\beta < 1$ indicates a lower risk. This β effectively common sizes the models, allowing a comparison between models of how the risk rating provided by the model fluctuates from year to year. We compare the β's for each model against benchmark β's for actual U.S. delinquent loans as provided by the U.S. Federal Reserve (2013), and actual Moody's corporate default data for each year (for all ratings). These benchmarks provide an indication of credit risk conditions in the market. For example, if the annual

β's of our benchmark data fluctuated between 1.0 and 2.0 over the 12-year period, but a particular credit model showed a β of 1 for each year, this would indicate that the model was remaining inappropriately static and not responding adequately to changes in credit risk.

CRITIQUE

Critique of Ratings-Based Models

A strength of external credit ratings is that they are formulated through a comprehensive analysis of an entity's business, financial, and economic environmental risks. A further plus is that the ratings are readily available to banks and researchers, thus requiring no modeling to produce them. However, it should be noted that rating agencies such as Standard & Poor's and Moody's stress that ratings are not absolute measures of default, but rather, a relative ranking of one entity to another, which do not ratchet up and down with economic conditions. Standard & Poor's (2014) maintains that "Ratings opinions are not intended as guarantees of credit quality or as exact measures of the probability that a particular debt issue will default. Instead, ratings express relative opinions about the creditworthiness of an issuer or credit quality of an individual debt issue, from strongest to weakest, within a universe of credit risk."

Although credit ratings are meant to be relative risk ratings and not absolute measures of default, they are nonetheless used by banks for measuring default probabilities and credit VaR. In addition, external credit ratings are used by banks under the standardized Basel approach for allocating capital. If the ratings themselves do not fluctuate with market conditions, then neither does the capital allocated. Allen and Powell (2011), in an Australian study, found that despite impaired assets of banks having increased fivefold over the GFC period, the underlying external credit ratings of corporate assets indicated that there had been negligible change to credit risk over this period. Thus, a weakness of the ratings models is that they can remain static for lengthy periods of time, not changing with dynamic economic circumstances.

CreditMetrics is based on external ratings and therefore has many of the same advantages and disadvantages as the external ratings we have already discussed. However, the model does have an advantage over the straight rating approach in that it links the transition to market spreads, and to default probabilities provided by external raters. Therefore, whilst the underlying rating may not have changed, modelers can update the VaR measurement by incorporating updated default probabilities into the model. However, these default probabilities are usually only provided annually by raters, meaning the transition model is nowhere near as responsive to market conditions as the structural model which can incorporate continuously changing market conditions. The CreditMetrics model uses a VaR approach that measures risk below a threshold. VaR has had many criticisms, most notably because it says nothing of the extreme risks beyond VaR—for example, Allen and Powell (2009) and Samanta, Azarchs, and Hill (2005). It is precisely in times of extreme risk that firms are most likely to fail, such as happened during the global financial crisis, and the criticisms of VaR escalated since the onset of this crisis (see, e.g., Krokhmal, Palmquist and Uryasev 2002; World Federation of Exchanges 2011).

As CreditPortfolioView is also based on a transition matrix, it has similar strengths and weaknesses to the CreditMetrics model. The exception is that it recognizes that different industries can transition differently, and has the advantage of incorporating industry adjustment factors, which are obtained through multiple regression of macroeconomic factors to obtain an industry index. However, a downside of the model is that it requires extensive analysis of the current state of the economy to determine conditional transition probability, using factors such as GDP growth, unemployment rates, and interest rates. Simpler approaches to incorporate market conditions into credit models have been proposed through the use of shared market prices by Allen and Powell (2009) and Jarrow (2001).

Table 11.2 provides results of our empirical analysis for external credit ratings. Column 1 shows the year. Columns 2 and 4 show our benchmark data, being delinquent loans for U.S. commercial banks (Federal Reserve Bank 2013) and Moody's default ratings. Column 6 shows the weighted average external rating of our portfolio (obtained by allocating AAA loans a weighting of 1, Aa1 ratings a weighting of 2, and so on, and then obtaining the average rating, weighted by the outstanding debt of each firm). Column 8 shows the capital that would need to be allocated to our portfolio, based on applying the Basel Risk weighted percentages, which we discussed in the external ratings services section, to each firm in our mid-cap portfolio. Note that the capital in column 8 will not exactly equal that applicable to the rating in column 6, as column 6 is an "averaged" rating whereas column 8 has been accurately calculated firm by firm.

Table 11.2 shows a great deal of fluctuation in the betas of delinquent loans (between 0.57 and 1.92, peaking in 2009), and for defaults (between 0.24 and 3.61, also peaking in 2009). Yet the average credit rating stayed unchanged throughout the period, causing the amount of capital adequacy indicated to be fairly static. Indeed, at the peak of defaults in 2009, the capital beta was almost 1. During the GFC, many banks experienced severe capital shortages, and if capital adequacy was being based on the Basel

TABLE 11.2 Results from Ratings-Based Models.

Year	Delinquent Loans (%)	β	Defaults (%)	β	Weighted Average Rating of Portfolio	β	Capital	β
2003	3.23	1.44	2.01	1.22	Baa	1.00	7.07%	1.00
2004	2.18	0.97	0.91	0.55	Baa	1.00	6.93%	0.98
2005	1.51	0.67	0.73	0.44	Baa	1.00	6.91%	0.97
2006	1.27	0.57	0.72	0.44	Baa	1.00	6.91%	0.97
2007	1.22	0.55	0.40	0.24	Baa	1.00	6.26%	0.88
2008	1.88	0.84	2.24	1.36	Baa	1.00	6.70%	0.95
2009	4.29	1.92	5.93	3.61	Baa	1.00	7.26%	1.02
2010	3.46	1.55	1.40	0.85	Baa	1.00	7.51%	1.06
2011	2.01	0.90	0.86	0.52	Baa	1.00	7.68%	1.08
2012	1.34	0.60	1.25	0.76	Baa	1.00	7.70%	1.09

standardized model, we see that it would have fallen woefully short of what was required.

In terms of the transition models, these are modified by transition factors, so, for example, a Moody's transition to default would be modified by default factors such as shown in column 4. As these factors are fluctuating, so, too, would the betas associated with a transition model, more or less in line with the betas for defaults shown in column 5. This, of course, improves the fluctuations for a transition model beyond that seen by a solely ratings-based approach such as that used by the Basel standardized model. Nonetheless, the underlying ratings are only undertaken on a periodic basis, and could therefore be out of date with the underlying risk of the firm (similar to the Basel model ratings); and the default factors used are usually modeled annually, which is usually after the event. So the response to market factors will be much more sluggish than a structural model, which can respond immediately, even daily (or intraday) if necessary.

Critique of Financial Statement Analysis (Accounting) Models

Accounting models have some strong points. They are generally easy to use. In most cases, all that has to be done is to plug the financial figures into the model, which will calculate the ratios for the user. It is relatively straightforward to replicate the models on a spreadsheet, as they comprise a few basic ratios. The models have also been shown to be fairly accurate when applied to industries and economic conditions that were used to develop the model. For example, Ohlson (1980) identified about 88 percent of

105 bankrupt firms accurately one year before bankruptcy. Altman (1968) showed bankrupt accuracy rates of up to 95 percent using a sample of 91 manufacturing firms over the same period as his model was developed. The accounting models have also attracted criticism. They were generally designed using specific industries; for example, the z-score was developed using manufacturing firms, which raises the question as to their applicability to other industries. Platt and Platt (1990) found accuracy lower when applied to other industries, and recommended that industry-relative ratios should be used in model development. Grice and Dugan (2001) also found low accuracy when the models were applied to industries, time periods, or stress situations different from those used to develop the model. Gutzeit and Yozzo (2011) found that during times of recession, the model accurately determined which firms failed but classified many survived firms as potential bankrupts, and the model was shown to have low accuracy when prediction period was more than two years out. Peel (1988) was concerned about the time lag in receiving the financial information. Vassalou and Xing (2004) criticized accounting models as being backward looking as opposed to the Merton model, which uses market prices reflecting investor expectations of future performance. Vassalou and Xing also make the point that accounting models imply that firms with similar financial ratios will have similar default probabilities, whereas firms with similar debt and equity levels might have very different default probabilities if the volatility of their assets differ.

The first four columns in Table 11.3 contain our benchmarks, the same as in Table 11.2. We have calculated a z-score for each loan in our portfolio based on Altman (1968), and column 6 shows the average z-score for our portfolio, with the corresponding β in column 7.

TABLE 11.3 Results from Accounting-Based Models.

Year	Delinquent Loans (%)	β	Defaults (%)	β	Average z-score	β	% Distressed z-score	β
2003	3.23	1.44	2.01	1.22	3.69	1.02	7.51%	1.02
2004	2.18	0.97	0.91	0.55	3.82	0.98	4.53%	0.61
2005	1.51	0.67	0.73	0.44	3.92	0.96	5.13%	0.69
2006	1.27	0.57	0.72	0.44	3.96	0.95	4.14%	0.56
2007	1.22	0.55	0.40	0.24	3.78	0.99	6.07%	0.82
2008	1.88	0.84	2.24	1.36	3.44	1.09	11.49%	1.55
2009	4.29	1.92	5.93	3.61	3.34	1.12	11.16%	1.51
2010	3.46	1.55	1.40	0.85	4.53	0.83	7.11%	0.96
2011	2.01	0.90	0.86	0.52	3.52	1.07	7.44%	1.01
2012	1.34	0.60	1.25	0.76	3.54	1.06	9.39%	1.27

Again, we see very little fluctuation in credit risk from the accounting model based on the average z-score β. The higher the z-score the better, and yet in 2009 when delinquent loans and defaults were the peak of the crisis, the average z-score indicates that credit risk was at its lowest. However, perhaps an average z-score is not the best way to show it, as the main concern from a credit risk perspective is the loans at the higher end of the credit risk spectrum. Thus, we show the percentage of loans classified as "distressed" under the Altman model (this is a score below 1.81). This reveals a different picture, with β more in line with the β for delinquent loans (though at a somewhat lesser spread), peaking in 2008 and 2009, meaning that the z-score does have some ability to identify changing credit risk. However, it should be emphasized that these data were obtained from year-end financials, which are generally released some months after the financial year end, so, for example, factors that contributed to the score from the beginning of 2008 may only be reflected in the score some months after the end of 2008.

Critique of Structural Credit Models

Unlike ratings- and accounting-based models, structural models do incorporate up-to-date market data as a key component, making the models responsive to changing conditions. This is a major advantage over most models, as it allows banks to identify potential problems at an early stage. A downside is that commercial structural models can be prohibitively expensive to purchase, and their complexity makes them very time consuming to replicate. Criticism of structural models has predominantly focused on the information contained in the model being insufficient to generate meaningful default probabilities or spreads, and that the model therefore suffers from incomplete causality. Huang and Huang (2003) find that structural models generate extremely low spreads for investment grade bonds.

Eom, Helwege, and Huang (2004) find the Merton model provides spreads that are too low, but also examine four other variations of structural models, finding them all to have difficulty in accurately predicting credit spreads since they provide spreads on the high side. KMV (Crosbie and Bohn 2003) finds the probabilities of default generated by the Merton model are too small to be of practical use. Allen and Powell (2011) found that the structural model understated credit risk in the pre-GFC period, but overstated it during the highly volatile GFC times. KMV calculates DD based on the Merton approach, but instead of using a normal distribution to calculate PD, KMV uses its own worldwide database, which contains information on thousands of corporate defaults, to determine PD associated with each default level.

TABLE 11.4   Results from Structural Credit Models.

Year	Delinquent Loans (%)	β	Defaults (%)	β	DD	β
2003	3.23	1.44	2.01	1.22	8.96	0.83
2004	2.18	0.97	0.91	0.55	9.20	0.81
2005	1.51	0.67	0.73	0.44	10.05	0.74
2006	1.27	0.57	0.72	0.44	9.50	0.78
2007	1.22	0.55	0.40	0.24	5.47	1.35
2008	1.88	0.84	2.24	1.36	1.69	4.38
2009	4.29	1.92	5.93	3.61	6.19	1.20
2010	3.46	1.55	1.40	0.85	8.26	0.90
2011	2.01	0.90	0.86	0.52	5.64	1.31
2012	1.34	0.60	1.25	0.76	9.09	0.81

Accuracy of a structural model can be improved by calibrating the DD values to a more accurate source such as the KMV EDF values. Du and Suo (2007) find that DD on its own is an insufficient determinant of credit quality and that results can be significantly improved by adding additional variables. Sy (2007) maintains that distance to default is not a sufficient determinant of default as many firms continue to trade while technically insolvent due to liabilities exceeding assets, and the author proposes a revised causal framework for estimating default, which incorporates serviceability. The structural model has also been criticized because it assumes exact information about the point of default (which the model takes as the point where asset values fall below liability values), which some deem as unrealistic, preferring instead a reduced-form approach (see Jarrow, Lando and Turnbull 1997), which views default as an unexpected event (a jump to default).

We see from Table 11.4 that DD fluctuates well, but with β peaking somewhat higher than the defaults β, showing that it has somewhat overshot the mark. DD peaks in 2008, whereas defaults only peak in 2009, meaning that DD is measuring stress in the market before the defaults occur, thus serving as an early warning indicator, as compared to ratings and accounting models, which usually respond far more sluggishly.

Comparison of Strengths and Weaknesses

The strengths and weaknesses of each model are compared in Table 11.5, where H shows that the criteria in column 1 is met to a high degree, M is moderate, and L is low.

TABLE 11.5 Summary of the Strengths and Weaknesses of Each Model.

	External Ratings	Accounting	Structural
Detailed customer specific financial analysis	H Detailed analysis of financials incorporated in the ratings process	H Detailed analysis of financials	L Only debt, equity, and asset values
Industry differentiation	M Industry factors incorporated at time of rating	L Most accounting models do not differentiate between industries	H Based on market fluctuations which will vary with industry risk
Fluctuates with market (no time delays)	L No fluctuations with market in the external ratings themselves. If a transition component is added, then this improves fluctuation, but the model will still lag the market	L No fluctuations with market	H Highly responsive to market fluctuations
Easy to model	H Ratings readily available to researchers	M Relatively easy to duplicate models on a spreadsheet	L Complex modeling techniques
Accuracy	High at time of rating Lower as time passes	High at time of rating Lower as time passes	Medium: Does fluctuate with market, but can over- or understate default risk depending on market volatility

CONCLUSIONS

The analysis shows that there is no one best model, with each model having its strengths and weaknesses. External ratings-based models (including transition models) and accounting models provide a comprehensive analysis of the individual customer's financial strength, but are static and don't fluctuate with the market. The structural model provides the opposite. Banks should (and larger ones generally do) make use of more than one approach. The external ratings and accounting-based models allow banks to measure and provide for individual customer circumstances, whereas the market-based structural model allows banks to continuously monitor fluctuating default risk, thus detecting potential problems at an early stage.

Acknowledgments: The authors would like to thank the Edith Cowan University Faculty of Business and Law Strategic Research Fund and the Australian Research Council for funding support.

REFERENCES

Allen, D., and R. Powell. 2009. Transitional credit modeling and its relationship to market at value at risk: An Australian sectoral perspective. *Accounting and Finance*, 49(3): 425–444.

_____. 2011. Customers and markets: Both are essential to measuring credit risk in Australia. *Australasian Accounting, Business & Finance Journal*, 5(1): 57–75.

Altman, E. 1968. " Financial ratios, discriminant analysis and the prediction of corporate bankruptcy. *Journal of Finance*, 23(4): 589–609.

Bank for International Settlements. 2014. Long-term rating scales comparison. www.bis.org/bcbs/qis/qisrating.htm.

Bharath, S., and T. Shumway. 2008. Forecasting default with the Merton distance-to-default model. *The Review of Financial Studies*, 21(3): 1339–1369.

Crosbie, P., and J. Bohn. 2003. *Modeling Default Risk*, www.moodysanalytics.com.

Crouhy, M., D. Galai, and R. Mark. 2000. A comparative analysis of current credit risk models. *Journal of Banking and Finance*, 24(1): 59–117.

D'Vari, R., K. Yalamanchili, and D. Bai. 2003. Application of quantitative credit risk models in fixed income portfolio management. www.rondvari.com/CIEF%202003_Final.pdf.

Du, Y., and W. Suo. 2007. Assessing credit quality from the equity market. Can a structural forecast credit ratings? *Canadian Journal of Administrative Sciences*, 24(3): 212–228.

Eom, Y., J. Helwege, and J. Huang. 2004. Structural models of corporate bond pricing: An empirical analysis. *Review of Financial Studies,* 17: 499–544.

Federal Reserve Bank. 2013. U.S. Federal Reserve Statistical Release. Charge-off and Delinquency Rates. www.federalreserve.gov/releases/ChargeOff/delallsa.htm.

Grice, J., and M. Dugan. 2001. The limitations of bankruptcy prediction models: Some cautions for the researcher. *Review of Quantitative Finance & Accounting*, 17(2): 151–156.

Gupton, G., C. Finger, and M. Bhatia. 1997. CreditMetrics—Technical document. www.riskmetrics.com/publications/techdoc.html.

Gutzeit, G., and J. Yozzo. 2011. Z-score performance amid great recession. *American Bankruptcy Institute Journal*, 30(2): 44–66.

Huang, M., and J. Huang. 2003. *How Much of the Corporate-Treasury Yield Spread Is Due to Credit Risk?* Unpublished Manuscript, Stanford University.

Jarrow, R., D. Lando, and S. Turnbull. 1997. A Markov model for the term structure of credit spreads. *Review of Financial Studies* 10: 481–523.

Jarrow, R. A. 2001. Default parameter estimation using market prices. *Financial Analysts Journal*, 57(5): 75.

Kealhofer, S., and J. Bohn. 1993. Portfolio management of default risk. www.moodysanalytics.com.

Krokhmal, P., J. Palmquist, and S. Uryasev. 2002. Portfolio optimization with conditional value-at-risk objective and constraints. *Journal of Risk*, 4: 2.

Moody's KMV Company. 2006. *Moody's KMV RiskCalc 3.1 United States.* www.moodys.com.

Ohlson, J. A. 1980. Financial ratios and the probabilistic prediction of bankruptcy. *Journal of Accounting Research*, Spring: 109–131.

Peel, M. 1988. A multilogit approach to predicting corporate failure—Some evidence for the UK corporate sector. *Omega* 16 (4): 309–318.

Pesaran, M., T. Schuermann, B. Treutler, and S. Weiner. 2003. *Macroeconomic Dynamics and Credit Risk: A Global Perspective.* www.papers.ssrn.com/sol3/papers.cfm?abstract_id=432903.

Platt, H., and M. Platt. 1990. Development of a class of stable predictive variables: The case of bankruptcy prediction. *Journal of Business, Finance and Accounting* 17 (1): 31–51.

Samanta, P., T. Azarchs, and N. Hill. 2005. *Chasing Their Tails: Banks Look Beyond Value-At-Risk,* www.standardandpoors.com.

Saunders, A., and L. Allen. 2002. *Credit Risk Measurement.* Hoboken, NJ: John Wiley & Sons.

Standard & Poor's. 2014. Ratings definitions. www2.standardandpoors.com.

Sy, W. 2007. A causal framework for credit default theory, www.apra.gov.au.

US Federal Reserve. 2013. *Federal Reserve Statistical Release.* Charge-off and Delinquency Rates on Loans and Leases at Commercial Banks, www.federalreserve.gov/.

Vassalou, M., and Y. Xing. 2004. Default risk in equity returns. *Journal of Finance* 59: 831–868.

Wilson, T. 1998. Portfolio credit risk. *Economic Policy Review* 4 (3): 71–82.

World Federation of Exchanges. 2011. WFE Market Highlights. www.world-exchanges.org/statistics.

Zimjewski, M. 1984. Methodological issues related to the estimation of financial distress prediction models. *Journal of Accounting Research*, 22(1): 59–82.

CHAPTER 12

Predicting Credit Ratings Using a Robust Multicriteria Approach

Constantin Zopounidis
Technical University of Crete, School of Production Engineering,
and Management Financial Engineering Laboratory,
Audencia Nantes School of Management, France

INTRODUCTION

Credit risk refers to the probability that an obligor will not be able to meet scheduled debt obligations (i.e., default). Credit risk modeling plays a crucial role in financial risk management, in areas such as banking, corporate finance, and investments. Credit risk management has evolved rapidly over the past decades, but the global credit crisis of 2007–2008 highlighted that there is still much to be done at multiple levels. Altman and Saunders (1997) list five main factors that have contributed to the increasing importance of credit risk management:

1. The worldwide increase in the number of bankruptcies
2. The trend toward disintermediation by the highest quality and largest borrowers
3. The increased competition among credit institutions
4. The declining value of real assets and collateral in many markets
5. The growth of new financial instruments with inherent default risk exposure, such as credit derivatives

Early credit risk management was primarily based on empirical evaluation systems. CAMEL has been the most widely used system in this context, which is based on the empirical combination of several factors related to capital, assets, management, earnings, and liquidity. It was soon realized, however, that such empirical systems cannot provide a sound basis for credit risk management. This led to an outgrowth of attempts from academics and practitioners, focused on the development of new credit risk assessment systems. These efforts were also motivated by the changing regulatory framework that now requires banks to implement analytic methodologies for managing and monitoring their credit portfolios (Basel Committee on Banking Supervision 2004).

The existing practices are based on sophisticated quantitative techniques, which are used to develop a complete framework for measuring and monitoring credit risk. Credit rating systems are in the core of this framework, and they are widely used for estimating default probabilities, supporting credit-granting decisions, pricing loans, and managing loan portfolios. Credit ratings are either obtained through scoring models developed internally by financial institutions (Treacy and Carey 2000) or are provided externally by credit rating agencies (CRAs).

The risk ratings issued by CRAs have received heavy criticism on their scope and predictive accuracy (e.g., Frost 2007; Pagano and Volpin 2010; Tichy et al. 2011), especially after the recent global credit crunch. The results from several studies actually indicate that such ratings are inferior to internal scoring systems for assessing the risk of financial distress and default. Hilscher and Wilson (2013), however, argue that focusing solely on a firm's default risk may lead to considerable loss of information in credit risk assessment, as systematic risk is also an important yet distinct dimension. Their empirical findings show that this risk dimension is best modeled through credit ratings issued by CRAs. This explains their widespread use by investors, financial institutions, and regulators, and their extensive analysis by academic researchers (for a recent overview, see Jeon and Lovo 2013). In this context, models that explain and replicate the ratings issued by CRAs can be useful in various ways, as they can facilitate the understanding of the factors that drive CRAs' evaluations, provide investors and regulators with early-warning signals and information for important rating events, and support the credit risk assessment process for firms not rated by the CRAs.

Previous studies have focused on analyzing and predicting credit ratings using mostly firm-specific data (usually in the form of financial ratios) and market variables, using different model building techniques. For instance, Huang et al. (2004) compared two data-mining methods (neural networks and support vector machines) using two data sets from Taiwan and U.S.A. for predicting credit ratings using purely financial ratios. Pasiouras et al. (2006) analyzed the bank credit ratings issued by Fitch for a cross-country sample, using explanatory factors covering the regulatory and supervisory framework and bank-specific characteristics. Hwang et al. (2010) employed an ordered nonlinear semiparametric probit model to predict the ratings issued by Standard and Poor's (S&P) for a static sample of listed U.S. companies, using financial and market variables as well as industry effects. In a similar framework, Mizen and Tsoukas (2012) found that using a non-linear probit model with state dependencies improves the prediction results, whereas Hwang (2013) further found time-varying effects to be important. On the other hand, Lu et al. (2012) analyzed the information in news articles, combined with financial and market variables, to predict changes in the S&P ratings for firms in the United States. Some studies have also considered default risk estimates from structural models (Hwang et al. 2010; Hwang 2013; Lu et al. 2012), which are based on the contingent claims approach introduced by Black and Scholes (1973) and Merton (1974).

In this study, a multicriteria decision aid (MCDA) methodology is employed. MCDA is well suited to the ordinal nature of credit ratings and the features of studies, through easy-to-comprehend decision models and model fitting techniques that do not rely on statistical assumptions. The applicability of the proposed MCDA approach is tested on a sample of European companies from different countries over the period 2002–2012. While most of the past studies related to the analysis of the ratings issued by CRAs have focused on the United States and the United Kingdom, the ratings of firms in European countries (other than the United Kingdom) have been relatively underexamined.

The focus on European data has some interesting aspects. First, during the past decade, particularly after the outbreak of the European sovereign debt crisis, the role of CRAs has received much attention from authorities, regulators, and governments in Europe. Furthermore, in contrast to U.S. firms, which operate out of a single country, European firms face different economic and business conditions, and the global crisis has not affected all European countries in the same manner. These particular features make it interesting to examine how the findings of studies conducted in other regions and time periods translate into a cross-country European setting, and to investigate the existence of time-varying effects, particularly in light of the ongoing turmoil in the European economic environment.

The rest of the chapter is organized as follows. The next section discusses construction of credit scoring and risk rating models and analyzes the contribution of multicriteria techniques in this field. The following section presents the multicriteria methodology adopted in this study, whereas the fourth section is devoted to the empirical analysis and the discussion of the results. Finally, this chapter proposes some future research directions.

CREDIT SCORING AND RATING

General Framework

Credit risk is defined as the likelihood that an obligor (firm or individual) will be unable or unwilling to fulfill its debt obligations toward the creditors. In such a case, the creditors will suffer losses that have to be measured as accurately as possible.

The expected loss L_i over a period T (usually one year) from granting credit to a given obligor i can be measured as follows:

$$L_i = PD_i LGD_i EAD_i$$

where PD_i is the probability of default for the obligor i in the time period T, LGD_i is the percentage of exposure the bank might lose in case the borrower defaults, and EAD_i is the amount outstanding in case the borrower defaults.

Under the existing regulatory framework of Basel II, default is considered to have occurred with regard to a particular obligor when one or more of the following events has taken place (Basel Committee on Banking Supervision 2004; Hayden 2003):

- It is determined that the obligor is unlikely to pay its debt obligations in full.
- There is a credit loss event associated with any obligation of the obligor.
- The obligor is past due more than 90 days on any credit obligation.
- The obligor has filed for bankruptcy or similar protection from creditors.

The aim of credit-rating models is to assess the probability of default for an obligor, whereas other models are used to estimate LGD and EAD. Rating systems measure credit risk and differentiate individual credits and groups of credits by the risk they pose. This allows bank management and examiners to monitor changes and trends in risk levels, thus promoting safety and soundness in the credit-granting process. Credit-rating systems are also used for credit approval and underwriting, loan pricing, relationship management and credit administration, allowance for loan and lease losses and capital adequacy, credit portfolio management, and reporting (Comptroller of the Currency Administrator of National Banks 2001).

Generally, a credit-rating model can be considered as a mapping function $f : \mathbb{R}^K \to C$ that estimates the probability of default of an obligor described by a vector $\mathbf{x} \in \mathbb{R}^K$ of input features and maps the result to a set C of risk categories. The feature vector $\mathbf{x}$ represents all the relevant information that describes the obligor, including financial and nonfinancial data. For instance, corporate loans, financial ratios, measuring the company's profitability, liquidity, leverage, and so on are usually considered to be important quantitative attributes. Nonfinancial criteria are related to the company's activities, its market position, management quality, growth perspectives, credit history, and the trends in its business sector, for example. Empirical evidence has shown that such nonfinancial attributes significantly improve the estimates of credit scoring and default prediction models (Grunert et al. 2005). Furthermore, market data and estimates from the Black–Scholes–Merton model have also been shown to be strong predictors of credit risk (Doumpos et al. 2014a; Vassalou and Xing 2004).

The development of a rating model is based on the process of Figure 12.1. The process begins with the collection of appropriate data regarding known cases with known creditworthiness status (e.g., defaulted and nondefaulted borrowers). These data can be taken from the historical database of a credit institution or from external resources. At this stage, some preprocessing of the data is necessary in order to transform them into useful features, to eliminate possible outliers, and to select the appropriate set of features for the analysis. These steps lead to the final data $\{\mathbf{x}_i, y_i\}_{i=1}^{M}$, where $\mathbf{x}_i$ is the input feature vector for obligor i, y_i is the actual credit status of the obligor, and M in the number of observations in the data set. These data, which are used for model development, are usually referred to as *training data*.

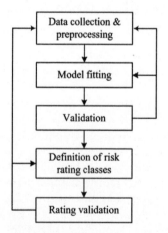

FIGURE 12.1 The process for developing credit-rating models.

The second stage involves the optimization process, which refers to the identification of the model's parameters that best fit the training data. In the simplest case, the model can be expressed as a linear function of the form:

$$f(\mathbf{x}) = \mathbf{x}\boldsymbol{\beta} + \beta_0$$

where $\boldsymbol{\beta} \in \mathbb{R}^K$ is the vector with the coefficients of the selected features in the model, and β_0 is a constant term. Under this setting, the objective of the optimization process is to identify the optimal parameter vector $\boldsymbol{\alpha} = (\boldsymbol{\beta}, \beta_0)$ that best fits the training data. This can be expressed as an optimization problem of the following general form:

$$\min_{\boldsymbol{\alpha} \in A} L(\boldsymbol{\alpha}, \mathbf{X}) \tag{12.1}$$

where A is a set of constraints that define the feasible (acceptable) values for the parameter vector $\boldsymbol{\alpha}$, $\mathbf{X}$ is the training data set, and L is a loss function measuring the differences between the model's output and the given classification of the training observations.

The results of the model optimization process are validated using another sample of obligors with known status. This is referred to as the *validation sample*. Typically, it consists of cases different than the ones of the training sample and for a future time period. The optimal model is applied to these new observations, and its predictive ability is measured. If this is acceptable, then the model's outputs are used to define a set of risk rating classes (usually, 10 classes are used). Each rating class is associated with a probability of default, and it includes borrowers with similar credit risk levels. The defined rating needs also to be validated in terms of its stability over time, the distribution of the borrowers in the rating groups, and the consistency between the estimated probabilities of default in each group and the empirical ones that are taken from the population of rated borrowers.

Multicriteria Aspects of Credit Rating

From the methodological point of view, credit scoring for business and consumer loans is a statistical pattern classification problem, as the decision models are constructed on the basis of historical default data. Nevertheless, some features that analysts often require scoring models to have (Krahnen and Weber 2001) make MCDA techniques appealing in this context. In particular (Doumpos and Zopounidis 2014):

- *Credit scoring models are usually required to be monotone with respect to the inputs.* From an economic and business perspective, the monotonicity assumption implies that as the input information for a given applicant improves, the estimated probability of default should decrease. Assuming that all attributes are in a maximization form, the monotonicity assumption can be formally expressed as follows:

$$\Pr(D|\mathbf{x}_i) \leq \Pr(D|\mathbf{x}_j) \quad \forall \mathbf{x}_i \succ \mathbf{x}_j \tag{12.2}$$

where $\Pr(D|\mathbf{x}_i)$ is the estimated probability of default for credit applicant i, and f represents the dominance relationship, defined as follows: $\mathbf{x}_i \succ \mathbf{x}_j \iff \mathbf{x}_i \geq \mathbf{x}_j$ and $x_{ik} > x_{jk}$, for at least one attribute k.

Models that violate monotonicity in an arbitrary manner may fail to be accepted, simply because they lack economic sense, thus providing counterintuitive results from an economic perspective. Furthermore, empirical results have shown that introducing monotonicity in credit-scoring models actually improves their predictive performance and robustness, through the elimination of the overfitting effect (Doumpos and Zopounidis 2009).

■ *Credit-scoring models should be transparent and comprehensible.* The predictive ability of credit-rating models is not the sole decisive factor for their success in practice. In addition to being accurate, credit risk– rating models should also be easy to understand by analysts, end users, and regulators. A comprehensible model enables its user to understand its underlying logic and provide justifications on its recommendations (Martens and Baesens 2010; Martens et al. 2011), instead of simply being used as a blackbox analytic recommendation tool.

■ *Risk grades are ordinal.* This is often ignored by many popular statistical and computational intelligence techniques used for model building, which often assume that the classes are nominal (i.e., in no particular order).

Multicriteria decision models fit well these requirements: (1) they are by definition ordinal; (2) they provide evaluation results that are monotone with respect to the evaluation criteria; and (3) they promote transparency, enabling the credit analyst to calibrate them on the basis of his/her expert domain knowledge and allowing for justification of the obtained results. Among others, MCDA methods have been used in the area of credit scoring and risk-rating (and the relevant field of financial distress prediction) in four different ways:

1. As tools for building accurate and transparent credit-risk assessment systems, customized to the needs of particular financial institutions (Bana e Costa et al. 2002; García et al. 2013). This is particularly important for special types of credit (e.g., project finance) for which historical data may

be lacking. In such cases, MCDA methods can greatly enhance peer expert judgment systems, facilitating the structuring of the credit-granting evaluation process and providing formal procedures for aggregating multiple credit evaluation criteria.

2. In combination with other modeling and learning techniques, including rough sets, fuzzy models, case-based reasoning, and neural networks (Capotorti and Barbanera 2012; Hu 2009; Vukovic et al. 2012; Yu et al. 2009). Such computational intelligence techniques provide strong data analysis capabilities. MCDA, on the other hand, provides axiomatic decision models of different forms.

3. As optimization approaches for model fitting under multiple performance measures (He et al. 2010; Li et al. 2011; Odeh et al. 2011). The performance of a credit-rating model has different aspects, including statistical (e.g., different measures of predictive accuracy) and economic (profit/costs derived from actions taken on the basis of the results of a risk assessment model). Multi-objective optimization techniques enable the consideration of such multiple performance measures when building a credit-rating model.

4. As alternatives to popular statistical and machine learning approaches providing more accurate rating results (Doumpos and Pasiouras 2005; Doumpos and Zopounidis 2011; Hu and Chen 2011). The results from several studies show that credit-scoring models constructed using MCDA techniques provide robust and accurate results, often actually outperforming other popular approaches. Thus, they could be considered as potential candidates for constructing credit scoring and rating models.

MULTICRITERIA METHODOLOGY

Modeling Approach

MCDA provides a variety of approaches for credit risk modeling and the construction of credit scoring systems, including outranking techniques (Doumpos and Zopounidis 2011; Hu and Chen 2011), rule-based models (Capotorti and Barbanera 2012; Vukovic et al. 2012; Yu et al. 2009), and value models (Bana e Costa et al. 2002; Doumpos and Pasiouras 2005; Doumpos 2012).

To facilitate the presentation this study focuses on additive value models in the framework of the UTADIS method (Doumpos and Zopounidis 2002; Zopounidis and Doumpos 1999). Additive models are popular approaches for credit risk modeling, as they are intuitive scoring systems that are simple to understand and implement, and they are compatible with the scorecard structure of credit rating systems used in practice (Siddiqi 2006).

For instance, Krahnen and Weber (2001) conducted a survey among major German banks and found that all of them used credit scoring models expressed in the form of an additive value function:

$$V(\mathbf{x}_i) = \sum_{k=1}^{K} w_k v_k(x_{ik}) \tag{12.3}$$

where the global value $V(\mathbf{x}_i)$ is an estimate of the overall creditworthiness and default risk of obligor i.

In this model, the overall assessment is a weighted average of partial scores $v_1(x_{i1}), \ldots, v_k(x_{iK})$ defined over a set of K credit risk assessment criteria. Without loss of generality, we shall assume that the weighting trade-off constants are non-negative and normalized such that $w_1 + w_2 + \cdots + w_K = 1$. On the other hand, the marginal value functions $v_1(\cdot), \ldots, v_K(\cdot)$, which define the partial scores, are scaled such that $v_k(x_{k*}) = 0$ and $v_k(x_k^*) = 1$, where x_{k*} and x_k^* are the most and least risky level of risk attribute k, respectively. For simplicity, henceforth it will be assumed that all risk assessment criteria are expressed in maximization form (thus implying that all marginal value functions are nondecreasing).

The construction of the credit-scoring model (12.3) can be simplified by setting $u_k(x_k) = w_k v_k(x_k)$, which leads to a rescaled set of marginal value functions $u_1, \ldots, u_K$ normalized in $[0, w_k]$. With this transformation, the evaluation model (12.3) can be rewritten in the following equivalent form:

$$V(\mathbf{x}_i) = \sum_{k=1}^{K} u_k(x_{ik}) \tag{12.4}$$

This decision model can be linear or nonlinear, depending on the form of the marginal value functions. The marginal value functions can be either prespecified by risk analysts or inferred directly from the data using a preference disaggregation approach. In the context of credit rating, the latter approach is the preferred one, particularly when there are historical data available for constructing the model. Under this scheme, a convenient and flexible way to take into consideration a wide class of monotone marginal value functions is to assume that they are piecewise linear. In that regard, the range of each risk criterion k is split into $s_k + 1$ subintervals defined by s_k breakpoints $\beta_0^k < \beta_1^k < \cdots < \beta_{s_k+1}^k$, between the least and the most preferred levels of the criterion (denoted by β_0^k and $\beta_{s_k+1}^k$, respectively), as illustrated in Figure 12.2. Thus, the marginal value of any alternative i on criterion k

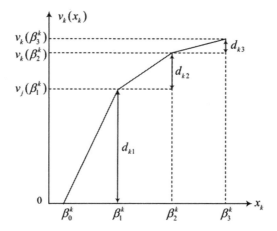

FIGURE 12.2   Piecewise linear modeling of a marginal value function.

can be expressed as:

$$u_k(x_{ik}) = \sum_{r=1}^{s_k} p_{ik}^r d_{kr} \qquad (12.5)$$

where $d_{kr} = u_k(\beta_r^k) - u_k(\beta_{r-1}^k) \geq 0$ is the difference between the marginal values at two consecutive levels of criterion k and

$$p_{ik}^r = \begin{cases} 0 & \text{if } x_{ik} < \beta_{r-1}^k \\ \dfrac{x_{ik} - \beta_{r-1}^k}{\beta_r^k - \beta_{r-1}^k} & \text{if } x_{ik} \in \left[\beta_{r-1}^k, \beta_r^k\right] \\ 1 & \text{if } x_{ik} > \beta_r^k \end{cases} \qquad (12.6)$$

With the above piecewise linear modeling of the marginal value functions, the scoring model (12.4) can be expressed as a linear function of the step differences in the marginal values between consecutive breakpoints in the criteria's scale:

$$V(\mathbf{x}_i) = \sum_{k=1}^{K} \mathbf{p}_{ik}^{\mathsf{T}} \mathbf{d}_k \qquad (12.7)$$

where $\mathbf{p}_{ik} = (p_{ik}^1, p_{ik}^2, \ldots, p_{ik}^{s_k})$ and $\mathbf{d}_k = (d_{k1}, d_{k2}, \ldots, d_{ks_k})$.

The parameters of model (12.7) can be estimated in the context of the MCDA disaggregation paradigm (Jacquet-Lagrèze and Siskos 2001) with nonparametric linear programming formulations, using data for obligors classified into predefined risk classes. In a general setting, assume that reference (training) data for $M_1, M_2, \ldots, M_N$ obligors are available from N risk classes $C_1, \ldots, C_N$, defined such that C_1 is the low-risk category and C_N the higher-risk one. The rating imposed by model $V(\mathbf{x})$ are made on the basis of the following classification rule:

Obligor i belongs in risk category 1 if and only if

$$t_\ell < V(\mathbf{x}_i) < t_{\ell-1} \tag{12.8}$$

where $1 > t_1 > t_2 > \cdots > t_{N-1} > 0$ are score thresholds that distinguish the risk classes.

The scoring model and thresholds that best fit the previous rule, according to the available training data, can be estimated through the solution of the following linear programming problem:

$$\min \sum_{\ell=1}^{N} \frac{1}{M_\ell} \sum_{\mathbf{x}_i \in C_\ell} (\varepsilon_i^+ + \varepsilon_i^-)$$

$$\text{s.t.} \quad V(\mathbf{x}_i) = \sum_{k=1}^{K} \mathbf{p}_{ik}^\top \mathbf{d}_k \qquad\qquad i = 1, 2, \ldots, M$$

$$V(\mathbf{x}_i) - t_n + \varepsilon_i^+ \geq \delta, \qquad \forall \mathbf{x}_i \in C_\ell, \ell = 1, \ldots, N-1$$

$$V(\mathbf{x}_i) - t_{n-1} - \varepsilon_i^- \leq -\delta, \qquad \forall \mathbf{x}_i \in C_\ell, \ell = 2, \ldots, N$$

$$t_{\ell-1} - t_\ell \geq 0, \qquad\qquad \ell = 2, \ldots, N-1$$

$$\sum_{k=1}^{K} \mathbf{1}^\top \mathbf{d}_k = 1$$

$$\mathbf{d}_k, t_\ell, \varepsilon_i^+, \varepsilon_i^- \geq 0 \qquad\qquad \forall i, k, \ell \tag{12.9}$$

where $\mathbf{1}$ is a vector of ones. The first set of constraints defines the credit scores for the training cases according to the additive model (12.7). The second set of constraints defines the violations (ε^+) of the lower bound of each risk class (this applies only to obligors belonging to classes $C_1, \ldots, C_{N-1}$), whereas the third set of constraints defines the violations (ε^-) of the upper bound of each risk category (this applies only to the obligors belonging to classes $C_2, \ldots, C_N$). In both constraints δ is a small positive user-defined constant used to model the strict inequalities of the classification rule (12.8). The fourth constraint is used to ensure that the thresholds are monotonically nonincreasing, whereas the last constraint normalizes the additive model so that the maximum score for any obligor is one.

The objective function involves the minimization of the model's fitting error. This is defined as the weighted sum of the errors for cases belonging into different classes, where the weights are defined in terms of the number of sample observations in each class. In this way, it is possible to handle training sets with considerable imbalanced class sizes, which are very common in credit rating (e.g., the number of obligors is default is much lower than the nondefaulted obligors).

The use of linear programming for model fitting enables the handling of big data sets. This is particularly important for credit scoring, as the available data become larger, particularly after the introduction of the Basel II regulatory framework. Furthermore, a linear programming model enables the risk analyst to incorporate special domain knowledge, which can be very useful for calibrating the model with expert judgment, in order to capture aspects of the problem not adequately covered by the data.

Robust Formulation

Robustness analysis has emerged over the past decade as a major research issue in MCDA. Vincke (1999) emphasized that robustness should not be considered in the restrictive framework of stochastic analysis and distinguished between robust solutions and robust methods. He further argued that although robustness is an appealing property, it is not a sufficient condition to judge the quality of a method or a solution. Roy (2010), on the other hand, introduced the term *robustness concern* to emphasize that robustness is taken into consideration a priori rather than a posteriori (as is the case of sensitivity analysis). In the framework of Roy, the robustness concern is raised by *vague approximations* and *zones of ignorance* that cause the formal representation of a problem to diverge from the real-life context, due to: (1) the way imperfect knowledge is treated; (2) the inappropriate preferential interpretation of certain types of data (e.g., transformations of qualitative attributes); (3) the use of modeling parameters to grasp complex aspects of reality; and (4) the introduction of technical parameters with no concrete meaning.

The robustness concern is particularly important when inferring MCDA decision models from data through disaggregation formulations. The quality of the inferred models is usually described in terms of their accuracy, but their robustness is also a crucial issue. Recent experimental studies have shown that robustness and accuracy are closely related (Doumpos et al. 2014b; Vetschera et al. 2010). However, accuracy measurements are done ex-post and rely on the use of additional test data, while robustness is taken into consideration ex-ante, thus making it an important issue that is taken into consideration before a decision model is actually put into practical use.

The robustness concern in this context arises because, in most cases, alternative decision models can be inferred in accordance with the information embodied in a set of training cases. This is evident in cases where the solution of optimization formulations such as (12.9) is not unique. Different optimal solutions may result in very different decision models, yielding results that may vary significantly when used to evaluate the risk level for cases outside the training set. Furthermore, even if the optimal solution is unique under the selected model fitting criterion for a given training sample, near optimal solutions may actually yield more meaningful models with improved robustness with regard to data variations.

The complexity of the inferred decision model is also an issue that is related to its robustness. Simpler models are more robust compared to more complex nonlinear models. The latter are defined by a larger number of parameters and, as a result, the inference procedure becomes less robust and more sensitive to the available data. Therefore, care should be given to the selection of the appropriate modeling form, taking into account the available data. This issue has been studied extensively in areas such as the statistical learning theory (Schölkopf and Smola 2002; Vapnik 2000).

Following this direction, Doumpos and Zopounidis (2007) presented simple modifications of traditional optimization formulations (such as the one discussed in previous section) on the grounds of the regularization principle, which is widely used in data mining and statistical learning (Vapnik 2000). From a data mining/statistical learning perspective, robustness involves the ability of a prediction model (or learning algorithm) to retain its structure and provide accurate results in cases where the learning process is based on data that contain imperfections (i.e., errors, outliers, noise, missing data, etc.). Given that the robustness of a prediction model is related to its complexity, statistical learning has been founded on a rigorous theoretical framework that connects robustness, complexity, and the accuracy of prediction models.

The foundations of this theoretical framework are based on Tikhonov's regularization principle (Tikhonov et al. 1995), which involves systems of linear equations of the form $\mathbf{Ax} = \mathbf{b}$. When the problem is ill-posed, such a system of equations may not have a solution and the inverse of matrix $\mathbf{A}$ may exhibit instabilities (i.e., $\mathbf{A}$ may be singular or ill-conditioned). In such cases, a numerically robust solution can be obtained through the approximate system $\mathbf{Ax} \approx \mathbf{b}$, such that the following function is minimized:

$$\|\mathbf{Ax} - \mathbf{b}\|^2 + \lambda \|\mathbf{x}\|^2 \tag{12.10}$$

where $\lambda > 0$ is a regularization parameter that defines the trade-off between the error term $\|\mathbf{Ax} - \mathbf{b}\|^2$ and the "size" of the solution (thus controlling the solution for changes in $\mathbf{A}$ and $\mathbf{b}$).

Following this approach, Doumpos and Zopounidis (2007) reformulated problem (12.9) as follows:

$$\min \sum_{\ell=1}^{N} \frac{1}{M_\ell} \sum_{x_i \in C_\ell} (\varepsilon_i^+ + \varepsilon_i^-) + \lambda \sum_{k=1}^{K} 1^T d_k$$

s.t. $V(x_i) = \sum_{k=1}^{K} p_{ik}^T d_k$ $i = 1, 2, \ldots, M$

$V(x_i) - t_n + \varepsilon_i^+ \geq 1,$ $\forall x_i \in C_\ell, \ell = 1, \ldots, N-1$

$V(x_i) - t_{n-1} - \varepsilon_i^- \leq -1,$ $\forall x_i \in C_\ell, \ell = 2, \ldots, N$

$t_{\ell-1} - t_\ell \geq 0,$ $\ell = 2, \ldots, N-1$

$d_k, t_\ell, \varepsilon_i^+, \varepsilon_i^- \geq 0$ $\forall i, k, \ell$ (12.11)

In this formulation, the objective function combines two terms. The first involves the minimization of the model's fitting error, similarly to formulation (12.9). The second term in the objective function is in accordance with Tikhonov's regularization. The parameter $\lambda > 0$ defines the trade-off between the minimization of the fitting error and the complexity of the model, which can be set by trial-and-error or with statistical resampling techniques.

Denoting by $d_k^*(k = 1, \ldots, K)$ the optimal parameters of the model resulting from the solution of the earlier linear program, the constructed additive value function is scaled between zero and $\theta = \sum_{k=1}^{K} 1^T d_k$. Rescaling the model in [0, 1] can be easily done simply by dividing the optimal solution by θ.

EMPIRICAL ANALYSIS

Data and Variables

The empirical analysis is based on a panel data set consisting of 1,325 firm-year observations involving European listed companies over the period 2002–2012. The sample covers eight different countries and five business sectors, as illustrated in Table 12.1.

Financial data for the firms in the sample were collected from the Osiris database, whereas Bloomberg was used to get the firms' ratings from S&P. Due to the sparsity of the data set with respect to the number of observations from each rating grade in the S&P scale, the observations were regrouped. In particular, a two-group setting is considered distinguishing between firms

TABLE 12.1 Sample Composition (Number of Observations) by Year, Country, and Business Sector.

Year	No. of Observations	Country	No. of Observations	Sector	No. of Observations
2002	38	Germany	308	Manufacturing	853
2003	102	France	303	Information and communication	220
2004	115	United Kingdom	298	Wholesale and retail trade	130
2005	126	Switzerland	135	Transportation and storage	90
2006	135	Netherlands	130	Construction	32
2007	138	Italy	88		
2008	140	Spain	33		
2009	139	Belgium	30		
2010	149				
2011	151				
2012	92				
Total	1,325	1,325		1,325	

in speculative (D to BB+) and investment grades (BBB to AAA). The percentage of observations in each rating group under these schemes is shown in Table 12.2.

For every observation in the sample for year t, the S&P long-term rating is recorded at the end of June, while annual financial data are taken from the end of year $t - 1$. The financial data involve four financial ratios: ROA (earnings before taxes/total assets), interest coverage (earnings before interest and taxes/interest expenses, EBIT/IE), solvency (equity/total assets, EQ/TA), and the long-term debt leverage ratio (equity/long term debt, EQ/LTD). ROA is the primary indicator used to measure corporate profitability. Interest coverage assesses firms' ability to cover their debt obligations through their operating profits. The solvency ratio analyzes the capital adequacy of the firms, whereas the long-term debt leverage ratio takes into consideration the long-term debt burden of firms relative to their equity. In addition to these financial ratios, we also take into account the size of firms, as measured by the logarithm of their market capitalization (CAP).

Table 12.3 presents the averages (over all years) of the financial variables for the two rating groups in the sample. All variables have a clear monotone (increasing) relationship with the ratings. In particular, firms in investment grades are more profitable, have higher interest coverage, are better

TABLE 12.2 Percentage of Sample Observations in Each Risk Category.

	Investment	Speculative
2002	76.3	23.7
2003	79.4	20.6
2004	78.3	21.7
2005	75.4	24.6
2006	75.6	24.4
2007	76.8	23.2
2008	72.1	27.9
2009	71.2	28.8
2010	70.5	29.5
2011	70.9	29.1
2012	78.3	21.7
Overall	74.5	25.5

TABLE 12.3 Averages of Independent Variables by Rating Group.

	Investment	Speculative
ROA	7.64	2.47
EBIT/IE	7.56	2.46
EQ/TA	33.26	26.17
EQ/LTD	1.23	0.85
CAP	16.27	14.26

capitalized and leveraged in terms of long-term debt, and have higher market capitalization. The differences between the rating groups are statistically significant at the 1 percent level for all variables under the Mann–Whitney nonparametric test.

Results

Given that during the time period spanned by the data, the European economic environment has experienced significant changes (e.g., the outbreak of the global crisis and the European sovereign debt crisis), the dynamics and robustness of the results over time are tested by developing and validating a series of models through a walk-forward approach. In particular, the data for the period 2002–2005 are first used for model fitting, whereas the subsequent period, 2006–2012, serves as the holdout sample. In a second run, the training data are extended up to 2006, and the holdout data span the period 2007–2012. The same process is repeated up to the case where the training data cover the period 2002–2010. Thus, six training and test runs are performed. Henceforth, these walk-forward runs will be referred to as F05 (model fitting on data up to 2005) up to F10 (model fitting on data up to 2010).

Table 12.4 summarizes the trade-offs of the predictor attributes in all models constructed through the walk-forward approach. It is evident that the size of the firms as measured by their capitalization is the dominant factor that explains the ratings, even though its relative importance has decreased over the years. The significance of market capitalization has also been reported by Hwang et al. (2010) and Hwang (2013), who derived similar results for U.S. firms. The profitability of the firms is also an important dimension, as evident by the relative importance of the ROA indicator. On the other hand, interest coverage was mainly important in the first years of the analysis, but its explanatory power appears to be weaker in the models that consider more recent data. At the same time, the importance of the equity to long-term debt has increased considerably, thus indicating that over the crisis leverage has become a crucial factor for explaining the credit ratings of the firms. Finally, the solvency ratio (equity to assets) appears to be the weaker predictor overall, throughout all years of the analysis.

Figure 12.3 provides further information on the marginal value functions of the attributes in the models, which indicate how the firms are evaluated under each risk-assessment criterion. The results are quite robust over all six models developed over different time periods. In terms of the ROA indicator, the form of the corresponding marginal value function shows that firms with positive ROA receive much higher rating compared to firms whose profitability is negative. A similar result is also evident for the long-term leverage ratio (EQ/LTD). Finally, as far as size is concerned, the performance

TABLE 12.4 Trade-offs (in %) of the Attributes.

	ROA	EBIT/IE	EQ/TA	EQ/LTD	CAP
F05	23.77	18.07	0.00	4.77	53.38
F06	19.39	13.17	0.00	12.29	55.15
F07	6.98	19.41	0.00	8.52	65.08
F08	20.50	6.75	3.21	17.69	51.85
F09	21.56	7.61	5.55	17.04	48.23
F10	18.44	7.80	5.44	24.07	44.25

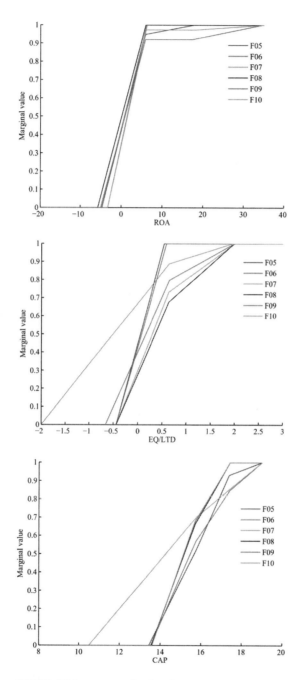

FIGURE 12.3 Marginal value functions.

TABLE 12.5   Classification Accuracies (in %) for the Holdout Samples.

	Investment	Speculative	Overall	LR
F05	87.28	70.24	82.73	82.73
F06	84.41	75.80	82.08	80.96
F07	83.26	75.40	81.07	79.28
F08	84.33	74.32	81.54	79.85
F09	86.62	70.37	82.14	80.10
F10	86.59	73.44	83.13	80.25

score of the firms increases (almost in a linear way) for firms with market capitalization approximately above 700 million euros. Such insights provide analysts with useful information about the rating models, thus enhancing their transparency and comprehensibility, which has been found to be important for their successful use in practice (Martens and Baesens 2010; Martens et al. 2011).

Table 12.5 presents results for the classification accuracies of all models in the holdout samples. Classification accuracy is defined as the ratio between the number of correct class assignments by a model (i.e., cases where the ratings estimated by the model coincide with the actual ratings) to the total number of observations being rated. All the reported results involve the holdout samples, which correspond to future time periods compared to the data used to fit the models. Table 12.5 reports the accuracy rates separately for cases in investment and speculative grades, together with the overall accuracy. For comparative purposes, the overall accuracies of models fitted with logistic regression (LR) are also presented. LR is probably the most popular method used by researchers and practitioner for constructing credit scoring and rating models. The results indicate that the accuracy rates of the multicriteria models are consistently higher for investment-rated firms, whereas firms rated in speculative grades are more difficult to describe. The overall accuracy of all models is consistently higher than 81 percent, and the proposed multicriteria methodology provides more accurate results compared to logistic regression.

CONCLUSIONS AND FUTURE PERSPECTIVES

The analysis of the ratings issued by CRAs has received much attention in the financial literature, due to their significance in the context of credit risk management and their widespread use by investors, policy makers, and managers. In this study, we sought to explain and predict the credit ratings issued by S&P on the basis of financial and market data, using a cross-country panel data set from Europe over the period 2002–2012. For the analysis, an innovative nonparametric multicriteria technique was employed, which is based on a linear programming formulation for fitting additive credit-risk rating models to data.

The results showed that the market capitalization appears to be the dominant factor for explaining the credit ratings of European firms. Profitability was also found to be an important dimension, together with long-term leverage, which has become an important issue, particularly after the outbreak of the crisis. The developed multicriteria models exhibit good and robust behavior, whereas its performance was found to be superior to logistic regression.

These empirical results could be extended in a number of directions. First, additional predictor attributes could be considered, focusing on macroeconomic factors, which could be of particular importance over the business cycle and during economic turmoil, providing a better description of cross-country differences. Data related to market sentiment and information from the CDS markets could also be useful for predicting credit ratings by complementing the estimates of structural models with timely findings on market trends. Variables related to regulatory frameworks (Cheng and Neamtiu 2009) and corporate governance (Alali et al. 2012) are also important for the analysis of credit ratings in a comprehensive context. Second, except for only focusing on static analyses of credit ratings, the explanation and prediction of rating changes is also a crucial point of major interest to market participants. The investigation could also be extended to cover nonlisted companies. Finally, the combination of financial data, structural models, and credit ratings in an integrated risk management context could be considered, in accordance with the findings reported in recent studies (e.g., Das et al. 2009; Hilscher and Wilson 2013) on the possible synergies that can be derived by combining different types of risk models and measures in credit risk assessment.

REFERENCES

Alali, F., A. Anandarajan, and W. Jiang. 2012. The effect of corporate governance on firms credit ratings: Further evidence using governance score in the United States. *Accounting and Finance* 52 (2): 291–312.

Altman, E. I., and A. Saunders. 1997. Credit risk measurement: Developments over the last 20 years. *Journal of Banking and Finance* 21 (11–12): 1721–1742.

Bana e Costa, C. A., L. Barroso, and J. O. Soares. 2002. Qualitative modeling of credit scoring: A case study in banking. *Journal of European Research Studies* 5 (1–2): 37–51.

Basel Committee on Banking Supervision. 2004. International convergence of capital measurement and capital standards: A revised framework. Bank for International Settlements, Basel, Switzerland.

Black, F., and M. Scholes. 1973. The pricing of options and corporate liabilities. *Journal of Political Economy* 81 (3): 637–659.

Capotorti, A., and E. Barbanera. 2012. Credit scoring analysis using a fuzzy probabilistic rough set model. *Computational Statistics and Data Analysis* 56 (4): 981–994.

Cheng, M., and M. Neamtiu. 2009. An empirical analysis of changes in credit rating properties: Timeliness, accuracy and volatility. *Journal of Accounting and Economics* 47 (1–2): 108–130.

Comptroller of the Currency Administrator of National Banks. 2001. *Rating Credit Risk: Comptroller's Handbook.* Washington, DC: U.S. Department of Treasury.

Das, S. R., P. Hanouna, and A. Sarin. 2009. Accounting-based versus market-based cross-sectional models of CDS spreads. *Journal of Banking and Finance* 33 (4): 719–730.

Doumpos, M. 2012. Learning non-monotonic additive value functions for multicriteria decision making. *OR Spectrum* 34 (1): 89–106.

Doumpos, M., D. Niklis, C. Zopounidis, and K. Andriosopoulos. 2014a. Combining accounting data and a structural model for predicting credit ratings: Empirical evidence from European listed firms. *Journal of Banking & Finance* (forthcoming).

Doumpos, M., and F. Pasiouras. 2005. Developing and testing models for replicating credit ratings: A multicriteria approach. *Computational Economics* 25 (4): 327–341.

Doumpos, M., and C. Zopounidis. 2002. *Multicriteria Decision Aid Classification Methods.* New York: Springer.

_____. 2007. Regularized estimation for preference disaggregation in multiple criteria decision making. *Computational Optimization and Applications* 38 (1): 61–80.

_____. 2009. Monotonic support vector machines for credit rating. *New Mathematics and Natural Computation* 5 (3): 557–570.

_____. 2011. A multicriteria outranking modeling approach for credit rating. *Decision Sciences* 42 (3): 721–742.

_____. 2014. *Multicriteria Analysis in Finance.* Berlin, Heidelberg: Springer.

Doumpos, M., C. Zopounidis, and E. Galariotis. 2014b. Inferring robust decision models in multicriteria classification problems: An experimental analysis. *European Journal of Operational Research* 236: 601–611.

Frost, C. A. 2007. Credit rating agencies in capital markets: A review of research evidence on selected criticisms of the agencies. *Journal of Accounting, Auditing and Finance* 22 (3): 469–492.

García, F., V. Giménez, and F. Guijarro. 2013. Credit risk management: A multicriteria approach to assess creditworthiness. *Mathematical and Computer Modeling* 57 (7–8): 2009–2015.

Grunert, J., L. Norden, and M. Weber. 2005. The role of non-financial factors in internal credit ratings. *Journal of Banking and Finance* 29 (2): 509–531.

Hayden, E. 2003. Are credit scoring models sensitive with respect to default definitions? evidence from the Austrian market. Tech. rep., University of Vienna.

He, J., Y. Zhang, Y. Shi, and G. Huang. 2010. Domain-driven classification based on multiple criteria and multiple constraint-level programming for intelligent credit scoring. *IEEE Transactions on Knowledge and Data Engineering* 22 (6): 826–838.

Hilscher, J., and M. Wilson. 2013. Credit ratings and credit risk: Is one measure enough? Tech. rep., AFA 2013 San Diego Meeting.

Hu, Y.-C. 2009. Bankruptcy prediction using ELECTRE-based single-layer perception. *Neurocomputing* 72: 3150–3157.

Hu, Y.-C., and C.-J. Chen. 2011. A PROMETHEE-based classification method using concordance and discordance relations and its application to bankruptcy prediction. *Information Sciences* 181 (22): 4959–4968.

Huang, Z., H. Chen, C.-J. Hsu, W.-H. Chen, and S. Wu. 2004. Credit rating analysis with support vector machines and neural networks: A market comparative study. *Decision Support Systems* 37 (4): 543–558.

Hwang, R.-C. 2013. Forecasting credit ratings with the varying-coefficient model. *Quantitative Finance* 13 (2): 1–19.

Hwang, R.-C., H. Chung, and C. Chu. 2010. Predicting issuer credit ratings using a semiparametric method. *Journal of Empirical Finance* 17(1): 120–137.

Jacquet-Lagrèze, E., and Y. Siskos. 2001. Preference disaggregation: Twenty years of MCDA experience. *European Journal of Operational Research* 130 (2): 233–245.

Jeon, D.-S., and S. Lovo. 2013. Credit rating industry: A helicopter tour of stylized facts and recent theories. *International Journal of Industrial Organization* 31 (5): 643–651.

Krahnen, J. P., and M. Weber. 2001. Generally accepted rating principles: A primer. *Journal of Banking and Finance* 25 (1): 3–23.

Li, J., L. Wei, G. Li, and W. Xu. 2011. An evolution strategy-based multiple kernels multi-criteria programming approach: The case of credit decision making. *Decision Support Systems* 51 (2): 292–298.

Lu, H.-M., F.-T. Tsai, H. Chen, M.-W. Hung, and H. Li. 2012. Credit rating change modeling using news and financial ratios. *ACM Transactions on Management Information Systems* 3 (3): 14:1–14:30.

Martens, D., and B. Baesens. 2010. Building acceptable classification models. In *Data Mining*, edited by R. Stahlbock, S. F. Crone, and S. Lessmann, 53–74, New York: Springer.

Martens, D., J. Vanthienen, W. Verbeke, and B. Baesens. 2011. Performance of classification models from a user perspective. *Decision Support Systems* 51 (4): 782–793.

Merton, R. C. 1974. On the pricing of corporate debt: The risk structure of interest rates. *The Journal of Finance* 29 (2): 449–470.

Mizen, P., and S. Tsoukas. 2012. Forecasting U.S. bond default ratings allowing for previous and initial state dependence in an ordered probit model. *International Journal of Forecasting,* 28 (1): 273–287.

Odeh, O., P. Koduru, A. Featherstone, S. Das, and S. M. Welch. 2011. A multi-objective approach for the prediction of loan defaults. *Expert Systems with Applications* 38 (7): 8850–8857.

Pagano, M., and P. Volpin. 2010. Credit ratings failures and policy options. *Economic Policy* 25 (62): 401–431.

Pasiouras, F., C. Gaganis, and C. Zopounidis. 2006. The impact of bank regulations, supervision, market structure, and bank characteristics on individual bank ratings: A cross-country analysis. *Review of Quantitative Finance and Accounting* 27 (4): 403–438.

Roy, B. 2010. Robustness in operational research and decision aiding: A multi-faceted issue. *European Journal of Operational Research* 3: 629–638.

Schölkopf, B., and A. Smola. 2002. *Learning with Kernels: Support Vector Machines, Regularization, Optimization and Beyond.* Cambridge, MA: MIT Press.

Siddiqi, N. 2006. *Credit Risk Scorecards.* Hoboken, NJ: John Wiley & Sons.

Tichy, G., K. Lannoo, O. Gwilym, R. Alsakka, D. Masciandaro, and B. Paudyn. 2011. Credit rating agencies: Part of the solution or part of the problem? *Intereconomics* 46 (5): 232–262.

Tikhonov, A., A. Goncharsky, V. Stepanov, A. G., Yagola, A. G. 1995. *Numerical Methods for the Solution of Ill-Posed Problems.* Dordrecht: Springer.

Treacy, W. F., and M. Carey. 2000. Credit risk rating systems at large U.S. banks. *Journal of Banking and Finance* 24 (1–2): 167–201.

Vapnik, V. 2000. *The Nature of Statistical Learning Theory*, 2nd ed. New York: Springer.

Vassalou, M., and Y. Xing. 2004. Default risk in equity returns. *Journal of Finance* 59 (2): 831–868.

Vetschera, R., Y. Chen, K. W. Hipel, and D. Marc Kilgour. 2010. Robustness and information levels in case-based multiple criteria sorting. *European Journal of Operational Research* 202 (3): 841–852.

Vincke, P. 1999. Robust solutions and methods in decision-aid. *Journal of Multi-Criteria Decision Analysis* 8 (3): 181–187.

Vukovic, S., B. Delibasic, A. Uzelac, and M. Suknovic. 2012. A case-based reasoning model that uses preference theory functions for credit scoring. *Expert Systems with Applications* 39 (9): 8389–8395.

Yu, L., S. Wang, and K. Lai. 2009. An intelligent-agent-based fuzzy group decision making model for financial multicriteria decision support: The case of credit scoring. *European Journal of Operational Research* 195 (3): 942–959.

Zopounidis, C., and M. Doumpos. 1999. A multicriteria decision aid methodology for sorting decision problems: The case of financial distress. *Computational Economics* 14 (3): 197–218.

Financial Markets

Parameter Analysis of the VPIN (Volume-Synchronized Probability of Informed Trading) Metric

Jung Heon Song
Kesheng Wu
Horst D. Simon
Lawrence Berkeley National Lab

INTRODUCTION

The Flash Crash of 2010

The May 6, 2010, Flash Crash saw the biggest one-day point decline of 998.5 points (roughly 9 percent) and the second largest point swing of 1,010.14 points in the Dow Jones Industrial Average. Damages were also done to futures trading, with the price of the S&P 500 decreasing by 5 percent in the span of 15 minutes, with an unusually large volume of trade conducted. All of these culminated in market value of $1 trillion disappearing, only to recover the losses within minutes—20 minutes later, the market had regained most of the 600 points drop (Lauricella 2011). Several explanations were given about the market crash. Some notable ones are:

1. Phillips (2010) listed a number of reports, which pointed out that the Flash Crash was a result of a fat-finger trade in Procter & Gamble, leading to a massive stop-loss orders (this theory, however, was quickly dismissed, as the Procter & Gamble incident came about after much damage had already been done to the E-mini S&P 500).

2. Some regulators attributed it to high-frequency traders for exacerbating pricing. Researchers at Nanex argued that *quote stuffing*—placing and then immediately canceling a large number of rapid-fire orders to buy or sell stocks—forced competitors to slow down their operations (Bowley 2010).
3. *The Wall Street Journal* reported a large purchase of put options by the hedge fund Universa Investments, and suggested that this might have triggered the Flash Crash (Lauricella and Patterson 2010).
4. Flood (2010) attributed technical difficulties at the NY Stock Exchange (NYSE) and ARCA to the evaporation of liquidity.
5. A sale of 75,000 E-mini S&P 500 contracts by Waddell & Reed might have caused the futures market to collapse (Gordon and Wagner 2010).
6. Krasting (2010) blamed currency movements, especially a movement in the U.S. dollars to Japanese yen exchange rate.

After more than four months of investigation, the U.S. Securities and Exchange Commission (SEC) and Commodity Futures Trading Commission (CFTC) issued a full report on the Flash Crash, stating that a large mutual fund firm's selling of an unusually large number of E-Mini S&P 500 contracts and high-frequency traders' aggressive selling contributed to the drastic price decline of that day (Goldfarb 2010).

VPIN: A Leading Indicator of Liquidity-Induced Volatility

A general concern in most of these studies is that the computerized high frequency trading (HFT) has contributed to the Flash Crash. It is critical for the regulators and the market practitioners to better understand the impact of high frequency trading, particularly the volatility. Most of the existing market volatility models were developed before HFT had widely been used. We believe that disparities between traditional volatility modeling and high-frequency trading framework have led to the difficulty in CFTC's ability to understand and regulate the financial market. These differences include new information arriving at irregular frequency, all models that seek to forecast volatility treating its source as exogenous, and volatility models being univariate as a result of exogeneity (López de Prado 2011).

A recent paper by Easley, Lopez de Prado, and O'Hara (2012) applies a market microstructure model to study behavior of prices a few hours before the Flash Crash. The authors argue that new dynamics in the current market structure culminated to the breakout of the event and introduced a new form of probability of informed trading—volume synchronized probability of informed trading (VPIN)—to quantify the role of order toxicity in determining liquidity provisions (Easley, López de Prado, O'Hara 2011).

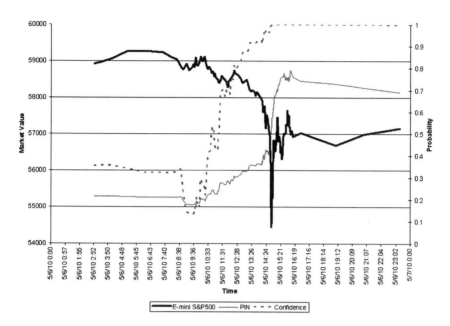

FIGURE 13.1 E-mini S&P 500s VPIN metric on May 6.
Source: López de Prado 2011

The paper presents an analysis of liquidity on the hours and days before the market collapse, and highlights that even though volume was high and unbalanced, liquidity remained low. Order flow, however, became extremely toxic, eventually contributing to market makers leaving the market, causing illiquidity.

Figure 13.1 shows the VPIN values of E-mini futures during the day of the Flash Crash. Near 11:55 A.M. on May 6, the value of VPIN exceeded 90 percent threshold value, and around 1:08 P.M., it passed 95 percent. The VPIN value attained its maximum by 2:30 P.M., and the market crash starts to occur at 2:32 P.M., which agrees with the CFTC/SEC report. This and other tests on different trading instruments provide anecdotal evidences that VPIN is effective.

Systemic Validation of VPIN

To explore whether VPIN is effective in a generic case, one needs to define an automated testing mechanism and execute it over a large variety of trading instruments. To this end, Wu, Bethel, Gu, Leinweber, and Rüebel (2013) adopted a simple definition for VPIN events. A VPIN event starts when the VPIN values cross over a user-defined threshold from below and last for a user-defined fixed duration. We also call each event a VPIN prediction, during which we expect the volatility to be higher than usual. If the volatility is indeed above the average of randomly selected time intervals of the same duration, we say that the event is a true positive; otherwise, it is labeled as a false positive. Alternatively, we may also say that the prediction is a true prediction or a false prediction. Given these definitions, we can use the false positive rate (FPR) to measure the effectiveness of VPIN predictions. Following the earlier work by López de Prado (2012), Wu, Bethel, Gu, Leinweber, and Rüebel (2013) chose to use an instantaneous volatility measure called Maximum Intermediate Return (MIR) to measure the volatility in their automated testing of effectiveness of VPIN.

In order to apply VPIN predictions on a large variety of trading instruments, Wu, Bethel, Gu, Leinweber, and Rüebel (2013) implemented a C++ version of the algorithm. In their test involving 97 most liquid futures contracts over a 67-month period, the C++ implementation required approximately 1.5 seconds for each futures contract, which is many orders of magnitude faster than an alternative. This efficient implementation of VPIN allows them to examine the effectiveness of VPIN on the largest collection of actual trading data reported in literature.

The VPIN predictions require the user to set a handful of different parameters, such as the aforementioned threshold on VPIN values and duration of VPIN events. The choices of these free parameters can affect FPR, the measured effectiveness of VPIN predictions. The authors computed the number of VPIN events and number of false positive events, and used FPR as the effectiveness score for VPIN predictions. The computation of VPIN involves a number of free parameters that must be provided by the users. For each of these parameter choices, the average FPR value over all 97 futures contracts was computed. After examining 16,000 parameter combinations, the authors found a collection of the parameter combinations that can reduce the average false positive rates from 20 percent to 7 percent. The best of these parameter combinations are shown in Table 13.1. We will provide definitions of the parameters as we describe the details of VPIN computation in the next section.

From Table 13.1, we see that these parameter combinations differ from each other in many ways, making it difficult to provide a concise recommendation on how to set these free parameters of VPIN. This chapter attempts a more systematic search of the parameter space. We plan to accomplish this goal in two steps: parameter optimization and sensitivity analysis. First, we search for the optimal parameters with a popular optimization library NOMAD (Nonlinear Mesh Adaptive Direct Search) by Audet, Le Digabel,

TABLE 13.1 The 10 Parameter Combinations That Produced the Smallest Average False Positive Rate α.

π (Nominal Price)	β (Buckets per Day)	σ (Support Window)	η (Event Horizon)	ν (Bucket Volume Classification Parameter)	τ (Threshold for VPIN)	α (False Positive Rate)
Median	200	1	0.1	1	0.99	0.071
Weighted median	1000	0.5	0.1	1	0.99	0.071
Weighted median	200	0.5	0.1	0.25	0.99	0.072
Weighted median	200	0.5	0.1	1	0.99	0.073
Median	200	1	0.1	10	0.99	0.073
Median	600	0.5	0.1	0.1	0.99	0.074
Median	200	1	0.1	Normal	0.99	0.074
Weighted median	200	1	0.1	1	0.99	0.074
Weighted median	200	1	0.25	1	0.99	0.074
Weighted mean	200	1	0.1	1	0.99	0.075

Source: Wu, Bethel, Gu, Leinweber, Rüebel 2013

and Tribes (2009), and Le Digabel (2011). Once the parameters with the minimal FPR values are found, we carry out sensitivity analysis using an uncertainty quantification software package named UQTK (Uncertainty Quantification Toolkit) by Sargsyan, Safta, Debusschere, and Najm (2012).

DEFINITION OF VPIN

Based on an idealized trading model shown in Figure 13.2, Easley, Kiefer, O'Hara, and Paperman (1996) defined a way to measure the information imbalance from the observed ratio of buys and sells in the market.

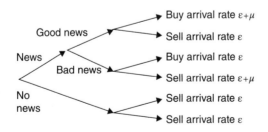

FIGURE 13.2 Idealized trading model.

The authors termed the measure probability of informed trading and used PIN as the shorthand. To compute PIN, one classifies each trade as either buy or sell, following some classification rule (Ellis, Michaely, O'Hara 2000), bins the trades buckets, and then calculates the relative difference between the buys and sells in each bucket. The probability of informed trading is the average buy–sell imbalance over a user-selected time window, which we will call the support window. This support window is typically expressed as the number of buckets.

In their analysis of the Flash Crash of 2010, Easley, López de Prado, and O'Hara (2011) proposed grouping the trades into equal volume bins and called the new variation the volume synchronized probability of informed trading (VPIN). The new analysis tool essentially stretches out the busy periods of the market and compresses the light trading periods. The authors termed this new virtual timing measure the volume time. Another important parameter in computing VPIN is the number of buckets per trading day.

An important feature in computing the probability of informed trading is that it does not actually work with individual trades, but, rather, with groups of bars, treating each as if it is a single trade. The trade classification is performed on the bars instead of actual trades. Both bars and buckets are forms of binning; the difference is that a bar is smaller than a bucket. A typical bucket might include tens or hundreds of bars. Based on earlier reports, we set the number of bars per bucket to 30 for the remainder of this work, as it has minor influence on the final value of the VPIN as shown from the published literature (Easley, López de Prado, O'Hara 2012; Abad, Yague 2012).

The price assigned to a bar is called the nominal price of the bar. This is a second free parameter for VPIN. When the VPIN (or PIN) value is high, we expect the volatility of the market to be high for a certain time period. To make this concrete, we need to choose a threshold for the VPIN values and a size for the time window.

Following the notation used by Wu, Bethel, Gu, Leinweber, and Rüebel (2013), we denote the free parameters needed for the computation of the VPIN as follows:

- Nominal price of a bar π
- Parameter for the bulk volume classification (BVC) ν
- Buckets per day (BPD) β
- Threshold for VPIN τ
- Support window σ
- Event horizon η

Next, we provide additional details about these parameters.

Pricing Strategies

VPIN calculations are typically performed in time bars or volume bars. The most common choice of nominal price of a bar used in practice is the closing price—that is, the price of the last trade in the bar. In this work, we consider the following five *pricing options* for our analysis: closing prices, unweighted mean, unweighted median, volume-weighted mean, and volume-weighted median.

Bulk Volume Classification

A common method used to classify a trade as either buyer-initiated or seller-initiated is via the tick rule, or more formally, the Lee-Ready trade classification algorithm. The method assigns a trade as buy if its price is higher than the preceding, and as sell if otherwise. This convention depends on the sequential order of trades, which is not the ideal approach in high-frequency trading. Instead, the bulk volume classification (BVC) assigns a fraction of the volume to buys and the rest to sells based on the normalized sequential price change (Easley, López de Prado, and O'Hara 2012). Let V_j^b denote the buy volume for bar j, and the volume of bar to be V_j. We follow the definitions by Easley, López de Prado, and O'Hara (2012) for the computation of V_j^b:

$$V_j^b = V_j Z\left(\frac{\delta_j}{\zeta}\right)$$

where Z denotes the cumulative distribution function of either the normal or the student t-distribution, ζ the standard deviation of $\{\delta_j\}$, where $\delta_j = P_j - P_{j-1}$, $\{P_j\}$ are the prices of a sequence of volume bars. We also denote the degrees of freedom of Z by v, and in the case of the standard normal distribution, we let $v = 0$. The rest of the volume bar is then considered as sells

$$V_j^s = V_j - V_j^b$$

Even though this formula uses a cumulative distribution function, it does not imply that the authors have assumed this distribution has anything to do with the actual distribution of the data. The actual empirical distribution of the data has been used, but according to Easley, López de Prado, and O'Hara (2012) no improvement was seen in empirical testing. We decided to use the BVC for its computational simplicity and, as noted by Easley, López de Prado, and O'Hara (2012), its accuracy, which parallels those of other commonly used classification methods.

The argument of the function Z can be interpreted as a normalizer of the price changes. In a traditional trading model, the average price change is subtracted first before dividing by the standard deviation. In HFT, however, the mean price is much smaller than the standard deviation ζ (Wu, Bethel, Gu, Leinweber, Ruebel 2013). We make use of the results from earlier works by Easley, López de Prado, and O'Hara (2012) by always using zero as the center of the normal distribution and the student-t distribution.

By definition, only the most recent few buckets are needed for the computation of the VPIN value (Easley, Kiefer, O'Hara, Paperman, 1996). We call this the support window, represent it as a fraction of the number of buckets in a day, and denote it by σ. The formula used to compute the VPIN is (Easley, López de Prado, O'Hara 2012)

$$VPIN = \frac{\sum \left\| V_j^b - V_j^s \right\|}{\sum V_j}$$

Following the works of earlier authors, we normalize the VPIN values by working with the following transformation:

$$\Phi(x) = \frac{1}{2} \left[1 + erf\left(\frac{x - \mu}{\sqrt{2}\sigma} \right) \right]$$

where erf is the error function measured by a normal distribution, μ the mean of the VPIN values, σ the standard deviation.

VPIN Event

If the value x is a normal distribution with mean μ and standard deviation σ, then the value $\Phi(x)$ denotes the fraction of values that are less than the specific value. This is a useful transformation, as it transforms the value of x from an open range to a close range between 0 and 1. The transformation allows using a single threshold τ for a variety of different trading instruments convenient. For example, in earlier tests, Easley, López de Prado, and O'Hara (2011; 2012) typically used the value 0.9 as the threshold for $\Phi(x)$. Had the VPIN values followed the normal distribution, this threshold would have meant that a VPIN event is declared when a VPIN rises above 90 percent of the values. One might expect that 10 percent of the buckets will produce VPIN values above this trigger. If one divides a day's trading into 100 buckets, one might expect 10 of the buckets to have VPIN values greater than the threshold, which would produce too many VPIN events to be useful. However, Wu, Bethel, Gu, Leinweber, and Rüebel (2013) reported seeing a relatively small number of VPIN events—about one event every two months. The reason for this observation is the following. First off, the VPIN values do not follow the normal distribution. The above transformation is a convenient shorthand for selecting a threshold, not an assumption or validation that VPIN values follow the normal distribution. Furthermore, we only declare a VPIN event if $\Phi(x)$ reaches the threshold from below. If $\Phi(x)$ stays above the threshold, we will not declare a new VPIN event. Typically, once $\Phi(x)$ reaches the threshold, it will stay above the threshold for a number of buckets; thus, many large $\Phi(x)$ values will be included in a single VPIN event. This is another way that the VPIN values do not follow the normal distribution.

Our expectation is that immediately after a VPIN event is triggered, the volatility of the market would be higher than normal. To simplify the discussion, we declare the duration of a VPIN event to be η days. We call this time duration the event horizon for the remainder of the discussion.

False Positive Rate

After we have detected a VPIN event, we next determine if the given event is a true positive or a false positive. As indicated before, we use MIR to measure the volatility. Since the MIR can be both positive and negative, two separate average MIR values are computed: one for the positive MIR and one for the negative MIR. These two values then establish a normal range. If the MIR of a VPIN event is within this normal range, then it is a false event; otherwise, it is a true event. We denote the false positive rate by α, where α is

$$\alpha = \frac{\#\ of\ False\ positive\ events}{\#\ of\ VPIN\ events}$$

The flowchart in Figure 13.3 summarizes how a VPIN event is classified. When the number of VPIN events triggered is 0, the above formula is ill defined. To avoid this difficulty, when no event is detected, we let the number of false positive events to be 0.5 and the number of events 0.5 as well, hence FPR = 1.

To quantify the effectiveness of VPIN, we compute the average false positive rate over the 97 most active futures contracts from 2007 to 2012. For each futures contract, we compute the VPIN values to determine the number of VPIN events and number of false positive events. The average FPR reported later is the ratio between the total number of false positive events and the total number of events. Note that we are not taking average of FPRs of different futures contracts to compute the overall FPR. Assuming that each time a VPIN that crosses the threshold from below signals an opportunity for investments—a true event leads to a profitable investment and a false positive event leads to a losing investment—the FPR we use is the fraction of

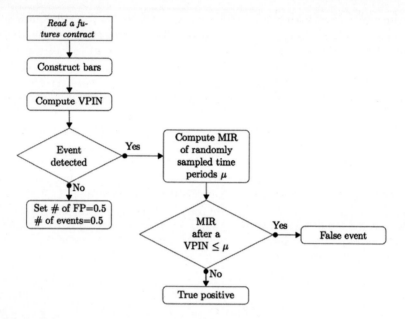

FIGURE 13.3   Flowchart of how a VPIN event is classified.
Source: Wu, Bethel, Gu, Leinweber, Rüebel 2013

"losing" investments. Thus, the overall FPR we use is a meaningful measure of the effectiveness of VPIN.

COMPUTATIONAL COST

From our tests, we observe that reading the futures contracts and constructing bars are one of the most time-consuming steps within the algorithm. For example, an analysis on the computation of VPIN on nine metal futures contracts over the 67-month period shows that reading the raw data took 11.93 percent of the total time, and constructing the bars took 10.35 percent, while the remaining computation required 10.59 percent second. In addition, we ranked the computational cost of each parameter in VPIN. Results show that the construction of the bars is the most time consuming, followed by bucket volume classification, evaluation of VPIN, transformation of VPIN using the error function, and calculation of MIR value—that is, $\beta > v > \sigma > \tau > \eta$.

To reduce the computational cost, the data are read into memory, and the computations are arranged so that the constructed bars are stored in memory. This allows all different computations to be preformed on the bars, with reading the original data again. Furthermore, we arrange our computations so that the intermediate results are reused as much as possible. For example, the same VPIN values can be reused when we change the threshold for event triggers and the event horizon. This knowledge is particularly useful for efficiently testing the sensitivity of the parameters (we need to calculate VPIN values of a large number of points to construct the surrogate model to be later used in sensitivity analysis).

Figure 13.4 shows a breakdown of time needed to construct volume bars with different pricing options. We see that for the weighted median, it requires as much as seven times more time than those of closing, mean, and weighted mean, and for median, as much as five times more.

To better take advantage of the multiple cores in a typical CPU, we implemented multithreaded program to compute false positive rate for each contract independently. Our tests are performed on an IBM DataPlex machine at the NERSC, which imposes a maximum run time of single computational job of 72 hours. For almost all tests, our program terminated in less than 72 hours. For those that did not terminate within the time limitation, we restart the test program using the latest values of the free parameters as their new starting points. Although this approach does succeed in finding the optimal solution, it loses track of the computational history, and therefore the overall optimization process is not as efficient as if we had run through the whole test without interruption. This restart requires more computation time, but should not have affected the final answers we have found.

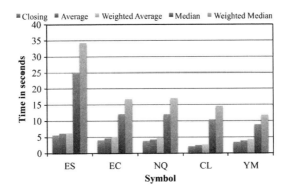

FIGURE 13.4 Time (seconds) needed to construct volume bars with different nominal prices.
Source: Wu, Bethel, Gu, Leinweber, Rüebel 2013

OPTIMIZATION OF FPR

The main goal of an optimization software is solving problems of the form

$$\min_{x \in \Omega} f(x)$$

where Ω is a subset of n-dimensional space with constraints denoted by c_j. The dual of this problem, finding the maximum, can be easily computed by multiplying the objective function by -1. There are many ways to numerically solve an optimization. For simple linear programming, the simplex method is available. For nonlinear problems, one approach is via iterative methods. Depending on the nature of the objective function, specifically differentiability, one can select from a number of existing algorithms.

Popular iterative methods that make use of derivative (or by approximation through finite differences) include quasi-Newton, conjugate gradient, and steepest-descent methods. A major advantage of using the derivatives is improved rate of convergence. There are also well-known software packages such as L-BFGS that implement quasi-Newton methods to solve large-scale optimization problems (Nocedal, Liu 1989).

In the computation of VPIN, the relationship between the free parameters and the final FPR values is defined through a lengthy computation procedure. There is no obvious ways to evaluate whether a small change in any of the parameters will produce small changes in FPR. For such a nonsmooth objective function, approximation of its derivative may not lead to desirable answers. The computational cost of optimization algorithms designed to work without a derivative can also vary greatly from one problem to another. In this case, a successful search strategy is via generalized pattern search (GPS) (Audet, Béchardand, Le Digabel 2008). We say a problem is a blackbox problem if either the objective function(s) or constraints do not behave smoothly. The MADS algorithm (Audet, Dennis 2006) is an extension of the GPS algorithm (Torczon, 1997; Audet, Dennis 2003), which is itself an extension of the coordinate search (Davidon 1991). NOMAD is a C++ implementation of MADS algorithm designed for constrained optimization of a blackbox problem. In this chapter, we deliberately chose NOMAD, as it not only extends the MADS algorithm to incorporate various search strategies, such as VNS (variable neighborhood search), to identify the global minimum of the objective function(s) (Audet, Béchardand, Le Digabel 2008), but also targets blackbox optimization under general nonlinear constraints.

MADS (Mesh Adaptive Direct Search) Algorithm

The main algorithm utilized in NOMAD is the MADS (Audet, Le Digabel, Tribes 2009; Le Digabel 2011), which consists of two main steps: search and poll. During the poll step, it evaluates the objective function f and constraints c_j at mesh points near the current value of x_k. It generates trial mesh points in the vicinity of x_k. It is more rigidly defined than the search step, and is the basis of the convergence analysis of the algorithm (Audet, Le Digabel, and Tribes 2009). Constraints can be blackboxes, nonlinear inequalities, or Boolean. As for x, it can also be integer, binary, or categorical (Le Digabel 2011). Readers interested in detailed explanation on how different constraints and x are treated can refer to Le Digabel (2011).

The MADS algorithm is an extension of the GPS algorithm for optimization problems, which allows polling in a dense set of directions in the space of variables (Audet, Dennis 2008). Both algorithms iteratively search for a solution, where the blackbox functions are repeatedly evaluated at some trial points. If improvements are made, they are accepted, and rejected if not. MADS and GPS generate a mesh at each iteration, and it is expressed in the following way (Audet, Béchardand, and Le Digabel 2008):

$$M(k, \Delta_k) = \bigcup_{x \in V_k} \{x + \Delta_k D_z : z \in \mathbb{N}^{n_D}\}$$

where V_k denotes the collection of points evaluated at the start of kth iteration, $\Delta_k \in \mathbb{R}^+$ the mesh size parameter, and D a constant matrix with rank n. D is, in general, simply chosen to be an orthogonal grid of I_n augmented by $-I_n$, that is, $[I_n \ -I_n]$. The poll directions are not a subset of this matrix D, and can still have much flexibility. This is why no more complicated D is used. For readers interested in a detailed discussion of the algorithm, see the paper by Audet, Béchardand, and Le Digabel (2008).

The search step is crucial in practice for its flexibility, and has the potential to return any point on the underlying mesh, as long as the search does not run into an out-of-memory error. Its main function is narrowing down and searching for a point that can improve the current solution.

Figure 13.5 shows the pseudocode of the MADS algorithm.

NOMAD Optimization Results

Although NOMAD can solve minimization problem involving categorical variables, doing so will significantly reduce the efficiency of the algorithm for this particular case. A breakdown of time needed to construct volume bars with different pricing options shows that weighted median is the most computationally heavy pricing option, with closing price located at the opposite end of the spectrum. Each pricing strategy was considered separately to reduce the amount of time needed for each run of the program submitted to the computer. This arrangement also reduces the complexity of

[0] **Initializations**

> $x_0 \in X, \Delta_0 \in \mathbb{R}^+$
> $k \leftarrow 0$

[1] **Poll and search steps**

> Search step
>> evaluate the functions on a finite number
>> of points of $M(k, \Delta_k)$
>
> Poll step
>> compute p MADS directions $D_k \in \mathbb{R}^{n \times p}$
>> construct the frame $P_k \subseteq M(k, \Delta_k)$
>> with x_k, D_k, and Δ_k
>> evaluate the functions on the p points of P_k

[2] **Updates**

> determine the type of success of iteration k
> solution update (x_{k+1})
> mesh update (Δ_{k+1})
> $k \leftarrow k + 1$
> check the stopping conditions, **goto** [1]

FIGURE 13.5 MADS algorithm.
Source: Audet, Béchardand,
Le Digabel 2008

understanding of the parameter space and allows for obtaining a better solution set. Solutions obtained from different starting points are shown in Table 13.4. The optimal parameter combination from Table 13.4 is

π	β	σ	η	υ	τ	α
Median	1528	0.1636	0.033	0.4611	0.9949	0.0340

However, varying initial choices of the parameters under the same pricing strategy is shown to be inconsistent, which suggests that the global optimal solution might still be out of reach. We attempted to reach this global optimal solution by enabling the variable neighborhood search (VNS) strategy.

Variable Neighborhood Search (VNS) Strategy

The VNS is a metaheuristic strategy proposed by Mladenović and Hansen (1997) for not only solving global optimization problems, but also combinatorial problems. It incorporates a descent method and a neighborhood structure to systematically search for the global minimum. For an initial solution x, the descent method searches through a direction of descent from x with respect to the neighborhood structure $N(x)$, and proceeds to find the minimum of $f(x)$ within $N(x)$. This process is repeated until no improvement is possible.

[0] **Initializations**

$$it_{max}, \xi_{max}, \xi_0, \delta \in \mathbb{N}^+$$
$$x_0 \in X$$
$$k \leftarrow 0, \; it \leftarrow 0$$

[1] **while** $(it \leq it_{max})$

$\xi_k \leftarrow \xi_0$

    while $(\xi_k \leq \xi_{max})$

        $x' \leftarrow shaking(x_k, \xi_k)$

        $x'' \leftarrow descent(x')$

        if $\left(f(x'') < f(x_k)\right)$

            $x_{k+1} \leftarrow x''$

            $\xi_{k+1} \leftarrow \xi_0$

        else

            $x_{k+1} \leftarrow x_k$

            $\xi_{k+1} \leftarrow \xi_k + \delta$

        $k \leftarrow k + 1$

$it \leftarrow it + 1$

FIGURE 13.6 Pseudocode of VNS.
Source: Audet, Béchardand, and Le Digabel 2008

The neighborhood structure could play a critical role in finding the global optimum. VNS makes use of a random perturbation method when the algorithm detects it has found a local optimum. This perturbed value generally differs to a large extent so as to find an improved local optimum and escape from the previous localized subset of Ω. The perturbation method, which is parameterized by a non-negative scalar ξ_k, depends heavily on the neighborhood structure. The order of the perturbation, ξ_k, denotes the VNS amplitude at kth iteration. Figure 13.6 succinctly summarizes the algorithm into two steps: the current best solution is perturbed by ξ_k, and VNS performs the descent method from the perturbed point. If an improved solution is discovered, it replaces the current best solution, and ξ_k is reset to the initial value. If not, a non-negative number δ (the VNS increment) is added to ξ_k, and resumes the descent method. This process is repeated until ξ_k reaches/exceeds a maximum amplitude ξ_{max} (Audet, Le Digabel, and Tribes 2009; Audet Béchardand, Le Digabel 2008; Mladenović, and Hansen 1997).

VNS in NOMAD

The VNS algorithm is incorporated in NOMAD as a search step (called the VNS search). If no improvement is achieved during MADS's iteration, new trial points are created closer to the poll center. The VNS, however, focuses its search on a distant neighborhood with larger perturbation amplitude. Since the poll step remains the same, as long as the following two conditions are met, no further works are needed for convergence analysis (Audet, Béchardand, and Le Digabel 2008).

1. For each ith iteration, all the VNS trial points must be inside the mesh $M(i, \Delta_i)$.
2. Their numbers must be finite.

To use VNS strategy in NOMAD, the user must define a parameter that sets the upper bound for the number of VNS blackbox evaluations. This number, called VNS_SEARCH, is expressed as the ratio of VNS blackbox evaluations to the total number of blackbox evaluations. The default value is 0.75 (Audet, Le Digabel, and Tribes 2009).

VNS Optimization Results

Table 13.5 shows a collection of optimization results with VNS strategy enabled. The two lowest FPRs obtained are 2.44 percent and 2.58 percent, using the following parameter set, respectively.

Even though the improvement is a mere 1 percent, these data sets are much more valuable for practical uses (especially the second set). The number of events detected for

π	β	σ	η	υ	τ	α
Median	1528	0.1636	0.033	0.4611	0.9949	0.0340

is 1518, whereas those for the two sets in Table 13.2 are 2062 and 2298. These two sets convey improved accuracy and precision. Furthermore, the second set of Table 13.2 detected more VPIN events than the first and is computationally more efficient. Given the difference in FPR is minimal,

TABLE 13.2 Non-VNS Optimal Parameter Sets.

π	β	σ	η	υ	τ
Weighted median	1784	0.0756	0.0093	49.358	0.9936
Mean	1836	0.0478	0.0089	0.9578	0.9952

π	β	σ	η	υ	τ	α
Mean	1836	0.0478	0.0089	0.9578	0.9952	0.0258

is more suited to be used in practice. Even so, VNS strategy failed to address the divergence of FPR when different starting parameters are chosen. We attempted to resolve this issue by increasing both the maximum blackbox evaluations and VNS_SEARCH (Table 13.3).

These two sets were both found with maximum blackbox evaluations of 5,000 and VNS_SEARCH = 0.75. However, no direct correlation of the values of these parameters with consistent FPR was observed. Maximum blackbox evaluations was set to 6,000 and VNS_SEARCH = 0.85. Yet, NOMAD returned FPR that is inferior to the two above.

π	β	σ	η	υ	τ	α
Closing	1799	0.6274	0.0662	0	0.9786	0.0578

From Table 13.5, we observe that the majority of FPR falls consistently within the range of 3 percent to 5 percent. Even though the optimization procedure consistently produces parameter combinations that give us FPR between 3 percent and 5 percent, the parameter values are actually different. Our next task is to understand the sensitivity of these parameter choices, that is, how the different parameter choices affect our effectiveness measure, FPR (Table 13.4).

UNCERTAINTY QUANTIFICATION (UQ)

In many cases of mathematical modeling, we do not have complete knowledge of the system or its intrinsic variability. These uncertainties arise from

TABLE 13.3 VNS Optimal Parameter Sets.

π	β	σ	η	υ	τ	α
Closing	1888	0.1578	0.0480	45.221	0.9942	0.0412
Closing	1600	0.3586	0.0482	10.371	0.9847	0.0458

TABLE 13.4 Optimization Results with Different Starting Points.

	Starting Point					Final						
	β	σ	η	υ	τ	β	σ	η	υ	τ	α	# of Events
Closing	200	1	0.25	0	0.99	243	1.0009	0.2484	9.613	0.9902	0.0668	1026
	20	1	0.25	0	0.8	121	1.6966	0.3311	5.2338	0.9917	0.0736	746
	2000	2	1	50	0.9999	1797	0.1314	0.0130	8.6047	0.9928	0.0401	2058
Mean	200	1	0.25	0	0.99	198	0.9970	0.2520	5.0195	0.9896	0.0759	1126
	20	1	0.25	0	0.99	314	1.0003	0.2500	10.061	0.9899	0.0752	995
Median	200	1	0.25	0	0.99	175	1.0205	0.2451	10.954	0.9905	0.0632	1087
	20	1	0.25	0	0.8	219	1.0880	0.2500	24.600	0.9937	0.0773	608
	2000	2	1	50	0.999	1528	0.1636	0.0327	0.4611	0.9949	0.0340	1518
WMean	200	1	0.25	0	0.99	200	1.0003	0.2501	4.9970	0.9900	0.0787	1073
	20	1	0.25	0	0.8	135	1.2246	0.2939	41.608	0.9858	0.0869	1393
WMedian	200	1	0.25	0	0.99	200	0.7063	0.4495	14.9968	0.9900	0.0720	1331
	20	1	0.25	0	0.8	273	1.2496	0.4738	9.9808	0.9908	0.0783	832
	2000	2	1	50	0.999	1998	1.116	0.9977	49.952	0.9934	0.1060	533

TABLE 13.5 VNS Optimization Results with Different Starting Points.

	Starting Point					Final						
	β	σ	η	υ	τ	β	σ	η	υ	τ	α	# of Events
Closing	1300	1.2	0.25	4	0.99	1799	0.6274	0.0662	0	0.9786	0.0578	1455
	200	1	0.003	0	0.99	1888	0.1578	0.0480	45.221	0.9942	0.0412	1184
	2000	2	1.0	50	0.9999	1600	0.3586	0.0482	10.371	0.9847	0.0458	1724
Mean	2000	2	1	50	0.9999	1606	0.0565	0.0118	35.361	0.9944	0.0306	2177
	200	1	0.003	0	0.99	1845	0.0401	0.0093	14.943	0.9972	0.0319	2300
	1300	1.2	0.25	4	0.99	1836	0.0478	0.0089	0.9578	0.9952	0.0258	2298
Median	1300	1.2	0.25	4	0.99	1745	0.0798	0.0156	7.0073	0.9937	0.0369	2005
	200	1	0.003	0	0.99	624	0.4338	0.0449	47.891	0.9905	0.0457	1369
WMean	200	1	0.003	0	0.99	1789	0.4539	0.0639	2.4991	0.9905	0.0442	878
WMedian	1300	1.2	0.25	4	0.99	1784	0.0756	0.0093	49.358	0.9936	0.0244	2062
	200	1	0.003	0	0.99	1631	0.0433	0.0098	33.763	0.9943	0.0329	2651

different places such as parameter uncertainty, model inadequacy, numerical uncertainty, parametric variability, experimental uncertainty, and interpolation uncertainty (Kennedy and O'Hagan 2001). Therefore, even if the model is deterministic, we cannot rely on a single deterministic simulation (Le Maître and Knio 2010). We must, therefore, quantify the uncertainties through different methods. Validation of the surrogate model and analysis of variance are frequently used to carry out UQ and sensitivity analysis.

Validation involves checking whether the surrogate model constructed from the original model correctly represents our model. Analysis of variance provides users with important information relevant to design and optimization. The user can identify the controllability of the system, as measured through sensitivity analysis, and characterize the robustness of the prediction (Najm 2009). There are two ways to approach UQ: forward UQ and inverse UQ. UQTK makes use of the former to perform its tasks.

UQTK

A UQ problem involves quantitatively understanding the relationships between uncertain parameters and their mathematical model. Two methodologies for UQ are forward UQ and inverse UQ. The spectral polynomial chaos expansion (PCE) is the main technique used for forward UQ. First introduced by Wiener (1938), polynomial chaos (PC) determines evolution of uncertainty using a nonsampling based method, when there is probabilistic uncertainty in the system parameters. Debusschere, Najm, Pébay, Knio, Ghanem, and Le Maître (2004) note advantages to using a PCE:

1. Efficient uncertainty propagation
2. Computationally efficient global sensitivity analysis
3. Construction of an inexpensive surrogate model, a cheaper model that can replace the original for time-consuming analysis, such as calibration, optimization, or inverse UQ

We make use of the orthogonality and structure of PC bases to carry out variance-based sensitivity analysis.

From a practical perspective, understanding how the system is influenced by uncertainties in properties is essential. One way of doing so is through analysis of the variance (ANOVA), a collection of statistical models that analyzes group mean and variance. The stochastic expansion of the solution provides an immediate way to characterize variabilities induced by different sources of uncertainties. This is achieved by making use of the orthogonality of the PC bases, making the dependency of the uncertain data and model solution obvious.

The Sobol (or the Hoeffding) decomposition of any second-order deterministic functional f allows for expressing the variance of f in the following way (Le Maître and Knio 2010)

$$V(f) = \langle (f - f_\emptyset)^2 \rangle = \sum_{\substack{s \in \{1,\ldots,N\} \\ s \neq \emptyset}} f_s^2$$

where $f_\emptyset \equiv \langle f \rangle$. Since $V_s(f) \equiv \langle f_s \rangle$ contributes to the total variance among the set of random parameters $\{x_i,\ i \in s\}$, this decomposition is frequently used to analyze the uncertainty of the model. Then for all $s \in \{1, \dots, N\}$, we can calculate sensitivity indices as the ratio of the variance due to x_i, $V_i(f)$, to $V(f)$, such that summing up the indices yields 1 (Le Maître and Knio 2010).

$$\sum_{\substack{s \in \{1, \dots, N\} \\ s \neq \emptyset}} S_s = 1, \ S_s = \frac{V_{s(f)}}{V(f)}$$

The set $\{S_s\}$ is *Sobol sensitivity indices* that are based on variance fraction—that is, they denote fraction of output variance that is attributed to the given input.

UQTK first builds quadrature using a user-specified number of sampled points from each parameter. For each controllable input, we evaluate it with each point of the quadrature to construct PCE for the model. Next, we create the surrogate model and conduct global sensitivity analysis using the approach just described.

UQ Results

Based on the formulation of VPIN, it can be readily understood that the objective function behaves smoothly with respect to the CDF threshold, τ. The higher the cutoff, the smaller the number of events detected. The objective function must behave smoothly with respect to its controllable input, so we conducted sensitivity analysis with τ as the controllable input, consisting of 19 equidistant nodes in the corresponding interval of Table 13.6. The quadrature is generated by taking samples of five points from each of β, σ, η, *and* υ. The pricing strategy used here is closing, and this is for practical reasons: Wu, Bethel, Gu, Leinweber, and Rüebel reported in 2013 relative computational costs for five largest futures contracts with different nominal prices, ranking weighted median, median, weighted average, average,

TABLE 13.6 Parameter Bounds Using Five Sampled Points, with τ as the Controllable Input.

	Lower Bound	Upper Bound
π	0	0
β	20	2000
σ	0.04	2.0
η	0.003	1.0
υ	0	50
τ	0.98	0.9999

and closing in descending order (see Figure 13.4). Because these five futures contracts (S&P 500 E-mini, Euro FX, Nasdaq 100, Light Crude NYMEX, and Dow Jones E-mini) constitute approximately 38.8 percent of the total volume, closing price will still be the most efficient strategy for our data set. In addition, many high-frequency traders opt to use closing price in their daily trading.

From Table 13.7, β and σ are the two most influential parameters. Sobol index of v is reasonable as well, given no uniform behavior of v was observed from outputs of NOMAD and Wu's paper. We interpret these numbers in the following way: Assuming the inputs are uniformly distributed random variables over their respective bounds, then the output will be a random uncertain quantity whose variance fraction contributions are given in Table 13.7 by Sobol indices. We then plot the semilog of the indices for each value of CDF threshold (Figure 13.7).

We see from Figure 13.7 consistent Sobol indices of BPD and its dominance over those of other parameters. The indices of support window and event horizon do behave similarly until $\tau \approx 1$, at which point we observe sudden fluctuation of the numbers. This is largely due to abnormal behavior of the objective function when the CDF threshold is close to 1. If we set the threshold too high, only a small fraction of events will be detected, in which case the objective function would return high FPR (refer to Figure 13.4). Hence, the anomaly is not too unreasonable. The plot also shows a nonuniform behavior of BVC parameter's Sobol indices. In addition, its contribution to overall sensitivity is minimal. When the degree of freedom (v) for the Student's t-distribution is large enough, the t-distribution behaves very much like the standard normal distribution. Figure 13.7 shows minimal sensitivity from BVC parameter. As such, we let $v = 0$ for the remainder of our studies for computational simplicity. In order to see the sensitivity due to τ and how the model behaves with different π, we set π to be the controllable input and changed the bounds to reflect more practical choices of the parameters.

Even though π is a categorical variable, it is used here as the index at which the sensitivities are computed. The controllable input is a way to index multiple sensitivity analysis being performed at once—that is, the

TABLE 13.7 Joint Sobol Sensitivity Indices.

	β	σ	η	v
β	0.14684	0.00521	0.02406	8.2694e-05
σ	0	0.74726	0.02441	0.00022
η	0	0	0.05407	7.0616e-05
v	0	0	0	0.00020

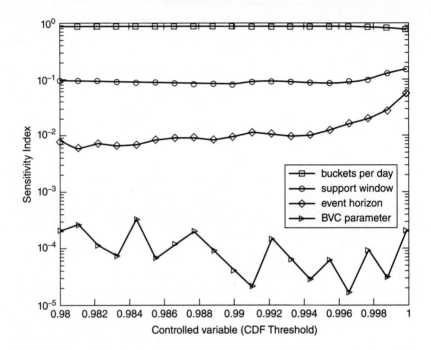

FIGURE 13.7 Semilog of Sobol indices of the four parameters.

controllable input can be the x location where we compute the sensitivities of the observable of interest, or it could be the index of the categorical value at which we want to get the sensitivities, or it could even be the index of multiple observables in the same model for which we want sensitivities. As such, using π as the controllable input does not bar us from carrying out sensitivity analysis (Tables 13.8, 13.9).

We then made the mesh even finer by setting the lower and upper bounds to include the majority of output parameters found in Table 13.5. The ranges are shown in Table 13.10. We sought to find out which parameter is the most influential one in these bounds. From Table 13.11, we see that no other parameters except η behave in a volatile way. As these bounds did not provide much insight to other variables, we changed the bounds so that they correspond to the parameters of the lowest FPRs. Ranges are specified in Table 13.12. The Sobol indices in Table 13.13 tell us that β and τ become insignificant when they are chosen in these intervals. σ and η, however, are extremely volatile, and most responsible for the variance of the objective function. We see from Table 13.11 and 13.13 that pricing options play minimal role in contributing to the overall sensitivity. Within the bounds

TABLE 13.8 Parameter Bounds with π as Controllable Input (5 Sampled Points).

	Lower Bound	Upper Bound
π	All Five Pricing Strategies	
β	200	2000
σ	0.05	1.0
η	0.01	0.2
υ	0	0
τ	0.98	0.999

TABLE 13.9 Sobol Sensitivity Indices.

	Pricing Strategies				
	Closing	Mean	Median	WMean	WMedian
β	0.01485	0.01653	0.01369	0.014465	0.012892
σ	0.42402	0.42017	0.41921	0.424548	0.415468
η	0.47059	0.46618	0.47463	0.465356	0.478596
τ	0.05595	0.05951	0.05672	0.058370	0.059124

TABLE 13.10 Parameter Bounds with π as Controllable Input (7 Sampled Points).

	Lower Bound	Upper Bound
π	All Five Pricing Strategies	
β	1400	2000
σ	0.04	0.5
η	0.003	0.01
υ	0	0
τ	0.98	0.999

prescribed in Table 13.10 and 13.12, it is suggested that the user select closing, unweighted mean, or weighted mean for computational efficiency.

The sensitivity analysis tells us that the range of each parameter we specify affects each one's relative importance. Initially, the support window and buckets per day were the dominant variables. As we made the mesh finer and changed it to correspond to the best results from NOMAD, we see that the event horizon and the support window become the determining parameters that control the variance of the objective function. This indicates that when

TABLE 13.11   Sobol Sensitivity Indices.

	Pricing Strategies				
	Closing	Mean	Median	WMean	WMedian
β	0.0083	0.0096	0.0096	0.0120	0.0088
σ	0.0416	0.0468	0.0480	0.0449	0.0471
η	0.9302	0.9269	0.9255	0.9258	0.9267
τ	0.0154	0.0124	0.0128	0.0131	0.0126

TABLE 13.12   Parameter Bounds with π as Controllable Input (7 Sampled Points).

	Lower Bound	Upper Bound
π	All Five Pricing Strategies	
β	1600	1888
σ	0.04	0.628
η	0.008	0.067
υ	0	0
τ	0.97	0.998

TABLE 13.13   Sobol Sensitivity Indices.

	Pricing Strategies				
	Closing	Mean	Median	WMean	WMedian
β	0.00040	0.00011	0.00011	0.00020	0.00050
σ	0.21397	0.22682	0.22386	0.22622	0.21967
η	0.70543	0.68904	0.69084	0.68912	0.69510
τ	0.05749	0.06118	0.06136	0.06090	0.06101

the number of buckets per day is between 1600 and 1888, and the VPIN threshold is between 0.97 and 0.998, their exact values have little influence on the resulting FPR.

CONCLUSION

We have analytically explored the parameter space of VPIN by rigorously searching for the global minimum FPR and conducting sensitivity analysis on a number of parameter bounds. Although we were not successful in finding the global minimizer of FPR, our test results from VNS optimization displayed some degree of consistency.

To better understand the parameter choices, we used uncertainty quantification to analyze the objective function's sensitivity with respect to each parameter. Results indicate oscillatory behavior of BVC parameter and minimal fluctuations observed in buckets per day, support window, and event horizon for τ not too close to 1. Studying changes in variance under different pricing strategies informed us that within the bounds obtained from NOMAD output, they play minimal role in determining the FPR.

From our analysis, we suggest using the following ranges of parameters for practical applications of VPIN:

- Using the mean price within a bar as the nominal price for the bar. Computing mean is quite efficient. Although there was little to no variation when using other pricing options, mean did yield one of the lowest FPRs.
- Sensitivity analysis shows the contribution from buckets per day is negligible when its values are between 1600 and 1800. We suggest using a number that lies in an interval of about 1836.
- Support window is an important parameter. Even a small perturbation can cause a drastic difference in FPR. We suggest the user to use a number very close to 0.0478.
- Event horizon is another important variable to consider. Like support window, it is highly volatile. We suggest the user to use 0.0089.
- CDF threshold is important. However, the analysis shows that as long as we are working with $\tau > 0.98$, its influence becomes minimal (but it should never be too close to 1).

Easley, López de Prado, and O'Hara (2010) stated some potential applications of the VPIN metric:

- Benchmark for execution brokers filling their customers' orders. The clients can also monitor their brokers' actions and measure how effectively they avoided adverse selection.
- A warning sign for market regulators who can regulate market activity under different flow toxicity level.
- An instrument for volatility arbitrage.

We believe that results from our optimization and sensitivity analysis can aid in improving the efficiency of the VPIN metric.

Acknowledgments: We would like to thank the Department of Energy's Workforce Development of Teachers and Scientists as well as Workforce

Development and Education at Berkeley Lab for initially supporting this research. We would also like to thank Dr. Bert Debusschere for his help with UQTK.

REFERENCES

Abad, D., and J. Yague. 2012. From PIN to VPIN: An introduction to order flow toxicity. *The Spanish Review of Financial Economics* 10 (2):74–83.

Audet, C., V. Béchardand, and S. Le Digabel. 2008. Nonsmooth optimization through mesh adaptive direct search and variable neighborhood search. *Journal of Global Optimization* 41 (2): 299–318.

Audet, C., S. Le Digabel, and C. Tribes. 2009. NOMAD user guide. *Technical Report G-2009–37.*

Audet, C., and J. E. Dennis Jr., 2006. Mesh adaptive direct search algorithms for constrained optimization. *SIAM Journal on Optimization* 17 (1): 188–217.

_____. 2003. Analysis of generalized pattern searches. *SIAM Journal on Optimization,* 13 (3): 889–903.

Bowley, G. 2010. Lone $4.1 billion sale led to "Flash Crash" in May. *The New York Times.*

_____. 2010. Stock swing still baffles, ominously. *The New York Times.*

Debusschere, B. J., H. N. Najm, P. P. Pébay, O. M. Knnio, R. G. Ghanem, and O. P. Le Maître. 2004. Numerical challenges in the use of polynomial chaos representations for stochastic processes. *SIAM J. Sci. Comp.* 26 (2): 698–719.

Easley, D., N. M. Kiefer, M. O'Hara, and J. B. Paperman. 1996. Liquidity, information, and infrequently traded stocks. *The Journal of Finance* 51 (4): 1405–1436.

Easley, D., M. López de Prado, and M. O'Hara. 2011. The microstructure of the "Flash Crash": Flow toxicity, liquidity crashes and the probability of informed trading. *Journal of Portfolio Management* 37 (2): 118–128.

_____. 2012. Flow toxicity and liquidity in a high frequency world. *Review of Financial Studies* 25 (5): 1457,1493.

_____. 2012. The Volume Clock: Insights into the High Frequency Paradigm. http://ssrn.com/abstract=2034858.

Ellis, K., R. Michaely, and M. O'Hara. 2000. The accuracy of trade classification rules: Evidence from NASDAQ. *Journal of Financial and Quantitative Analysis.*

Flood, J. 2010. *NYSE* confirms price reporting delays that contributed to the Flash Crash. *AI5000.*

Goldfarb, Z. 2010. Report examines May's Flash Crash, expresses concern over high-speed trading. *The Washington Post.*

Gordon, M., and D. Wagner. 2010. "Flash Crash" report: Waddell & Reed's $4.1 billion trade blamed for market plunge. *Huffington Post.*

Kennedy, M., and A. O'Hagan. 2001. Bayesian calibration of computer models. *Journal of the Royal Statistical Society.* Series B Volume 63, Issue 3.

Krasting, B. 2010. *The yen did it. Seeking Alpha.*

Lauricella, T. 2010. Market plunge baffles Wall Street—Trading glitch suspected in "mayhem" as Dow falls nearly 1,000, then bounces. *The Wall Street Journal*, p. 1.

Lauricella, T., and S. Patterson. 2010. Did a big bet help trigger "black swan" stock swoon? *The Wall Street Journal*.

Lauricella, T., K. Scannell, and J. Strasburg. 2010. How a trading algorithm went awry. *The Wall Street Journal*.

Le Digabel, S. 2011. Algorithm 909: NOMAD: Nonlinear optimization with the MADS algorithm. *ACM Transactions on Mathematical Software* 37 (4): 44:1–44:15.

Le Maître, O., P. Knio, and M. Omar. 2010. *Spectral Methods for Uncertainty Quantification: With Applications to Computational Fluid Dynamics (Scientific Computation)*, 1st ed. New York: Springer.

López de Prado, M. 2011. *Advances in High Frequency Strategies*. Madrid, Complutense University.

Mladenović, N., and P. Hansen. 1997. Variable neighborhood search. *Computers and Optimization Research* 24 (11): 1097–1100.

Najm, H. N. 2009. Uncertainty quantification and polynomial chaos techniques in computational fluid dynamics. *Annual Review of Fluid Mechanics* 41: 35–52.

Nocedal, J., and D. C. Liu. 1989. *On the Limited Memory for Large Scale Optimization*. *Mathematical Programming B* 45 (3): 503–528.

Phillips, M. 2010. SEC's Schapiro: Here's my timeline of the Flash Crash. *The Wall Street Journal*.

Sargsyan, K., C. Safta, B. Debusschere, and H. Najm. 2012. Uncertainty quantification given discontinuous model response and a limited number of model runs. *SIAM Journal on Scientific Computing* 34 (1): B44–B64.

Wiener N. 1938. The homogeneous chaos. *American Journal of Mathematics* 60 (4): 897–936.

Wu, Ke., W. Bethel, M. Gu, D. Leinweber, and O. Ruebel. 2013. A big data approach to analyzing market volatility. *Algorithmic Finance* 2 (3-4): 241–267.

CHAPTER 14

Covariance Specification Tests for Multivariate GARCH Models[1]

Gregory Koutmos

Charles F. Dolan School of Business, Fairfield University

INTRODUCTION

Proper modeling of the variances and covariances of financial assets is extremely important for many reasons. For example, risk premia are typically a function of risk that is mostly measured by the variance or the covariance of the asset of interest with some market index. Similarly, risk management requires the use of the variance–covariance matrix of portfolios of risky assets.

Recently, research interest has focused on the time variability of variances and covariances with the use of ARCH-type models. The autoregressive conditionally heteroskedastic model (ARCH) was proposed by Engle (1982) as a way of modeling volatility clustering. Even though the model was originally applied to UK unemployment data, it has been particularly successful in the modeling of variances of financial time series. There is a plethora of applications of univariate ARCH-type models in the area of finance (see Bollerslev, Chou, and Kroner 1992, for an excellent survey). Bollerslev, Engle, and Wooldridge (1988) introduced and estimated the first multivariate GARCH class of models. Koutmos and Booth (1995) introduced a multivariate exponential GARCH model to study volatility spillovers across major national stock markets.

---

[1] The title of an earlier version of this paper was: "Cross-Moment Specification Tests" Working paper, Charles F. Dolan School of Business, Fairfield University.

The class of ARCH-type models has been extremely useful in terms of accommodating various hypotheses as well as stylized facts observed in financial time series. Consequently, there have been several versions of these models at both the univariate and the multivariate level (see for example Andersen et al. 2006). Such variety, however, created the need to discriminate among different versions in terms of how well they fit the data. To facilitate the model selection process Engle and Ang (1993) introduced a series of diagnostics based on the news impact curve implied by the particular ARCH model used. The premise is that if the volatility process is correctly specified, then the squared standardized residuals should not be predictable on the basis of observed variables. Using these tests, we can determine how well the particular model captures asymmetries in the variance, and how well it accommodates large negative and positive innovations.

These tests have been proven very useful and easy to implement. However, there has been no similar set of tests to evaluate the performance of multivariate versions of ARCH-type models. In this chapter, I propose a set of covariance diagnostics along the lines of Engle and Ng (1993). These diagnostics can guide the researcher in terms of the appropriateness of the particular specification for the covariance function. Such diagnostics are essential for multivariate ARCH models, especially since in many instances the various covariance specifications cannot be nested making it impossible to use nested hypotheses testing to decide among models.

The rest of this chapter is organized as follows: First is the description of the covariance specification tests and the estimation procedures, followed by a comparison of three covariance specifications using standard traditional tests as well as the proposed covariance specification tests.

COVARIANCE SPECIFICATION TESTS

The volatility specification tests proposed by Engle and Ng (1993) can be described by the following set of equations:

$$\text{Sign bias test: } z^2_t = a + b\,S^-_{t-1} + e_t \tag{14.1}$$

$$\text{Negative sign bias test: } z^2_t = a + b\,S^-_{t-1}\varepsilon_{t-1} + e_t \tag{14.2}$$

$$\text{Positive sign bias test: } z^2_t = a + b(1 - S^-_{t-1})\varepsilon_{t-1} + e_t \tag{14.3}$$

$$\text{Joint test: } z^2_t = a + b_1 S^-_t + b_2 S^-_{t-1}\varepsilon_{t-1} + b_3(1 - S^-_{t-1})\varepsilon_{t-1} + e_t \tag{14.4}$$

where ε_t and σ_t are the estimated residuals and the standard deviations from the particular ARCH type model used, $z_t = \varepsilon_t/\sigma_t$ are the standardized residuals, S^-_{t-1} is a dummy variable that takes the value of unity if ε_{t-1} is negative and zero otherwise, and e_t is an error term. The premise is that if the volatility process is correctly specified, then the squared standardized residuals should not be predictable on the basis of observed variables.

The first test examines the impact of positive and negative innovations on volatility not predicted by the model. The squared residuals are regressed against a constant and the dummy S^-_{t-1}. The test is based on the t-statistic for S^-_{t-1}. The negative size bias test examines how well the model captures the impact of large and small negative innovations. It is based on the regression of the standardized residuals against a constant and $S^-_{t-1}\varepsilon_{t-1}$. The calculated t-statistic for $S^-_{t-1}\varepsilon_{t-1}$ is used in this test. The positive sign bias test examines possible biases associated with large and small positive innovations. Here, the standardized filtered residuals are regressed against a constant and $(1 - S^-_{t-1})\varepsilon_{t-1}$. Again, the t-statistic for $(1 - S^-_{t-1})\varepsilon_{t-1}$ is used to test for possible biases. Finally, the joint test is an F-test based on a regression that includes all three variables; that is, $S^-_{t-1}, S^-_{t-1}\varepsilon_{t-1}$, and $(1 - S^-_{t-1})\varepsilon_{t-1}$.

As mentioned earlier, even though these diagnostics are applied routinely to determine the fit of volatility models, they provide no evidence regarding the fit of covariance models in the case of multivariate ARCH models. As such, I propose extending the Engle and Ng (1993) tests to the specification of the covariance function. The idea is that if the covariance of the returns of two assets i and j is correctly specified, then information regarding the past sign and size of the innovations of the two assets should not be able to predict the product of cross-standardized residuals.

Let $\xi_{i,j,t} = (\varepsilon_{i,t}/\sigma_{i,t})(\varepsilon_{j,t}/\sigma_{j,t})$ be the product of standardized residuals, $S^-_{i,t}$ a dummy that takes the value of 1 if $\varepsilon_{i,t} < 0$ and zero otherwise and $S^-_{j,t}$ a dummy that takes the value of 1 if $\varepsilon_{j,t} < 0$ and zero otherwise. The proposed tests can then be based on the following regressions:

Sign bias test: $\xi_{i,j,t} = b_0 + b_1 S^-_{i,t-1} + b_2 S^-_{j,t-1} + u_t$ (14.5)

Negative size bias test: $\xi_{i,j,t} = b_0 + b_1 S^-_{i,t-1}\varepsilon_{i,t-1}$

$$+ b_2 S^-_{j,t-1}\varepsilon_{j,t-1} + u_t \qquad (14.6)$$

Positive size bias test: $\xi_{i,j,t} = b_0 + b_1(1 - S^-_{i,t-1})\varepsilon_{i,t-1}$

$$+ b_2(1 - S^-_{j,t-1})\varepsilon_{j,t-1} + u_t \qquad (14.7)$$

Joint test: $\xi_{i,j,t} = b_0 + b_1 S^-_{i,t-1} + b_2 S^-_{j,t-1} + b_3 S^-_{i,t-1}\varepsilon_{i,t-1}$

$$+ b_4 S^-_{j,t-1}\varepsilon_{j,t-1} + b_5(1 - S^-_{i,t-1})\varepsilon_{i,t-1} + b_6(1 - S^-_{j,t-1})\varepsilon_{j,t-1} + u_t \quad (14.8)$$

If the covariance model is correctly specified, then we should expect the coefficients in regressions above to be jointly zero. Thus, individual t-tests and/or F-tests could be used to test the null hypothesis of correct specification. Given that these are multivariate regressions, the F-statistics is more appropriate.

APPLICATION OF COVARIANCE SPECIFICATION TESTS

In this section, I estimate a bivariate GARCH model with three different covariance specifications. The bivariate model used can be described by the following set of equations:

$$r_{i,t} = \mu_{i,t} + \varepsilon_{i,t} \tag{14.9}$$

$$r_{j,t} = \mu_{j,t} + \varepsilon_{j,t} \tag{14.10}$$

$$\sigma^2_{i,t} = \alpha_{i,0} + \alpha_{i,1}\varepsilon^2_{i,t-1} + \alpha_{i,2}\sigma^2_{i,t-1} + \delta_i S_{i,t-1}\varepsilon^2_{i,t-1} \tag{14.11}$$

$$\sigma^2_{j,t} = \alpha_{j,0} + \alpha_{j,1}\varepsilon^2_{j,t-1} + \alpha_{j,2}\sigma^2_{j,t-1} + \delta_j S_{j,t-1}\varepsilon^2_{j,t-1} \tag{14.12}$$

where, $r_{i,t}$ and $r_{j,t}$ are the continuously compounded returns on assets i and j; $\mu_{i,t}$ and $\mu_{j,t}$ are the conditional means; $\sigma^2_{i,t}, \sigma^2_{j,t}$ are the conditional variances; and $\varepsilon_{i,t}$ and $\varepsilon_{j,t}$ are innovations or error terms. Equations (14.11) and (14.12) specify the conditional volatility along the lines of a standard GARCH(1,1) process amended by the terms $\delta_i S_{i,t-1}\varepsilon^2_{i,t-1}$ and $\delta_j S_{j,t-1}\varepsilon^2_{j,t-1}$ where, $S_{k,t-1} = 1$ if $\varepsilon_{k,t-1} < 0$ and zero otherwise for $k = i, j$. These terms are designed to capture any potential asymmetry in the conditional variance (see Glosten, Jagannathan, and Runkle 1989). Such asymmetries have been attributed to changes in the financial leverage so much so that asymmetric volatility has been termed *the leverage effect*, even though such an explanation is not very convincing (see, e.g., Bekaert and Wu 2000; Koutmos 1998; and Koutmos and Saidi 1995).

Completion of the system requires that the functional form of the covariance be specified. I use three alternative specifications for the purpose of applying the cross-moment tests discussed earlier. It should be pointed out that in the context of the bivariate model the cross-moment is simply the covariance. The three alternative covariance specifications are as follows:

$$\sigma_{i,j,t} = \rho_{i,j}\sigma_{i,t}\sigma_{j,t} \tag{14.13a}$$

$$\sigma_{i,j,t} = \gamma_0 + \gamma_1\varepsilon_{i,t-1}\varepsilon_{j,t-1} + \gamma_2\sigma_{i,j,t} \tag{14.13b}$$

$$\sigma_{i,j,t} = \gamma_0 + \gamma_1\varepsilon_{i,t-1}\varepsilon_{j,t-1} + \gamma_2\sigma_{i,j,t} + \delta_3 S_{i,t-1}\varepsilon_{i,t-1} + \delta_4 S_{j,t-1}\varepsilon_{j,t-1} \tag{14.13c}$$

The first model (14.13a) is the *constant correlation model* introduced by Bollerslev (1990). This model assumes that the conditional correlation

$\rho_{i,j}$ is constant. It has been used extensively in the literature, especially for large-scale systems because of its simplicity. Model (14.13b) is the vector GARCH model introduced by Bollerslev, Engle, and Wooldridge (1988). It models the covariance as function of the product of past innovations and past covariances. It has more flexibility because it allows for a time varying conditional correlation. Model (14.13c) is the *asymmetric vector GARCH model*. It is basically an extended version of (14.13b), where the extension consists of allowing the covariance to respond asymmetrically to past innovations from assets i and j in which $S_{i,t-1}$ and $S_{j,t-1}$ are dummy variables taking the value of 1 if the corresponding past innovations are negative and zero otherwise.

The bivariate GARCH model is estimated allowing alternatively the covariance to follow (14.13a), (14.13b), and (14.13c). Subsequently the residuals from the three models are subjected to the covariance specification diagnostics.

EMPIRICAL FINDINGS AND DISCUSSION

The data set used to estimate the three versions of the model are the returns of the stock market portfolio (U.S. market index) and the returns of the portfolio of the banking sector. The data are obtained from the data library of professor Kenneth French (http://mba.tuck.dartmouth.edu /pages/faculty/ken.french/data_library.html).

The market index is value weighted and includes all firms listed in the NYSE, AMEX, and Nasdaq. The sample period extends from January 2, 1990, until December 31, 2013, for a total of 6,048 daily observations. Table 14.1 presents some basic diagnostics on the standardized residuals obtained by the three models. The variance ratio tests are based on the notion

TABLE 14.1   Specification Tests for Standardized Residuals.

	Constant Correlation Model	Vector GARCH Model	Asymmetric Vector GARCH Model
$\text{Var}(\sigma^2_{i,t})/\text{Var}(\varepsilon^2_{i,t})$	0.0384	0.0226	0.0157
$\text{Var}(\sigma^2_{j,t})/\text{Var}(\varepsilon^2_{j,t})$	0.0322	0.0286	0.0177
$\text{Var}(\sigma_{i,j,t})/\text{Var}(\varepsilon_{i,t}\varepsilon_{j,t})$	0.0148	0.0175	0.0139
$Q_{i,j}(10)$	18.7112*	6.6979	5.7067

Note: (*) denotes significance at the 5 percent level at least. $Q_{i,j}(10)$ is the Ljung-Box statistics calculated for the cross-product of the standardized residuals of portfolios i and j. It follows χ^2 with degrees of freedom equal to the number of lags used in the test. The variance ratio diagnostics are based on equations (8)–(10).

that the forecast of a variable should have a lower variance than the variable itself; see Shiller (1981). For example, $\sigma^2_{i,t}$ is the conditional forecast of $\varepsilon^2_{i,t}$. Therefore, the variance of $\sigma^2_{i,t}$ should be smaller than the variance of $\varepsilon^2_{i,t}$. Similarly, $\sigma_{i,j,t}$ is the conditional forecast of $\varepsilon_{i,t}\varepsilon_{m,t}$. Therefore, $\text{Var}(\sigma_{i,j,t})$ < $\text{Var}(\varepsilon_{i,t}\varepsilon_{j,t})$. On these tests, there is no evidence of misspecification in the variance or the covariance functions across all three models. Likewise, the Ljung–Box statistics shows no evidence of autocorrelation in the cross product of standardized residuals for the vector GARCH and the asymmetric vector GARCH models. It does show significant autocorrelation in the case of the constant correlation model, suggesting that this particular specification fails to capture persistence in the covariance.

Though the above tests are very useful, they are not designed to capture asymmetries and nonlinearities in the covariance. For this we turn to the estimated covariance specification tests discussed earlier.

Table 14.2 reports the covariance specification tests. The results are rather interesting. Looking at the constant correlation model, it can be seen that this particular covariance specification fails to capture the sign of positive and negative residuals (sign bias test). Simply put, the covariance exhibits a type of asymmetry that the model fails to capture. Also, the model fails to capture the size of negative residuals as can be seen by the negative size bias test. The joint test also rejects the hypothesis that the product of standardized residuals cannot be predicted using past information.

TABLE 14.2 Covariance Specification Tests.

	Constant Correlation Model	Vector GARCH Model	Asymmetric Vector GARCH Model
Sign bias test $F(2,6048)$	7.8003*	4.0226*	1.0157
Negative size bias test $F(2,6048)$	6.6741*	1.0286	0.0177
Positive size bias test $F(2,6048)$	2.0148	0.0175	0.0139
Joint test $F(6,6048)$	2.7112*	1.5976	0.7067

Note: (*) denotes significance at the 5 percent level at least. The critical values for $F(2,6048)$ and $F(6,6048)$ are 3.00 and 2.10, respectively.

Sign bias test: $\xi_{i,j,t} = b_0 + b_1 S^-_{i,t-1} + b_2 S^-_{j,t-1} + u_t$

Negative size bias test: $\xi_{i,j,t} = b_0 + b_1 S^-_{i,t-1}\varepsilon_{i,t-1} + b_2 S^-_{j,t-1}\varepsilon_{j,t-1} + u_t$

Positive size bias test: $\xi_{i,j,t} = b_0 + b_1(1 - S^-_{i,t-1})\varepsilon_{i,t-1} + b_2(1 - S^-_{j,t-1})\varepsilon_{j,t-1} + u_t$

Joint test: $\xi_{i,j,t} = b_0 + b_1 S^-_{i,t-1} + b_2 S^-_{j,t-1} + b_3 S^-_{i,t-1}\varepsilon_{i,t-1} + b_4 S^-_{j,t-1}\varepsilon_{j,t-1}$
$\qquad\qquad + b_5(1 - S^-_{i,t-1})\varepsilon_{i,t-1} + b_6(1 - S^-_{j,t-1})\varepsilon_{j,t-1} + u_t$

Moving on to the vector GARCH model, the evidence suggests that the covariance specification fails that sign bias test, but it passes the rest of the tests. These findings point in the direction of using a covariance specification that is capable of capturing asymmetry. This conclusion is supported by the evidence regarding the asymmetric vector GARCH model. The covariance specification tests fail to reject the hypothesis that the sign and the size of past residuals cannot be used to better predict the conditional covariance.

It should be pointed out that in this particular application, the covariance models used were nested so that other tests can also be used, in addition to the covariance tests. The advantage of the proposed covariance tests, however, is that they can be applied equally well in cases were competing models are not nested.

CONCLUSION

This paper proposes a set of covariance specification tests analogous to the tests suggested by Engle and Ang (1993) for the conditional variance. The tests are applied to a bivariate model, with three possible covariance specifications. The tests allow the researcher to discriminate among competing hypotheses regarding the covariance, whether the models are nested or not. Since efficient covariance estimates are important for pricing and risk-managing portfolios, these tests could provide additional information and guidance in the process of selecting the appropriate covariance models in different applications.

REFERENCES

Andersen, T. G., T. Bollerslev, P. F. Christoffersen, and F. X. Diebold. 2006. Volatility and correlation forecasting. In *Handbook of Economic Forecasting*, edited by G. Elliot, C. W. J. Granger, and A. Timmermann, 778–878. Amsterdam: North-Holland.

Bekaert, G., and G. Wu. 2000. Asymmetric volatility and risk in equity markets. *The Review of Financial Studies* 13: 1–42.

Bollerslev, T. 1990. Modeling the coherence in short-run nominal exchange rates: A multivariate generalized ARCH model. *Review of Economics and Statistics* 72: 498–505.

Bollerslev, T., R. Y. Chou, and K. F. Kroner. 1992. ARCH modeling in finance: A review of the theory and empirical evidence. *Journal of Econometrics* 52: 5–59.

Bollerslev, T., R. Engle, and J. M. Wooldridge. 1988. A capital asset pricing model with time varying covariance. *Journal of Political Economy* 96: 116–131.

Engle, R. F. 1982. Autoregressive conditional heteroskedasticity with estimates of the variance of U.K. inflation. *Econometrica* 50: 286–301.

Engle, R. F., and V. K. Ang. 1993. Measuring and testing the impact of news on volatility. *Journal of Finance* 48: 1749–1778.

Glosten, L., R. Jagannathan, and D. Runkle. 1989. *Relationship Between the Expected Value and the Volatility of the Nominal Excess Return on Stocks*, Working paper, Department of Finance, Columbia University.

Koutmos, G., and G. G. Booth. 1995. Asymmetric volatility transmission in international stock markets. *Journal of International Money and Finance* 14: 55–69.

Koutmos, G., and R. Saidi. 1995. The leverage effect in individual stocks and the debt to equity ratio. *Journal of Business Finance and Accounting* 22: 1063–1075.

Koutmos, G. 1998. Asymmetries in the conditional mean and the conditional variance: Evidence from nine stock markets. *Journal of Economics and Business* 50: 277–290.

_____. 1999. *Cross-Moment Specification Tests*. Working paper, Charles F. Dolan School of Business, Fairfield University.

Shiller, R. 1981. Do prices move too much to be justified by subsequent changes in dividends? *American Economic Review* 71: 421–435.

CHAPTER 15

Accounting Information in the Prediction of Securities Class Actions

Vassiliki Balla

INTRODUCTION

After the tenth anniversary of the passage of the Sarbanes-Oxley Act, there has been an increase in allegations related to SOX reporting requirements. According to the "2011 Review and Analysis" of Cornerstone Research, there has been an increase in Class Actions (CAs) in 2011 contrary to 2010, originating from accounting misstatements and financial restatements. It is worth noting that CAs, which are linked to accounting, take longer to resolve and are less likely to result in dismissal than settlement. However, accounting cases result in higher settlement outcomes. The year 2011 was characterized by increased stock market volatility, creating a dynamic environment for securities class action litigation. In recent years, there has been an increase in the number and value of securities class actions (SCAs), attracting the attention of various stakeholders such as investors, managers, policy makers, lawyers, and so on. Over the years numerous class action lawsuits have been in the spotlight, most of them involving securities fraud. It is worth noting that even in regular securities class actions that received less media attention in recent years, the compensation exceeded $500 million. By and large, even median class action cases may reach settlements of millions of dollars (Buckberg et al. 2003).

Importance of the Study

In recent years, there has been an increase in securities class action lawsuits indicating another type of risk: namely, the securities class action risk (Ryan and Simmons 2007). It has been made evident that companies should operate in a way to avoid all type of risks including the risk stemming from mass litigations. Pellegrina and Saraceno (2009) highlight the significance of the phenomenon in the banking sector, indicating that the size of a class action may be a warning signal about the bank's stability. Accordingly, it is vital for all business sectors, as well as investors and stakeholders (e.g., creditors, debtors, staff), to be aware of the risk exposure that stems from a class action before making an investment decision. For this reason, it would be beneficial to investors, who do not participate in a class action, to be able to know if the company will face a class action in the future, long before it is announced. Current research builds on this and focuses on the development of a model to predict securities class actions.

There are many studies that prove the negative effect of security class actions on stock returns. Abnormal security returns will be observed not only when misrepresentations are discovered in a company's financial statements, but also in periods preceding the discovery. Kellogg (1984) and Alexander (1996) agree that the non-disclosure of adverse information that inflates the price of a stock harms the investors who purchase the stock.

Supporting evidence suggests that a security class action might be seen as an event of three stages (Ferris and Pritchard 2001). The first stage is the revelation of a potential fraud, in which there is significant negative reaction to stock price. The second stage is the filing of the fraud to court, in which the significance is smaller but still the reaction to stock price is negative. Lastly, there is the third stage of the judicial resolution, during which there is no reaction to stock price. This evidence shows that only the revelation of a potential fraud has immediate reaction to stock price. Shareholders are not much interested about the outcome of the lawsuit (third stage); rather, they are concerned about the revelation of the incidence (first stage) and its filing (second stage). A related empirical study proved that the revelation of a potential fraud is linked to an abnormal negative return of 21.5 percent during a three-day period surrounding the announcement of negative information, 23.5 percent during the formation of the class and until two days before the announcement, and 43.8 percent during the entire class period (Niehaus and Roth, 1999).

According to Chava et al. (2010), security class actions are likely to increase a firm's perceived risk in corporate governance, information asymmetry, and operation, and therefore its cost of equity capital. They found that after the lawsuit is filed, a firm's cost of equity capital increases significantly. Also, security class actions are associated with indirect costs such as difficulty in recruiting directors and auditors after a lawsuit has occurred. More importantly, security class actions disrupt the relationships between an entity and its suppliers and customers (Black et al. 2006).

Securities class actions affect CEO turnover, too. Out of a sample of 309 companies that were sued and settled between 1991 and 1996, their board structure did not change significantly after a lawsuit, whereas insider holdings declined. The probability of CEO turnover increases for both high and low settlement cases, from about 9 percent per year before to about 23 percent per year after the settlement (Strahan 1998). A class action's announcement harms CEOs' and CFOs' future job prospects. After such an event, CEO turnover takes place as well as pay-cuts and takeovers, causing a negative market reaction (Humphery-Henner 2012).

A class action results in decrease of overinvestment. This decrease matches with an increase in cash holdings, a decrease in pay-outs, and an increase in leverage. Firms that have faced a class action in the past change their behavior toward better governance, greater focus, and lower overinvestment (McTier and Wald 2011).

The existing literature presents descriptive and statistical evidence for securities class actions trying to investigate the factors that cause this phenomenon. Part of the literature applies statistical analysis, which either relates to the consequences of SCAs as explained earlier or investigates its effect to the share price. Conclusively, this research employs five classification techniques, plus an integrated method, in order to predict the phenomenon of security class actions. In other words, it is the first study that examines the prediction of securities class actions in industrial sector basing on data from the most recent period (2003–2011) and while employing the largest sample so far.[1]

Focusing on Industrial Sector

Prior research in the field has covered the examination of banking sector (Pellegrina and Saraceno 2011; Balla et al. 2014). This is surprising, since the industrial sector has been subject to the highest class actions of all time, such as the case of Master Tobacco ($206 billion) and the case of Dukes v. Wal-Mart Stores ($11 billion). Furthermore, the recent financial crisis resulted in a number of credit-crisis cases filed since 2007. BP in the energy sector, NOVARTIS in the healthcare-sector, and NOKIA and YAHOO! in

---

[1] Existing literature concentrates on corporate events such as bankruptcy, mergers, and acquisitions. Most of it shows encouraging results in predictive accuracy, even though they seem to differ according to the event, the country, as well as the methodology used.

the information technology sector are some characteristic examples that prove that the industrial sector is a major target of securities class actions.

Focusing on the United States

The legal framework of the United States that covers securities class actions is clearer than in any other country for many years now. Security class actions operate in a specific legal context, which is approved by the United States, blocking ineligible and inappropriate securities class actions to take place that would be incorrectly traced. European jurisdictions and the EU have different features compared to the U.S. class actions system. Therefore, it is not only the fact that U.S. firms were chosen because they are all subject to the same jurisdiction as previously explained, but also because this jurisdiction is considered to be more integrated than any other in the world. Hence, the lack of a common base upon which class actions operates causes difficulties in creating a homogeneous sample with comparable data, highlighting the appropriateness of a US dataset.

LITERATURE REVIEW

It is not surprising that a growing strand of the literature examines the causes of securities class actions, providing insights into the litigation process and analyzing the effects of lawsuits on corporations (e.g., McTier and Wald 2011). Others examine the factors that influence the probability of a security class action (e.g., Strahan 1998). However, there are no studies on the development of quantitative multicriteria models to predict security class actions (apart from Balla et al. 2014, who focused on banking sector), in advance of their occurrence. This chapter attempts to fill this material gap.

The disclosure of bad news increases the probability of security class actions. Kinney et al. (1989) claim that when firms restate their financial statements due to material errors, the yield of the stock returns is directly affected, increasing once more the probability of a lawsuit. There is evidence to link the size of the company with the lawsuit, proposing that larger companies have higher probability to face a class action, as they promise large damage compensation (Sarra and Pritchard 2010).

The first issue that should be noted is that of methodology. Half of the papers used logistic regression and the other half probit regression, in order to determine the variables that play an important role. This is considered as sufficient, given the fact that they did not aim to develop prediction models. This chapter will apply more advanced techniques (UTADIS, MHDIS, SVMs), filling in this way this gap and enriching a rather poor literature, as far as the methodology is concerned.

Even though the first study comes from Kellogg (1984), including data from 1967 to 1976, the researchers that followed did not include in their analysis data between 1977 and 1990 due to the stagnant legal framework that repelled researchers from investigating this phenomenon. The era that most authors examined is between 1996 and 2004, mainly because during that period the enactment of PSLRA and SLUSA took place, giving incentive to academicians to investigate its impact on the phenomenon. The current study ranks among three other studies (Poulsen et al. 2010; Pellegrina et al. 2011; Balla et al. 2014) that account for the most recent period of 2003–2011.

The only literature that directly relates to the current study comes from McShane et al. (2012), who use Hierarchical Bayesian model, and Balla et al. (2014), who developed classification models to forecast the incidence of security class action. All other researches examine whether certain variables affect the filing of a lawsuit. Consequently, this is the third study that will research the prediction of securities class actions and the second that will apply multicriteria techniques in order to predict the phenomenon of securities class action.

METHODOLOGY

UTilités Additives DIScriminantes (UTADIS)

UTADIS is a classification method that uses an additive utility function in order to score firms and decide upon their classification. It is a variant of the well-known UTA method (UTilités Additives) (Zopounidis and Doumpos 1999).

Its general form is:

$$U(g) = \sum_{i=1}^{n} p_i u_i(g_i),$$

Where $g_i = (g_1, g_2, \dots, g_n)$ is the vector of evaluation criteria, p_i is a constant indicating the significance of criterion g_i ($p_1 + p_2 + \dots p_n = 1$), and $u_i(g_1)$ is the marginal utility of criterion g_i. The evaluation criteria $g_1, g_2, \dots, g_n$ involve all the characteristics (qualitative and/or quantitative) of the alternatives that affect their overall evaluation. In the case of the class action's prediction, the evaluation criteria involve the financial ratios. The alternatives under consideration are classified by the decision maker into q classes $C_1, C_2, \dots, C_q$ (in our case there are two classes: the first contains the firms that faced CA at least once in the past; and the second, firms that never faced CAs so far).

Multi-group Hierarchical Discrimination (MHDIS)

An alternative MCDA non-parametric approach is the multi-group hierarchical discrimination (MHDIS) method. MHDIS has been successfully applied in classification problems in finance, such as credit risk (e.g., Doumpos and Zopounidis 2002) and M&A's (Zopounidis and Doumpos 2002). MHDIS distinguishes the groups progressively, starting by discriminating the first group from all the others, and then proceeds to the discrimination between the alternatives belonging to the other groups.

$$U_k(x) = \sum_{i=1}^{m} p_{ki}\, u_{ki}(g_i) \quad \text{and} \quad U_{\sim k}(x) = \sum_{i=1}^{m} p_{\sim ki}\, u_{\sim ki}(g_i),$$
$$k = 1, 2, \ldots, q - 1$$

The utility functions in MHDIS do not indicate the overall performance but, rather, serve as a measure of the conditional similarity of an alternative to the characteristics of group C_k when the choice among C_k and all the lower groups $C_{k+1}, \ldots, C_q$ is considered. However, similarly to the UTADIS, the estimation of the weights of the criteria in the utility functions, as well as the marginal utility functions, is accomplished through mathematical programming techniques. More specifically, at each stage of the hierarchical discrimination procedure, three programming problems (two linear and one mixed-integer) are solved to estimate the utility thresholds and the two additive utility functions in order to minimize the classification error, as summarized.

Support Vector Machines (SVMs)

Support vector machines (SVMs) can be used for regression as well as for classification. SVMs are a family of learning algorithms first introduced by Vapnik in 1995 that can solve linear and nonlinear problems. In current research, SVM$_{light}$ was applied in classifying SCAs. SVM$_{light}$ is an implementation of basic SVM for the problem of pattern recognition. The optimization algorithms used in SVM$_{light}$ can handle problems with many thousands of support vectors efficiently. This can be represented by the following equation:

$$y = b + \sum y_i a_i x \bullet x_i$$

Where y is the outcome, y_i is the class value of the training example x_i, and $\bullet$ is the dot product. The vector x corresponds to an input, the vectors x_i are the support vectors, and b and a_i are parameters that determine the hyperplane ($a \geq 0$).

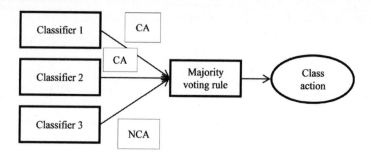

FIGURE 15.1   Majority voting rule.

Majority Voting

Majority voting (MV) is a simple framework that allows us to combine different methods operating on binary classification outputs (class actions / non–class actions). The MV method goes with the decision where there is a consensus that at least half of the classifiers agree on it. Let us assume that there is a system L of K classifiers, $L = \{l1, \ldots, lM\}$, and $yk(x_i)$, $i = 1, \ldots, n$ and $k = 1, \ldots, K$, that denote the output of the kth classifier for the ith multi-dimensional input sample x_i. Given the binary outputs from the M classifiers for a single input sample, the decision of the MV classifier can be represented as follows:

$$y_i^{MV} = 0 \text{ if } \sum_{k=1}^{K} y_k(x_i) \leq K/2$$

$$y_i^{MV} = 1 \text{ if } \sum_{k=1}^{K} y_k(x_i) \leq K/2$$

Figure 15.1 illustrates the application of the majority voting combining the output of three classifiers. Classifiers 1 and 2 indicate that the firm has faced a class action, whereas classifier 3 indicates the opposite. Therefore, just because two out of three classify the firm as facing a class action, the final decision under majority voting rule is that the firm will be classified in the group with the class action firms.

The combination of multiple classifiers has received increased attention in recent applications in finance, such as credit scoring and the prediction of acquisitions (Pasiouras et al. 2005).

DATA

The current research investigates firms that faced a security class action lawsuit at least once during the period 2003 to 2011. These firms are matched with another set of firms that did not face a security class action lawsuit during the same period:

1. The financial data are drawn from the OSIRIS Database of Bureau van Dijk, as it has been extensively used for research in the area of accounting and finance (Lara et al. 2006).
2. The list of firms that faced SCAs is drawn from the Securities Class Action Clearinghouse maintained by the Stanford Law School in cooperation with Cornerstone Research.

In order to include firms subject to SCAs in the sample, they should meet the following criteria:

a. Only filings that took place between January 1, 2003, January 1, 2003, and December 31, 2011, and December 31, 2011, are considered for inclusion in the sample. This is due to unavailability of financial data in the online version of OSIRIS Database of Bureau van Dijk, prior to 2001.
b. SCAs should be filed to USA courts.
c. All firms should be classified in OSIRIS as industrial companies.
d. Data should be available in OSIRIS for at least one year prior to the SCA—that is, if a SCA took place in 2004, then financial data of 2003 should be retrieved from OSIRIS.
e. To include NCAs firms into the matching sample, they should meet the same criteria, the only exception being that they should not have been subject to a SCA. To be more specific, when a company in the energy sector faced a SCA in 2007, it should be matched with another company of the same sector that did not face a class action in the same year. In both cases, financial data from the year prior to the event (i.e., 2006) should be available in OSIRIS.

Sample Construction

Initially, we identified a total of 1,204 U.S, firms that faced a SCA, which were matched by size and industry with an equal number of NSCA firms. Then, 168 firms were excluded due to unavailability of data, reducing the sample to 1,036 SCA and 1,036 NSCA firms. Therefore, the total number of filings is 2,072 companies operating in the United States over the period 2003 to 2011.

Figure 15.2 presents the distribution of the SCAs over the period of the analysis. For example, our sample includes 136 companies that faced a SCA during 2005.

Table 15.1 presents the nine sectors that were used in the analysis. For example, the "Manufacturing" sector contains firms that relate to

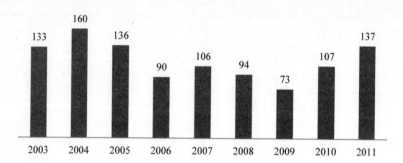

FIGURE 15.2 Number of SCAs per year.

TABLE 15.1 Description and Number of Filings by Sector.

	Sector	Details	Number of SCAs
1	Utilities	Electric, gas, and water firms as well as integrated providers	23
2	Telecommunication Services	Cable, satellite, TV, Internet, radio, radio, and telephone companies	25
3	Materials	Mining and refining of metals, chemical producers, and forestry products	37
4	Information Technology	Electronics manufacturing, software creation, products and services relating to information technology	278
5	Manufacturing firms	Construction and manufacturing firms, aerospace and defense, industrial machinery, tools production, cement, and metal fabrication firms	107
6	Healthcare	Healthcare management firms, health maintenance organizations, biotechnology	240
7	Energy	Oil, gas companies, and integrated power firms	59
8	Consumer Staples	Essential products such as food, beverages, tobacco, and household items	63
9	Consumer Discretionary	Retailers, consumer services companies, consumer durables and apparel companies, and automobiles and components companies	204

manufacturing and construction industry; the "Consumer Staples" sector contains products that satisfy essential needs such as food, beverages, tobacco items, and so on. The "Information Technology," the "Healthcare," the "Consumer Discretionary," and the "Manufacturing" are the sectors with the largest average number of class action filings for the period under examination. Table 15.1 also presents the total number of class actions per sector under investigation. Therefore, we collected financial data of 23 SCA firms from the same sector ("Utilities"), lagged by one year, and so on.

The matching was made according to the sector and to the year the class action took place. For example, for a company in the "Energy" sector that faced a class action during the year 2003, financial data from the prior year (i.e., 2002) were gathered and were matched to another company from the "Energy" sector that was not subject to a SCA, using data from the same year (i.e., 2002). In other words, in both cases (SCA and NSCA firms), financial data from the previous year (i.e., 2002) were used.

The total sample must be split into two subsamples: the training sample and the validation sample. The training sample will be used for model development and the validation sample will be used to test the predictive ability of the models. The current research splits the sample in the two subsamples under the "2/3 rule" (Panel A, Model A) and under the "Crisis rule" (Panel B, Model B), as will be explained further.

Training and Validation Sample (Model A) As mentioned earlier, the total sample consists of 1,036 firms that faced a SCA during 2003 to 2011 and 1,036 firms that were not subject to a SCA over the same period. The training sample amounts a total of 1,382 firms so that two-thirds of the sample will be used for training purposes (66 percent).

The validation sample consists of the remaining 345 firms (i.e., not used in the training dataset) that faced a SCA during 2010 to 2011 matched with another 345 firms that did not face a SCA during the same period. That makes a total validation sample of 690 firms, which is around 33 percent of our total sample (see Table 15.2).

Training and Validation Sample (Model B) A further test will be applied over the credit crisis period to examine whether the performance of the models is robust. On the basis of a cut-off point in time, the two subsamples that are produced correspond to the precredit and postcrisis period. So, the training sample contains data from 2003 until 2007.

The validation sample consists of 411 firms that faced a SCA between 2008 and 2011 and 411 firms that did not face a SCA. Therefore, the total size of the validation sample is 822 firms, corresponding to 40 percent of the

TABLE 15.2 Summary of Training and Validation Samples.

Panel A (Model A)				
Sample		Securities Class Action	NonSecurities Class Action	Total
Training sample	2003–2009	691	691	1,382
Financial data (1 year lag)	2002–2008			
Validation sample	2010–2011	345	345	690
Financial data (1 year lag)	2009–2010			
Total sample	2003–2011	1,036	1,036	2,072

Panel B (Model B)				
Samples	Years	Securities Class Action	NonSecurities Class Action	Total
Training sample	2003–2007	625	625	1,250
Financial data (1 year lag)	2002–2006			
Validation sample	2008–2011	411	411	822
Financial data (1 year lag)	2007–2010			
Total sample	2003–2011	1,036	1,036	2,072

total sample. Table 15.2 summarizes the construction of the training and validation samples under the division of the 2/3 rule (Panel A Model A), as well as the construction of training and validation samples taking into consideration the crisis that occurred in 2008 (Panel B Model B).

Variables

OSIRIS contains numerous quantitative variables. In the beginning, various basic pre-calculated ratios were extracted. After the above data were exported, variables with missing values of more than 5 percent were excluded from the analysis. So, the final set of accounting variables is limited to the remaining eight:

1. Return on assets (ROA), measuring the profitability of a firm
2. Current ratio (CR), measuring the liquidity level of a firm
3. Equity to total assets (E/TA), measuring the leverage of a firm
4. Total assets (TA), measuring the size of a firm
5. Total of all immediate negotiable medium of exchange or instruments normally accepted by banks for deposit and immediate credit to a customer account (CE/TLD), measuring the liquidity level of a firm

6. Goodwill to total assets (G/TA), measuring the goodwill of a firm
7. Historical background of each company to SCAs (PAST), measuring the repetition of an action after a SCA has already taken place in the past
8. Net sales to total assets (NS/TA) measuring the productivity of a firm

Variables Reduction Process

We applied descriptive statistics for the two groups in order to investigate the main characteristics of target firms and further a correlation analysis.

The main results from the descriptive statistics are summarized below:

- As far as the *profitability* is concerned, the results offer a preliminary indication that earnings generated from invested capital (assets) are more in firms belonging in the NSCA group than those belonging in the SCA group. In other words, firms belonging in NSCA group make use of their assets more efficiently than firms belonging in SCA group. Gande and Lewis (2009) provide supporting evidence that firms that have lower profitability ratio will face a SCA.
- In terms of *liquidity*, the firms that belong in the SCA group have better liquidity than those belonging in the NSCA group. This suggests that firms that belong in SCA group have better working capital management than those firms that belong in the other group.
- Concerning the *productivity*, the firms that belong in the SCA group have lower ratio of net sales to total assets than those that belong in the NSCA group. High ratio indicates effective pricing strategy. Firms with low profit margins tend to have high asset turnover, while those with high profit margins have low asset turnover. So, it is clear that firms belonging in SCA group have lower productivity than firms belonging in the NSCA.
- The firms that belong in the SCA group are firms with low level of total assets (measuring the *size* of the entity) compared to the NSCA group. This is an indication that small entities are SCA targets, even though Pellegrina and Saraceno (2011) and Donelson et al. (2012) proved that the log of TA is positively linked to the litigation.
- Firms belonging in SCA group do not have high *goodwill* compared to firms belonging in the NSCA category. This stems from the fact that G/TA is lower in the SCA group than that of firms than belong in NSCA group, although the difference is quite small.
- The figures for *leverage* suggest that SCA is attracted by firms with high level of equity, given that the SCA firms tend to have higher levels of equity to total assets ratio than the NSCA firms. This indicates that shareholders will file a class action against a firm that has increased equity in relation to total assets. McTier and Wald (2011) found that

TABLE 15.3 Descriptive Statistics for the Two Groups and Nonparametric Test.

Variables	NCA/CA	N	Mean	Std. Devia- tion	Mann Whitney U	Wilcoxon W	Z	Asymp- totic Sig. (2-tailed)
1 ROA	SCA	1,036	2.808	21.018	433976.0	971142.0	7.540	0.000
	NSCA	1,036	3.896	11.489				
	TOTAL	2,072	0.543	17.262				
2 NS/TA	SCA	1,036	0.904	0.782	459674.0	996840.0	5.653	0.000
	NSCA	1,036	1.107	0.988				
	TOTAL	2,072	1.005	0.897				
3 CR	SCA	1,036	2.995	2.771	440453.0	977619.0	7.065	0.000
	NSCA	1,036	1.960	2.505				
	TOTAL	2,072	2.477	2.691				
4 Log TA	SCA	1,036	5.824	0.932	332805.0	869971.0	14.97	0.000
	NSCA	1,036	6.308	0.567				
	TOTAL	2,072	6.066	0.808				
5 E/TA	SCA	1,036	50.577	28.746	435581.5	972747.5	7.422	0.000
	NSCA	1,036	42.965	25.404				
	TOTAL	2,072	46.771	27.386				
6 G/TA	SCA	1,036	0.120	0.157	473457.0	1010623.0	4.690	0.000
	NSCA	1,036	0.141	0.161				
	TOTAL	2,072	0.130	0.159				
7 PAST	SCA	1,036	0.190	0.439	513086.0	1050252.0	2.776	0.006
	NSCA	1,036	0.144	0.400				
	TOTAL	2,072	0.167	0.420				
8 CE/TLD	SCA	1,036	0.619	1.003	429495.0	966661.0	7.869	0.000
	NSCA	1,036	0.289	0.464				
	TOTAL	2,072	0.454	0.798				

Notes: ROA: profit & loss for the period/total assets; NS/TA: net sales/total assets; CR: current assets/current liabilities; log TA: total current assets, long–term receivables, investments in unconsolidated companies, other investments, net property, plant and equipment and other assets, including intangibles; E/TA: shareholders' funds/total assets; G/TA: the excess of cost over equity of an acquired company. The item is a component of total intangible assets; PAST: the number of SCA that each company has faced in the past; CE/TLD: the total of all immediate negotiable medium of exchange or instruments normally accepted by banks for deposit and immediate credit to a customer account.

leverage[2] is negatively correlated with statistical significance at the 1 percent level in all models except one, in which the correlation is not statistically significant.

■ Finally, it seems that the firms belonging in the SCA group are those that have *historical background in litigation*. This is supported by the higher mean of SCA group. Gande and Lewis (2009) used a dummy called "previous lawsuit" in order to examine whether the legal past of a business plays significant role. The results showed that this dummy is positively correlated and statistically significant at the 1 percent level.

Univariate Test of Two Groups

A parametric approach applied, in order to test whether the means of the retained variables differ among the two groups of firms. The results are the same when a non-parametric approach is applied. All the variables are statistically significant at the 1 percent level. Thus, all the variables seem to have discriminative power between SCA and NSCA firms under the assumption that the two groups are not normally distributed.

Correlation Analysis

An important issue of concern is multicollinearity. If there is a strong correlation among the variables, the estimates of the regression model may become unstable. The outcome of the non-parametric test shows that further attention needs to be paid on the statistical significant variables. Thus, we examine the correlation among the variables. Table 15.4 shows the correlation coefficients.

The variable CE/LTD is considered to highly correlated with CR, which is somehow expected, since they belong to the same category representing liquidity. Therefore, CE/TLD will be excluded from further analysis. The rest of the variables do not seem to correlate with each other, a fact that allows us to consider them in further analysis. The final set of variables to be included to the classification models are the ones shown in Table 15.5.

---

[2]Leverage is calculated as the company's total debt divided by the sum of the company's market value of equity and total debt.

TABLE 15.4 Pearson Correlation among the Variables.

Variables	ROA	NS/TA	CR	Log TA	E/TA	G/TA	PAST	CE/LTD
ROA	1							
NS/TA	0.165**	1						
CR	0.037	0.129**	1					
Log TA	0.202**	0.118**	0.290**	1				
E/TA	0.134**	0.075**	0.420**	0.311**	1			
G/TA	0.049*	0.100**	0.129**	0.129**	0.027	1		
PAST	0.062**	0.029	0.014	0.041	0.007	0.014	1	
CE/ TLD	0.067**	0.144**	0.554**	0.377**	0.501**	0.166**	0.031	1

*Correlation is significant at the 0.05 level (two two-tailed).
**Correlation is significant at the 0.01 level (two two-tailed).
Notes: ROA: profit & loss for the period/total assets; NS/TA: net sales/total assets; CR: current assets/current liabilities; log TA: total current assets, long–term receivables, investments in unconsolidated companies, other investments, net property, plant and equipment and other assets, including intangibles; E/TA: shareholders' funds/total assets; G/TA: the excess of cost over equity of an acquired company. The item is a component of total intangible assets; PAST: The number of SCA that each company has faced in the past; CE/TLD: the total of all immediate negotiable medium of exchange or instruments normally accepted by banks for deposit and immediate credit to a customer account.

TABLE 15.5 Final Set of Input Variables.

	Balance Sheet and Other Characteristics	Variables
1	Profitability	ROA
2	Productivity	NS/TA
3	Liquidity	CR
4	Size	Log TA
5	Leverage	E/TA
6	Size	G/TA
7	Historical background	PAST

Notes: ROA: profit & loss for the period/total assets; NS/TA: net sales/total assets; CR: current assets/current liabilities; log TA: total current assets, long-long-term receivables, investments in unconsolidated companies, other investments, net property, plant and equipment and other assets, including intangibles; E/TA: shareholders' funds/Total assets; G/TA: the excess of cost over equity of an acquired company. The item is a component of total intangible assets; PAST: the number of SCA that each company has faced in the past; CE/TLD: the total of all immediate negotiable medium of exchange or instruments normally accepted by banks for deposit and immediate credit to a customer account.

RESULTS

Before moving to the discussion of the results, it should be reminded that two approaches are followed for the analysis of the models: that is, the Model A (where two-thirds of the sample will be used for training purposes) and the Model B[3] (where the training and validation samples were constructed in such way as to correspond to the pre- and post-crisis period).

Table 15.6 shows the coefficients of LA. All signs are as expected. First of all, ROA, NS/TA, Log TA, and G/TA are negatively related to the probability of a SCA, while all the rest carry a positive sign. The variable PAST is statistically significant and positively related to the probability of SCAs. Apart from E/TA and G/TA, all the rest variables are statistically significant in both cases.

Supporting results are provided by DA and SVMs in Table 15.7 showing the coefficients of these variables. Once more, all signs are as expected. As in the case of LA, the variables ROA, NS/TA, log TA, and G/TA are negatively related to the probability of a SCA. Moreover, results do not differ materially in the case of the crisis robustness test (Model B).

Table 15.8 presents the UTADIS and MHDIS weights of the model in both cases. As far as the UTADIS results are concerned, the ratio CR contributes the most to the classification (36.41 percent and 38.41 percent in

TABLE 15.6 Coefficients of LA.

	Variables	Model A	Model B
1	ROA	0.022^{***} (0.000)	0.024^{***} (0.000)
2	NS/TA	0.292^{***} (0.000)	0.292^{***} (0.000)
3	CR	0.105^{***} (0.005)	0.101^{***} (0.010)
4	Log TA	0.722^{***} (0.000)	0.752^{***} (0.000)
5	E/TA	0.003 (0.308)	0.002 (0.422)
6	G/TA	0.027 (0.944)	0.105 (0.797)
7	PAST	0.339^{**} (0.012)	0.342^{**} (0.014)

*Significant at $p < 0.10$, **Significant at $p < 0.05$, ***Significant at $p < 0.01$.
Notes: ROA: profit & loss for the period/total assets; NS/TA: net sales/total assets; CR: current assets/current liabilities; log TA: total current assets, long-long-term receivables, investments in unconsolidated companies, other investments, net property, plant and equipment and other assets, including intangibles; E/TA: shareholders' funds/total assets; G/TA: The excess of cost over equity of an acquired company. The item is a component of total intangible assets; PAST: the number of SCA that each company has faced in the past.

---

[3] The empirical work for LA and DA was performed in SPSS, while rest methodologies were applied in MATLAB.

TABLE 15.7 Coefficients of DA and SVMs.

Methods	Discriminant Analysis		Support Vector Machines	
Variables	Model A	Model B	Model A	Model B
1 ROA	0.372	0.375	0.350	0.355
2 NS/TA	0.331	0.324	0.329	0.335
3 CR	0.230	0.222	0.217	0.212
4 Log TA	0.697	0.711	0.767	0.783
5 E/TA	0.102	0.080	0.047	0.031
6 G/TA	0.005	0.017	0.004	0.009
7 PAST	0.178	0.181	0.144	0.144

Notes: ROA: profit & loss for the period/total assets; NS/TA: net sales/total assets; CR: current assets/current liabilities; log TA: total current assets, long–term receivables, investments in unconsolidated companies, other investments, net property, plant and equipment and other assets, including intangibles; E/TA: shareholders' funds/total assets; G/TA: the excess of cost over equity of an acquired company. The item is a component of total intangible assets; PAST: the number of SCA that each company has faced in the past.

TABLE 15.8 Weights of Variables in the UTADIS and MHDIS.

Methods	UTADIS		MHDIS			
	Model A	Model B	Model A		Model B	
Variables	TOTAL	TOTAL	NSCA	SCA	NSCA	SCA
1 ROA	9.91%	11.02%	0.62%	6.88%	10.93%	0.34%
2 NS/TA	12.42%	13.47%	0.61%	11.55%	0.50%	12.03%
3 CR	36.41%	38.41%	86.82%	0.00%	62.02%	24.00%
4 Log TA	36.19%	32.34%	8.38%	12.62%	23.58%	0.00%
5 E/TA	0.98%	1.12%	0.16%	2.03%	2.21%	0.00%
6 G/TA	0.00%	0.00%	0.69%	66.93%	0.77%	60.49%
7 PAST	4.09%	3.64%	2.72%	0.00%	0.00%	3.14%

Notes: ROA: profit & loss for the period/total assets; NS/TA: net sales/total assets; CR: current assets/current liabilities; log TA: total current assets, long–term receivables, investments in unconsolidated companies, other investments, net property, plant and equipment and other assets, including intangibles; E/TA: shareholders' funds/total assets; G/TA: the excess of cost over equity of an acquired company. The item is a component of total intangible assets; PAST: the number of SCA that each company has faced in the past.

both cases respectively). The log TA variable follows by contributing 36.19 percent and 32.34 percent. NS/TA weights 12.42 percent and 13.47 percent again in both cases, and ROA contributes by 11.91 percent and 11.02 percent. Also, the variable PAST plays a role, although small to the classification of the firms, weighting 4.09 percent and 3.64 percent in both cases, respectively. Thus, when a firm has faced a massive lawsuit in the past, it has many chances to face another one in the future. It is worth noting that once more all variables play a significant role to the classification, apart from G/TA, which does not affect the classification of firms in the two groups.

As far as MHDIS is concerned, CR contributes more to the classification 86.82 percent and 62.02 percent in NSCA group and in SCA group 0.00 percent and 24.00 percent under Model A and Model B, respectively. The Log TA contributes 8.38 percent and 23.58 percent in NSCA group and 12.62 percent and 0.00 percent in SCA group, in both models, respectively. The NS/TA ratio follows weighting 0.61 percent and 0.50 percent in NSCA group and in SCA group 11.55 percent and 12.03 percent in both cases. ROA weights 0.62 percent and 10.93 percent in NSCA group and 6.88 percent and 0.34 percent. G/TA ratio influences by 0.69 percent and 0.77 percent in NSCA group and 66.93 percent and 60.49 percent the classification of SCA firms in both cases, respectively. Once more, all variables play a significant role to the classification.

This above clarifies that there is consistency in the results regardless of the employed method. Most of the selected accounting variables play a significant role in the classification. Four out of the seven variables are statistically significant in discriminating between SCA and NSCA firms. These results can be linked to the weights given by UTADIS and MHDIS, which indicates that these four variables play the most important role in classifying firms into SCA and NSCA group.

The results provided by the techniques proved that there are differences in classification accuracies even when the dataset is the same. In some cases, LA provided higher classification accuracy than UTADIS, and vice versa. This happens because each technique processes differently the information given. In other words, even though the dataset employed is the same, there are differences in the implicit criteria for solving the problem. As a result, some methods are more accurate in classifying SCA firms and others are more accurate in classifying NSCA firms.

Each technique employs different algorithms for the development of a prediction model and utilizes different objective functions. Even techniques that belong to the same category may provide totally different results.

For instance, UTADIS and MHDIS belong to multicriteria decision aid models group. UTADIS solves one linear programming formulation to minimize the sum of all misclassifications. MHDIS solves three mathematical programming formulations, two linear and one mixed-integer, involving (1) minimization of overall classification error, (2) minimization of the number of misclassifications, and (3) maximization of the minimum distance between the global utilities of the correctly classified banks. These techniques generate different weights affecting the utility scores, and consequently provide different classification accuracies (Doumpos and Zopounidis 2002). Discriminant analysis on the other hand as a multivariate statistical technique develops a linear discriminant function in order to maximize the ratio among–group to within-group variability, assuming that the variables follow a multivariate normal distribution and that the dispersion matrices of the groups are equal (Zopounidis and Doumpos 1999). These assumptions do not apply in real world problems, like security class actions. As such, DA (as well as LA) was used for comparison purposes.

Profile of SCA Target Firms

The analysis of the examined variables will assist us provide a profile of the target firms that have more probabilities to face a security class action. Let's examine the variables in more detail.

ROA & CR ROA relates negatively to SCA. The lower the ratio is, the more likely it is for a firm to face a SCA. This result is in line with CR, which is linked to the SCAs in a positive way, implying that firms, that are SCA targets are the ones that present increased current assets compared to current liabilities to the financial statements. Firms with high liquidity and low profitability have more chances of facing a massive litigation, due to the fact that the shareholders expect to be compensated by firms that have high liquidity. When a firm achieves high profitability compared to its total assets (high ROA), the shareholders are not willing to proceed to a SCA, showing a sense of trust to the financial management, as well as to generate expectations for a prosperous future performance (i.e., continuous and hopefully increased profitability in the future). It would not have been to the shareholders interest to turn against the firm disturbing its day to day operation, with unexpected consequences; either positive or negative.

ROA and CR are statistically significant at 1 percent level, meaning that these variables are statistically reliable. Also, the weights in UTADIS are 9.91 percent and 11.02 percent in Model A and Model B accordingly; that is the fourth most significant variable playing an important role in the classification of the firms. As for CR, the weights in UTADIS are 36.41 percent and 32.34 in the Model A and the Model B accordingly, making it the second most significant variable. The weights in MHDIS are 0.00 percent (Model A) in SCA and 86.82 percent in NSCA. In the Model B the weight in SCA is 24.00 percent, while in NSCA is 62.02 percent. The results agree with those of Gande and Lewis (2009) and Peng and Röell (2008), who found ROA to be negatively related to the SCA with statistical significance at 5 percent level.

NS/TA NS/TA ratio is used to capture the productivity level of a firm. It turns out that NS/TA ratio is negatively related to SCA. The firm's productivity is directly affected, when it utilizes its assets inefficiently, and therefore a satisfactory level of sales cannot be generated. From the shareholders' point of view, this is translated as a sign of inefficient financial management, a fact that that makes them willing to start thinking of creating a class. Linking this productivity ratio with the profitability ratio discussed above (ROA), firms with inefficient use of assets will likely face a SCA. NS/TA ratio is also statistically significant at the 1 percent level. Regarding UTADIS, it the third most influencing factor with 12.42 percent and 13.47 percent in both cases, showing that this variable plays a significant role along with ROA, CR, and Log TA. MHDIS is also consistent with UTADIS results, generating 11.55 percent in SCA and 0.61 percent in NSCA (Model A) and 12.03 percent in SCA and 0.50 percent in NSCA (Model B).

Log TA Log TA is negatively related to SCA. Small-size firms measured in terms of the log of total assets have increased possibility to face a SCA, compared to their larger rivals. This is explained by the fact that the shareholders target small firms, which are probably being run by inexperienced managers, and they can be an easier target in the case of a lawsuit compared to large corporations. Log TA is statistically significant at the 1 percent level in Model A and also when crisis robustness is tested (Model B). McTier and Wald 2011 found that small firms are less likely to face a SCA provided they paid a high dividend. It can be assumed that the shareholders may be biased by this kind of dividend policy. However, it is doubtful whether this would be the case if a small firm did not distribute profits. Pellegrina and Saraceno (2011) conclude that banks with high total assets have high probability to face a SCA, but they avoid such legal actions as they please shareholders through compensation mechanisms. Large banks in terms of total assets have the capability to distribute dividends, whereas small firms usually do not have this kind of flexibility, thereby increasing the possibility to face SCA. It should be kept in mind that Pellegrina and Saraceno (2011) focused only on banking sector, whereas the current study focuses on the industrial one. Moreover, the findings of the current study support the findings of Poulsen et al. (2010), who also found that the logarithm of total assets and ROA are negatively related to a SCA.

G/TA G/TA ratio relates negatively to the SCA, indicating that the lower the G/TA ratio is, the higher the possibility that a firm does not manage its intangible assets in the most effective way. The firms that receive lawsuits are the ones that have not paid significant attention to build their good-will. Although it is not a statistically significant variable at all levels in either Model A or Model B, it is still included in the analysis as a measure of size control in addition to log TA. According to MHDIS, G/TA ratio weights 66.93 percent in SCA and 0.69 percent in NSCA and 60.49 percent in SCA and 0.77 percent in NSCA in Model A and Model B accordingly.

PAST PAST is positively related to SCA. This indicates that massive lawsuits will take place in firms that faced SCAs in the past. Donelson et al. (2012) examine the incidence of a SCA in the case where the firm operates in a high litigation risk industry. They support that a firm in a high litigation risk industry is more likely to be sued compared to one belonging in an industry with no historical background in litigations. Gande and Lewis (2009) and Pellegrina and Saraceno (2011) agree with these findings, showing that firms that experienced litigation activity in the past have higher likelihood of being sued again.

E/TA E/TA ratio is positively related to SCA. The higher a company's equity against its debt is, the higher is the probability of SCA. When existing share-holders invest more and/or new shareholders invest in a firm, this increases the possibility of SCA. Increased equity reflects increased expectations from the side of investors/shareholders. Hence, they would be willing to proceed to a SCA in case they would not be compensated for their investment. Additionally, increased equity stemming from new shareholders increases the possibility of finding a group of unsatisfied ones who would be willing to proceed to a SCA. Previous literature captures the leverage characteristic through the use of total debt to total assets claiming that higher leverage leads to higher probability of a SCA (Amoah and Tang 2010; Poulsen et al. 2010). Evidence from Peng and Röell (2008) and Strahan (1998) support the idea that high debt may indicate a recent history of poor performance, asset write-downs, or forced heavy borrowing that fuels shareholder dissatisfaction and leads to massive litigations. So, the higher the firm's leverage, the higher the risk, and consequently the higher the probability of a SCA.

Results of Six Classification Methods

Table 15.9 summarizes the results of all six classification methods. The comparison of the results obtained in the training and validation datasets show that the models are quite stable, achieving similar accuracies in the two datasets.

Panel A summarizes the overall accuracy in the validation sample. We observe that UTADIS provides the highest classification of 70.72 percent,

TABLE 15.9 Summary of results.

Panel A (Model A)			
Training (percent)	Accuracy of SCA	Accuracy of NSCA	Overall
LA	62.10	74.80	68.50
DA	61.50	75.80	68.70
UTADIS	54.56	84.52	69.54
SVMs	57.31	83.07	70.04
MHDIS	58.90	69.18	64.04
MV	59.18	80.46	69.82
Validation (percent)			
LA	54.80	80.00	67.40
DA	55.70	79.40	67.50
UTADIS	51.59	89.86	70.72
SVMs	49.57	88.12	68.84
MHDIS	57.97	75.94	66.96
MV	53.62	84.05	68.84
Panel B (Model B)			
Training (percent)	Accuracy of SCA	Accuracy of NSCA	Overall
LA	62.20	75.00	68.60
DA	61.60	76.80	69.20
UTADIS	52.80	87.20	70.00
SVMs	57.60	84.32	70.96
MHDIS	60.32	69.28	64.80
MV	61.44	45.49	53.46
Validation (percent)			
LA	53.80	80.80	67.30
DA	54.50	79.80	67.20
UTADIS	45.01	95.13	70.07
SVMs	50.36	87.83	69.10
MHDIS	56.45	74.45	65.45
MV	45.49	45.25	45.37

followed by SVMs and MV (68.84 percent). DA and LA follow with 67.50 percent and 67.40 percent, respectively. Turning to the accuracies in the SCA group, MHDIS provides the best classification with 57.97 percent, DA with 55.70 percent, and LA with 54.80 percent. As for the NSCA group, UTADIS provides the best classification with 89.86 percent, SVMs with 88.12 percent, and MV (as an integrated method) with 84.05 percent.

Panel B summarizes the results of all six classification methods when the crisis robustness test is applied (Model B). The classification results are generally in line with the previous ones. As far as the overall accuracy in validation sample is concerned, UTADIS provides the highest classification of 70.07 percent, followed by SVMs and MV (69.10 percent). LA and DA follow with slightly lower accuracy (67.30 percent and 67.20 percent, respectively). As it regards the accuracy in the SCA group, MHDIS provides the best classification with 56.45 percent, DA with 54.50 percent, LA with 53.80 percent, and SVMs with 50.36 percent. Turning to the NSCA group, UTADIS provides again the best classification with 95.13 percent, followed by SVMs and LA with 87.83 percent and 80.80 percent, respectively.

MV as a popular integration technique is applied in order to examine whether the combination of different methods can lead to better classification results. It is clear from both tables that its application has not resulted in a significant improvement in the recorded classification accuracies. In more detail, in Table 15.9 (Panel A) the overall accuracy under MV in the training sample is 69.82 percent and in the validation sample is 68.84 percent. The overall accuracy in Table 15.9 (Panel B) in the training sample is 53.46 percent and in the validation sample is 45.37 percent.

CONCLUSIONS

Focusing on the industrial sector, this study explores the predictability of the five separate classification techniques plus an integration technique, so as to value the probability that a firm will face a class action in the future. It is important that we utilized the largest sample size so far, counting 2,072 cases from the industrial sector in the United States. In addition, the data collected cover a wide period of time, 2003 to 2011, which is immediately after the Sarbanes–Oxley Act took place in 2002.

Firms with high liquidity and low profitability have more chances of facing a massive litigation due to the fact that the shareholders expect to be compensated by firms that have high liquidity. According to UTADIS, the profitability ratio (ROA) is the fourth most significant variable in the classification of the firms, and liquidity ratio (CR) is the second most significant variable. These results are in line with those of Gande and Lewis (2009) and Peng and Röell (2008). Inefficient financial management (low NS/TA ratio) drives the shareholders to form a class and go against the firm. Regarding UTADIS, this variable plays also a significant role. Against McTier and Wald (2011) and Pellegrina and Saraceno (2011), this research reveals that small-size firms have increased possibility to face a security class action, compared to their larger rivals. Poulsen et al. (2010) provides

TABLE 15.10 Accounting Information.

Overall Accuracy			
Model A	Percentage	Model B	Percentage
UTADIS	70.72	UTADIS	70.07
SVMs	68.84	SVMs	69.10
MV	68.84	LA	67.30
SCA group			
MHDIS	57.97	MHDIS	56.45
DA	55.70	DA	54.50
LA	54.80	LA	53.80

supporting evidence that the logarithm of total assets and ROA are negatively related to a security class action.

Moreover, the firms that that receive lawsuits are the ones that have not paid significant attention to build their goodwill and have experienced litigation activity in the past. Once more, the results are in line with Donelson et al. (2012), Gande and Lewis (2009), and Pellegrina and Saraceno (2011). Also, the higher the firm's leverage, the higher the risk, and consequently, the higher the probability of a security class action supporting results by Peng and Röell (2008) and Strahan (1998).

The classification techniques provide consistent results, and the order in which the methods provide the highest accuracies are the same for the two models, as shown in Table 15.10.

Undoubtedly, MHDIS, UTADIS, and MV are the best classifiers in all models providing over 60 percent accuracy. Interestingly in overall accuracy UTADIS and MHDIS takes the first place in all models in overall accuracy and SCA group, respectively.

REFERENCES

Alexander, J. C. 1996. Rethinking damages in securities class actions. *Stanford Law Review* 48 (6): 1487–1537.

Amoah, N., and A. Tang. 2010. Board, audit committee and restatement-induced class action lawsuits. *Advances in Accounting, Incorporation Advances in International Accounting,* 26 (2): 155–169.

Balla, V., C. Gaganis, F. Pasiouras, and C. Zopounidis. 2014. Multicriteria decision aid models for the prediction of securities class actions: evidence from the banking sector. *OR Spectrum* 36: 57–72.

Black, B. S., B. R. Cheffins, and M. Klausner. 2006. Outside Director Liability. *Stanford Law Review* 58: 1055–1159.

Buckberg, E., T. Foster, and R. Miller. 2003, June. Recent trends in securities class action: Will Enron and Sarbanes-Oxley change the tides? *NERA Economic Consulting.*

Chava, S., C. A. Cheng, H. Huang, and G. J. Lobo. 2010. Implications of securities class actions for cost of equity capital. *International Journal of Law and Management* 52 (2): 144–161.

Donelson, D. C., J. J. McInnis, R. D. Mergenthaler, and Y. Y. Yu. 2012. The timeliness of earnings news and litigation risk. *Accounting Review.*

Doumpos, M., and C. Zopounidis. 2002. Business failure prediction: A comparison of classification methods. *Operational Research* 2 (3): 303–319.

Ferris, S., and A. A. Pritchard. 2001. Stock price reactions to securities fraud class actions under the private securities litigation reform act. *Michigan Law and Economics Research Paper No. 01–009.*

Gande, A., and C. Lewis. 2009. Shareholder-initiated class action lawsuits: Shareholder wealth effects and industry spillovers. *Journal of Financial and Quantitative Analysis* 44 (4): 823–850.

Humphery-Jenner, M. L. 2012. Internal and external discipline following securities class actions. *Journal of Financial Intermediation* 21: 151–179.

Kellogg, R. 1984. Accounting activities, security prices and class action lawsuits. *Journal of Accounting and Economics* 6: 185–504.

Kinney, W., and L. L. McDaniel. 1989. Characteristics of firms correcting previously reported quarterly earnings. *Journal of Accounting and Economics* 1: 71–93.

Lara, J. M. G., B. G. Osma, and B. G. D. A. Noguer. 2006. Effects of database choice on international accounting research. *ABACUS* 42 (3–4): 426–454.

McShane, B., O. O. Watson, T. Baker, and S. S. Griffith. 2012. Predicting securities fraud settlements and amounts: A hierarchical Bayesian model of federal securities class action lawsuits. *Journal of Empirical Legal Studies* 9 (3): 482–510.

McTier, B. C., and J. K., Wald. 2011. The causes and consequences of securities class action litigation. *Journal of Corporate Finance* 17: 649–665.

Niehaus, G., and G. Roth. 1999. Insider trading, equity issues, and CEO turnover in firms subject to securities class action. *Financial Management* 28 (4): 52–72.

Pasiouras, F., S. Tanna, and C. Zopounidis. 2005. *Application of Quantitative Techniques for the Prediction of Bank Acquisition Targets.* Singapore: World Scientific Publishing Co.

Pellegrina, L. D., and M. Saraceno. 2011. Securities class actions in the US banking sector: Between investor protection and bank stability. *Journal of Financial Stability* 7: 215–227.

Peng, L., and A. Röell. 2008. Executive pay and shareholder litigation. *Review of Finance* 12 (1): 141–184.

Poulsen, T., T. T. Strand, and S. S. Thomsen. 2010. Voting power and shareholder activism: A study of Swedish shareholder meetings. *Corporate Governance: An International Review* 18 (4): 329–343.

Ryan and Simmons. 2007. Securities class action settlements. *2006 Review and Analysis Cornerstone Research, Inc.*

Sarra, J., and A. Pritchard. 2010. Securities class actions move north: A doctrinal and empirical analysis of securities class actions in Canada. *Alberta Law Review,* 47: 881–927.

Strahan, P. 1998. Securities class actions, corporate governance and managerial agency problems. *Boston College—Department of Finance; National Bureau of Economic Research.* Working paper series.

Zopounidis, C., and M. M. Doumpos. 1999. A multicriteria decision aid methodology for sorting decision problems: The case of financial distress. *Computational Economics* 14: 197–218.

_____. 1999. Business failure prediction using the UTADIS multicriteria analysis method. *Journal of the Operational Research Society* 50: 1138–1148.

_____. 2002. Multicriteria classification and sorting methods: A literature review. *European Journal of Operational Research* 138 (2): 229–246.

About the Contributors

CHRIS ADCOCK

Professor of Financial Econometrics at the University of Sheffield, he is also a visiting professor of Quantitative Finance at the University of Southampton and a visiting professor at Durham Business School. Research interests are in portfolio selection, asset pricing theory and the development of quantitative techniques for portfolio management. He has acted as advisor to several international investment managers. Founding editor of *The European Journal of Finance*, he has been an associate editor of several finance journals and Series C and D of the Journal of the *Royal Statistical Society*. Current research projects are in downside risk, portfolio selection, skewness, and option returns, involving collaborations with universities in the United Kingdom, the European Union and China.

DAVID E. ALLEN

David E. Allen is an adjunct professor in the Centre for Applied Financial Studies at the University of South Australia and a visiting professor in the School of Mathematics and Statistics at the University of Sydney. He was previously professor of Finance at Edith Cowan University, Perth, Western Australia. He has a Ph.D. in Finance from the University of Western Australia, an M.Phil. in the History of Economic Thought from the University of Leicester in England, plus an M.A. in Economics from the University of St. Andrews in Scotland.

He is the author of three monographs and more than 90 refereed publications on a diverse range of topics covering corporate financial policy decisions, asset pricing, business economics, funds management and performance benchmarking, volatility modeling and hedging, and market microstructure and liquidity.

VASSILIKI BALLA

Dr. Vassiliki Balla has been a member in the Financial Engineering Laboratory of Technical University of Crete for the last five years. Her Ph.D.

thesis focuses on Multicriteria Decision Aid Models for the prediction of securities class actions. She holds a first M.Sc. in Banking and Finance from Athens University of Economics and Business and a second M.Sc. in Audit and Applied Accounting from National and Kapodistrian University of Athens. She also holds a B.Sc. in Economics from University of Piraeus and a B.A. in Accounting from Technological Educational Institution of Chalkida. Her research interests are accounting and corporate governance in public as well as industrial sector.

MARIDA BERTOCCHI

Marida Bertocchi is a full professor of applied mathematics in economics and finance at the University of Bergamo. She taught numerous courses at the Universities of Bergamo, Urbino, and Milan, including basic and advanced calculus, portfolio theory, advanced mathematical finance, stochastic optimization, and parallel processing. She has been director of the Department of Mathematics, Statistics, Computer Science, and Applications at the University of Bergamo. She is scientific coordinator of the Ph.D. program in Analytics for Economics and Business. Her research interests are stochastic programming and its applications, especially to bond portfolio management, energy, and financial applications. She has been responsible for many grants from national and international sources as well as from private firms.

IAIN CLACHER

Iain Clacher is an associate professor in Accounting and Finance at Leeds University Business School and the co-director of the Retirement Savings Research Group at the International Institute of Banking and Financial Services. Iain has a B.A.(Hons) in Finance from the University of Strathclyde and a Ph.D. in Accounting from the University of Leeds. His main area of research focuses on corporate pension schemes and he has a number of papers covering pension accounting, pension plan solvency, and pension system design. His research has attracted funding from bodies, including the Actuarial Profession and the Rotman International Centre for Pensions Management. He has also published articles and book chapters in a number of other areas including corporate governance, sovereign wealth funds, financial accounting, precious metals, and intangible assets, as well as being a co-author on the European version of *Fundamentals of Corporate Finance*. Iain is a regular commentator on range of financial and economic issues in the media as well as being an invited speaker at a wide range of national and international conferences and events. In addition to his academic work, he also works as a consultant with previous clients including FTSE 100 companies, a large international pension fund, the NAPF, the City of London Corporation, and the Work Foundation.

JITKA DUPAČOVÁ

Jitka Dupačová is professor at the Department of Probability and Mathematical Statistics of Charles University, Prague. She is known for her results in stochastic programming and related areas of statistics and optimization, which is also the subject of her books and more than 150 published scientific papers. She has participated in applied research (water management and planning, financial management, optimization of technological processes). In consideration of her merits in the development of stochastic programming she was awarded one of twelve memorial plaques during the X. Symposium on Stochastic Programming (2004).

MARK FREEMAN

Mark Freeman is professor of Finance at Loughborough University, where he is also the co-director of the Centre for Post-Crisis Finance and Academic Leader for the University research challenge of "Secure & Resilient Societies." He has previously held full-time academic appointments at the Universities of Bradford, Exeter and Warwick, and visiting positions at Northwestern University, the University of California, Irvine, the University of Technology, Sydney and the University of Leeds. He holds a first class undergraduate degree in mathematics from Nottingham University (1986) and a Ph.D. in finance from Warwick University (1997). His research focusses on long-term financial problems, with particular interest in the long-run investment outlook for pension funds and intergenerational discount rates. His involvement with professional organizations includes, amongst many other things, presenting his research at the World Bank and the UK Treasury and providing advice to the Financial Conduct Authority and the OECD.

HIROFUMI FUKUYAMA

Professor Hirofumi Fukuyama serves on the Faculty of Commerce at Fukuoka University. He earned a Ph.D. in Economics from Southern Illinois University–Carbondale in 1987. His research and teaching interests involve measuring efficiency and productivity change accounting for jointly produced desirable and undesirable outputs. He has published widely in journals such as *Omega, European Journal of Operational Research, Journal of Productivity Analysis,* and *Japan and the World Economy.*

ROSELLA GIACOMETTI

Rosella Giacometti is associate professor at the University of Bergamo, where she teaches Credit and Operational Risks, Mathematical Finance, and Statistics for Financial Markets. She worked for Cambridge Econometric as European Analyst and collaborated with many banks on teaching and consultancy activities. She received a Ph.D. in Mathematics applied to the analysis of Financial Markets from the University of Brescia (Italy), and an M.Sc. in Statistics and Operational Research from Essex University (UK). Her research interests are pricing of financial products, portfolio management, and credit and operational risk.

DAVID HILLIER

David Hillier is vice-dean and professor of Finance at Strathclyde Business School in the University of Strathclyde, Glasgow. He earned a Ph.D. in Finance on Corporate Insider Trading and a B.Sc.(Hons) in Mathematical Sciences. David was previously Ziff Chair in Financial Markets at the University of Leeds. His research has attracted an ANBAR citation and best paper prizes, and he has been ranked in the top 3% most prolific finance researchers in the world over the period 1958 to 2008 (Heck, 2007). He is the editor of *Journal of Economics & Business* and on the editorial board of a number of international journals, including *Journal of International Business Studies.* David is the co-author of a number of textbooks on corporate finance. His research interests are in corporate finance, corporate governance, and insider trading.

MICHAEL JACOBS JR., Ph.D., CFA

Mike is a director in PwC's risk advisory practice in risk and regulation, and has 20 years of experience in the risk-modeling practice across various risk types (credit, market, enterprise, and operational), leading projects in model development and validation using advanced econometric techniques, economic capital modeling, capital adequacy analysis, stress testing, loss forecasting, credit risk of wholesale loan portfolios, and optimizing portfolio risk measurement and management through use of advanced econometric and computational statistical modeling approaches. Just prior to joining PwC, Mike led engagements in development and validation of models for stress testing, credit and operational risk, and ALLL at Deloitte Enterprise Risk Services/Models and Methodologies. Prior to Deloitte, Mike was a senior economist and lead modeling expert in the Enterprise Risk Analysis Division of the OCC, advising senior bank examiners and policy makers on risk-modeling issues and model risk management. Prior to the OCC, Mike led the Empirical Research Group in the Risk Methodology Division at JPMorgan Chase, building models for wholesale and counterparty credit risk, as well as design of the proprietary credit capital and market VaR models.

Education: Ph.D. in Finance, June 2001, Graduate School and University Center of the City University of New York, Zicklin School of Business Program in Finance; M.A. in Economics, May 1994, State University of New York at Stony Brook, Institute for the Decision Sciences, Applied Stochastic Processes and Game Theory; B.S. in Engineering Science, December 1990, State University of New York at Stony Brook, School of Engineering and the Applied Sciences, Applied Mathematics & Statistics, Engineering Mathematics.

Publications: *Journal of Fixed Income, Research in International Business and Finance, The Journal of Portfolio Management, Journal of Credit Risk, Applied Financial Economics, The Journal of Risk Finance, The Journal of Financial Transformation, Journal of Risk Management in Financial Institutions, The Journal of Risk and Financial Management, The Journal of the Risk Management Association*; Books chapters: *Managing and Measuring Risk: Emerging Global Standards and Regulation after the Financial Crisis* (London: World Scientific Publishing Co. Pte. Ltd., London), *Rethinking Risk Measurement and Reporting* (London: Risk Books).

MALCOLM KEMP

Malcolm Kemp is a leading expert in risk and quantitative finance with over 30 years' experience in the financial services industry. He is currently managing director of Nematrian, a company he founded in 2009 that specializes in intellectual property development and provision of consultancy services to the financial services sector. Between 1996 and 2009, Malcolm was an executive director and head of Quantitative Research at Threadneedle Asset Management. This role included responsibility for Threadneedle's derivatives, performance measurement, risk management, liability-driven investment, and other quantitative investment activities.

Prior to working at Threadneedle, Malcolm was a partner at Bacon & Woodrow in its investment consultancy practice, having joined them on graduation from Cambridge University with a first class honors degree in mathematics. Malcolm is a fellow of the Institute and Faculty of Actuaries, a Chartered Enterprise Risk Actuary, and an adjunct professor at Imperial College Business School, London (where he teaches courses in *Enterprise Risk Management*) and has written two books on quantitative finance, Market Consistency: Model Calibration in Imperfect Markets (2009) and Extreme Events: Robust Portfolio Construction in the Presence of Fat Tails (2011).

MILOŠ KOPA

Miloš Kopas is an assistant professor at the Department of Probability and Mathematical Statistics of Charles University in Prague. His research is focused on stochastic programming applications in finance, especially on the portfolio optimization models, including risk measuring and managing, utility theory, and stochastic dominance.

GREGORY KOUTMOS

Dr. Gregory Koutmos is the Gerald M. Levin Endowed Professor of Finance and Graduate Programes Coordinator at the Charles F. Dolan School of Business at Fairfield University in Fairfield, Connecticut. He has published extensively in the areas of financial markets volatility, equilibrium asset pricing models, fixed income securities, and risk hedging. He coedited with Dr. George Philippatos the book *International Securities* Volumes I & II, published by Edgar Elgar Publishing Inc., 2001. He holds a Ph.D. from the Graduate Center of the City University of New York (1990), an M.A. from City College of the City University of New York (1984), and a B.S. from the Graduate School of Business and Economic Studies (ASOEE), Athens-Greece (1980). He has been awarded with a Doctor Honoris Causa from the Hanken School of Economics, Helsinki, Finland, 2009.

RAIMUND M. KOVACEVIC

Raimund M. Kovacevic is currently a research assistant at the Department of Operations Research and Control Systems at the Technical University of Vienna, Austria. Before, he had the position of an assistant professor at the Department of Statistics and Operations Research at the University of Vienna. Previously, he worked as a consultant, project manager, and risk manager in insurance, banking, and energy management for Siemens AG Austria, Feilmeier & Junker GmbH, and Financial Soft Computing GmbH. His main research interests involve stochastic modeling and optimization with applications in risk management for finance, insurance, and energy production and trading. He has published in the *International Journal of Theoretical and Applied Finance, Journal of Risk and Insurance, IMA Journal of Management Mathematics, Statistics and Risk Modeling, Operations Research Spectrum,* and *IIE Transactions* and holds a Ph.D. in economic sciences (statistics) from the University of Vienna.

RENATA MANSINI

Renata Mansini is associate professor of Operations Research at the Department of Information Engineering of the University of Brescia. She received her M.S. degree in Business Economics at the University of Brescia (Italy) and got her Ph.D. in Computational Methods for Financial Decisions at the University of Bergamo (Italy), spending one year at the Olin Business School, Washington University in St. Louis (United States) and working as researcher in the Center for Optimization and Semantic Control at the System Science Department of the same university. She is author of more than 70 scientific papers, most of which were published in international volumes and journals such as *Computers and Operations Research, Discrete Applied Mathematics, European Journal of Operational Research, IIE Transactions, INFORMS Journal on Computing, Journal of Banking & Finance, OMEGA The International Journal of Management Science, Transportation Science,* and *Transportation Research.* Her primary research interests are models and solution algorithms for optimization problems in different application areas including finance, transportation, and procurement.

WLODZIMIERZ OGRYCZAK

Wlodzimierz Ogryczak is professor of Operations Research in the Institute of Control and Computation Engineering at the Warsaw University of Technology. Earlier he was with the Institute of Computer Science, University of Warsaw, while temporally he served as the H.P. Kizer Eminent Scholar Chair in Computer Science at Marshall University and as a visiting professor at Service de Mathématiques de la Gestion, l'Université Libre de Bruxelles and at Laboratoire d'Informatique de Paris 6 (LIP6), l'Université Pierre et

Marie Curie. He received both his M.Sc. and Ph.D. in Mathematics from University of Warsaw, and D.Sc. in Computer Science from Polish Academy of Sciences. His research interests are focused on models, computer solutions, and applications in the area of optimization and decision support. He has published in many international journals, including *European Journal of Operational Research, Annals of Operations Research, Mathematical Programming, SIAM Journal on Optimization, Computational Optimization and Applications, OMEGA The International Journal of Management Science,* and *Control and Cybernetics,* among others.

Research conducted by W. Ogryczak was supported by the National Science Centre (Poland) under grant DEC-2012/07/B/HS4/03076.

GEORG CH. PFLUG

Georg Pflug studied Law (Mag. iur, 1974) and Mathematics and Statistics (Ph.D., 1976) at the University of Vienna. He was professor at the University of Giessen, Germany, and since 1989 has been full professor at the University of Vienna and head of the Computational Risk Management Group. He was dean of the faculty of Business, Economics and Statistics (2008–2010). He is also part-time research scholar at the International Institute of Applied Systems Analysis, Laxenburg, Austria.

Pflug is author of four books: *Stochastic Approximation and Optimization of Random Systems* (CA: H. Walk and L. Ljung, Birkhäuser, 1992); *Optimization of Stochastic Models,* Kluwer, 1996); *Modeling, Measuring and Managing Risk* (CA: W. Roemisch, World Scientific, 2007); *Multistage Stochastic Optimization* (CA: A. Pichler, New York: Springer, 2014); and of over 70 scientific papers in refereed journals.

Pflug's interests include stochastic modeling, stochastic optimization, measuring and managing of risks, and applications in finance, energy, pension funds, and insurance.

ROBERT J. POWELL

Robert J. Powell is an associate professor at the School of Business, Edith Cowan University. He has 20 years banking experience in South Africa, New Zealand, and Australia. He has been involved in the development and implementation of several credit and financial analysis models in banks. He has an honors degree in commerce from Rhodes University, an M.Com. from the University of South Africa and a Ph.D. in finance from Edith Cowan

University. He has published several journal articles and book chapters on value at risk, conditional value at risk, credit risk, and hedge fund regulation.

HORST D. SIMON

Horst D. Simon is Berkeley Lab's deputy director. He holds a Ph.D. in Mathematics from the University of California, Berkeley.

ABHAY K. SINGH

Abhay K. Singh is a Post-Doctoral Research Fellow at the School of Business, Edith Cowan University. He is a Btech graduate with an MBA in finance from the Indian Institute of Information Technology, Gwalior, India, and has a Ph.D. in finance from Edith Cowan University in Western Australia.

JUNG HEON SONG

Jung Heon Song graduated from University of California, Berkeley, with a B.A. in Applied Mathematics. He is currently an affiliate at Lawrence Berkeley National Lab's Scientific Data Management group.

M. GRAZIA SPERANZA

M. Grazia Speranza is full professor of Operations Research at the Department of Economics and Management of the University of Brescia. She is currently president of the Transportation Science and Logistics Society of INFORMS.

She is author of about 150 papers that appeared in international journals and volumes. She is editor of international journals such as *Transportation Science, EURO Journal on Transportation and Logistics, International Transactions in Operational Research, and TOP*. She is editor-in-chief of the series *Advanced Tutorials in Operational Research*. She has given seminars at numerous universities and has been spoken at several international conferences and international schools. She organized international conferences and was a member of the Scientific Committee or of the Program Committee of several international conferences.

MARIA TERESA VESPUCCI

Maria Teresa Vespucci is associate professor of operations research at the University of Bergamo, Italy. She received the Ph.D. degree in numerical optimization from the University of Hertfordshire, United Kingdom. Her research interests include linear algebra, numerical optimization, mathematical programming, and stochastic programming, with applications to operations, planning, and economics of electric energy systems. She is coordinator of many grants from the electric power sector.

WILLIAM L. WEBER

William L. Weber is professor of Economics in the Department of Economics and Finance at Southeast Missouri State University. He earned a Ph.D. in Economics from Southern Illinois University–Carbondale in 1986. He teaches classes in environmental economics, econometrics, and financial institutions management. His research interests include using distance functions to measure the efficiency and productivity change of producers such as banks and other financial institutions, vineyards, primary and secondary schools, and universities. He has published papers in journals such as *Review of Economics and Statistics, European Journal of Operational Research, Journal of Econometrics,* and *Management Science.* His book *Production, Growth, and the Environment: An Economic Approach* was published in 2014 by The CRC Press.

KESHENG WU

Kesheng Wu is a staff computer scientist at Lawrence Berkeley National Lab. He holds a Ph.D. in Computer Science from University of Minnesota, Twin Cities.

QI ZHANG

Qi Zhang is an associate professor in Finance in the Accounting and Finance Division at Leeds University Business School. He gained his B.A. and M.A. in Economics from the School of Economics and Management at Tsinghua University, China. His Ph.D. was awarded by Leeds University Business School.

Qi is a member of European Finance Associate and American Accounting Associate. Qi's research interests are in the areas of financial reporting and price discovery, financial econometrics, financial market anomalies, and banking and emerging markets. He has had papers published in the *Journal of Accounting and Economics, the Journal of Forecasting,* and the *Journal of Banking and Finance.*

WILLIAM T. ZIEMBA

Dr. William T. Ziemba is the Alumni Professor (Emeritus) of Financial Modeling and Stochastic Optimization in the Sauder School of Business, University of British Columbia, where he taught from 1968–2006. His Ph.D. is from the University of California, Berkeley. He currently teaches part time and makes short research visits at various universities. Recently, he is the distinguished visiting research associate, Systemic Risk Centre, London School of Economics.

He has been a visiting professor at Cambridge, Oxford, London School of Economics, University of Reading and Warwick in the United Kingdom; Stanford, UCLA, Berkeley, MIT, Universities of Washington and Chicago in the United States; Universities of Bergamo, Venice, and Luiss in Italy; the Universities of Zurich (Cyprus), Tsukuba (Japan), and KAIST (Korea); and the National University and the National Technological University of Singapore.

He has been a consultant to a number of leading financial institutions, including the Frank Russell Company, Morgan Stanley, Buchanan Partners, RAB Hedge Funds, Gordon Capital, Matcap, Ketchum Trading and, in the gambling area, to the BC Lotto Corporation, SCA Insurance, Singapore Pools, Canadian Sports Pool, Keeneland Racetrack, and some racetrack syndicates in Hong Kong, Manila, and Australia. His research is in asset-liability management, portfolio theory and practice, security market imperfections, Japanese and Asian financial markets, hedge fund strategies, risk management, sports and lottery investments, and applied stochastic programming. His co-written practitioner paper on the Russell-Yasuda model won second prize in the 1993 Edelman Practice of Management Science Competition. He has been a futures and equity trader and hedge fund and investment manager since 1983.

He has published widely in journals such as *Operations Research, Management Science, Mathematics of OR, Mathematical Programming, American Economic Review, Journal of Economic Perspectives, Journal of Finance, Journal of Economic Dynamics and Control, JFQA, Quantitative Finance, Journal of Portfolio Management* and *Journal of Banking and Finance,* and in many books and special journal issues.

Recent books include *Applications of Stochastic Programming* with S.W. Wallace, SIAM-MPS, 2005; *Stochastic Optimization Models in Finance*, 2nd edition with R.G. Vickson (World Scientific, 2006); and *Handbook of Asset and Liability Modeling, Volume 1: Theory and Methodology* and *Volume 2: Applications and Case Studies* with S. A. Zenios (North Holland, 2006, 2007); *Scenarios for Risk Management and Global Investment Strategies* with Rachel Ziemba (John Wiley & Sons, 2007); *Handbook of Investments: Sports and Lottery Betting Markets,* with Donald Hausch (North Holland, 2008); *Optimizing the Aging, Retirement and Pensions Dilemma* with Marida Bertocchi and Sandra Schwartz (Wiley Finance, 2010); *The Kelly Capital Growth Investment Criterion,* 2010, with legendary hedge fund trader Edward Thorp and Leonard MacLean (World Scientific, 2010); *Calendar Anomalies and Arbitrage, The Handbook of Financial Decision Making* with Leonard MacLean; and *Stochastic Programming* with Horand Gassman (World Scientific, 2012, 2013). In progress in 2014 are *Handbooks on the Economics of Wine* (with O. Ashenfelter, O. Gergaud, and K. Storchmann) and *Futures* (with T. Mallaris).

He is the series editor for North Holland's Handbooks in Finance, World Scientific Handbooks in Financial Economics and Books in Finance, and previously was the CORS editor of INFOR and the department of finance editor of *Management Science,* 1982–1992. He has continued his columns in Wilmott and his 2013 book with Rachel Ziemba have the 2007–2013 columns updated with new material published by World Scientific. Ziemba, along with Hausch, wrote the famous *Beat the Racetrack* (1984), which was revised into Dr Z's *Beat the Racetrack* (1987) and presented their place and show betting system, and the *Efficiency of Racetrack Betting Markets* (1994, 2008)—the so-called bible of racetrack syndicates. Their 1986 book *Betting at the Racetrack* extends this efficient/inefficient market approach to simple exotic bets. Ziemba revised BATR into *Exotic Betting at the Racetrack* (World Scientific, 2014), which adds Pick 3,4,5,6, etc. and provides other updates.

CONSTANTIN ZOPOUNIDIS

Constantin Zopounidis is professor of Financial Engineering and Operations Research at Technical University of Crete (Greece), distinguished research professor in Audencia Nantes, School of Management (France), and senior academician of both the Royal Academy of Doctors and the Royal Academy of Economics and Financial Sciences of Spain. He is editor-in-chief of *Operational Research: An International Journal* (Springer), *International Journal of Multicriteria Decision Making* (Inderscience), *The International Journal of Financial Engineering and Risk Management* (Inderscience), *The Journal of Computational Optimization in Economics and Finance*

(Nova Publishers), and *The International Journal of Corporate Finance and Accounting* (IGI Global). He is also associate editor in international transactions in *Operational Research* (Wiley), *New Mathematics and Natural Computation* (World Scientific), *Optimization Letters* (Springer), *International Journal of Banking, Accounting and Finance* (Inderscience), *International Journal of Data Analysis Techniques and Strategies* (Inderscience), and the *European Journal of Operational Research* (Elsevier). He also has served as president since early 2012 of the Financial Engineering and Banking Society (FEBS).

In recognition of his scientific work, he has received several awards from international research societies. In 1996, he received the Gold Medal and Diploma of Social and Human Sciences from the MOISIL International Foundation for his research in multicriteria intelligent decision support systems and their applications in financial management. In 2000, he received the Best Interdisciplinary Research Paper Award from the Decision Sciences Institute, and in 2010, he received the highly commended paper award from the Emerald Literati Network. The European Journal of Operational Research has awarded him the Best Reviewer Award in 2010 and the Certificate of Excellence in Reviewing in 2012. Also, in 2012, he was the recipient of the Long-lasting Research Contribution Award in the field of Financial Engineering & Decision Making by ESCP Europe. In 2013, he received the Edgeworth-Pareto prestigious Award from the International Society of Multicriteria Decision Making.

He has edited and authored 75 books in international publishers and more than 450 research papers in scientific journals, edited volumes, conference proceedings, and encyclopedias in the areas of finance, accounting, operations research, and management science.

He is a frequent invited speaker in international conferences, and he has given several invited lectures as visiting professor in many European universities.

Glossary

Accounting-based credit models   Models that measure credit risk based on an analysis of financial ratios.

Additive value function   A type of multicriteria evaluation model where the overall performance of an available option is obtained as a weighted sum of partial performance assessments. It is a compensatory model, in which the weak performance on one dimension can be compensated by strong performance on others.

Akaike Information Criterion (AIC)   A measure of the quality of a statistical model for a given dataset allowing for selection of the best model.

Asset/liability management   A risk-management process used by financial institutions to manage their assets and cash flows in accordance with their obligations (liabilities).

Banking stability index   An index that describes the degree to which a banking system as a whole can withstand the financial distress of some financial agents.

Basel accords   A set of international standards issued by the Basel Committee on Banking Supervision, with a strong focus on the capital adequacy of banks.

Beta   The relative risk of an asset in comparison to the market or other defined benchmark.

Budget constraint   Restriction that the sum of a set of investment weights equals the investor's budget, which is usually normalized to one.

Bulk volume classification   A common method used to classify a trade as either buyer-initiated or seller-initiated.

CEO   Chief executive officer, usually the most senior corporate officer managing a corporation.

CFO   Chief financial officer, reports to CEO and the board of directors.

Cholesky decomposition   A decomposition of a negative (positive) semi-definite matrix into a lower triangular matrix, a diagonal matric of Cholesky values, and the transpose of the lower triangular matrix. This decomposition can be used to impose concavity (convexity) on a function.

Class actions   Collective lawsuits in which there is a group of people in similar circumstances suing another party in order to be compensated.

Classification technique   A technique in which a new observation will be classified into a set of categories (sub-populations). The problem bases on a training set of data containing observations whose category membership is known.

CMR   A multiperiod PD rate, structurally equivalent to pricing EPE as the contingent leg of a CDS, by applying the counterparty spread to it.

Conditional distress probability   The probability that given the distress or bankruptcy on one specific agent, another financial agent comes under financial distress as a consequence.

Conditional Value at Risk $CVaR_\alpha$ (at the confidence level α) is a coherent risk measure defined as the mean of the α-tail distribution of losses.

Contamination bounds   Upper and lower bounds for the optimal performance of the objective constructed for purposes of stress testing.

Copula models   Mathematical models which formalize the joint and conditional distress probabilities.

Counterparty credit risk measurement and management (CCR) exposure   Quantifies how much money the counterparty might owe the bank in the event of default.

Covariance matrix   Square symmetric matrix in which elements in the leading diagonal are the asset variances. Entry in row i column j is the covariance between returns on assets i and j, respectively.

Covariance specification tests   A set of statistical tests for assessing the performance of various covariance specifications in the context of multivariate GARCH-type models.

Credit default swap (CDS)   A bilateral agreement between counterparties to insure against the loss of risky reference debt.

Credit ratings   Classifications of obligors into credit risk categories, prepared either internally by a credit institution or provided externally by credit-rating agencies.

Credit risk   The risk due to the failure of an obligor to meet scheduled debt obligations.

Credit scoring   The process of evaluating and scoring the creditworthiness of obligors, usually based on quantitative models.

Credit valuation adjustment (CVA)   The product of the EPE times the LGD times the CMR.

Current exposure (CE)   Measures the exposure if the counterparty were to default today.

Cut-off point   It is the higher value an observation can take in order to be categorized categorized to a predefined group (e.g., CA/NSCA group).

Delinquent loans   Loans with repayments more than thirty days overdue.

Distance to default   A numerical indicator describing the danger of default in the next period of a firm. This indicator is related—but not identical—to the probability of default in the next period.

Directional output distance function   A function that seeks the maximum expansion in desirable outputs and contraction in undesirable outputs.

Economic capital (EC)   The difference between a UL measure, or some extreme loss at some confidence level (e.g., a high quantile of a loss distribution) and the associated EL measure.

Efficient portfolio   A portfolio of assets with the highest possible return for a given level of risk or with the lowest risk for a given level of expected return.

Efficient frontier   A concave curve, which relates the expected return on efficient portfolios to their volatility.

Efficient portfolio A portfolio, which has the minimum variance (or, equivalently, volatility) for a given level of expected return; alternatively, the maximum expected return for a given level of variance (or volatility).

Energy trading Exchange of contracts for buying and selling electricity in a regulated market or in an OTC market.

Eigenvector A vector that when a square matrix multiplies this vector, it yields a constant multiple of the vector.

Expected loss (EL) A measure generally thought of as some likely loss measure over some time horizon (e.g., an allowance for loan losses amount set aside by a bank).

Expected positive exposure (EPE) The average of a simulation of a large number (on the order of 10^2 to 10^3) different paths for the various underlying future prices in the possible market environments.

Expected return The expected value of the portfolio return.

Exposure-at-default (EAD) The economic exposure on a claim to a counterparty that defaults.

External ratings A credit rating provided by an independent rating firm.

Financial system The universe of all financial agents of a country (central bank, private and governmental banks, and other financial intermediaries as, e.g., insurance companies) with all the interdependencies, as mutual share holdings and mutual loans.

Firm value models Mathematical models describing the future development of the value (assets minus liabilities) of a firm using stochastic variables.

Fixed transaction costs Transaction costs that are charged independently of the amount of capital invested.

Forward market Special financial contracts that allow hedging against future movements of the price of a commodity or of a financial activity.

Forward zero curve The forward spread curve between a rated bond and the risk free rate on a zero coupon bond.

Futures contract An agreement between two parties to perform a transaction for an asset in the future with pre-agreed terms (date of the transaction, its volume, and price).

GARCH models Generalized autoregressive conditionally heteroskedastic models. Statistical models describing the conditional variance of a random variable, mostly times series of returns on speculative assets.

Hedonic prices A method of obtaining the price of a single characteristic from a good or service that consists of a bundle of characteristics.

Heteroskedasticity Subpopulations within a data set have different variability across groups.

Hierarchical Bayesian model A model that allows researchers and practitioners to develop more realistic models in decision making. The promise of Bayesian statistical methods lies in the ability to deal with problems of high complexity.

High frequency trading The use of computational algorithms and electronic systems to perform financial transactions rapidly in investment strategies that seek to make short-term profits.

Hypergeometric functions   Special functions that are solutions of second order linear ordinary differential equations. These are usually infinite series.

i.i.n.d   Independent and identical normal distribution.

Individual distress probability   The probability that one specific financial agent suffers distress in the next period.

Integrated method   A method of bringing together two systems into one, on the basis that the new one will deliver better classification results.

Joint distress probability   The probability that a given group of financial agents all suffer distress in the next period.

Kurtosis   A measure of the peakedness of the distribution of a random variable.

Leptokurtosis   A random distribution with higher kurtosis than a normal distribution as there is a greater concentration of observations around the mean.

Linear programming (LP) model   An optimization model where constraints and objective function are linear.

Logistic regression   A regression that measures the relationship between a categorical dependent variable and one or more independent variables.

Loss cascade   Due to interrelations between financial agents, the default of one may cause the default of others in a cascading series, like falling dominoes.

Loss-given-default (LGD)   The ultimate economic loss on a claim to a counterparty that defaults.

Market portfolio   A portfolio consisting of all assets in a market, with each asset weighted in proportion to its market value relative to the total market value of all assets.

MCDA   Multicriteria decision aid models that consider multiple criteria in decision–making environments.

Mid-cap   Companies with a medium-sized market capitalization.

Minimum variance portfolio   A portfolio on the efficient frontier, which has the minimum possible variance.

Mixed-integer linear programming (MILP) model   An optimization model where constraints and objective function are linear, and possibly some variables are constrained to take integer values.

Monte Carlo modeling   The simulation of multiple random scenarios of asset returns.

Multicriteria decision aiding   A field of operations research dealing with decision support in problems involving multiple conflicting decision criteria.

News impact curve   A graphical representation of the degree of asymmetry of volatility to positive and negative innovations.

Nonperforming loan   A loan that is past due more than three months, a loan to a borrower who is bankrupt, or a loan that is in the process of being restructured.

Nuisance parameters   Parameters in a probability distribution which cannot be removed by standardization or transformation and thus confound statistical tests.

Output analysis   Aims at analysis of the obtained results in connection with uncertainty or perturbation of input data.

Pay-out   The expected financial return from an investment or the expected income/salary/bonus.

Polynomial chaos   An approach to determine the evolution of uncertainty using a nonsampling based method, when there is probabilistic uncertainty in the system parameters.

Portfolio   Amount of capital invested in each asset of a given set.

Portfolio optimization   The process for defining the best allocation of capital to assets in terms of risk-return criteria.

Portfolio selection   The process of constructing an efficient portfolio.

Potential exposure (PE)   Measures the potential increase in exposure that could occur between today and some time horizon in the future.

Power capacity planning   Planning for future development of plants to produce electricity.

Preference disaggregation analysis   A methodological field in multicriteria decision aiding involved with the elicitation of preferential information from data using nonparametric regression techniques.

Probability of default   The likelihood that an obligor will fail to meet scheduled debt payments in a given time period.

Probit regression   A type of regression that aims to estimate the probability that an observation with particular characteristics will be classified into a predetermined category.

Quadratic utility function   A utility function that is a quadratic function of its argument.

Ratings based models   Models that incorporate credit ratings such as those provided by Standard & Poor's, Moody's, and Fitch.

Revenue function   Maximum potential revenues that a firm can produce, given output prices and costs of production.

Regime-switching model   A model with more than one state where the switching between regimes is governed by a transition matrix.

Regulatory capital (EC)   The difference between a UL measure, or some extreme loss at some confidence level (e.g., a high quantile of a loss distribution) and the associated EL measure as dictated by a supervisory model.

Risk appetite   A non-negative real number that describes an investor's appetite for risk, with higher values corresponding to a greater degree of aggression. The reciprocal is risk aversion.

Risk aversion   The attitude of investors toward risk. Risk aversion is described by a concave utility function, risk-neutral investors have a linear utility function, and risk-prone investors have a convex utility function.

Risk constraints   Prescribe the upper bound of the portfolio risk (expressed by means of a risk measure).

Risk-free rate   A rate of return that is known for certain in advance and for which there is no default risk.

Risk measure   Quantitative measure of the variability of losses or profits due to uncertain and undesired events.

Risk premium The extra return that investors require for risky investments over risk-free return.

Robustness analysis The examination of the validity of a solution and the results of an analysis to changes in the decision and modeling context (data, hypotheses, modeling assumptions).

Robustness test A test that investigates the degree to which a method/technique provides correct results in the presence of invalid inputs.

Safety measure A function, complementary to a risk measure, that measures the portfolio performance in terms of risk with respect to the expected return (level of safety of a portfolio). A safety measure has to be maximized when it is the objective function of a portfolio optimization model.

Second-order stochastic dominance Relationship between two random variables based on comparison of expected utilities for all non-satiate and risk-averse decision makers.

Security market line The tangent to the efficient frontier corresponding to the risk-free rate. All portfolios on this line consist of a holding in the market portfolio and a long or short position in the risk-free rate.

Self-financing portfolio A portfolio with both long and short positions for which the net investment required is zero.

Shadow output prices Unobservable price ratio that supports a given output mix and equals the opportunity cost of production.

Sharpe ratio The ratio of the expected excess return on a portfolio to its volatility.

Simultaneous confidence intervals A set of confidence intervals constructed with a specified overall probability.

Single-period portfolio optimization model An optimization model that provides the optimal portfolio at a given point in time for a single investment period.

Skewness A measure of the distributional asymmetry of a random variable.

SOX The Sarbanes–Oxley Act of 2002; an act intended intended to protect investors by improving the accuracy and reliability of corporate disclosures made pursuant to the securities laws.

Standard constants Three real scalars that determine the location, slope, and curvature of the efficient frontier.

Stationarity The property of a stochastic process with constant mean and variance where the covariance between two points in the process is determined by the distance between the two points.

Stein's lemma A mathematical result that plays an important result in portfolio selection.

Stochastic programming An optimization modeling approach for dealing with decision problems under uncertainty.

Stress testing The investigation of unexpected loss (UL) under conditions outside our ordinary realm of experience (e.g., extreme events not in our reference datasets).

Structural credit models Models that measure distance to default based on the debt and equity structure of a company and fluctuations in the market values of that company's assets.

Tangency portfolio A synonym for the market portfolio.

Tikhonov's regularization   Robust solution of an approximate system of linear equations, taking into account the errors in the solution and its stability to changes in the problem data.

Time substitution   Given a fixed amount of input that can be used over some range of time, time substitution is the process of choosing when and how intensively to use that input so as to maximize production.

Transaction costs   Costs that are charged when a transaction (buying or selling) takes place.

Transition credit models   Models that measure credit risk based on the probability of a borrower transitioning from one credit rating to another.

Transition probability matrix   The probability matrix that governs the switching between regimes.

Trapezoidal rule   A standard technique for numerical integration.

Unexpected loss (UL)   A measure generally thought of as some unlikely loss measure over some time horizon (e.g., an allowance for loan losses amount set aside by a bank).

Utility function   A nondecreasing and usually nonlinear function that maps an outcome to its importance. In portfolio selection, the outcome is usually return and the utility function is invariably concave.

Variable neighborhood search   A metaheuristic approach for solving complex optimization problems (combinatorial and global optimization), which is based on the idea of improving a solution by systematically searching in distant neighborhoods of the solution.

Variable transaction costs   Transaction costs that depend on the amount of capital invested.

Value at risk (VaR)   The potential loss over a given time period for a selected level of confidence.

Volatility specification tests   Statistical tests for assessing the performance of various volatility models.

Volume synchronized probability of informed trading (VPIN)   A procedure used to estimate the probability of informed trading based on volume imbalance and trade intensity. VPIN quantifies the role of order toxicity (adverse selection risk in high frequency trading) in determining liquidity provisions.

Index